ISBN 978-1-332-01658-7
PIBN 10269290

1 MONTH OF
FREE
READING

at

www.ForgottenBooks.com

By purchasing this book you are
eligible for one month membership to
ForgottenBooks.com, giving you
unlimited access to our entire
collection of over 1,000,000 titles via
our web site and mobile apps.

To claim your free month visit:
www.forgottenbooks.com/free269290

HISTORY

OF THE

UNIVERSITY OF EDINBURGH

FROM ITS FOUNDATION.

BY ANDREW DALZEL

PROFESSOR OF GREEK IN THAT UNIVERSITY

WITH A MEMOIR OF THE AUTHOR

VOL. II.—HISTORY.

EDINBURGH

EDMONSTON AND DOUGLAS

1862.

13776
11/7/91

PREFATORY NOTICE.

In printing the following work, the Author's MS. has been carefully adhered to, with only a few verbal corrections. PROFESSOR DALZEL'S intention evidently was to have continued his HISTORY OF THE UNIVERSITY, in the form of Annals, to the commencement of the present century, but it terminates abruptly about the year 1723, when the University had laid the foundation of its eminence as a School of Medicine. This intention appears from the table of Contents prefixed to his MS., in which he has given the titles of two additional chapters, but which, judging from the state of the existing manuscript, were probably never written. We cannot, therefore, but feel regret that this portion of Professor Dalzel's History, which would have embraced an account of his own times, was left unfinished, if we consider the facilities of daily and familiar intercourse that existed at a period when several of the Professors resided within the Collegiate buildings, and when so many eminent men were associated with the University. The titles of these two chapters are as follows :—

"Chapter VII. From the institution of the Medical
" Faculty to the time of Dr. Robertson as Principal,
" in 1762.

"Chapter VIII. From the beginning of Dr. Robert-
" son's presiding over the College, till the end of the
" eighteenth century."

There however remains, as materials to be employed
for the illustration of this part of his subject, a series
of extracts from the Records of the Town-Council,
between August 1724 and May 1779, which the
Author had made with considerable labour and care.
These extracts have been compared with the Council
Records; and as furnishing a variety of facts illustrative of the history of the University during that
period, they have been inserted in the Appendix,
No. V.

In connexion with the History of the University,
Professor Dalzel intended to have prepared lists and
biographical notices of the Professors in the various
chairs. Having only partially completed this part of
his plan, the portions which were actually written are
given in the subsequent pages;[1] and a few documents
marked to be inserted, have been supplied in the Appendix. It may also be mentioned, that a complete
Chronological List of the Principals, Regents, and Professors is contained in the volume entitled " A Cata-

---

[1] See footnote to page 330.

logue of the Graduates in the Faculties of Arts, Divinity, and Law, of the University of Edinburgh," published in 1858. I find, however, from Mr. Dalzel's
researches, as embodied in the present work, that the
above List of Regents, from 1583 to 1707, needs re-
vision, by forming a separate list of Professors of
Humanity during that period.

Having been requested to act as Editor of the following work, as I could not, without assistance, devote
to it the time that would be requisite, it is but proper
to state, that I was assisted by the Rev. James Anderson, author of the "Ladies of the Covenant," and
other works ; and that he undertook not only the
necessary task of searching out and collating the
various papers to which reference is made in the
course of the History, but also the more serious part
of transcribing and arranging the Author's manuscript
for the press.

DAVID LAING.

CONTENTS.

CONTENTS.

APPENDIX.

HISTORY

UNIVERSITY OF EDINBURGH.

CHAPTER I.

FROM THE INSTITUTION OF THE COLLEGE IN 1582 TO THE ACCESSION
OF JAMES VI. TO THE CROWN OF ENGLAND IN 1603.

SOON after the reformation of religion in Scotland, which was established in the year 1560, the Magistrates and Town-Council of Edinburgh, with the Ministers and other respectable Citizens, were solicitous to promote the cause of learning and the liberal education of the youth, which had, during the troubles of the kingdom, been much neglected. They considered, also, that it was attended with great inconvenience and expense to send away the youth from the capital of the kingdom to be educated at St. Andrews, or any other university at a distance ; and especially that parents in narrow circumstances, however willing, were altogether unable to bestow a learned education on such of their sons as seemed to be possessed of talents fitted for literary pursuits.[1] They therefore proposed that a University should be founded in their own city ; and

1561.
Proposal to
have a University
founded in
Edinburgh.

[1] Robertson, Vitæ et Mortis Rob. Rolloci Narratio, p. 5.

A

they were encouraged in having this scheme carried into execution by a legacy of 8000 merks Scots, which had been bequeathed for that purpose, about the year 1558, by Robert Reid, Bishop of Orkney. But the Abbot of Kinloss and others, who had possession of this money, being unwilling to give it up, the Town-Council were not able to recover it till the year 1582.

1563.
A site for it
provided. They purchased, however, in the year 1563, for the sum of one thousand pounds Scots,[1] the right to a great part of the ground and buildings which had belonged to the Provost and Prebendaries of the Collegiate Kirk of Field, anciently denominated "Templum et Præfectura Sanctæ Mariæ in Campis," to be a site for their intended College. This is the very place which the University buildings now partly occupy, and which, before the South Bridge was erected, included also the space betwixt the east front of the New College and the Royal Infirmary, through which the street now passes, but which was formerly garden ground.

This place was soon after rendered remarkable by the unhappy fate of Henry Lord Darnley, husband to the Queen. The apartments where he lodged, and which were blown up by gunpowder on the 10th of February 1567, were either the same which had been possessed by the Provost of the Kirk of Field, or the lodgings of the Prebendaries in the vicinity of the Provost's house to the east. This house was afterwards

---

[1] Pennycuick, Parson of that Ilk, and Provost of the Kirk of Field, dispones to the town the haill bigging called the Kirk of Field, with the kirkyeard, for the sum of 1000 pounds Scots.—Town-Council Records, vol. iv. June 21, 1563.

Nicol Hutcheson, one of the Prebendaries of the Kirk of Field, resigns his prebend in favour of the town, for payment of 70 merks.—*Ibid.* vol. v. Dec. 30, 1579.

repaired, and appropriated as a habitation for the Principal of the College. It yet remains (1803), situated almost upon the spot which the centre of the Museum and Library are destined to occupy in the plan of the new fabric. But neither the house, nor the garden to the eastward, were got possession of by the Town-Council till several years after the foundation of the College. They had entered into a contract with John Gib, servitor to the King's Grace, whereby they obliged themselves to convey to John Fenton, Comptroller's Clerk, and Agnes Lindsay, his spouse, and the said John's heirs, that tenement or lodging, then waste and decayed, sometime pertaining to the Provost of the Kirk of Field, with the garden, etc., upon this condition, that Fenton and his wife should pay a feu-annual of 50 shillings Scots yearly, and acknowledge the Town as their Superior; and the said John Gib renounces his pretended right of superiority for the sum of 300 merks paid to him by the town.[1]

In the year 1579, by the strenuous exertions of Mr. Clement Little, Advocate, and one of the Commissaries of Edinburgh, Mr. Henry Charteris, a respectable citizen, Mr. James Lawson, a minister of the city, a man of talents and of considerable learning, and who had formerly been sub-Principal of King's College, Aberdeen, the Town-Council at length determined to begin the work; but the Archbishop of St. Andrews and the Bishop of Aberdeen had still sufficient influence to suspend the undertaking, as injurious to the Universities

1579. The Town Council determine to begin the work;

but are prevented.

---

[1] Town-Council Records, vol. vi. p. 128.

already established in the kingdom.   The High Grammar School, however, was built and endowed at this
time in the place where the monastery of the Blackfriars, then in ruins, was formerly situated.

1581.
The College
buildings
commenced. But in the year 1581, the Episcopal faction having
lost its power in the Church of Scotland, the Ministers
of Edinburgh, particularly Mr. James Lawson and Mr.
Walter Balcanquhal, supported by Mr. William Little,
afterwards Provost of the city, and his brother, Mr.
Clement, the Commissary, seized the opportunity to
urge the design of erecting a College.   The work of
building and repairing was accordingly begun, and
carried forward with great diligence and industry.
The accommodation, however, thus provided, did not
consist of one regularly designed magnificent structure,
such as was then, and is now, exhibited by a College
in either of the two Universities of England ; but was
patched up, partly by repairing such old buildings as
were found upon the spot, and partly by the addition
of others constructed upon the most frugal plan.   An
old irregular pile of building, adjoining to the Kirk of
Field, which had been the town residence of the Duke
of Chatelherault and his family, but now obtained by
the Town-Council of Edinburgh, in consequence of the
forfeiture of the Hamiltons by the Regent, Earl of
Morton, was fitted up and converted into apartments
for different classes of students, to be there instructed
by the new Professors ; and it remained appropriated
for this purpose for more than two centuries, when it
was lately demolished to give way for the new buildings.   It stood in a transverse direction from north to

south, in the place now occupied by the classes for the practice of Physic and Moral Philosophy, in the very centre of the north side of the great inner quadrangle of the New College. Other buildings were gradually added, but according to no regular plan; so that the whole academical fabric, even in its most complete state, exhibited but a mean and motley appearance. Such as it was, however, it might be regarded as a great exertion made in behalf of learning, considering the state of the city of Edinburgh, and the finances of the country at that period.

Antecedent to the Reformation, a Bull of the Pope used to be considered as necessary for giving the proper authority to erect a college or university; and, accordingly, the ancient Universities of St. Andrews and of Glasgow, and King's College, Aberdeen, had derived their privileges and authority from that source. But the Papal influence being annihilated in Scotland previous to the existence of the College of Edinburgh, the citizens looked towards the King as possessed of the only legal power for giving a sanction to their new institution. James the Sixth was then upon the throne; and, fortunately, his education had been so conducted by his chief preceptor, the celebrated George Buchanan, as to inspire him with a great respect and an uncommon passion for learning. Even at the age of twelve, he himself had made considerable progress in it, and discovered then such a maturity of judgment, that, with the approbation of his subjects, he had superseded the Earl of Morton, Regent of the kingdom, and assumed the reins of government into

his own hands.[1]   He was now in his seventeenth year,
and gave his countenance to the Magistrates and Town-
Council of Edinburgh in their scheme of erecting a
College.   His mother, Queen. Mary, by her charter,
dated the 13th of March 1566, had bestowed many of
the church's possessions and emoluments within the
liberties of Edinburgh upon the Provost, Magistrates,
Council, and community of that city, for the behoof of
the ministers of the gospel and support of the poor,
under the general appellation of " The Foundation for
the Ministers and Hospitality of Edinburgh."   The

1582.
April 14.
King James
VI. grants a
Charter
under the
Great Seal
authorizing
the founding
of a Univer-
sity.

King now granted a new charter under the Great Seal,
containing a confirmation of this deed, and by an
additional grant not only conferring anew upon the
said corporation the above-mentioned church possessions and emoluments, to be applied by them for the
maintenance of the ministers, support of the poor, repairing of schools, and propagation of letters and
sciences, according as they and their successors should
think fit; but also giving them full power to receive
from all persons who, hereafter, out of their great zeal,
might be disposed to bestow yearly profits or rents
within or without the said town for the same purposes ;
which gifts or bequests are declared to be as fully
ratified, confirmed, and freely mortified as any other
such donations and possessions were ever before bequeathed or granted in perpetuity to the church.   This
charter also confirms and ratifies the renunciation by
John Gib, his Majesty's servant, in favour of the said
corporation and community, of all right or title which

[1] Robertson's History of Scotland, Book vi.

he, in virtue of the King's gift, may or can pretend to have to the provostry and church of the Kirk of Field, and possessions or revenues thereof; ratifying, moreover, and confirming all the rights the said town has to those void and spacious places which lately belonged to the Provost, prebendaries, priests, and friars of the said Kirk of Field; which situation is declared to be extremely commodious for " the erection of apartments and edifices, where professors of liberal science and literature, and students thereof may reside and hold their daily exercises, apart from the other places destined for the foundation of hospitality." Wherefore, the King's Majesty, earnestly desirous for the honour of God, and the common good of the realm, that learning should daily increase, wills and permits by the said charter, THAT IT SHALL BE LAWFUL FOR THE FORESAID PROVOST AND TOWN-COUNCIL, AND THEIR SUCCESSORS, TO BUILD AND REPAIR HOUSES FOR THE RECEPTION, HABITATION, AND ENTERTAINMENT OF PROFESSORS OF GRAMMAR, HUMANITY, AND LANGUAGES, PHILOSOPHY, THEOLOGY, MEDICINE, AND LAW, AND ALL OTHER LIBERAL SCIENCES--which is declared to be no violation of the above-mentioned foundation: and further, THAT THE SAID PROVOST, BAILIES, AND TOWN-COUNCIL, AND THEIR SUCCESSORS, SHALL IN ALL TIME COMING, WITH ADVICE, HOWEVER, OF THE MINISTERS OF THE CITY, HAVE FULL FREEDOM TO ELECT THE BEST-QUALIFIED PERSONS THEY MOST CONVENIENTLY CAN, FOR THE DISCHARGE OF THE SAID OFFICES, WITH POWER TO INSTAL AND REMOVE THEM AS IT SHALL BE FOUND EXPEDIENT: and prohibiting all other persons from teaching the said sciences within the said town, unless by permission of the said Provost, Bailies, and Council.

The Charter
ratified in
Parliament. This charter, which is dated at the Castle of Stirling the 14th of April 1582, was afterwards in the year 1621, ratified by Act of Parliament, and the College, which had been built by the Provost, Magistrates, and Council, in consequence thereof, endowed anew with all liberties, rights, immunities, and privileges appertaining to a free college ; and that in as ample form and extensive manner as those enjoyed by any college within his Majesty's realm.

By the original charter, the privilege of instituting a *Studium Generale* is clearly and obviously granted to the corporation of the city of Edinburgh, which is, to all intents and purposes, the same with what is now called a University. That this was the original appellation given to universities, is evident from the style adopted by the Popes in their bulls authorizing such institutions.

But, though the patrons of this foundation had thus obtained full powers of erecting professorships of languages, and of all the different branches of liberal science, commonly called the four Faculties of Arts, Theology, Law, and Medicine, composing a *Studium Generale* or University, they, at the beginning, confined their views to the two first, Arts and Theology, comprehended in one college, to be called THE COLLEGE OF EDINBURGH.

Plan of In-
struction. The plan of instruction in view for this new seminary seems to have been borrowed from that which was adopted in the other colleges of Scotland; divested,

however, as much as possible, of those antiquated forms and monastic ceremonies practised in the times of Popery, and with which the other colleges seem to have been very much embarrassed at the era of the Reformation.

The first object of the patrons was to institute such a course of instruction as should accomplish the youth in general literature, or prepare them for entering with advantage upon the study of Theology or of Law or Medicine. The election of a Professor of Theology was deemed necessary, as soon as the students intended for the holy ministry should be ready for profiting by his lectures, but it was late before the sciences of Law and Medicine were regularly taught in the University of Edinburgh ; and it long remained the custom for such of the youth as were designed for the practice of either of these, to acquire a knowledge of them in foreign universities, from whence many of them who studied physic, and some who studied law, returned to their native country decorated with the doctor's degree.[1]

Four Regents or Professors of Philosophy, with a Principal, who was also Professor of Theology, were therefore all the instructors employed in the College of Edinburgh for some time after its origin. A Professor of Humanity or Philosophy, whose chief business was to teach Latin to the younger part of the students, upon their first entry to the College, was afterwards added ; and in process of time a Professor of

[1] In King's College, Aberdeen, among the original members founded by Bishop Elphinston, soon after the institution of the University in the year 1494, there were professors of the Civil and Canon Law, and also a professor of Medicine. —See Statistical Account, p. 63.

Mathematics, a Professor of Hebrew, and others, were gradually introduced.

The duty of the Regents or Professors of Philosophy. The duty of the four Regents or Professors of Philosophy was to instruct their pupils in the knowledge of the Greek language, and in the different branches of philosophy, as logic, metaphysics, ethics, physics, including the elements of mathematics and astronomy ; a previous acquaintance with the Latin tongue, in which these instructions were to be conveyed, being deemed absolutely necessary. All the different parts of that course, which was to last for four years, with an annual vacation of six weeks or two months, were taught by each of the four Professors to that class of students who entered under his tuition at their first coming to College ; so that, when one Professor was in the first year of the course, another was in the second, another in the third, and another in the fourth, always in rotation.

The four Classes of Greek and Philosophy. Those students who were in the first year of the course, and employed for the first month in learning Latin, and afterwards Greek, were called " Classis Bejanorum," or " The Bejan Class ;" those in the second year, during which logic and metaphysics were chiefly taught, were called " Classis Semi Bejanorum," or the " Semi Class ;" those in the third year, when ethics and mathematics were the chief subjects of instruction, were called " Classis Baccalaureorum," or " The Bachelor Class ;" and those in the fourth year, which was chiefly spent upon physics and astronomy, were styled "Classis Magistrandorum," or " The Magistrand Class." The Professor who had the charge of the Magistrand Class concluded the quadriennial course by having the degree of M.A. conferred upon all his students, after they had held a solemn public disputation upon those branches of science, in which he had instructed them. This act was commonly called "The Laureation of the Class." The session of the College The Graduation or Laureation. commenced about the 10th, or, as it was then, the 1st of October, and continued till about the beginning of August. After the students had received the degree of M.A., they were understood to be qualified for entering upon the study of Theology, Law, or Physic.

In the month of March 1583, the Town-Council 1583. March. gave orders to complete the enclosure of the College buildings; and that the instruction of youth in their new institution might be no longer delayed, they invited from St. Andrews Mr. Robert Rollock, to be the first who should enter upon that charge. He was a man of great reputation for prudence, piety, and learning, and was well acquainted with the academical method of teaching then practised; for he had for several years held the office of Professor of Humanity in St. Salvator's College, and being afterwards promoted to a professorship of Philosophy, was at the time carrying forward a class of students in the fourth year of their course, with a view to laureate or graduate them in the beginning of the next August. Having accepted of the invitation of the Town-Council of Edinburgh, he prepared for commencing his instructions in their new College in the following October.

On the 11th of that month proclamation was made Oct. 11. Proclamation requiring students to enrol their names. by the Town-Council, requiring all scholars and students who desired to be instructed in the College to present themselves before one of the Magistrates, and enrol their names.[1] A great number appeared, attracted by the reputation of Rollock. With these it was his intention to enter upon the usual employment of the first year of the quadrennial course ; and ac-

October. Session I. Rollock begins his lectures.

cordingly he began to teach in the lower hall of Hamilton House, now converted into rooms for the accommodation of the College. But finding that, of the great number who had enrolled under his tuition, many were too deficient in the knowledge of Latin for entering with advantage upon the philosophical course, and no Professor of Humanity being yet established in this new seminary, whose business it would have been to remedy this defect, he recommended to the patrons

Mr. Duncan Nairne, Second Regent or Professor of Philosophy.

Mr. Duncan Nairne, a young man of good abilities and learning, to be one of the four intended Regents or Professors of Philosophy ; but proposed that this second Professor should, in the meantime, take under his charge, for the first year, those who were deficient in Latin, so as to prepare them for a new Bejan class the ensuing session, when those under his own immediate care would be in the second year of their course,

Novem. 8.

and compose the Semi class. Nairne was accordingly chosen, and this plan adopted, so that during the first session, or first term of the College of Edinburgh, which lasted from October 1583 till the end of August 1584, there were only two classes of students : a Bejan class under Mr. Robert Rollock, followed by a Latin class under Mr. Duncan Nairne.

It seems to have been the intention of the patrons

---

[1] Town-Council Records, vol. vii. in Latin.

that all the students should be accommodated with lodgings, and remain in them nightly, within the College ; and accordingly mention is made in the Town-Council Records of certain regulations that were enacted for this purpose about this time. It was ordered, likewise, that all of them should wear gowns, on pain of expulsion. The custom for at least a considerable number of students to lodge within the College appears to have been kept up for many years ; but at length it went gradually into disuse, and has long ago been entirely abandoned, as quite inconsistent with the mode of instruction which has long prevailed. It is probable that the order for wearing gowns was never complied with. A proposal of this kind was revived in the year 1690, during the time of the Parliamentary Visitation, but does not appear to have been insisted on, and certainly was not carried into effect ; nor is it to be regretted that such a badge was never adopted. It is not easy to see with what advantage it could be attended, at-least in the present state of the University. That the Professors should have a distinction of this kind, when they appear officially, is of more evident utility, and therefore this custom with respect to them continues to prevail.

For the more decent attendance on public worship, the gallery in the east end of the High Church was allotted for the Professors and students, until the patrons should find reason for a different arrangement in this particular.[1]

About this time the state of political parties seemed

---

[1] Town-Council Records, vol. vii. Dec. 13, 1583.

1584.
State of po-
litical parties
in the king-
dom.
rather unfavourable to the prosperity of the College. After the fall of the Earl of Morton, Regent of the kingdom, the Duke of Lennox and the Earl of Arran, formerly Captain James Stewart, with the French faction, had obtained an ascendant over the King. A conspiracy of the nobles had been formed for depriving them of their power; and the King, having been decoyed into the Earl of Gowrie's castle of Ruthven, was seized by the conspirators, an enterprise which is known in history by the appellation of "The Raid of Ruthven;" and though at first Arran had been committed to prison, Lennox obliged to leave the kingdom, and James himself under the necessity of publishing a proclamation vindicating the measures of the conspirators, whose conduct was also approved by an assembly of the Church, and a convention of the Estates, yet the King at length, by his own address and vigilance, had contrived to escape out of their hands. Upon which Arran, soon after regaining his freedom and his influence, had not only prevailed over his opponents among the nobility, but had also induced the King to take severe measures against the Church, which occasioned the confinement or banishment of several of the most eminent and zealous of the Presbyterian Ministers. Among those who had been banished were Mr. James Lawson and Mr. Walter Balcanquhal, the former of whom, who had strenuously promoted the foundation of the College, died at London much regretted.

But all these unfavourable circumstances, and the distracted and convulsed state of the kingdom, did not interfere with the King's passion for learning, nor prevent him from patronizing and endowing the infant College. By a charter under the Great Seal, dated the 4th of April 1584, he granted for its use, and for maintaining the Rector and Regents thereof, the parsonage and vicarage of. Currie, with the tithes and church lands thereunto belonging, anciently called the Archdeaconry of Lothian. Thus protected by the King's favour, and encouraged by his bounty, the Town-Council persevered steadily in carrying on the College buildings; and that the business might be conducted with every possible advantage, they had named one of the late magistrates,[1] to be master of work, and treasurer or collector of the College revenue. A legacy, too, of books, consisting of about 300 volumes, which Mr. Clement Little had in the year 1580 bequeathed to the town, and which had been deposited in a gallery contiguous to Mr. Lawson's house, being removed to the College, and delivered to the charge of Mr. Rollock, furnished a commencement to what is now the public Library of the University.

Perseverance of the Town-Council in carrying on the College buildings.

Sept. 18. The commencement of the Public Library.

The two professors, Rollock and Nairne, having, in the month of August, concluded the first session of the College, the latter, at the commencement of a new one in October, undertook the charge of a new Bejan class, consisting of such students as had recently entered to the College, together with those whom he had prepared with that view during the preceding session, while the former went forward with his own students in the second year of the course, and now composing the Semi class. But unfortunately, towards the end of

1584. October. Session II.

[1] Mr. Andrew Sclater.

1585.
May.
The students
dispersed on
account of
the Plague.
the year, the plague began to make its appearance, and it increased to such a degree of violence in the course of the following year, that in the month of May the students were all dispersed, and the two Professors were under the necessity of concluding the session prematurely, and retiring from the city.

Fall of the
Earl of
Arran.
The power and insolence of Arran, grown at last intolerable, were not of long duration. The banished noblemen, protected by Elizabeth, Queen of England, returned into their native country at the head of 10,000 men. They took possession of the town of Stirling, and invested its castle, where the King was, who thought it prudent to come to an accommodation with them ; and they obtained from him a pardon in the most ample form. A Parliament was held at Linlithgow on the 10th of December, where the banished The Exiles
restored. noblemen and gentlemen were restored to their ancient honours and estates ; but Arran, who had been obliged to save himself by a precipitate flight, was degraded, stripped of his wealth, and declared an enemy to his country.

The restoration, however, of the family of Hamilton proved of some detriment to the College. The large fabric which composed the chief part of the College building, and which the Duke of Chatelherault had formerly obtained from the Provost and Prebendaries of the Kirk of Field, at an annual feu-rent of forty merks, but which, during the forfeiture of the Hamilton family, had been granted to the town of Edinburgh, for the use of the College, was now claimed by Lord, afterwards the Marquis of Hamilton ; and after a disagreeable litigation occasionally carried on, and which was not terminated till the year 1613, James, the second Marquis, with great difficulty, was prevailed on to accept of 3000 pounds Scots from the town as a compensation for all further claim.

Instead of the Earl of Arran, who had been made Provost of the city, by means of a letter procured from the King, William Little, a great promoter of the interest of the College, and brother of Mr. Clement formerly mentioned, was elected to that office in the end of the year. About the same time, a "Short and General Confession of the true Christian Religion, according to God's Word," was subscribed in the College by Mr. John Craig and Mr. James Hamilton, the two professors, Rollock and Nairne, and soon after by Charles Lumisden ; and it was resolved and ordained that all those who afterwards received degrees from the College should subscribe this solemn engagement. The original of this deed, with a great number of subscriptions annexed, is still extant at the beginning of the Graduation-book, the most curious and valuable record in the possession of the University of Edinburgh.[1]

Dec. 11. William Little, Provost of the city.

About the beginning of the year 1586, the fear of the plague having subsided, the two professors, with the students, returned to the College in the month of February, and resumed their studies, which had been intermitted for about nine months.[2] Rollock's students, being now in the third year of their course,

1586. Feb. 3. Session III.

[1] This Covenant and Confession is published in Dunlop's Collection of Confessions of Faith, printed at Edinburgh by James Watson, 1722, vol. ii. p. 103. This printed copy bears that it was carefully collated with a MS. in the Graduation-Book of the University of Edinburgh.

[2] Town-Council Records, vol. vii. January 14, 1585.

were, therefore, denominated the Bachelor class; Nairne's, of consequence, was now the Semi; but, as the College had not met in the preceding October, there was no new Bejan class this session; and,

Feb. 9.
Rollock
elected Prin-
cipal.
though Rollock was elected Principal of the College on the 9th of the same month, he continued to teach his class till the conclusion of the course.

Feb. 16.
Mr. Charles
Lumisden,
third Pro-
fessor of
Philosophy.
Nairne did not long survive this event, but, dying about this time, much lamented, Mr. Charles Lumisden, who had been educated at St. Andrews under Rollock, was chosen to succeed him, and carried forward the Semi class till the end of August, when it was thought proper to grant a vacation to the College for one month.

October.
In the beginning of October, Lumisden resigned his Professorship, and accepted of a call to be minister of Duddingston; and, as it was now thought proper that a new Bejan class should be assembled, it was resolved to elect two new Regents by a comparative trial. Candidates being invited by means of public

Mr Adam
Colt the
fourth, and
Mr. Alexr.
Scrimger the
fifth Profes-
sor of Philo-
sophy.
programs, six young men appeared and entered their names. A public disputation was held for ten days, and the judges appointed by the patrons decided in favour of Mr. Adam Colt and Mr. Alexander Scrimger, who were accordingly elected, and received as two of the Professors of Philosophy.

Session IV.
The classes being assembled after the vacation, Principal Rollock's students, now in the fourth year of their course, composed the Magistrand class; Mr. Colt had the charge of the Bachelor, which had been begun by Nairne, and carried on by Lumisden; but

there was no Semi class this session, no Bejan having existed the foregoing year. The new class entered under the tuition of Mr. Scrimger.

The 8th of February this year was rendered remarkable for the tragical death of Mary, mother to the King ; an event which leaves an indelible stain on the memory of Queen Elizabeth her rival. Though James be properly considered as the founder of the University of Edinburgh, Mary had the merit of paving the way for that establishment by her original grant of the 13th of March 1566, by which she bestowed upon the Provost, Magistrates, Council, and Community of Edinburgh the church-possessions and emoluments within the liberties of the city, of which a part was, by her son's deed of confirmation, afterwards appropriated to the use of the College.

In the month of August, Mr. Robert Rollock, now Principal of the College, conferred the degree of M.A. on the students of the first class educated under his own immediate charge. Upon which occasion all of them, being forty-seven in number, subscribed the above-mentioned covenant. Among those who had particularly distinguished themselves were Charles Ferme, Philip Heslope, Henry Charteris, and Patrick Sands, all of them afterwards Professors, and the two last also Principals of the College.

After the solemnity of the graduation, Rollock resigned the office of Regent, or Professor of Philosophy ; and the Town-Council, with the Ministers and Kirk-Session of the city, by the advice and approbation of the Presbytery, called him to the

(Marginal notes:)
1587.
Feb. 8
Death of
Queen Mary

August.
First Class
graduated.

August 27
Rollock
resigns his
Regency,
and is made
Professor of
Divinity.
This office
held jointly
with that of
Principal till
the year
1620

Professorship of Divinity, which office continued to be united with that of the Principal of the College until the year 1620.

In October, at a public comparative trial for a successor to Mr. Rollock, in the Professorship of Philosophy, the four scholars above-mentioned, with some others, appeared as candidates. The judges declared all the four, formerly named, well qualified, but, as they approved most of Mr. Philip Heslope, the patrons elected him to supply the vacated place. He, accordingly, on the assembling of the College, undertook the charge of the new Bejan class, Mr. Scrimger's being the Semi (there being no Bachelor Class for the reason formerly mentioned), and Mr. Colt's being the Magistrand.[1]

In August 1588, this class, now under the tuition of Mr. Colt, and which had been begun by Mr. Duncan Nairne, and continued by Mr. Charles Lumisden, received the master's degree, with the solemnity usual on such occasions, being thirty in number, and the second class which was graduated in the College of Edinburgh.

On the meeting of the College in October, after the vacation, Mr. Colt undertook the charge of the new Bejan class, Mr. Heslope carried forward the Semi, Mr. Scrimger the Bachelor; but, as there was no Magistrand class, there could be no graduation at the conclusion of this session.

---

[1] This year some of the houses and garden-ground within the precincts of the Kirk of Field, which belonged to Mr. James Ritchie, a writer, were purchased for the use of the College.

Meanwhile, in January 1589, Mr. Charles Ferme, who had been the second in order approved by the judges at the last comparative trial, was elected Regent, that he might be prepared for beginning the Bejan class the following October.

1589.
January.
Mr. Charles
Ferme the
seventh,

But after the vacation, when the College assembled in October, two of the other places had also become vacant. Mr. Alexander Scrimger had, in a private manner, been removed from his office by the Principal, on account of some misconduct in the case of a meeting of his students ; and Mr. Philip Heslope had embraced an opportunity of travelling into Germany. The patrons, therefore, elected in their stead Mr. Henry Charteris and Mr. Patrick Sands, the two remaining candidates who had been approved by the judges in the late comparative trial.

Mr. Henry
Charteris the
eighth, and
Mr. Patrick
Sands the
ninth Pro-
fessor of
Philosophy.

The Philosophy class being thus at length completed, the Senatus Academicus, at the beginning of this session, consisted of the following members :—

October
Session VII.

Mr. Robert Rollock, Principal and Professor of Divinity ; Mr. Charles Ferme, Mr. Adam Colt, Mr. Patrick Sands, Mr. Henry Charteris, Regents or Professors of Philosophy.

In February 1590, a contract was entered into by the Town-Council and the College of Justice, by which the Lords of Session in the first place, the Town-Council of Edinburgh in the second, and the Faculty of Advocates and Writers to the Signet in the third, agreed that each of the three parties should contribute the sum of 1000 pounds Scots, making up the sum of 3000 pounds, for which the Town-Council obliged

1590.
February.
A Contract
by the Town-
Council and
College of
Justice, for
instituting a
Law Pro-
fessor.

themselves to pay 300 pounds a year for maintaining a Professor of Law. Mr. Adam Newton, Advocate, entered accordingly upon this office, but gave public lectures only on Humanity, or the Latin language and literature, without any instructions on the science of law. These he continued during the usual sessions of the College, till the month of June 1594, when the Town-Council thought proper to remove him, as he had assumed the office without receiving instalment from them as patrons of the University. In his place was substituted, by consent of all the three parties, Sir Adrian Damman of Bysterveldt, a native of Ghent, and resident at the court of Scotland, as consul or agent for the Estates of the Low Countries. This new professor, in the same way with Mr. Newton, gave public lectures only on Humanity. But he did not continue long in office, as shall be afterwards mentioned.

In the meantime, in August 1590, the third class, under the tuition of Mr. Henry Charteris, consisting but of thirteen students, received the degree of master of arts.

In October the same year, Mr. Charteris of course assembled the new Bejan class, Mr. Ferme having now the charge of the Semi ; and, as Mr. Colt had accepted of a call to be minister of Borthwick,[1] Mr. Philip Heslope, who had returned from Germany, was substituted in his place in the charge of the Bachelor class, Mr. Patrick Sands having that of the

Mr Adam Newton gives lectures on Humanity instead of Law.

He is removed by the Town.

Sir Adrian Damman substituted, who also gives lectures on Humanity.

August. The third Class graduated.

October. Session VIII.

---

1 Mr. Adam Colt was afterwards translated to Inveresk, where he died at an advanced age, in great estimation for learning, prudence, and piety.

Magistrand, on whom, at the conclusion of the course 1591. August. The fourth Class graduated. in August, he conferred the master's degree with the usual solemnity.

At the opening of the College, after the vacation, October. Session IX. Mr. Sands undertook the tuition of the new Bejan class; and, at the conclusion of the session, the 1592. The fifth Class graduated. Magistrand class, under the charge of Mr. Heslope, being twenty-eight in number, was graduated in the usual manner.

This year the King appeared to be remarkably indulgent to the Presbyterian form of Church Government. Though his own principles were favourable to the Episcopal hierarchy, as his conduct with regard to the Church in the year 1584, and the whole course of it after his accession to the throne of England, evidently showed, yet, as the Presbyterian ministers had greatly contributed to the promotion of that peace and good order which had prevailed in the kingdom during his absence in the year 1589-90, when he visited the court of Copenhagen on the occasion of his marriage with the Princess Anne of Denmark, he became greatly reconciled not only to their persons, but to their form of ecclesiastical government. Being himself present in an Assembly on the 4th of August 1590, he applauded the Presbyterian doctrine and discipline, promised to adhere to both, and allowed the Assembly to frame such acts as tended gradually to subvert all remains of Episcopal jurisdiction; and at last, in a Parliament held in June 1592, he consented Presbyterian Church Government established by law. to a law rescinding or explaining the acts which had been passed in 1584, unfavourable to the Presbyterian government, and permitted the Parliament now to establish it in the most ample manner.[1]

In October, at the commencement of a new session of the College, Mr. Heslope, in his turn, had the charge of the new Bejan class; and, on the 12th of the following August, the Magistrand class, nineteen in number, under the tuition of Mr. Ferme, was graduated as usual. It is remarkable that John, second Earl of Gowrye, made a distinguished figure among the candidates on this occasion. He took a principal share in the disputation and defence of the Theses, and his name appears in the graduation-book[2] among the subscribers of the Confession and Covenant. This is the famous Earl of Gowrye, who afterwards gave name to that mysterious conspiracy which has so much puzzled the historians to explain.

At the beginning of the new session in October, Mr. Charles Ferme undertook the charge of the new Bejan class; but in November, Mr. Heslope having received a call to be minister of Inveresk,[3] Mr. George Robertson, the son of a burgess of Edinburgh, who had taken the master's degree in 1588, was elected to succeed him; and entered to the charge of the Semi class; Mr. Patrick Sands advanced with the Bachelors; and Mr. Henry Charteris brought the Magistrand class, consisting of twenty students, to the usual degree on the 7th of the following August.[4]

---

[1] Robertson's Hist. of Scotland, b. viii.

[2] William Rynd, Lord Gowrye's private tutor, and Will. Bowy, are also subscribers.

[3] He died a few years after he was admitted minister of Inveresk. He was the son of an Edinburgh burgess, and eminently learned, particularly in mathematical science.

[4] This and the following year,'provisions being extremely dear, the Town-Council repeatedly gave the Regents a handsome allowance in addition to their ordinary salaries.

Mr. Henry Charteris began the new session in October. Session XII. October, with the charge of the Bejan class; and at the conclusion of it, on the 12th of August 1595, 1595. August. Mr. Sands graduated the Magistrand class, consisting The eighth Class graduated. of twenty-nine students.

Mr. Sands, in October, entered of course upon the October. Session XIII. charge of the new Bejan class; and at the termination of the session, Mr. George Robertson, who had succeeded Mr. Heslope, brought the Magistrand class, 1596. The ninth Class graduated. consisting of twenty-four students, to the usual degree. He was the first who caused the Theses, which were the subjects of the public disputation, to be printed.

In October, the College, as usual, met after the October. Session XIV. vacation; and Mr. George Robertson undertook the charge of the new Bejan class. But on the 13th of Dec. 13. A tumult in the city, and its consequences. December the tranquillity of the city was disturbed by a dreadful tumult, by which the King's life was exposed to danger; and which afterwards well nigh proved fatal to the city of Edinburgh, and to the existence of the Presbyterian Church Government in Scotland. The excessive lenity on the part of the King to the Popish Lords, and the suspicion, violence, and rash proceedings of the Presbyterian clergy, were the causes of this shocking outrage against all law and good government. Although the Magistrates of Edinburgh had exerted themselves in repressing the commotion, and had succeeded so far as to preserve the King's life, and to hinder the effusion of blood; yet, because they had not prevented the commencement of this affair, of which it afterwards was proved that they had no previous suspicion, it was not till after the interposition of Queen Elizabeth, and the most abject submission which they made to the King, that they were restored to the Royal favour.[1] The Ministers of Edinburgh found it necessary to consult their safety by flight ; and though James at length suffered his resentment against them to be in some measure mitigated, by the mediation chiefly of Mr. Rollock, Principal of the College, of whom he always entertained a most favourable opinion, yet he had resolved in his own mind to humble the power of the Church, and he succeeded. He soon obliged the Clergy to submit to his own jurisdiction, and in other respects abridged their privileges ; and before the end of the year 1598, he prevailed with a majority of the Assembly to declare it lawful for ministers to accept of a seat in Parliament, and to agree that the Church should be represented in that Supreme Court by fifty-one of their number ; a circumstance which, under the appearance of favouring the Church, was, with reason, thought by many to point at the restoring of Episcopacy.

1597.
July 30.
The tenth
Class gradu-
ated.

The College, however, notwithstanding the great disturbance which had prevailed in the city, was regularly conducted to the conclusion of the session ; and, on the 30th of July, the tenth class, under the tuition of Mr. Charles Ferme, thirty-four in number, received the usual degree. Robert Ker, Lord Newbattle, afterwards Earl of Lothian, bore a share in the public disputation on this occasion, and also

---

[1] See Dr. Robertson's History of Scotland, Book viii., and Maitland's History of Edinburgh, chap. iii.

subscribed the Confession and Covenant. He soon after set out on foreign . travel, accompanied by Mr. Patrick Sands, which vacated one of the professorships. Upon which Mr. William Craig, a young man of talents and polite manners, who had taken his degree in 1593, and was recommended by Principal Rollock, was chosen; and admitted in October to the charge of Mr. Sands's class, then entering on the third year of their course; and he was the eleventh Professor of Philosophy.

October.
Mr. William Craig, eleventh Professor of Philosophy.

The same month, at the opening of the new session, Mr. Charles Ferme entered upon the charge of the Bejan class; Mr. George Robertson proceeded with the Semi; and the Magistrand was now conducted by Mr. Henry Charteris.

Session xv.

This year, Sir Adrian Damman, who, in consequence of a contract betwixt the Town-Council and the College of Justice formerly mentioned, had given public lectures annually on the Latin classics since the end of the year 1594, thought proper, on account of his other engagements, to resign this duty; and a new contract was entered into, on the 28th of December, by which it was stipulated that the interest of 2000 pounds Scots of the sum of 3000 formerly allotted for the support of a Professor of Law, should be employed for maintaining six bursars or exhibitioners; fifty marks being then esteemed a competent annual supply for an ordinary scholar; and the interest of the remaining 1000 was reserved for a salary to a Professor of Humanity or Philosophy : the other four Regents, at that time, having each no more than 100 pounds

Dec. 28.
A new Contract betwixt the Town and the College of Justice.

Six bursaries founded;

and a Professorship of Humanity.

Mode of
Electing,
Scots[1] yearly. It was agreed also that the election
of a Professor of Humanity should be made by six
delegates, of whom two should be from the Lords of
Session, two from the Town-Council, one from the
Faculty of Advocates, and one from the Society of
Writers to the Signet ; and that they should take the
advice of the Principal of the College. Previous to

and Regula-
tions for the
Professor.
the conclusion of the contract, the following regulations had been adopted :—That the Regent of
Humanity shall teach the Rhetoric of Cassander, and
the Orations of Cicero ; and shall cause his scholars to
make short declamations weekly ; that he shall also
teach Horace, Juvenal, Plautus, the Greek Grammar,
with certain Greek authors ; and as the scholars learn
an oration of Cicero, he shall cause them to declaim it
publicly in the school.

Mr. John
Ray, first
Professor of
Humanity.
Mr. John Ray, a native of the county of Angus,
well advanced in life, and who had great experience
in teaching, though he had only taken his degree at
the last laureation, was, by the approbation of all the
parties, elected ; and was properly the first Professor
of Humanity in the College of Edinburgh. He gave
instructions on the Latin language and literature, both
in public and private.

1598.
January.
In January 1598, Mr. George Robertson having
accepted a call to be one of the ministers of the town
of Edinburgh,[2] a public comparative trial was held for

---

[1] £8, 6s. 8d. sterling. It should seem
that ten per cent. at this time was not
thought exorbitant interest. Mr. Hume
says that interest in England, during the
reign of James, was never below eight
per cent. - Appendix to the Reign of
James I. About money see Chalmers's
Life of Ruddiman, pp. 196, 197, 321.

[2] Mr. George Robertson did not long
survive his admission as a minister of
Edinburgh. He lived just long enough
to compose an account of the life of

the election of a Professor to supply his place ; and, after a disputation continued for some days, Mr. John Adamson, son of Mr. Henry Adamson, Provost of Perth, proved the successful candidate, and entered upon the charge of the Semi class begun by Mr. Robertson. Mr. Adamson became a great ornament to the College, not only as one of the Regents, but afterwards as Principal. He had taken the master's degree in August 1597.[1] Mr. John Adamson, twelfth Professor of Philosophy.

On the 29th of July, the Magistrand class, consisting of thirty-two students, under the tuition of Mr. Henry Charteris, being the eleventh since the institution of the College, was graduated with the usual solemnity. July 29. The eleventh Class graduated.

At this time, Mr. James Bannatyne, brother to Mr. Patrick Bannatyne, Justice-Clerk Depute, bequeathed 100 merks to the College ; which was the first private donation bestowed upon this Seminary. The first private donation.

At the opening of a new session in October, the Senatus Academicus consisted of the following members :— October. Session XVI.

Mr. ROBERT ROLLOCK, Principal and Professor of Divinity.

Mr. HENRY CHARTERIS,	Professors of	The Bejan class.
Mr. CHARLES FERME,	Philosophy	The Semi class.
Mr. JOHN ADAMSON,	having the	The Bachelor class.
Mr. WILLIAM CRAIG,	charge of	The Magistrand class.

Mr JOHN RAY, Professor of Humanity.

But the society did not long remain in this state ;

Principal Rollock,—Vitæ et Mortis D. Roberti Rolloci Scoti, Narratio. Edinburgi, 1599, 12mo.

[1] On the 21st of March, William Muirhead was elected one of the six bursars by the Advocates and Writers to the Signet ; and in May Robert Gilmour, a bursar and student in the Magistrand class, was made Janitor of the College, the third who had held that office. He was afterwards minister at Calder-Clere.

for, on the 8th of February 1599, the College sustained an irreparable loss by the death of Principal Rollock in the forty-fourth year of his age. He was a man eminently qualified for the offices which he held, and had discharged them all with the greatest approbation. He was equally dear to the patrons, to his colleagues, and to the whole body of the students.

This excellent and useful man, for so he may be truly called, was born in the county of Stirling, in the year 1555, of an honourable family, being the second son of David Rollock of Powhouse, and of Marion Livingstone, daughter of Henry Livingstone of Westquarter.[1] His family was a branch of that of the ancient Barons of Duncrub, afterwards ennobled by the title of Lord Rollo.[2] He studied Latin at the grammar-school of Stirling, under Thomas Buchanan, a famous master, nephew to the celebrated George. Thence he was removed to St. Salvator's College in the University of St. Andrews, where he distinguished himself so much in passing through his philosophical course, that he soon after obtained first the Professorship of Humanity, and afterwards a regency of Philosophy in the same College. It was there, while he was carrying his first class of students towards the conclusion of their quadrennial course, that his reputation attracted the notice of the Magistrates and Town-Council of Edinburgh. He accepted of their invitation to be the first Professor in their newly-instituted College; and they could not have

---

[1] Vitæ et Mortis Rob. Rolloci Narratio. Auctore Georgio Robertson.

[2] Crawford's History of the University of Edinburgh.

made a more fortunate choice. He discharged the duty first of a Professor of Philosophy, and then of Principal and Professor of Divinity, with such industry, ability, and success, that he had the satisfaction before his death to see the society over which he presided one of the most flourishing in the kingdom.

According to the custom which then prevailed, Rollock conveyed his instructions to the students generally in the Latin tongue, of which the works he has left show him to have been a great master. He is said to have been profoundly skilled in the dogmatic philosophy of Aristotle, entertaining at the same time a disgust at the absurd wranglings which had long prevailed in the schools, and showing a high esteem for the dialectics of Ramus, of which no man knew how to make a better use.

As Principal of the College, it was his custom frequently to visit the Philosophy classes privately, in order to try the progress of the students, and to exhort them to the practice of piety and virtue. On Wednesday, in the afternoon, he gave public lectures on Divinity to the Philosophical classes, as well as the students in that faculty, from the former of whom he exacted an account in public of the knowledge they had acquired during the preceding week. After the lecture was ended, and the students of Theology dismissed, he proceeded to the exercise of discipline with the Philosophy classes; and, when any case of extraordinary negligence or transgression required to be corrected, he generally attained his purpose by means of earnest expostulation and admonition in preference to coercion, in the exercise of which he was very sparing, although in those days corporal punishment had not been laid aside in the Universities. But, whether he administered chastisement or rebuke, he always acted in so judicious a manner as to conciliate the respect and attachment of the students, and to allure their minds to the admiration and love of religion and virtue. With respect to the students of Divinity, he was so successful in his method of training them up for the proper exercise of the pastoral charge, that, for the space of twelve years, he had the most flourishing seminary of the kind known in that age.

Besides his double academical duty, as Principal and Professor of Divinity, he likewise, at the request of the Magistrates and Town-Council, preached weekly on Sunday mornings in the east church of St. Giles ; and, during the two last years of his life, he discharged the whole duty of one of the eight ministers of the city, and was much admired by his hearers as an eloquent and powerful preacher.

But such a variety of severe duty was calculated to impair a constitution much more vigorous than that which Rollock possessed. In the year 1596, he already felt the excruciating effects of a confirmed stone ; and the unfortunate tumult excited in the city about that time gave him additional anxiety and pain. He, indeed, had the satisfaction to perceive his interest, and the respect shown to his character so powerful as to give him a principal share in reconciling the King to the Magistrates of Edinburgh, and in procuring the return of the ministers to their charge in the city, but his health continued gradually to decline.

The ensuing year, however, he still retained a sufficient degree of vigour to enable him to act as Moderator of the General Assembly, which was held at Dundee, and where the King himself was present. Rollock's principles were decidedly loyal, and he was personally attached to the King; and, though a strict Presbyterian, he maintained the necessity and utility of a firm alliance betwixt the Church and State. He condemned the violence of the clergy discovered in the late tumult, and recommended to them a peaceful deportment, and the cultivation of harmony and a good understanding with the King, whose professions in favour of the Presbyterian doctrine and discipline he believed to be sincere, and never suspected him of any design to restore the Episcopal Hierarchy. In that Assembly, therefore, he promoted those measures which were agreeable to the King; and, being one of the number of the subsequent Commission, he, at the King's desire, supported the petition presented to Parliament by that body, praying that the Church might be represented in the Supreme Civil Court by a certain number of ecclesiastics to be chosen by the General Assembly. But this worthy man did not live to see the end of these concessions, which afterwards turned out so different from his expectations. Hence he was considered by some of his own party as too credulous, and better fitted for the duties of a College than the management of public affairs.

C

Meanwhile, on the approach of winter, his health was so much impaired, that he found it necessary to confine himself to his chamber, and soon after to his bed. He saw his dissolution gradually approaching, but did not decline the visits and the conversation of his friends. Two of these, Patrick Galloway and David Lindsay, he requested to go to the King, to whom he professed inviolable attachment, and, in his name, to exhort his Majesty to continue to the end of life in the paths of religion, which he had hitherto firmly trod, and not suffer himself to be diverted from that honourable course by the secret machinations of designing men, or the hope of aggrandizing his royal power, and always to think and speak with decent esteem of the Ministers of the Church.

With the Ministers of the city, who came to visit him in a body, he held an affectionate and pious discourse ; calling God to witness with what ardent affection he had ever regarded the University, and with what fidelity he had performed his academical duty, not doubting that his brethren would readily bear testimony to the great advantage derived both to the Church and State from that useful institution. And now that the end of his mortal state was at hand, he conjured them, when he should be no more, to support, to protect, to cherish it to the utmost of their power. In the exercise of the pastoral office, he could not, he said, affirm that he had in reality done any essential service, he only ventured to assert that it had been his earnest endeavour to do so. He put them in mind of his conduct in the late General

Assembly at Dundee, and declared that he reflected with satisfaction on the part he had taken in healing the wounds given to the peace of the Church by the late unhappy tumult. He expressed his approbation of a recent measure adopted, by which their number was doubled,[1] and his satisfaction in having recommended two of them on this occasion, who had been bred under his own tuition. He wished that the Church should ever maintain a firm alliance with the State, and confessed that he had exerted his influence in promoting that union, but without sacrificing the interest of the Church to his love of peace or his attachment to the King, with respect to whom he strongly recommended lenient rather than violent behaviour on the part of the clergy, as the surest method of obtaining their desire from a Prince, who, as he thought, had given strong evidence of a firm intention to support the cause of religion. He then took leave of them in the most pious and affectionate terms.

In the evening of the same day, when his physicians were endeavouring by medicines to palliate the violence of his malady, "God," said he, "shall now be my only physician;" and he persisted in an effusion of strains of the most fervent and pathetic devotion. Having taken each of the bystanders by the hand, he blessed them, one by one, with such pious and dignified expressions, "that he seemed," says his biographer,[2] "to be one of the patriarchs;" and he

---

[1] See Dr. Robertson's History of Scotland, Book viii.
[2] Georgii Robertsoni Narratio, etc., 1599.

accompanied his benediction with prudent exhortations suited to the disposition of each.

During that night he enjoyed some repose, contrary
to expectation ; and, on the following day, the Magistrates and several of the Town-Council came to
pay their respects to him. He spoke to them of his
approaching dissolution, as a thing he had long wished
for. He mentioned the anxious concern which he had
always felt for the prosperity of the College, and said
that he should not act consistently with this sentiment,
if he did not freely declare his opinion with respect
to a successor. "Why," continued he, " need you go
in quest of some stranger to undertake the office,
who may know nothing about the doctrine and dis--
cipline of this institution, when you have at hand a
person of excellent talents, and well prepared for
undertaking such a duty ? I mean Mr. Henry Charteris, who possesses every sort of knowledge which
he could derive from my own instructions, and who
has already, for ten years, discharged the office of a
Professor of Philosophy with the greatest applause.
Commit the helm of your College to his hands, and
you shall see that God will prosper his labours. You
ought to be its protectors as well as patrons ; let a
higher solicitude for its prosperity possess your minds."

He recommended to their care his wife, and his
only child, yet unborn, of whom, after being ten years
married, she was then pregnant ; he acknowledged
that his inattention to worldly affairs had been so
great, that he had saved nothing of the salaries which
he had enjoyed ; but he expressed a hope that the

affection with which they had ever regarded himself would still, after his death, be extended to his widow and his orphan child. The Magistrates assured him that everything should be done according to his wish. He next exhorted the Professors of Philosophy to persevere in the proper discharge of their duty, and to behave with due submission to his successor. Then he relapsed into the most fervent strains of devotion, beseeching his blessed Saviour to hasten the time of his dissolution.

At midnight he got some rest, which the force of his disease soon interrupted. He sent for his venerable colleague, Mr. Walter Balcanquhal, whom he addressed in most affectionate terms, and requested the assistance of his prayers ; but expressed a wish that he would put up no request for the prolonging of his life. After this religious service was concluded, he enlarged upon the great advantages derived from the preaching of the Gospel. Again he had recourse to prayer and to pious ejaculation, demeaning himself, and reposing his assurance of salvation in the merits of Christ. It was now Sunday, and he was asked whether he chose the conversation of any minister ; but he declined disturbing them in the exercise of their public function, and begged that he might himself be permitted to converse familiarly with his God.[1]

In the evening the Lord Provost of the city[2] went in to him, whom he thus addressed :—" I have earnestly recommended the University to the favour

---

[1] The words of his biographer are :— " Sinite," inquit, " me psittaci instar, cum Domino meo balbutire."

[2] Sir Alexander Seton, Lord Fyvie ; also President of the Court of Session, afterwards Earl of Dunfermline.

of the Magistrates, over whom you, my Lord, preside ;
and I have now to request that you may take her
under your particular protection. Your rank in the
State, and the high dignity with which you are invested, enable you also to succour the Church ; do
not, my Lord, withhold from her your good offices, or
forget that the source of your own salvation is from
Christ, and that present things are of a transient
nature, and will soon fade away."

During the ensuing night his disease became still
more excruciating ; and when his attendants observed
him resisting and sustaining the most vehement ago-
nies, and were unable to abstain from tears and
lamentations, he soothed and consoled them in the
tenderest manner, dissuading them from bewailing his
fate, for that he would soon arrive at the consumma-
tion of all his wishes. After this, he refused every
sort of sustenance, and recommended the care of his
funeral to his two highly esteemed friends, William
Little, late Lord Provost, and William Scott of Ely.
In the evening his discourse was observed to be less
diffuse ; but what he uttered was still full of energy
and ardent devotion, until he fell at length into a
gentle sleep ; and after continuing in that state for
some time, he resigned his breath without a struggle,
and with the greatest composure.

Such was the man who gave the first impulse to
those instructions which have been regularly delivered
in the University of Edinburgh for upwards of two
centuries. While the historians of kingdoms and
nations are ambitious of recording the minute circum-

stances in the lives and characters of those princes, statesmen, and warriors who, sometimes by their virtues, but far oftener by their crimes, have attracted the admiration of mankind, Literary History must move in an humbler sphere, and often be contented with celebrating the less splendid labours of those useful men who have employed their talents in diffusing the principles of virtue and of patriotism among the youth, in setting before them the true felicity of their nature, and teaching them how to counteract those fatal passions which are the source of so much misery to the human race.

After Mr. Rollock's death, the greatest respect was shown to his memory. He was followed to the grave by an immense concourse of all ranks, who lamented him with expressions of the deepest sorrow. Upwards of thirty copies of verses were composed in his praise by his literary friends; and the Magistrates of Edinburgh, mindful of his dying request, voted, on the 15th of the following June, 100 marks of annuity to his widow for five years, and the sum of 1000 marks as a portion for his posthumous daughter; and afterwards, on the 22d of February 1611, they bestowed upon her 100 marks yearly, to continue to the time of her marriage.[1]

On the 14th of February 1599, the Town-Council, in compliance with the recommendation of the late Mr. Rollock, elected Mr. Henry Charteris to be Principal and Professor of Divinity in his place. Mr.

1599.
Feb. 14.

Mr. Henry Charteris, second Principal and Professor of Divinity.

[1] Her name was Jean, and she was afterwards married to Mr. Robert Balcanquhal, minister of Tranent, son of Mr. Walter. Her mother, whose name was Helen Baron, was daughter to the Laird of Kinnaird in Fife.

Charteris had held the office of one of the Regents for almost ten years, and was a most learned, modest, and respectable man. A vacancy of one of the professorships of Philosophy being thus occasioned, and a public comparative trial being announced, two candidates entered their names, Mr. Robert Scott and Mr. Andrew Young, the former of whom had taken his degree in 1597, and the latter in 1598, and who had been recently elected a Professor of Philosophy at Aberdeen. Though both of them were much approved of, the judges gave the preference to Mr. Scott, who was accordingly elected; and he received from Mr. Charteris the charge of the Bejan class. Mr. Young, however, obtained a promise from the patrons, and was named by them to succeed upon the next vacancy that should happen. Mr. Charles Ferme having some time before accepted of a call to be Minister at Fraserburgh, Mr. James Knox, who, on a former trial, had given great satisfaction to the judges, and had by them been recommended to the Town-Council, who had elected him accordingly, now entered to the charge of the Semi class in place of Mr. Ferme.

Mr. James Knox, the thirteenth, and Mr. Robert Scott, the fourteenth Professor of Philosophy.

On the 28th of July, Mr. William Craig advanced the Magistrand class to the usual degree, in number thirty-five, being the twelfth since the institution of the College. This is the year in which the King published his book entitled *Βασιλικον Δωρον*, containing precepts concerning the art of government, addressed to Prince Henry his son.

July 28. The twelfth Class graduated.

In October, on the meeting of the College after the vacation, the state of the Senatus Academicus was as

October. Session XVIII.

follows :—Mr. Henry Charteris, Principal and Professor of Divinity ; Mr. William Craig, Mr. Robert Scott, Mr. James Knox, Mr. John Adamson, Professors of Philosophy ; Mr. John Ray, Professor of Humanity.

At the conclusion of the session, the thirteenth class, under the tuition of Mr. John Adamson, consisting of thirty-five students, received the degree in the usual manner. The Theses printed on this occasion are dedicated by Mr. Adamson to Alexander Seton, Lord Fyvie, President of the Court of Session, and Lord Provost of the city. 1600. July 29. The thirteenth Class graduated.

In October, at the opening of a new session, Mr. Adamson, in his turn, undertook the charge of the new Bejan class. October. Session XIX.

On the 10th of December, the Town-Council, finding that the accommodation formerly provided for the students to attend public worship in the East Church of St. Giles's, called the High Church, was not large enough to contain them all, allotted the east gallery of the Trinity College Church for their reception, till a more commodious place should be found. Dec. 10

On the 30th of July, Mr. James Knox brought the Magistrand class, consisting of twenty students, to the usual degree. Upon that occasion the Theses continued to be printed. 1601. July 30. The fourteenth Class graduated.

The Principal's annual salary having hitherto been no more than 400 marks, the patrons, on the 16th of September this year augmented it to 600. The Principal's salary augmented.

In October, at the opening of a new session, Mr. James Knox entered upon the charge of the new Bejan class ; and, in December, Mr. William Craig October. Session XX.

resigned his office, and went into France, where he was elected Professor of Divinity in the College of

Mr. Andrew Young, fifteenth Professor of Philosophy.

Saumur.[1] This opened a place for Mr. Andrew Young, who was accordingly brought from Aberdeen and set over the class vacated by Mr. Craig.

1602.
February 22.
The fifteenth Class graduated.

On the 22d of February, much sooner than the usual period (probably from some apprehension of the plague, which soon after broke out), Mr. Robert Scott advanced the Magistrand class, consisting of thirty-two students, to the Master's degree with the usual solemnity.

October.
Session XXI.

The College being again met in October, after the vacation, Mr. Scott undertook the charge of the new Bejan class; but continued in the office only till the

1603.
January.
Mr. James Reid, seventeenth Professor of Philosophy.

beginning of the ensuing January, having then accepted of a call to be one of the ministers of Glasgow. Upon which, a comparative trial for a successor being announced by programs, four competitors appeared, of whom Mr. James Reid was preferred by the judges; and being elected accordingly, he proceeded with the Bejan class.

March 24.
The King's accession to the throne of England.

The city of Edinburgh, its College, and the whole kingdom, were now to be deprived of the presence of their monarch. He was, in consequence of the death of Queen Elizabeth, which happened on the 24th of March, soon to take possession of the English throne. Previous to this event, he had granted to the Magistrates of Edinburgh a most ample Charter, dated at Holyroodhouse the 15th of that month, confirming all

---

[1] After holding this office but for a few years, Craig returned to Scotland, and died in his own house in Blackfriars Wynd, Edinburgh.

his former donations to them.   This is called the City
of Edinburgh's *Golden Charter*.   It contains, amidst
a great variety of other matter, a particular enumeration and confirmation of all the former grants respecting the College of Edinburgh.   On the 5th of April,
the King began his journey from his native kingdom,
and entered London on the 7th of May, amidst the
acclamations of the people.   But the vast accession
of power and importance which James acquired by
this event, and the dazzling objects of ambition which
it held out to him, did not alienate his affection
from the people of his native kingdom.   Even the
College of Edinburgh, humble as it was, and poorly
endowed, was not, amidst a variety of concerns of
superior moment, entirely effaced from his memory.
In his absence he showed himself not unmindful of
it ; and, when he revisited his native kingdom, after
an interval of fourteen years, it was destined to receive additional marks of his favour.

Meanwhile, on the 29th of July, Mr. Andrew Young's
pupils in the Magistrand class, now the sixteenth
from the institution of the College, and twenty-three
in number, received, as usual, the Master's degree.

July 29.
The six-
teenth Class
graduated.

Having brought the annals of the College of Edinburgh to the termination of the twenty-first session,
in the year 1603, when the accession of James the
Sixth to the crown of England forms a new era in the
political history of Scotland, and may be supposed to
have had some influence also on the state of its learning, it may be proper to introduce here some account
of that sort of literature and science which was taught

in this new institution, and of the method observed by the Professors in conveying their instructions to the students.

In a liberal education, the object next after the acquisition of reading and writing was then, and still is, a knowledge of the Latin tongue. Without this it is impossible to obtain an intimate acquaintance with the Roman authors, whose works, together with those of the ancient Greeks, have, ever since the revival of learning in the West in the fifteenth or sixteenth centuries, been justly considered as the only genuine standards of fine writing.

But scholars in those days had additional and indispensable motives for becoming proficients in Latin. It had long been the universal medium of communication among the learned ; it was the language in which the Professors in the Universities delivered their instructions, and in which the students not only performed most of their Academical exercises, but in which they were obliged, under a strict penalty, always to converse within the precincts of the College.

The knowledge of Latin had never been utterly extinguished, even in those dark ages which succeeded the subversion of the Roman Empire. The service of the Romish Church, by being performed in that language, obliged the priests to learn it. Many of these, indeed, contented themselves with a very limited acquaintance with it, and scarcely understood the Breviary which they were obliged daily to read. There are, however, some instances of persons distinguished for profound erudition so far back as the eighth and ninth centuries ; but such of their productions as have been preserved are so inelegant and so entirely destitute of classical purity, that they now attract no attention, unless from those who find it necessary to search into them, on account of the historical facts which they contain. In those gloomy periods books were extremely scarce, and libraries existed only in monasteries and cathedrals. In these recesses were preserved most of the MSS. of the Roman classics, which were brought to light upon the revival of learning ; and it appears that the most learned of the priests and monks were not unacquainted with them, but they made little use of them for the refinement of their taste, or as their masters in the art of composition. As no literary knowledge could be acquired, but by the ecclesiastics who frequented those sacred retreats, and as, previous to the origin of Universities and Colleges, no schools were to be found anywhere else, the great body of-the laity was plunged into the most profound and infamous ignorance. Even princes and persons of the highest rank who were employed in the administration of civil affairs, could neither read nor write. The field of battle was the only scene where they could acquire distinction.[1]

It may also be proper to introduce here some account of the method of examining the different classes at the opening of each session, and the trial of the Magistrand class at the conclusion, previous to their

[1] [This and the three preceding paragraphs occur as a detached fragment of Professor Dalzel's MS. He probably intended to have added some notice of other branches of learning taught in the Philosophical classes; but this intention he does not seem to have executed.—EDIT.]

receiving the degree, from which it will appear how
laborious the Professors were in the discharge of their
duty, and what diligence was required from the students
in performing their exercises.

Method of
Examination
at the be-
ginning of
the Session.

The month of October, during the course of which
the students were entering or returning to their studies,
was employed in the reading of Latin and Greek, and
other preparation for the business of the ensuing session ; and about[1] the beginning of November, when
the classes were fully met, the Principal, or, in his
absence, the Senior Regent, in a meeting in the public
hall, a little before nine in the morning, prescribed
to the Bejan class a piece of Scots, which was called

The Public
Theme to be
turned into
Latin.

the Public Theme. This being copied by each, and
then read aloud, the students were separated, and,
under the observation of the Regents who attended
them by turns, all except their own particular Professor, they translated it into Latin, and, having copied
their respective versions in a fair hand, and subscribed
them each with his own name, and the name of the
Master who had instructed him in Latin, they delivered them to the attending Regent before twelve
o'clock. At four o'clock in the afternoon, they met
again in the public hall in presence of the Principal
and the Regents, when each of them, upon being
called by name, read his Latin version aloud under
the particular inspection of one of the Regents, and
then returned the paper to be perused by the Principal and Regents ; and, if any one of them was
found so deficient in the knowledge of Latin, that

[1] This account is taken from Crawford's History of the University of Edinburgh.

there was no hope of his profiting by the instructions to be delivered in the class, he was advised to return to the study of that language.

The next day a Latin Theme was prescribed to the Semi class to be translated into Greek, and afterwards read and examined in the same manner. A Latin Theme to be turned into Greek.

The third day a passage of some Latin and Greek author was prescribed to the Bachelor class to be analysed logically, and an account was taken of this task also in the same manner. Analysis of a passage.

Previous to this, the Semi class, at the opening of the session, spent several days in repetition of what they had formerly learned, and then they were exa-- mined publicly by the Magistrand and Bachelor Regents and the Professor of Humanity. The eldest Philosophy Regent examined them on Ramus's Dialectic and the Compend of Ars Syllogistica, the second on the Greek poets, the Humanity Regent on the Greek prose authors ; and an account was taken not only of what had been taught publicly, but of what each student had acquired by his own private industry. Semi Class examined.

After the finishing of this trial, the Bachelors were examined by the Magistrand, Semi, and Bejan Regents, the first putting questions on Porphyry and the Categories, the second περὶ Ἑρμηνείας and the Priors, and the third on the Topics, Sophistics, Ramus, etc.

Lastly, the Magistrand class underwent a double examination by the Bachelor, Semi, and Bejan Regents. In the first place, the eldest Regent demanded an account of what was called the common part of Logic, the next of the Demonstration, and the last of the Topics, Sophistics, and Ramus ; and, in the second place, the eldest put questions on the Acroamatical books de Principiis, the second on the rest of the Acroasis, and the third on the Ethics.

A few days after the conclusion of this first examination of the Magistrand class, a second trial was held of all the classes, on account of such students as had been absent ; and whoever failed to appear at both examinations was called to a strict account in a third trial either in the public hall, or in the private schools.

Before the middle of July, near the close of the session, as preparatory to receiving the degree, the Magistrands gave up their names for trial in the public hall, by the Bachelor, Semi, Bejan, and Humanity Regents. This trial also consisted of two parts. In the first, the eldest Philosophy Regent demanded an account of the general part of Logic ; the next, of the Demonstration ; the third, of the Topics, Sophistics, and Ramus ; and the Humanist of the Ethics. In the second, the eldest Regent interrogated on the Acroamatics ; the next, de Cœlo and on Astronomy ; the third, de Ortu · and on the Meteors ; and the Humanist, de Anima.

The evening before the public disputation on the Theses, they met in presence of the Principal and Professors, and subscribed the Confession of Faith ; and this year likewise they subscribed for the first time a solemn engagement to persevere in affection to the College where they had received their education.[1] Then the Principal, upon finding that all of them had received a certificate of having performed all the necessary exercises, took the report of the five Regents respecting the behaviour and ability of every one in particular, and, according to their merit, enrolled their names, distinguishing them into certain ranks, some being styled Exortes, before all the circles; others being of the first circle, with some annexed to it; others of the second circle; the rest being arranged in a line, whose names it was thought proper to suppress in the public recitation. This was called " The circling of the class."

The day usually appointed for the graduation was Monday, as the Court of Session was sitting at that time of the year; and, as on Monday the Court never met, this afforded an opportunity for the Lord Chancellor and other Privy Councillors, the Lords of Exchequer, the Lords of Session, Advocates, and Clerks to the Signet, to be present at this solemnity, with the Lord Provost, Magistrates, and Town-Council, Patrons of the College, and other learned persons.

The disputation upon the Theses used to commence in the morning, and terminate in the evening about six o'clock, when the candidates were called in by name, according to the ranks previously determined, and made their appearance in a conspicuous place before the Principal, who first gave them a short exhortation to a virtuous and honourable life, and then performed the ceremony of graduation, by touching the head of every one of the candidates with a

---

[1] These subscriptions are still extant in the Graduation-Book.

bonnet, after which one of the number, in a short speech, concluded the solemnity.

The College of Edinburgh, for many years after its institution, conferred no other degree than that of Master of Arts, although the privilege of erecting a *Studium Generale,* or University, being originally granted to the patrons by the King, and afterwards ratified in Parliament, certainly gave a title to the College to confer degrees also in all the other faculties, Theology, Law, and Medicine ; a right, however, which it did not begin to exercise till after the beginning of the eighteenth century, when the number of Professors had considerably increased.

In the study of Philosophy, which, with Theology, was the principal employment of the youth in this Seminary during the four years' course, Aristotle was still regarded with peculiar respect. His doctrines, however, were in a great measure cleared from that gross and mysterious jargon which adhered to them in the ages which immediately preceded the revival of classical learning, the invention of printing, and the reformation of religion, as may be seen from the Theses which are still extant, and which formed the subjects of the philosophic disputations of the students previous to their receiving the degree. From inspecting these, it will appear that the students, as well as the Professors, were able to have recourse to Aristotle in the original, and to reason upon his tenets in a much more clear and intelligible manner than had been the case in the Schools, where he was known only through the medium of a barbarous Latinity.

The great Lord Bacon indeed existed at this period, was even in the prime of life, and occupied in those studies, the fruits of which were destined to bring about a complete revolution in the Schools of Philosophy, and to add lustre to James's reign in England. But his genius was yet unknown in the Colleges of his native country, as well as in those of Scotland, which last, however, were fully as forward in cherishing and admiring it when known, as well as that of the divine Newton which soon succeeded it, as the Universities of any other country.

CHAPTER II.

1603.
October.
Session
XXII.

ON the meeting of the College in October 1603, Mr. Andrew Young undertook the charge of the new Bejan class, Mr. James Reid proceeded with the Semi, Mr. James Knox with the Bachelor, and Mr. John Adamson with the Magistrand. But about the close of the year the plague broke out, and it increased to such a degree of violence, that before the

1604.
May 28.
The seven-
teenth Class
graduated.

end of May in the ensuing year, most of the students were dispersed, which obliged Mr. Adamson to anticipate the usual term for graduation, by admitting his class, in number twenty-six, to the degree on the 28th of that month, after publicly defending the Theses, without the usual form of previous examination ; after which he accepted of a call to be minister at North Berwick, and resigned his office in the College. He had, however, given such proofs of ability during the discharge of his duty as a Professor, that he was afterwards invited to return to the College, and to undertake the superintendence of it as Principal. In his

Mr. David
Monro,
eighteenth
Professor of
Philosophy.

place was substituted Mr. David Monro, who had been one of the candidates at the late comparative trial, and had acquitted himself with approbation.

No new class entered in October this session on account of the plague, and it was the beginning of the succeeding year before the other classes returned to the College. The plague having then much abated, these assembled at length in their usual number, but Mr. David Monro had no duty to perform till the ensuing session, as there was no Bejan class till then.[1]

October.
Session
XXIII.

Meanwhile, on the 27th of July 1605, the eighteenth class, educated by Mr. James Knox, and consisting of twenty-four students, were graduated in the usual manner.[2]

1605.
July 27.
The eighteenth Class
graduated.

Mr. Knox, soon after, having received a call to be minister of Kelso, resigned his professorship ; and in October, at the opening of the next session, Mr. David Monro undertook the charge of a new Bejan class ; Mr. Andrew Young proceeded with the Bachelor ; and Mr. James Reid with the Magistrand,—which, being the nineteenth class, and twenty-eight in number, he brought forward to the usual degree, on the last day of June 1606.

October.
Session
XXIV.

1606
June 30.
The nineteenth Class
graduated.

In the following vacation, a vacancy having happened in the Rectorship of the High School, by the resignation of Mr. Alexander Home, Mr. John Ray, who had been Professor of Humanity upwards of eight years, preferred the former office, and being translated thither accordingly, he held it for nearly

---

[1] On the 3d of April, James Shaw, student in the highest class, was admitted Porter of the College.

[2] The following is the title of the Theses published on this occasion :—
"Theses Philosophicæ, quas auspice et propitio Deo, Præside Jac. Knoxio, propugnabunt Adolescentes Magisterii Candidati è Scholis Edinburgi Philosophicis hoc Anno 1605, emittendi. Disputabuntur die Lunæ 4. Kal. Aug. à septima matutina in duodecimam, et hora prima pomeridiana usque ad vesperam Edinburgi in Æde sacra Regii Collegii." They are dedicated to the Earl of Dunfermline, Chancellor, etc.

twenty-four years.　He was esteemed an accomplished Latin scholar, and composed some Latin verses upon different occasions, which are not inelegant.[1]

Delegates from the College of Justice and the Town-Council having met to choose a successor to Mr. Ray,

Mr. Blase
Colt, second
Professor of
Humanity.

Mr. Blase Colt, son of Mr. Oliver Colt, Advocate, a young man who had distinguished himself as an excellent Greek as well as Latin scholar, and who had received the Master's degree in 1603, appeared as a candidate, and there being no competitor, he was unanimously elected, and was the second Professor of Humanity in the University of Edinburgh.

October.
Session
XXV.

In October, Mr. James Reid began the session with the new Bejan class, Mr. David Monro having the Semi ; and there being no Bachelor class this session, Mr. Andrew Young proceeded with the Magistrands

1607.
July 25.
The twen-
tieth Class
graduated.

to the close of their course, and graduated them on the 25th of July 1607, being twenty-eight in number.

October
Session
XXVI.

In October, at the opening of the new session, Mr. David Monro, for what reason is unknown, resigned his office ; and as his students had already passed through two years of their course, it was thought more proper that Mr. Young, on account of his experience, should take the charge of them, and that the new Bejan class should be committed to the person who should happen to be elected instead of Mr. Monro.

Candidates being invited by program to contend for the vacant office, three competitors appeared,—

---

[1] See them in Hunter and Low's edition of Buchanan's Psalms, Adamson's Muses' Welcome, 1617, Robertson's Life of Rollock, 1599, etc.

Mr. Matthew Crawford, Mr. James Fairly, and Mr. William King. The first had taken the degree in 1606, and the other two at the last graduation, neither of whom were above nineteen years of age, but both of distinguished abilities. The judges, after the trial, were greatly at a loss which of the two last to prefer, and as each of them had an equal number of votes, it was agreed to commit the decision to the arbitration of Mr. John Nicolson, an accomplished scholar, just returned from foreign travel, and he declared for Mr. James Fairly.

But the judges, at the same time, having also recommended Mr. King as well qualified to supply the next vacancy, the patrons soon had an opportunity of gratifying him, as well as the other candidate, for, on account of the plague, no Bejan class had entered in October 1604, and there had been only three Professors of Philosophy since the time of Mr. Adamson's resignation in the month of May that year. It therefore became necessary to complete the number of Philosophy professors, when a new class was to be assembled in October 1608. Accordingly, Mr. William King was elected before the close of the present session, that he might be ready to undertake the charge of the next Bejan class in October 1608. In the meantime, Mr. James Fairly took the charge of the present Bejan class, Mr. James Reid proceeding with the Semi, and Mr. Andrew Young with the Bachelor, instead of Mr. David Monro. There was no Magistrand class this session, and consequently no graduation.

Mr. James Fairly, the nineteenth, and Mr. William King, the twentieth Professor of Philosophy.

1608. July. No graduation.

Flourishing
state of the
College.

This year, the state of the College began to flourish in an unusual degree. The frequent resignation of professors had hitherto been attended with great disadvantage. Men of learning had been discouraged from holding those laborious offices long, while the provision made for them was so scanty, as scarcely to furnish the means of a decent subsistence. But the plague had now disappeared, and the country not only felt the effects of profound peace, but abounded in every kind of plenty. Greater encouragement was now held out to men of letters, and the present Regents, Mr. Andrew Young, Mr. James Reid, Mr. James Fairly, and Mr. William King, who were men of talents and of great industry, were induced to remain in office much longer than any of their predecessors, and having acquired much experience, they felt great authority and respect attached to their situation.

The original
Revenue
very scanty.

When the College was first instituted, it possessed but a very trifling revenue,—only the Archdeaconry of Lothian, consisting of the vicarage and parsonage teinds of the kirk of Currie, together with the rents of the Provostry of the Collegiate Church, called the Kirk of Field, consisting, for the most part, of ground-annuals paid from different houses in the town ; also the vicarage and parsonage teinds of Kirkurd.[1] The first accession obtained was the sum of 3000 pounds Scots, contributed by the Town-Council and the College of Justice, which went chiefly to the maintenance of a Professor of Humanity. Two small addi-

---

[1] In the Presbytery of Peebles.

tions were made by James Bannatyne and William Couper.[1]

But this year, Mr. Walter Balcanquhal, who had been a great promoter of the foundation of the College, and Mr. John Hall, who was studious of its prosperity, considering that the late pestilence, as well as other circumstances, had contributed much to the diminution of the city's revenue, and prevented the augmentation of the College income from that source, and knowing that a sum amounting to 8100 pounds, belonging to the Kirk-Session, was in the hands of the treasurer unemployed, they obtained the consent of the other Ministers of the city, and the Kirk-Session, that this money should be employed for the augmentation of the salaries of the Professors. A contract was therefore framed, on the 16th of December this year, by which this money was conveyed by the Kirk-Session to the Town-Council of Edinburgh, on condition that the latter should pay to the College, for augmentation of the salaries of the Masters, in all time coming, the sum of 1000 marks yearly, and grant to the Session that the Ministers, in name thereof, should,

Donation by the Kirk-Session of Edinburgh.

[1] In the year 1589, James Master of Lindsay, having obtained a lease of the Nunnery of Haddington, for payment of a small rent to a titular prioress, and thinking proper that this should be applied for the advancement of learning, at first assigned the complete profits of the crop 1588 to the Town of Edinburgh, for the use of the College ; which were received accordingly. Afterwards, about the beginning of the year 1600, the same worthy person, the Lord Lindsay of the Byres, by a contract with the Town-Council of Edinburgh, agreed to bestow eighty pounds yearly out of the teinds of Crail in Fife, which belonged to the Priory of Haddington, for maintaining two bursars in the College. This sum continued to be paid for eight or nine years, until the Lord Binning, then Clerk Register, having married his daughter into that family, obtained a sentence of the Court of Session, by which that donation made to the College of Edinburgh, and another to the New College, St. Andrews, were reduced and annulled.—Crawford's History of the University of Edinburgh.

Ministers to
haVe a Voice
in electing
Professors. for the future, have joint voice with the Town-Council in electing the Principal, Masters, and Regents of the College. The Town-Council, farther to show their willingness to promote the interest of the College, resolved, on their part, after holding a conference Donation by
the Town-
Council of
the public
Mortcloths. with the Ministers, to bestow the annual profits arising from the public mortcloths or palls, for the purpose also of augmenting the salaries of the Professors ; which resolution was ratified on the 22d of February 1609.

1608.
October.
Session
XXVII. In the beginning of October, the College having assembled, Mr. William King undertook the charge of the new Bejan class, Mr. James Fairly proceeded with the Semi, Mr. James Reid with the Bachelor, and Mr. Andrew Young with the Magistrand.

1609.
February 15. In consequence of the new donations which have been mentioned, the salary of Mr. Henry Charteris, Principal, was by an act of Council augmented from 400 to 500 pounds ; and whereas the Regents had formerly only 200 pounds annually a piece, each of the two eldest, Mr. Young and Mr. Reid, now received an addition of 100 marks, which made the salary of each to be 250 marks.

July 27.
The twenty-
first Class
graduated. On the 27th of July, Mr. Young's students, being the twenty-first class, and thirty-three in number, were advanced to the Master's degree ; and after the vacation he entered upon the charge of the new Bejan October.
Session
XXVIII. class in the beginning of October, the other Regents proceeding with the other classes in regular order.

1610.
June 22. On the 22d of June 1610, the Council accepted of an offer made by the widow of one Alexander Lindsay,

in consequence of which they agreed to receive from her 3000 marks, and to pay her twelve per cent. per annum during her life, and on her death to employ 2000 marks of that sum for maintaining two bursars.

On the 28th of July, the twenty-second class, under the charge of Mr. James Reid, consisting of twenty-six students, received the Master's degree, with the usual solemnity, on which occasion, Robert Ker, eldest son of Lord Roxburgh, a very young man, went through every part of the trials and disputations with the other candidates. He died abroad a few years after.

July 28. The twenty-second Class graduated.

At the opening of a new session in October, Mr. Reid, of course, undertook the charge of the Bejan class, but Mr. Andrew Young, who had been afflicted for some months with an alarming distemper, was obliged to devolve the care of the Semi class upon a young man whose name was Mr. Andrew Stevenson, and who had been one of his own graduates in 1609. As there seemed to be no hope of Mr. Young's recovery, a comparative trial for a successor was publicly announced. On the appointed day three candidates appeared,—Mr. Andrew Stevenson, already mentioned, the son of a burgess of Edinburgh; Mr. Robert Burnet, son to the Laird of Barns in Tweeddale; and Mr. James Ker, son to the Laird of Linton. They had all been lately graduated, and the youthfulness of their appearance occasioned a demur, and the affixing of fresh programs to invite more competitors, but without the desired effect. The trial therefore proceeded, and Mr. Stevenson being most approved of by

October. Session XXIX.

1611. Mr. Andrew Stevenson chosen an interim Professor of Philosophy.

the judges, the patrons elected him, but upon this condition, that if Mr. Young should recover his health, the newly elected Professor should retire, and suffer the other to resume his former station.[1]

Mr. Stevenson had scarcely taken possession of his office, when the Professorship of Humanity became vacant by the untimely death of Mr. Blase Colt, a young man greatly esteemed for his learning and the politeness of his manners. Upon this his elder bro-

Mr. Oliver Colt, third Professor of Humanity. ther, Mr. Oliver, who had practised as an advocate for several years, disliking that profession, offered himself as a candidate to succeed his brother, and was unanimously chosen. But he did not continue long in that office. Having betaken himself for some time before to the study of Divinity, he received a call to be minister of Holyroodhouse, and resigned his professorship in the end of November this year.[2]

July 27. The twenty-third Class graduated. On the 27th of the preceding July, Mr. James Fairly had brought the twenty-third class, consisting of twenty-two students, then under his charge, to the Master's degree, in the usual manner ; and in the be-

October. Session XXX. ginning of the following October he undertook the charge of the new Bejan class. Mr. Andrew Young, having recovered his health, after a long and severe illness, was allowed to resume his charge ; and he proceeded with the Bachelor class. Mr. Stevenson consequently withdrew, and for some time betook himself entirely to private study.

---

[1] Mr. Robert Burnet will be mentioned afterwards (see p. 61). Mr. James Ker, a few years after, was chosen a Regent in St. Leonard's College, St. Andrews, where, after a period of three years, he died of a hectic fever in 1617.

[2] He was soon after translated to the church of Foulden, in the Merse, where he died.

Soon after the commencement of the session, candidates for the vacant Professorship of Humanity being invited by means of public programs, Mr. Robert Burnet, formerly mentioned, and Mr. Galbraith, son to a burgess of Edinburgh, were the only two who gave in their names. After the trial, the judges being at a loss which of the two to prefer, it was agreed to decide the affair by lot. Mr. Burnet proved successful, and Mr. Galbraith went over to France, where he obtained a Professorship in one of the Colleges of that kingdom.[1]

Mr. Robert Burnet, fourth Professor of Humanity.

On the 25th of July, Mr. William King's students, twenty-four in number, making the twenty-fourth class since the foundation, were graduated in the usual way.[2] After the vacation, at the commencement of a new session he returned to the charge of a new Bejan class.

1612. The twenty-fourth Class graduated.

October. Session XXXI.

In July 1613, Charles Shearers, of Dort in Holland, conveyed to the Treasurer of the city of Edinburgh 500 marks for the use of the College, reserving the interest of that sum to himself and his friends for some time.

1613. Shearers' Donation.

On the 31st of the same month the twenty-fifth class, now under the charge of Mr. Andrew Young, consisting of thirty-one students, received the Master's degree. The printed Theses, a pretty large collection, are dedicated in elegant Latin to Sir John Maitland, Lord Thirlestane, the Chancellor, a man of great integrity, ability, and learning.

July 31. The twenty-fifth Class graduated.

---

[1] On the 19th of June, Mr. Alexander Douglas being called to be minister at Whittingham, William Watson, student in the highest class, was chosen Porter of the College.

[2] The Theses on this occasion have been preserved, and form a large collection contained in a quarto pamphlet, under the heads, "Theses Logicæ, Physicæ, Ethicæ, Astronomicæ."

October.
Session
XXXII.
At the opening of a new session in October, Mr. Young returned to the charge of the new class, and the other three Professors proceeded with the other classes in regular order.

1614.
A Visitation
of the Col-
lege.
In May 1614, the College was visited by a Committee, consisting of sixteen members of the Town-Council, five Ministers of the city, and three Advocates, assessors of the Town. The chief object of their meeting was to devise better accommodation for the public assemblies of all the five classes, and the students of Divinity. The graduations, for want of room in the College, had been for several years performed either in the Trinity College Church, or in that of the Greyfriars.

July 30.
The twenty-
sixth Class
graduated.
On the 30th of July, the twenty-sixth class, under the charge of Mr. George Reid, consisting of twenty-eight students, obtained the Master's degree ; and October.
Session
XXXIII. after the vacation Mr. Reid began another session with a new Bejan class.

1615.
July 22.
The twenty-
seventh Class
graduated.
On the 22d of July 1615, the Magistrand class, being the twenty-seventh, and consisting of thirty-five students, under the charge of Mr. James Fairly, were graduated in the usual manner. John Stewart, afterwards Earl of Traquair, and Great Treasurer of Scotland, distinguished himself among the candidates on this occasion.

October.
Session
XXXIV.
New Public
Hall and Lib-
rary
It was now Mr. Fairly's turn to take the charge of the Bejan class on the opening of the session in October ; and on the 27th of December in the same year, the Town-Council resolved, in consequence of the report of the late visitors, that a common hall and

room for a Library should be built, and they allotted the sum of 3000 marks for that purpose.[1] The work was soon after begun and carried on with great industry. The building still remains, and consists of an upper and under hall; the former of which is the Public Library, and the latter was, for many years, used as the common hall, where public discourses were delivered and degrees conferred. It extends from north to south, within the first quadrangle of the new fabric, for more than 100 feet, its north-west corner touching the south-east one of the new Chemical Laboratory.[2]

On the 27th of July, the twenty-eighth class, twenty-eight in number, under the charge of Mr. William King, obtained the usual degree. On this occasion, John Campbell, afterwards Earl of Loudon, and Chancellor of Scotland, was distinguished in the disputation, both in defending and impugning the Theses.[3]

1616.
July 27.
The twenty-eighth Class graduated.

At the beginning of the thirty-fifth session, Mr. William King had the charge of the new Bejan class, Mr. James Fairly proceeded with the Semi, Mr. James Reid with the Bachelor, and Mr. Andrew Young with the Magistrand.

October.
Session
XXXV.

The year 1617 is famous in the annals of the College of Edinburgh. The King, after an absence of fourteen years, resolved to visit his native kingdom, and at his arrival in Edinburgh on the 16th of May,

1617.

May 16.

---

[1] Town-Council Records, vol. xii.

[2] The inscription over the gate of the Common Hall fronting the west, is somewhat singular: "SENATUS POPULUSQUE EDINBURGENSIS HAS ÆDES CHRISTO ET MUSIS EXTRUENDAS CURARUNT. ANNO DOMINI M.DC.XVII."

[3] See, about establishing parish schools, December 10, 1616, Chalmers's Life of Ruddiman, p. 18.

he was received with great demonstrations of loyalty and affection by the Magistrates and Town-Council, and the principal citizens.[1] While he remained there, he discovered a great desire to be present at a philosophical disputation in the College, not only to give evidence of his passion for learning, but to show his own proficiency in it. But he was so much employed in the administration of public affairs, that he was not able, while in Edinburgh, to accomplish his purpose. He therefore commanded the Professors to attend him in the Castle of Stirling on the 19th of the ensuing July, where he intended to be on his return from a progress he was to make through several of the towns of the kingdom.

Meanwhile, the meeting of Parliament and other solemnities on account of the presence of the King, occasioned such a bustle in the city, that it was thought proper to indulge the students with a longer vacation than usual. For that reason the twenty-ninth class, under the charge of Mr. Andrew Young, was graduated on the 29th of June. It consisted of. forty-six students, the greatest number of graduates at one act of laureation known in Scotland.

June 29.
The twenty-ninth Class graduated.

At the time appointed the Professors repaired to Stirling Castle, and there, in the Chapel-Royal, about five o'clock in the evening, in presence of the King and many of the nobility and learned men of both kingdoms, commenced a disputation which lasted for three hours. Nothing could have been more agreeable to the King's taste than such a pedantic exhi-

July 19.
The Professors hold a Disputation in Stirling Castle before the King.

1 Adamson's Muses' Welcome to King James, p. 39; Maitland's History of Edinburgh, p. 58.

bition. He not only sat with great patience during the whole time, but was highly delighted with the performance.

Mr. Henry Charteris, Principal of the College, being a man of great modesty, though of profound learning, was averse to taking any share in the debate on such a public occasion. He therefore prevailed with Mr. John Adamson,. who had formerly been one of the professors of philosophy, but was then minister of Liberton, to preside in his place. Mr. James Fairly, one of the Regents, was pitched upon to draw up and defend the Theses; Mr. Patrick Sands, formerly a Regent, Mr. Andrew Young, Mr. James Reid, and Mr. William King, at that time the remaining three Regents or professors of philosophy, were appointed to impugn.

These Theses have been preserved in "The Muses Welcome to King James,"[1] a book published by Mr. John Adamson, who presided at the Disputa-

[1] The full title of the book is : " TA ΤΩΝ ΜΟΥΣΩΝ ΕΙΣΟΔΙΑ : The Muses Welcome to the High and Mighty Prince JAMES, by the Grace of God, King of Great Britaine, France, and Ireland, Defender of the Faith, etc. At his Majesties happie Returne to his olde and native Kingdome of Scotland, after 14. yeeres absence, in anno 1617. Imprinted at Edinburgh by Thomas Finlason, Printer to his most excellent Majestie, 1618." It contains the speeches and other addresses presented to the King at the different towns and places where he stopped in his progress through Scotland ; and from p. 221 to p. 237, are to be found the above mentioned Theses, with an account of several of the particulars attending the Disputation. The whole exhibits a striking picture of the literary attainments of the Scots at that period. Latin Poetry still makes the principal figure, but not in quite so good a taste as had been discovered by Buchanan. The book is dedicated to the King by John Adamson the editor. The Theses are entitled :— " Theses Philosophicæ, quas ad devotissimum obsequium testandum Jacobo Magnæ Britanniæ, Fran. et Hib. invictissimo, potentissimoque Monarchæ, eidemque omnium totius orbis Regum philosopho excellentissimo proponunt Phil. Professores in Academia Edinburgena, coram disputandas, A.D. XIX. Julii, Sterlini." There is added at the conclusion :—" Disputatæ sunt in Capella Regia ab hora quinta vespertina in octavam sine Regis fastidio. Præsidebat Joannes Adamsonus. Respondebat Jacobus Fairlæus. Opponebant Patricius Sandæus, Andreas Junius, Jacobus Reidus, et Gulielmus Regius, Philos. Prof." The

tion, and form a very curious specimen of the subjects of philosophic debate in those days. The topics selected from the rest, were such as, it was judged, would be most acceptable to the King and the rest of the audience. The first thing insisted on was, *That Sheriffs and other inferior Magistrates ought not to be hereditary.*[1] This was opposed by Mr. Sands with many apposite arguments, to which, however, such satisfactory answers were given, that the King, though he himself had for some time supported Mr. Sands, while the defender still directed all the answers to the latter, was so well pleased, that turning to the Marquis of Hamilton, heritable Sheriff of Clydesdale, who was standing behind his chair, " James," said he, " you see your cause is lost, and all that can be said for it distinctly answered and refuted."

The next topic insisted on was the nature of *Local Motion*, which Mr. Young illustrated by many arguments from the text of Aristotle. Upon which the King, addressing himself to certain English Doctors who attended him, observed that these men were as well acquainted with the meaning of Aristotle as he was himself when alive.

Mr. Reid disputed next upon the *Origin of Fountains*, and the King was so much entertained with the last argument which was used, that he desired to

introductory speeches of the Præses, and the other disputants are also preserved, and contain abundance of adulation to his learned Majesty.

[1] It forms the fourth head, as follows —" *Primus Motor simpliciter immobilis est et immutabilis : cæteri Motores a Primo pendent, et reguntur omnes.*

" 1. Licet supremus Magistratus omnino immobilis et immutabilis sit ; expedit tamen, ut inferiores Magistratus aut ad tempus duntaxat definitum præsint, aut prudentiæ formatoris et servatoris Reipublicæ relinquantur.

" 2. Inferiores igitur Magistratus non debent esse hæreditarii."

hear more upon the subject, even after the three-quarters of an hour, the time allotted, were elapsed. The King himself occasionally interfered in the debate, sometimes joining the impugner and sometimes the defender ; expressing himself in elegant Latin, and showing great acquaintance with the *arcana* of Philosophy.

Mr. King, in the last place, held a dissertation *de Spontaneo et Invito.* Upon which subject, as well as on all the rest, the King himself took notice of every argument and answer, with much intelligence, and in good expression.

When the Disputation was concluded, his Majesty went to supper, and, after a little time, commanded the Professors to be introduced, and he conversed with them in a very learned manner on all the subjects which had been handled in the Disputation. His Majesty then condescended to indulge himself in pleasant allusions to the names of the actors ; thus exercising a humble species of witticism altogether inconsistent with the principles of good taste. " Methinks," said he, " these gentlemen, by their very names, have been destined for the parts which they have performed to-day. *Adam* was the first father of all, and therefore, very fitly, Adamson had the first part in this act. The defender is justly called Fairly ; his Theses had some *fairlies ;*[1] and he sustained them very *fairly,* and with many *fair lies* given to his opponents. And why should not Mr. Sands be the first to enter the *sands ?* But now I clearly see that all sands are

---

[1] A *fairlie* in the Scots dialect signifies a *wonder.*

not barren, for certainly he hath shown a fertile wit. Mr. Young is very *old* in Aristotle; and Mr. Reid[1] need not be *red* with blushing for his manner of acting to-day. Mr. King disputed very *kingly*, and of a kingly purpose, concerning the royal supremacy of reason over anger and all passions. I am so well satisfied," continued his Majesty, "with this day's exercise, that I will be god-father to the College of Edinburgh, and have it called THE COLLEGE OF KING JAMES; for, after the foundation of it had been stopped for several years in my minority, as soon as I came to any knowledge, I zealously *held hand to it*, and caused it to be established. And, although many look upon it with an evil eye, yet I will have them to know that, having given it this name, I have espoused its quarrel." One of the attendants hinted to his Majesty that there was one of the company of whom he had taken no notice, Mr. Henry Charteris, Principal of the College, who sat, during the Disputation, on the President's right hand, and who was a man of profound and universal learning, though not forward to speak in so august an assembly. "Well," said his Majesty, "his name agreeth very well with his nature, for *charters* contain much matter, yet say nothing, but put great purposes in men's mouths."

The witty allusions thus made by the King to the names of the disputants being much applauded by those who stood by his chair, his Majesty signified his desire that they should be expressed in verse, in which he not only took much delight, but could

---

[1] Pronounced *Red* in the Scots way.

himself make verses with great readiness. Various attempts were accordingly made to versify them, both in English and in Latin; and some of these productions were afterwards printed.[1]

One of the English Doctors having expressed a wonder at the King's fluency and elegance in the speaking of Latin, " All the world," said his Majesty, " knew that my preceptor, George Buchanan, was a great master in that faculty. I follow his pronunciation both of the Latin and Greek, and am sorry that my people of England do not the like, for certainly their pronunciation utterly spoileth the grace of these two learned languages; but ye see that all the learned men of Scotland express the true and native pronunciation of both."[2]

The King continued his discourse on the subjects of

[1] See the "Muses Welcome," *ubi supra*. As it is almost impossible to translate puns into a different language, three different attempts to express these in Latin, selected from a great many others, have, as may be supposed, all failed. The following is the English, or rather Scottish version of them :—

" As *Adam* was the first of men, whence all beginning tak,
So *Adamson* was president, and first man in this Act," etc.

See the "Muses Welcome," p. 231.

But we must not suppose that a taste for such wretched witticisms was peculiar to James. It was the fashion of the times; and the disputants themselves had even given the King the hint; for the Præses concluded his introductory speech in these words :—
"Tu qui ab *arenis* nomen habes, Patrici Sandæe, primus in Arenam descendito."
To which Mr. Sands answered :—"Quòd ab *arenis* nomen habeam, dignissime Præses, ideòne me primum in Arenam hanc vocas? lepidè quidem, et argutè id à te dictum non inficior : mihi tamen hoc quicquid est nominis argumento potius esse debet, quò minùs in Arenam tam nobilem me temerè protrudam. Quid enim in philosophicis operæ pretii præstare poterunt, coram Rege omnium Φιλοσοφωτάτῳ, *steriles, mihi nomen, Arenæ*? conaborne ego soli lumen, aut cœlo sidera inferre ?"—P. 226. The writings of Shakspere, that transcendent genius in other respects, who died this very year, and, as well as Bacon, reflects ineffable lustre on this period, abound in this species of witticism, and show that it was then the prevailing taste also in England.

"Now it is room enough, and Rome indeed," etc.

See "Julius Cæsar," and innumerable other instances.

[2] His Majesty's partiality has carried him somewhat too far here; though something might be said in favour of his opinion. The Scots pronunciation is certainly much better understood

the disputation till ten at night; again expressed great satisfaction with the entertainment he had received; and promised that, as he had given the College of Edinburgh a name, he would also in due time give it a Royal God-bairn gift for enlarging its patrimony. He took occasion, from the subjects which had been handled that day, to speak on many points of philosophy with such subtilty and skill as very much surprised the learned hearers.[1]

Having taken his departure from Stirling he arrived at Glasgow on the 22d of July, where a deputation of the Town-Council of Edinburgh was directed to wait on him, and to offer him the thanks of the town for his great attention bestowed upon their College. Two days after, when at Paisley, he sent the following letter to the Town-Council :—

" JAMES R.—Trusty and well beloved, We greet you well. Being sufficiently persuaded of the good beginning and progress which you have made in repairing and building of your College; and of your commendable resolution instantly to proceed and persist therein, till the same shall be perfectly finished; for your better encouragement in a work so universally beneficial for our subjects, and of such ornament and reputation for our City in particular, We have thought

abroad than the English; but that the latter *spoileth the grace* of the learned tongues will not be so readily allowed.

[1] " That James was but a middling writer may be allowed; that he was a contemptible one can by no means be admitted. Whoever will read his Basi- licon Doron, particularly the two last books; the True Law of Free Monarchies; his Answer to Cardinal Perron; and almost all his speeches and messages to Parliament, will confess him to have possessed no mean genius."—Hume's Appendix to James the First.

good, not only to declare our special approbation thereof, but likewise, as we gave the first being and beginning thereunto, so we have thought it worthy to be honoured with our name of our own imposition; and the rather because of the late care, which we received of the good worth and sufficiency of the Masters thereof, at their being with us at Stirling: in which regard, these are to desire you to order the said College to be called in all time hereafter by the name of KING JAMES'S COLLEGE, which we intend for a special mark and badge of our favour toward the same. So, doubting not but you will accordingly accept thereof, We bid you heartily farewell. From our Court at Paisley, the 25th of July 1617."

About the beginning of October the Professors returned to their usual employment. Mr. Andrew Young undertook the charge of a new Bejan class, while Mr. William King carried forward the Semi, Mr. James Fairly, the Bachelor, and Mr. James Reid, the Magistrand.

October.
Session
XXXVI.

On the 4th of March this year, the sum of 200 marks had been received by the Treasurer, being a legacy bequeathed to the College by the late David Alexander, merchant; and on the 30th of December the following year, Hugh Wright, also a merchant, delivered to the Treasurer 1000 marks, to receive an annuity during his own life, which was afterwards to form part of a salary for a Professor of Divinity.

Mr. James Reid's students, thirty-four in number, and forming the thirtieth class, were graduated on the

1618.
July 25.
The thirtieth
Class gradu-
ated.
25th of July 1618. In the title of the Theses, which were published on this occasion, the College begins to take the name of ACADEMIA JACOBI REGIS.[1]

October.
Session
XXXVII.

1619.
July 24.
The thirty-
first Class
graduated.
On the meeting of the thirty-seventh session in October, Mr. Reid began the new Bejan class; and on the 24th of July 1619, the Magistrand, under the charge of Mr. Fairly, received the degree in the usual manner, being the thirty-first class, consisting of thirty-three students.

This year abounded in donations to the College. January 15th: Alexander Stobo, a messenger, bequeathed 300 marks for increasing the stock for a salary to a Professor of Divinity. May 28th: a legacy of 1000 marks for maintaining bursars,[2] by Archibald Johnston, was delivered to the Treasurer by Samuel Johnston the donor's son. June 2d: Sir William Nisbet of Dean, Lord Provost, paid to the Treasurer 1000 pounds for the Professor of Divinity's stipend. On the 25th of the same month, 100 marks were received as a legacy by William Justice, being a contribution to the College building. And on the 21st of July, James Young and Barbara Robertson, his wife, allotted 100 marks as part of a fund for the support of bursars.

October.
Session
XXXVIII.
The College as usual having assembled in October after the vacation, the charge of the Bejan class devolved on Mr. Fairly, while Mr. Reid proceeded with

---

[1] "Theses Philosophicæ, quas Dei Opt. Max. ductu, et auspiciis, ad diem 6 Kal. Augusti, Edinburgi, in Æde sacra Regii Collegii, propugnabunt Adolescentes Magisterii Candidati, ex ACADEMJA JACOBI REGIS; hoc anno 1618, cum laureâ emittendi. Præside Jacobo Reido. Edinburgi, excudebat Andreas Hart. Anno 1618." 4to.

[2] Bursars, or poor students, as in Crawfurd's History.

the Semi, Mr. Young with the Bachelor, and Mr. King with the Magistrand, till the 22d of July 1620, when this last class, being the thirty-second, and consisting of thirty-five students, received the degree. On this occasion Patrick Hume of Polwarth particularly distinguished himself both in defending and impugning the Theses.

During this year a new and remarkable arrangement was made in the College. Mr. Patrick Sands, after holding a Professorship of Philosophy for eight years, had resigned that office and gone abroad with Lord Newbattle, son of the Earl of Lothian. On his return he had been advised to engage in the study and practice of the law; but as he did not succeed according to his expectation in this profession, David Akinhead, whose sister he had married, being Dean of Guild, and having great influence in the Town-Council, set on foot a scheme for having him made Primar or Principal of the College. Towards the conclusion of the year 1618, Mr. Henry Charteris, who had only 500 pounds of salary, applied for an augmentation equal to the stipend of the ministers. The Dean of Guild admitted the reasonableness of his request, but, pretending that the revenue of the College was not sufficient for enabling the patrons to comply with his demand, he advised him to take the first opportunity of accepting of a call to be minister of any vacant parish. This learned and worthy man readily comprehended the hint, and immediately resolved to retire from the office of Principal, in hopes of finding some other station where the merit of his services would be better understood by his constituents. He was prevailed on, however, by the professors, who had the highest respect for his talents and character, to preside over them for a year longer. But having received a call to be minister of North Leith, he at last resigned his charge on the 20th of March 1620.

Mr. Henry
Charteris
resigns.

An opportunity was thus furnished for executing the scheme of accommodation in favour of Mr. Sands. The charge of Principal or Primar of the College, and Professor of Divinity, which had been hitherto united, was now divided. Mr. Andrew Ramsay, one of the ministers of the city, was elected by the Town-Council and the other ministers to be public Professor of Divinity, and also to be Rector of the College for the ensuing year, this last office being considered only as annual. At the same time, the two senior Regents, Mr. Andrew Young, and Mr. James Reid, were created public Professors, the former of the Mathematics, and the latter of the Metaphysics; and Mr. Patrick Sands was elected Primar or Principal, during the pleasure of the Town-Council.[1] And notwithstanding the pretence of the scantiness of the College revenue formerly held out to the late Principal, Mr. Ramsay, as Professor of Divinity, had an appointment of 500 pounds; Mr. Sands, 1000 marks, with 100 pounds for house rent; and the two senior Regents, the additional sum each of 250 marks, which was equal to their former salaries as ordinary Regents. The salaries also of the two junior Regents, Mr. James Fairly and Mr. William King, were augmented from 150 marks to 250 marks each. A committee was appointed by the Town-Council, the 22d of March, to receive the Library

The office of Principal and Professor of Divinity disjoined.

Mr. Andrew Ramsay elected Professor of Divinity, also Rector of the College.

The two senior Regents made also Professors of Mathematics and Metaphysics. Mr. Patrick Sands, Primar or Principal. Salaries arranged.

[1] Town-Council Records, vol. xiii. March 20.

from Mr. Henry Charteris, which was still kept in a private chamber, and to deliver it to the charge of the new Principal; and that Mr. Charteris might not appear to be altogether neglected, a gratuity of 1000 marks was bestowed upon him for his long and faithful services.[1]

The charge of the Library delivered to the new Principal.

This year Mr. William Rig senior, contributed to the College for the support of a Professor of Divinity the sum of 625 marks, which was received by the Treasurer on the 23d of August.

At the opening of the College in October, after the vacation, Mr. William King commenced the session with the charge of the new Bejan class, the other three Regents proceeding with the other classes in the usual order.

1620.
October.
Session
XXXIX.

On the 23d of January, the City Treasurer received a legacy of 1000 marks, bequeathed by Thomas Spear for the support of a Professor of Divinity; and on the 20th of April, Sir William Nisbet of Dean, having added a year's interest to his former donation of 1000 pounds, which made the principal sum 1100 pounds, stipulated with the Town-Council that an annuity of 100 pounds should be paid as part of a stipend also for a Professor of Divinity.

1621.
January 23.
Donations.

Mr. Andrew Young brought the students of the Magistrand class to the Master's degree on the 14th of July 1621, somewhat earlier than the usual period, on account of the meeting of that Parliament which was long known among the people by the appellation of the Black Parliament, because in it were ratified

July 14.
The thirty-third Class graduated.

[1] Town-Council Records, vol. xiii. March 22.

the five obnoxious Articles adopted in the year 1618 by the Perth Assembly, favourable to the Episcopal hierarchy, which James had it so much at heart to establish, upon the model of the Church of England. The gratitude, however, of the College of Edinburgh was due to this very Parliament. For, having met on the 4th of August, it passed an act wherein the different grants made by his Majesty to the Provost, Magistrates, Corporation and Community of the city of Edinburgh are particularly stated and ratified ; which ratification is declared to be "as valid, effectual, and sufficient in all respects as if the foresaid infeftments of the dates respective above written, were at length and word by word engrossed in this present Act." Likewise, "for the farther encouragement" of the said Provost, Bailies, Council, and Community of Edinburgh, "in repairing and re-edifying of the said College, and placing therein sufficient professors for teaching of all liberal sciences, ordains the said College in all time to come to be called King James's College ; and also, with advice of the said Estates of Parliament, his Majesty has of new again given, granted, and disponed to them and their successors, in favour of the said burgh of Edinburgh, patrons of the said College, and of the Rector, Regents, bursars, and students within the same, all liberties, freedoms, immunities, and privileges appertaining to a free College, and that in as ample form and large manner as any College has or bruiks within his Majesty's realm."[1]

At the commencement of a new session it was Mr.

[1] Acts of the Parliament of Scotland.

Young's turn to begin the Bejan class, the three other October. Session XL. Professors conducting the others in the usual order.

This session, a legacy by John Lawtie, apothecary, 1622. July 22. Donations. of 100 pounds, was delivered to the Treasurer on the 22d of July 1622. On the 27th of the same month, July 27. The thirty-fourth Class graduated. Mr. James Reid advanced his class, being the thirty-fourth, and consisting of thirty-six students, to the Master's degree, with the usual solemnity.

Mr. Patrick . Sands, Principal, having given small Mr. Sands resigns the office of Principal. satisfaction in the government of the College, resigned that charge on the 7th of August into the hands of David Akinhead, then Provost of the city, and received a gratuity of 1000 marks.[1] On the 30th of the same month, Mr. Robert Balcanquhal, minister of Tranent, gave security for the principal sum of 1000 marks, bequeathed to the College for the support of a Professor of Divinity, by the late Mr. Walter Balcanquhal his father, who had been a great promoter of the prosperity of the College from its foundation to the time of his death. At the same time he paid the arrears of interest due upon that sum. The same year a legacy of 300 marks, bequeathed for the same use by John Mason, merchant, was delivered to the Treasurer by Isobel Brown, his widow.

Soon after the commencement of a new session, October. Session XLI. when Mr. James Reid had undertaken the charge of the Bejan class, and the other three Regents were proceeding with the other classes in the usual order, the Town-Council appointed the Provost and Bailies, with some of the ministers, to inquire at Mr. Robert

[1] Town-Council Records, vol. xiii. August 7.

Boyd of Trochrig, Principal of the College of Glasgow, on what conditions he would accept of the same office in the College of Edinburgh.[1] In consequence of this he was chosen Principal, and also one of the

October 18.
Mr. Robert
Boyd, fourth
Principal.

eight ministers of Edinburgh, on the 18th of October, with 1200 marks of stipend and 200 marks as house rent. But he resigned the office on the 31st of January 1623, for what reason does not appear, after holding it for a few months.

1623.
July 26.
The thirty-
fifth Class
graduated.

On the 26th of July, the thirty-fifth class, under the charge of Mr. James Fairly, consisting of thirty students, received the Master's degree. Mr. Andrew Young, the senior Regent, and public Professor of the Mathematics, performed the ceremony of graduation, as the office of Principal was vacant by the resignation of Mr. Boyd.

Death of Mr.
Andrew
Young,
Senior
Regent and
Professor of
Mathema-
tics.

This was Mr. Young's last public appearance. He died very soon after, being about forty-five years of age. He had been a Professor of Philosophy in Aberdeen two years, and twenty-two in the College of Edinburgh, where he had received his education. He was distinguished as a very diligent and successful teacher, his lectures and dictates being very perspicuous, and at the same time, concise and comprehensive. He was said also to be a remarkably elegant classical scholar, and very well acquainted with the text of Aristotle, but to have had a great disgust at the wrangling of the scholastic philosophers.[2]

---

[1] Town-Council Records, vol. xiii. October 9th and 10th.

[2] By his wife Barbara Brown, a very frugal woman, by whose assistance he acquired considerable wealth, he had an only daughter, who was married to Sir Michael Nasmyth of Posso in Tweeddale.

Mr. Andrew Stevenson, Professor of Humanity,[1] who had formerly been elected his successor during his first illness, was, after the space of twelve years, substituted in his place the second time.

Mr. Andrew Stevenson, fifth Professor of Humanity, chosen twenty-first Professor of Philosophy.

The offices of Professor of Humanity and of Principal being now both vacant, a comparative trial was held for supplying the former. Four competitors appeared, Mr. William Hog, Mr. David Will, Mr. George Hannay, and Mr. Samuel Rutherford ; and the last, after some hesitation, was preferred by the judges, and elected sixth Professor of Humanity.

Mr. Samuel Rutherford, sixth Professor of Humanity.

At the opening of the forty-second session, Mr. James Fairly undertook the charge of the Bejan class, while Mr. James Reid proceeded with the Semi, Mr. Andrew Stevenson with the Bachelor, and Mr. William King with the Magistrand.

1623. October. Session XLII.

Meanwhile, the Town-Council, the Ministers and Professors, were unanimously of opinion that Mr. John Adamson would be the most proper person to preside over the College. He had formerly held the office of one of the Regents during seven years with great reputation, and was afterwards minister of North Berwick, from whence he was translated to Liberton. It was while he officiated in this last charge that he had the honour to preside in the disputation held at Stirling Castle before the King, in the year 1617, in place of Mr. Henry Charteris, who declined that public appearance. He was accordingly chosen Principal on the 21st of November, and remained longer in that

Nov. 21. Mr. John Adamson fifth Principal.

[1] Mr. Robert Burnet had been elected fourth Professor of Humanity in the year 1611, but how long he held the office, or at what particular time Mr. Andrew Stevenson succeeded him, I have not been able to ascertain.

situation than any person who enjoyed the office, except the late Dr. William Robertson. His annual salary was 1200 marks, with 200 marks as house rent.

Donations.

On the 10th of December, William Dick, merchant, delivered to the City Treasurer 300 marks, being a donation to the College by Margaret Stewart his mother; and on the 16th of January 1624, the Treasurer received also 500 marks, a legacy of James Ainslie, towards maintaining a Professor of Divinity.

1624.
July 25.
The thirty-sixth Class graduated.

On the 25th of July, the thirty-sixth class, under Mr. William King, in number twenty-seven, received the Master's degree with the usual solemnity.

October.
Session
XLIII.

After the commencement of a new session in October, Mr. King having the charge of the Bejan class, and the other professors proceeding as usual in their order with the other classes, towards the close of this year and beginning of the next, some apprehended appearance of the plague dispersed for a few days both the Court of Justice and the College; and though the alarm proved to be without foundation, yet the classes, especially the lowest, on this account lost a considerable number of students.

1625.
March 27.
Death of
King James.

During this session, on the 27th of March 1625, died James the Sixth of Scotland and First of Great Britain; a prince to whom the University of Edinburgh is indebted for its original institution, and for the unremitted attention with which he protected and cherished it in its infant state; and to whom the Lord Provost, Magistrates, and Council of Edinburgh owe a most important and honourable patronage, such as no other corporation in Great Britain can boast.

CHAPTER III.

THE accession of Charles, the only surviving son of the late King, made no immediate change upon the affairs of Scotland ; and the University of Edinburgh being in a flourishing condition, education proceeded there in the same manner which had been practised for many years. Commencement of the reign of Charles I.

On the 23d of July 1625, the thirty-seventh class, under the care of Mr. Andrew Stevenson, but which had been instructed the two first years of the course by Mr. Andrew Young, were graduated in the usual manner, being thirty-six in number. The Theses, printed by the heirs of Andrew Hart, were dedicated to the celebrated Thomas Hope of Craighall, a great promoter of the prosperity of the College, and who, about this time, was appointed King's Advocate. 1625. July 23. The thirty-seventh Class graduated.

During the vacation, Mr. James Fairly, who had been one of the Professors of Philosophy for seventeen years, having accepted of a call to be minister of Leith, resigned his academical charge. A comparative trial being announced, in the usual manner, for the election of a new Regent, eight candidates appeared, namely, Mr. Patrick Panter, Mr. Thomas Crawford, Mr. John Mr. James Fairly resigns, and a trial for a successor announced. Eight Candidates.

F

Brown, Mr. George Hannay, Mr. Robert Rankin, Mr. Alexander Hepburn, Mr. John Armour, and Mr. Samuel Fraser, the first two having received their degree at St. Andrews, and the other six at Edinburgh. The particulars of this trial have been preserved by Mr. Thomas Crawford, who, though one of the unsuccessful candidates on this occasion, afterwards became one of the greatest ornaments of the University.

Judges in trial.The judges appointed by the Town-Council, besides the ministers of the city, were Mr. Alexander Morison,[1] and Mr. Alexander Peirson, advocates, and assessors to the Magistrates, Mr. Patrick Sands, late Principal, and John Gelly, doctor of medicine.

The subjects assigned by lot.The subjects of the trial were distributed by lot, and were obtained as follows :—The 1st, *De Quanto*, by Mr. Brown ; the 2d, being chap. I. *De Demonstratione*, by Mr. Rankin ; the 3d, being the last chapter of the same, by Mr. Armour ; the 4th, being the chapter of book II. of the Ethics, *De Affectibus;* the 5th, viz., the last chapter of the first book of *Acroasis de Materia Prima*, by Mr. Crawford ; the 6th, viz., the second chapter of book I. *De Cœlo*, by Mr. Fraser ; the 7th, being chap. ii. book I. *De Ortu;* the last, viz. *De Facultatibus Animæ*, by Mr. Panter.

Mode of trial.These subjects were prescribed on a Saturday at eleven o'clock to be discussed by the candidates on the ensuing Monday, the time of three quarters of an hour being allowed to each. On Monday the trial commenced at eight o'clock in the morning, and continued till near seven . in the evening, the one half of the

---

[1] Afterwards Lord Prestongrange, and Rector of the University.

candidates discoursing in the forenoon, and the other in the afternoon, before a very numerous audience. The next day, in the afternoon, Mr. Brown defended his thesis *De Quanto*, against the other seven candidates, half an hour each, the dispute having been opened by the Principal. The following days, the rest, succeeding in their order, disputed in the same manner, excepting Mr. Samuel Fraser, who declined the contest after the first day's debate.

At the close of the trial the judges selected two of the number as particularly well qualified, but recommended Mr. Patrick Panter[1] as the best. But David Aikenhead, Lord Provost, and Mr. John Hay, townclerk, having a particular predilection for Mr. Robert Rankin, who was the son of a burgess of Edinburgh, and allowed to be a young man of great ability, and who had studied two years in the University of Cambridge, their interest in the Council had gained over a great party to support their views. Opinion of the judges.

On putting the vote, the Bailies, Dean of Guild, Treasurer, and principal Councillors, who were not under influence, supported the recommendation of the judges, but a majority following the Provost, the election was made in favour of Mr. Robert Rankin. Many of the most respectable members of the Council were Mr. Robert Rankin chosen twenty-second Professor of Philosophy.

---

[1] Mr. Patrick Panter was a native of Dundee, and became Professor of Divinity at St. Andrews; Mr. George Hannay, who was son to a burgess of Canongate, was afterwards minister of Torphichen; Mr. John Brown, who was son of Mr. William Brown, Clerk of Exchequer, and Mr. Alexander Hepburn, son of Mr. Thomas Hepburn, parson of Oldhamstocks, were afterwards Regents in the College of Edinburgh. Mr. John Armour the son of a burgess, was soon after chosen Professor of Humanity in the same University, and afterwards of Philosophy at St. Andrews. — Crawford's History of the University of Edinburgh.

much offended with the decision, and complained, with reason, that contrary to the fair mode of proceeding at all former elections, the opinion of the judges had not been followed. Mr. Rankin was installed next day, being the 18th of November.

1625.
October.
Session
XLIV.

At the commencement of the forty-fourth Session in October, Mr. Stevenson having undertaken the charge of the new Bejan class, Mr. King proceeded with the Semi, Mr. Fairly with the Bachelor, and Mr. Reid with the Magistrand. Towards the end of November, Mr. Rankin, the new professor, succeeded to Mr.

Mr. Samuel
Rutherford
resigns the
Professor-
ship of
Humanity.

Fairly's charge ; about which time Mr. Samuel Rutherford, professor of Humanity, having incurred some scandal on account of an irregular marriage, found it prudent to resign his office.

On this occasion it was apprehended that there would be a great number of competitors for the vacant chair, most of those especially who had stood a trial at the two last elections. In order to diminish the number, in the first place, a promise was given to Mr. John Brown of the first Professorship of Philosophy that should be vacant, in consideration of his father's steady attachment to the interest of the City. This too gave great disgust to several of the most respectable members of the Council, as they regarded it as another neglect of the opinion of the judges at the late trial. In the next place, as the Principal (who, by the terms of the foundation of the Professorship of Humanity, was entitled to give his advice in elections to that office), and also several of the Regents, were of opinion that the former mode of trial in the election of Professors of Humanity was too slight—an Ode of Horace to be explained and commented upon by the candidates for the space of three quarters of an hour being all that had been required; it was resolved, with the consent of the six delegates from the Town-Council and College of Justice, that candidates should be examined on a variety of Greek and Latin authors *ad aperturam libri*. This accordingly had the effect to intimidate competitors, insomuch, that on the 27th of March, the day appointed by the public program, there appeared only Mr. John Armour and Mr. Thomas Crawford. They were examined in the upper hall of the College, in presence of the six delegates, the Principal and Professors, and a great number of other men of letters.

It fell to the lot of Mr. Crawford to be tried first, *Comparative trial of a Professor of Humanity.* and in the meantime the other candidate was removed. The authors pitched upon were Plautus, Ovid, Horace, Lucan, Juvenal, Virgil, Hesiod, and Orphei θυμιάματα. Upon each of these the competitors were severally examined, as long as the Judges thought proper, and Mr. Crawford proving the successful candidate, he was *Mr. Thomas Crawford elected seventh Professor of Humanity.* appointed to hold an inaugural lecture (*ad clepsydram*) next day at two o'clock, upon an Ode of Horace. He was admitted to his office on the 29th of March 1626.[1]

On the 29th of July, Mr. James Reid promoted the *1626. July 29. The thirty-eighth Class graduated.* thirty-eighth class to the Master's degree, being twenty-four in number. Several of the students had retired

---

[1] The Town-Council made a handsome donation to Mr. Samuel Rutherford, the late Professor, on his resignation.

before this time, through an apprehension of some symptoms of the plague. The Theses at this graduation are dedicated to Thomas Earl of Melrose. The first article of them is entitled, *Theses de Disciplinis in genere.*

There, in one passage Mr. Reid takes occasion to expose the futility of certain modern theologians, who affect to despise the liberal sciences, and who are not afraid or ashamed to brand Philosophy with insolent and opprobrious epithets. " Whatever these persons may think of themselves," says he, " who thus contemn human Philosophy, such is its lustre in the Christian life, and so great its benefit to civil society, ·that Aristippus chose rather to be a Christian philosopher than an *ignorant* or *unphilosophic* divine."[1]

Dispute between Mr. James Reid and the Rev. Mr. William Struthers.

In this he particularly alluded to the conduct of Mr. William Struthers, one of the ministers of Edinburgh, and moderator of the Presbytery, who, on the trial of a certain candidate for the character of a preacher of the gospel before the Presbytery, had expressed himself in contemptuous terms of Philosophy, calling it the *dish-clout* to Divinity. This, the Professor at the public graduation took the opportunity of resenting, which cost him dear. For Struthers, being highly offended with the retort, and having formerly borne its author a secret grudge, he prevailed

---

[1] " Temere satis, salse, ac rigide satis perstringunt recentiores quidam Theologi disciplinas has liberaliores ; dum earum famulitium (quod certe honorarium Theologiæ præstant) cum *peniculis tantum inter dapes* conferre non verentur, non erubescunt.

" Quanticunque igitur sibi viderentur, qui humanam sic despicerent Philosophiam ; tanta tamen lux est ipsius in vita Christiana, tantus usus in Societate civili, ut Aristippus mallet esse Philosophus Christianus, quam Theologus Aphilosophus."

with the other ministers of the City, and also several
other distinguished members of the Presbytery, to
espouse his quarrel, and immediately after the graduation he brought a charge against the Professor before
the Town-Council. Mr. Reid, who was a man of a
most respectable character, and much esteemed by the
members of the Town-Council, and by a numerous
circle of friends, being then in a bad state of health,
was advised by his physicians to retire without loss
of time to a country-house he had in Fife ; and the
Council, being averse from entertaining any accusation
against him, concurred in the same advice, in hopes
that the resentment of Mr. Struthers and his brethren
would subside before the next assembling of the College. The event turned out otherwise, for in his absence his enemies were very active in carrying on their
designs against him, and the new elections happening
in the beginning of October, about the time of Mr.
Reid's return to town, the ministers, whose power in
the City was very great at that time, availing themselves of certain unfavourable circumstances in his
conduct, succeeded in stirring up a strong prejudice
against him. He had still, however, a great number
of friends in the Council, who secretly warned him of
the hazard to which he was exposed. He therefore,
by the advice of his lawyers, appealed his cause from
the Council of the town to the Privy-Council. This
circumstance, which went to deny the jurisdiction of
the Town-Council, was taken advantage of by those who
were hostile to the defendant ; and the Town-Council
instantly asserted what they apprehended to be their

Mr. Reid deprived of his office, and Mr. John Brown elected in his place twenty-third Professor of Philosophy. undeniable right, by pronouncing sentence of deprivation against him, and by electing immediately in his place Mr. John Brown, to whom the first vacant professorship of Philosophy had been promised. In the terms of the sentence, no other ground of procedure was stated than that the Council had acted so *for reasons known to themselves and moving them.* Mr. Reid complained of the injustice of this sentence, and had sufficient interest to procure a mandate from Court for reinstating him in his office. But compliance with this order being on some pretence or other eluded or delayed, he was at last prevailed with to give in a voluntary resignation, which he did on the 13th of July 1627,[1] and then retired to his own house, where he lived in tranquillity to a good old age. The Town-Council, however, to show their sense of his faithful services for twenty-four years, bestowed on him a donation of 1000 pounds Scots.[2] Indeed, they seem to have set him aside with great reluctance, and to have sacrificed him merely to the implacable resentment of Struthers and his friends.

1626. October. Session XLV. At the commencement of the forty-fifth session in the preceding October, Mr. Reid who had entered upon the charge of the new Bejan class, was, in the course of the session, in consequence of the above-mentioned procedure, superseded by Mr. John Brown, while Mr. Stevenson proceeded with the Semi, Mr. King with

---

[1] Reid resigned his public professorship of Metaphysics at the same time (Town-Council Records, July 13, 1627); an office which, after his time, continued dormant till the year 1708, when it was attached to the professorship of Logic with which it is still conjoined.

[2] Town-Council Records, July 18, 1627.

the Bachelor, and Mr. Rankin with the Magistrand class.

The Library which had been begun by Mr. Clement Little had greatly increased by donations from the candidates for the Master's degree, and from other generous benefactors ; and a private chamber being now unable to furnish proper accommodation for the books, they were removed into the upper great hall, until a room sufficiently capacious should be built for their reception. This was afterwards done, in consequence of an Act of Council passed in April 1642 ; and the apartment now called the Museum,[1] where the Professor of Natural History gives his lectures, and of which the west end is occupied by the Humanity class, was originally erected for a library, and was actually appropriated to that use till about the year 1760, as shall oe more particularly mentioned elsewhere. As the Principal, who hitherto had the sole charge of keeping the Library, found it now necessary to have some assistance in that duty, the patrons on the 26th of December 1626, allowed him a sum of money for employing a servant to attend to the situation of the books.

Mr. Andrew Ramsay, who for six years had been Rector of the University, and Professor of Divinity, the former of which offices he acknowledged to have been a mere title, had resigned them both on the 8th of March 1626, but continued to discharge the duties of the Professorship to the end of the year.

In the beginning of the next year, the Town-Council

Increase of the Library.

Mr. Andrew Ramsay resigns the offices of Rector and Professor of Divinity.

[1] Anno 1800.

were still of opinion that it would contribute to the more commodious government of the whole University that a Rector should be chosen, and having on the 5th of January 1627 held a meeting with the ministers of the City, first within the College, and afterwards within the Council-Chamber, they elected into that office for the ensuing year, Alexander Morison of Prestongrange, one of the Lords of Session, much distinguished for his learning. He appeared before the Council and took an oath *de fideli administratione*, but it does not appear that he entered any further into the duties of his new function.

1627.
January 5.
Alexander
Morison,
Lord Pres-
tongrange,
second Rec-
tor of the
University.

The vacant Professorship of Divinity was supplied on the 19th of April, by recalling into the College from the charge of the Church of North Leith, the venerable Mr. Henry Charteris, who had been formerly Principal, and also Professor of Divinity, when those offices were held in conjunction, but who now agreed to confine himself entirely to the duties of the latter.[1]

Mr. Henry
Charteris re-
called to the
Professor-
ship of
Divinity.

On the 28th of July, the thirty-ninth class, twenty-six in number, received the usual degree. They had been instructed the two first years of the course by Mr. Fairly, and the remaining two by Mr. Rankin. The Theses published on this occasion were dedicated to the Lord Provost David Aikenhead, the Bailies, and the rest of the Town-Council.

1627.
July 28.
The thirty-
ninth Class
graduated.

[1] The donations hitherto received for the support of a Professor of Divinity were still inadequate to the purpose. Mr. Charteris accepted of 1000 marks of annual salary, with a dwelling-house, agreeing that the excess of his salary above the interest of the donations should be refunded to the Town from the profits of succeeding gifts.

In the beginning of October, at the opening of a new session, the College consisted of the following members, viz. :— October. Session XLVI.

> Alexander Morison, Lord Prestongrange, Rector of the University.
> Mr. John Adamson, Principal.
> Mr. Henry Charteris, Professor of Divinity.
> Mr. Robert Rankin, \
> Mr. John Brown, \
> Mr. Andrew Stevenson, } Professors of Philosophy.
> Mr. William King, /
> Mr. Thomas Crawford, Professor of Humanity.

Mr. Rankin had the charge of the Bejan class, the other three Philosophy Professors proceeding in their order with the other classes, till the 27th of July 1628, when Mr. King brought the fortieth class to the Magisterial degree, consisting only of fifteen students ; the number being so small on account of the fear of the plague, which prevailed in the first year of the course. 1628. July 27. The fortieth Class graduated.

The new session in October 1628 opened with the Bejan class, under the care of Mr. King ; and the others proceeded under their respective Professors in the usual order. 1628. October. Session XLVII.

This year all the Laws or Regulations of the College were collected together and inserted into a Register. The greater part of them formerly had remained in the custody of the Principal, and used to be read annually in public after the examination of the classes in November. Laws of the College.

On the 3d of December the Town-Council passed an act ordaining the Laws to be observed for the future, and to be inserted in the Town-Council Records.[1]

In the month of July died Mr. Henry Charteris, Professor of Divinity, a man of profound erudition, being not only well acquainted with the ancient languages, but an excellent Philosopher and Theologian, and at the same time of singular modesty and sanctity of character.

A violent dispute arose about the election of his successor. The King was well known to inherit his father's partiality to the Episcopal form of church government, which was the source of many of those calamities which afterwards afflicted the kingdom, and which at last proved fatal to himself and to his family. William Laud, Bishop of London, and afterwards Archbishop of Canterbury, a bigoted and intolerant prelate, whose counsels had great influence with the King, had already gained many followers among the Scottish clergy. Of that number were Thomas Sydeserf and John Maxwell, afterwards Bishops, the one of Galloway, and the other of Ross. These, with others of their partisans, had pitched upon Mr. Robert Menteith, son to Alexander Menteith, a citizen, as a proper person for supplying the vacant Divinity chair. After taking his Master's degree in 1621, Menteith had gone abroad, and obtained a Professorship of Philosophy at Saumur, where he remained four years. He then returned to his native country, with the character of an accomplished scholar, and particularly noted for an

[1] The Laws are still to be seen in the Town-Council Records of the above date, expressed in English. In a Register belonging to the College they are in Latin.

agreeable delivery in the pulpit ; but his doctrines by many were regarded as erroneous, and strongly tainted with Arminianism.

A party, however, was prevailed with to favour his election, by means chiefly of Sydeserf, who had considerable interest in the Council. But this measure was violently opposed by Mr. William Struthers, supported by Mr. Andrew Ramsay and Mr. Henry Rollock, ministers of the City, with the Principal and Professors of the College, whose advice the patrons, averse from giving countenance to innovation in doctrine, thought it most prudent to follow ; and on the 24th of July, notwithstanding the keen struggle made for Menteith, they elected Mr. James Fairly, then Minister at South Leith, to succeed Mr. Charteris as Professor of Divinity.

Next day, Mr. Andrew Stevenson advanced the forty-first class to the usual degree, being thirty-eight in number. On this occasion the Theses were dedicated to Provost Aikenhead, and the other members of the Town-Council, from which the Laws of the College had received a new sanction. *1629. The forty-first Class graduated.*

After the usual vacation, the new session in October 1629 commenced, when Mr. Stevenson took upon him the charge of the new Bejan class ; and the other three Regents proceeded in their order with the other three Philosophy classes. *1629. October. Session XLVIII.*

In February 1630, Mr. John Ray, who had been Professor of Humanity in the College more than eight years, and afterwards Rector of the High School upwards of twenty-three, having died in the sixty-third year of his age, Mr. Thomas Crawford, Professor of Humanity, was, on the 26th of the same month, appointed by the Town-Council to succeed him in the Rectorship of the High School. Two competitors appeared for the vacant Professorship,—Mr. John Armour, formerly mentioned, and Mr. Humphrey Hood. They both declined the strict trial *ad aperturam libri;* and an Ode of Horace was prescribed, on which each of them was required to comment three-quarters of an hour. A majority of the judges declared in favour of Mr. Armour. He was elected accordingly, and was the eighth Professor of Humanity.[1]

1630.
March.
Mr. John Armour elected eighth Professor of Humanity.
1630.
July 29.
The forty-second Class graduated.

On the 29th of July, Mr. John Brown's class, being the forty-second since the institution of the College, were admitted to the usual degree, being thirty-one in number. At the graduations the custom still prevailed of arranging the candidates, and of bringing them forward or circulating them according to their respective merit. But on this occasion, Mr. Alexander Hope, son of Sir Thomas Hope, his Majesty's Lord Advocate, being dissatisfied with his place in the circulation, as it was called, although, in the general opinion, the rank he had obtained was quite equal to his merit; and others of the candidates having complained of a similar grievance, the practice of thus arranging or circulating the Magistrand class was laid aside for some time.

In the month of August, the Town-Council, being informed that Dr. John Sharp, Professor of Divinity

---

[1] Some years afterwards, Mr. Humphrey Hood was settled a minister in Nithsdale.

in the College of Die in Dauphiny, was expelled from France by the influence of Cardinal Richelieu, and had come over to London, thought proper to invite him to the Professorship of Divinity in the College of Edinburgh ; and in order to make way for this arrangement, Mr. James Fairly was called to exercise the ministry along with Mr. Andrew Ramsay in the south-west district of the city ; in consequence of which he resigned his office in the University, and on the 17th of November, Dr. John Sharp was elected to succeed him as Professor of Divinity.[1]

1630.
Nov. 17.
On the resignation of Mr Fairly, Dr. John Sharp is elected fourth Professor of Divinity.

On the 29th of December in the same year, Charles Shearer of Dort, in Holland, probably related to the former donor of the same name, delivered to the City Treasurer 1000 marks, the interest to be paid annually to himself during his life, and afterwards, in the same way to his cousin John Shearer, at Cambusmiln in Monteith, and then to remain as a donation for augmenting the salary of the Professor of Divinity.

Donation.

In October 1630, after the vacation, the new Bejan class assembled under the care of Mr. John Brown, the other Professors proceeding in rotation with the other classes, till the 23d of July 1631, when Mr. Robert Rankin brought the forty-third class to the usual degree, being forty-three in number.

1630.
October.
Session
XLIX.

1631.
July 23.
The forty-third Class graduated.

During the vacation, Mr. William King, after having been a Regent in the College twenty-three years, accepted of a call to be minister at Cramond ; upon which the Council, in consequence of a previous promise given to the Earl, of Airth and some others,

On the resignation of Mr. William King,

---

[1] Dr. Sharp had a salary allowed him of 1200 marks, with a house.

Mr. Alexander Hepburn elected twenty-fourth Professor of Philosophy.

1631. October. Session L.
elected Mr. Alexander Hepburn, formerly mentioned, to supply the vacant Professorship.

In the following October, at the opening of the ·fiftieth session, Mr. Rankin in course took the charge of the new class, while the other Professors proceeded in rotation with the other classes; Mr. Alexander Hepburn, the new Professor, having the charge of the Magistrand, in place of Mr. William King, till the 21st

1632. July 21. The forty-fourth Class graduated.
of July 1632, when the former graduated the forty-fourth class, which he had instructed during the preceding session, being thirty-three in number.

Legacy by John Byres, late Dean of Guild.
On the 18th of January this year, Thomas Charteris delivered to the City Treasurer 300 marks, a donation to the College by his father-in-law, John Byres of Coats, late Dean of Guild of the City.

October. Session LI.
In October, after the annual vacation, Mr. Alexander Hepburn took upon him the charge of the new Bejan class, and the other Professors proceeded in their order with the other classes.

1633. June 22. The forty-fifth Class graduated.
On 22d of June the forty-fifth class, under Mr. Andrew Stevenson, was advanced to the Master's degree. The graduation was performed in the lower hall of the College, as had been the case the preceding year, and as continued to be the case till the year 1655. This year the graduation was held at an earlier period than usual, on account of the bustle occasioned by the King's presence in the city, and the holding of the Parliament.

His Majesty had made a journey into Scotland in order to be crowned at Edinburgh, and on the 15th of June he entered the city, and was received with sincere affection and loud acclamations by all ranks of his subjects. The streets through which he proceeded were decorated in the most pompous and splendid manner. Ostentatious magnificence, rather than elegance of taste, was consulted on this occasion, and the Scots, preposterously enough, boasted that this exhibition was nothing inferior in grandeur to the entries of the mightiest princes in Christendom for 120 years before. All the pageantry and the speeches delivered at this splendid procession, were devised or composed by Mr. John Adamson, Principal of the University, and the celebrated William Drummond of Hawthornden, assisted by Mr. Thomas Crawford, then head-master of the High School, and a committee of citizens. The particulars of this splendid ceremony have been enumerated and recorded by different authors.[1] Nor was the College of Edinburgh deficient in loyalty and respect to his Majesty at this time. As the effusions of their gratitude to the former King, when he visited Scotland after an absence of fourteen years, had been published in *The Muses Welcome to the High and Mighty Prince James,* of which book Principal Adamson had been the editor ; so there now appeared a collection of poetical congratulations addressed to the less fortunate Charles when he came to be crowned at Edinburgh, published under the direction of the same learned person, and consisting of a great variety of copies of verses by different authors, in

---

[1] Rushworth's Historical Collections, part ii. p. 181. Maitland's History of Edinburgh, p. 65. "The King's entry," says Maitland (p. 69), "together with the present made, and the banquet given on this occasion, cost the citizens the sum of £41,489, 7s. Scottish money."

Greek, in Latin, and in English.[1]　But the rejoicing was not of long duration.

The King, by following too implicitly the advices of Laud, which coincided with his own passionate fondness for the complete establishment of Episcopacy in Scotland, and for accomplishing which his father had, not very auspiciously, begun, created a source of infinite calamity to the nation and to himself. In addition to the five obnoxious articles proposed by the late King, approved by the Perth Assembly in 1618, and ratified in Parliament in the year 1621, it was now determined to have a body of canons and a Liturgy introduced and obtruded upon the nation, the great majority of whom, it was easy to perceive, were entirely averse to that mode of conducting their religious worship. In the Parliament, which was dissolved on the 28th of June, evident symptoms of partiality to the hierarchy had been displayed; and from that time the King looked with an unfavourable aspect on those of his subjects who differed from him in their sentiments on ecclesiastical government.[2] On the other hand, the bishops and those who concurred with them were received with the greatest favour. But, while the Episcopal faction was elated, the great majority of the nation were disgusted; and to add to this discontent, many of the prelates, and those who adhered to them, were imprudent enough to inculcate

---

[1] [Under the following title :—
"ΕΙΣΟΔΙΑ ΜVSΑRVΜ ΕDINENSIUΜ IN CAROLI Regis, Musarum Tutani, ingressu in Scotiam. Edinburgi excudebant Hæredes Andreæ Hart 1633," 4to, 56 leaves, including the English poems by David Primrose and William Douglas.]

[2] Rushworth's Historical Collections, vol. ii. p. 183.

and disseminate Arminian doctrines. In this situation of affairs the Universities, it may be supposed, and as will presently appear, were not entirely exempted from the animosities and divisions which agitated the rest of the nation.

Meanwhile, the College having met after the vacation, Mr. Stevenson in rotation entered to the charge of the new Bejan class, while the other Professors conducted the other classes in the usual order.

1633.
October.
Session
LII.

In December, a vacancy happened in the Professorship of Humanity, by the resignation of Mr. John Armour, who had accepted of a Professorship of Philosophy in the old College of St. Andrews. A comparative trial being announced, three competitors appeared for the vacant office, Mr. James Adamson, nephew to the Principal, Mr. Archibald Newton, son to a citizen of Edinburgh, both of them masters in the High School, and Mr. Alexander Gibson, son to a writer. The subject of the trial was an ode of Horace, the seventh of the first book, upon which each of the candidates was required to speak nearly an hour. The first made a very respectable appearance; but the contest ran betwixt the other two. Mr. Newton was generally understood to be of superior ability; but as he was obnoxious to the Episcopal party, whose influence had now become formidable, the Judges, with an indecent partiality, declared in favour of Mr. Alexander Gibson, who was accordingly elected and admitted to the office on the 27th of December.[1]

Mr. John
Armour
resigns the
Professor-
ship of
Humanity.

Dec 27.
Mr. Alexan-
der Gibson
elected ninth
Professor of
Humanity.

---

[1] Mr. James Adamson afterwards was a minister in Ireland, and Mr. Newton minister of Liberton.

1634.
Feb. 19.
A donation. On the 19th of next February, the City Treasurer received from James Ellis a legacy of 1300 marks, which had been bequeathed by his father and grandfather for augmenting the provision for a Professor of Divinity.

July 26.
The forty-
sixth Class
graduated. On the 26th of July, Mr. John Brown's class, being the forty-sixth, and consisting of thirty-nine students, received the usual degree in the lower hall of the College.

1634.
October.
Session
LIII. In October after the vacation, Mr. Brown commenced a new course with a new Bejan class, while the other Professors proceeded in the usual mode with the other classes till the 25th of July, when the forty-1635.
July 25.
The forty-
seventh Class
graduated.seventh class, under Mr. Robert Rankin, obtained the Master's degree with the usual solemnity.

Ever since the first graduation, conducted by Mr. Robert Rollock in the year 1587, it had been the Subscrip-
tions.custom for the candidates to subscribe the short Confession of Faith or Covenant, which had been drawn up in the year 1581, and first subscribed by King James and his household,[1] and soon after by persons of all ranks, and again by all sorts of persons in the year 1590, and which afterwards made the first part of the National Covenant[2] adopted in the years 1638 and 1639 ; but the prelates and ministers who adhered to them, after many former fruitless attempts, succeeded this year in prevailing with the Masters of the College, with the exception

---

[1] See Collection of Confessions, published by James Watson, 1722, vol. ii. pp. 103, 120.

[2] [Professor Dalzel, in his MS., instead of "the National Covenant," has the words, "the famous Solemn League and Covenant," which was only first adopted in 1644. See p. 123.]

of Mr. Andrew Stevenson, who protested against the measure, to discontinue their subscription, and to cause the candidates to subscribe in place of it a short Oath containing a renunciation of Popery.[1] Accordingly this engagement still appears in the graduation-book, at the head of the subscriptions by Mr. Rankin's students graduated this year, and of those who were graduated the two succeeding years. In the year 1604, the Principal and Professors, as well as the graduates, had begun to subscribe also a solemn engagement to remain affectionate and dutiful to the University of Edinburgh where they had received their education ; and from that date till the year 1639, a double subscription appears regularly in the Graduation-Book, after which time the former of the two was omitted.

In the beginning of April this year, the Town-Council, from the sense they entertained of the merit of Dr. John Sharp, Professor of Divinity, allowed him 300 marks, as an augmentation of his stipend, which sum was paid annually till the year 1638.

On the 22d of the same month, the Council also agreed to relieve the Principal of the labour of keeping the Library, and they elected Mr. Kenneth Logie, son to Mr. James Logie, Advocate, who was recommended as a proper person for undertaking that charge. He had been employed to assist the Principal in arranging the books, and in making a catalogue of them, a copy of which the Principal delivered to the Council on

April 22. Mr. Kenneth Logie elected first Keeper of the Library.

---

[1] [This and the other Oaths to which the author refers, will be found in the volume lately published, containing "A Catalogue of the Edinburgh Graduates," etc. Edinb. 1858, 8vo.]

the same day. An annual salary of 400 marks was granted to the new Librarian, with certain fees and perquisites incident to the office, and regulations were drawn up respecting the times of the Librarian's attendance, and the admission of students to the use of the books, which still were kept in the higher hall.[1]

1685.
October.
Session
LIV.

At the opening of the fifty-fourth session in October 1635, Mr. Robert Rankin had the charge of the new Bejan class, which being matriculated after it was fully convened, according to the custom which now prevailed, amounted to the number of fifty-nine students.

In January 1636, a donation of 100 marks was delivered by James Muir to the City Treasurer, as a contribution towards the maintenance of bursars.

In April 1636, it was thought proper to augment the Principal's salary to 2000 marks including his house-rent, and to assist in completing that part of the old College fabric encompassing a small lower court, which formerly occupied the same ground where the Anatomical Theatre and Museum now stand. Mr. James Keith of Edmonston contributed 500 marks.

---

[1] A note about Porters : see Crawford's MSS. [The passage here referred to may be quoted :—" From the first times of the College, the Porter thereof was chosen, either out of the supreme class, or out of those who were lately graduated : These being always students in Divinity, and aiming at the ministry, had many avocations from their attendance : In consideration whereof, anno 1623, Mr. John Sinclair demitting (who thereafter was minister at Pennycuik), Mr. John Adamson, Principal, moved to the Council, that the Porter should be chosen such an one as had no avocation from his constant attendance, especially a bookbinder, who might employ himself at work within the gate of the College, in a room fit for the purpose : Hereupon, David Smith, bookbinder, was elected Porter ; who, dying this year, 1635, one Robert Binall succeeded to him ; and he dying also in the vacance 1639, one James Marshell filled his place."]

On the 23d of July, the graduation of the forty- 1636. July 23. The forty-eighth Class graduated. eighth class, under the care of Mr. Alexander Hepburn, twenty-four in number, was performed in the usual manner in the lower College hall.

The College being again met after the vacation, the October. Session LV. new Bejan class, now conducted by Mr. Hepburn, was found, at the matriculation, to consist of fifty-seven students. Meanwhile, before the end of October, Mr. Alexander Gibson, to the surprise of his friends, On the re-signation of Mr. Alexander Gibson, Mr. James Wiseman is appointed tenth Professor of Humanity, Nov. 11. resigned the Professorship of Humanity, and accepted of an invitation to be master of the Grammar School in the Canongate. Upon announcing the vacancy, and inviting candidates by means of public programs, to stand a comparative trial, Mr. James Wiseman, master of the Grammar School at Linlithgow, alone appeared; and, being without a competitor, he was required by the Judges to give a discourse upon an ode of Horace, the twenty-eighth of the first book, and was appointed to the office on the 11th of November.

On Monday, the 22d of July 1637, the forty-ninth 1637. July 22. The forty-ninth Class graduated. class, under the charge of Mr. Andrew Stevenson, forty-five in number, were graduated in the common hall of the college.

This was the day immediately after the famous check given to the encroachments of Prelacy in Scotland. The new Service-Book, or Liturgy for the Church of that kingdom, devised by the Scotish Prelates, under the auspices of Archbishop Laud, was now printed and ready to be introduced. The Book of Common Prayer of the Church of England had fur-

nished the model. A few deviations had been adopted,
but these seemed most imprudently calculated to
favour Popery and Arminianism; and the minds of
the people became so much incensed that the introduction of this new religious service was considered
by them as almost equivalent to the restoration of the
Mass.[1] By a royal mandate the Ministers of Edinburgh had been ordered to announce from the pulpit
on the preceding Sunday the intended commencement of this new ritual. Mr. Andrew Ramsay alone
had the boldness to refuse, and Mr. Henry Rollock,
after some hesitation, followed his example. During
the intervening week a general alarm prevailed among
the people. Edinburgh which, at the Reformation, was
not a bishopric, had been by King Charles himself
erected into an episcopal see so late as the year 1633,
and the Collegiate Church of St. Giles was made the
cathedral. David Lindsay the Bishop, on the day
appointed, attended by James Hannay the Dean, and
Alexander Thomson, a minister, came into the middle
district or nave of the cathedral, where a great congregation was assembled ; the eastern part or chancel
being yet under a state of repair for the altar and
other apparatus adapted to the Episcopal communion.
No sooner had the Dean begun the service than there
ensued a great tumult, the particulars of which have

[1] The book was printed under the
following title :—" The Booke of Common Prayer, and Administration of the
Sacraments. And other parts of Divine
Service for the use of the Church of
Scotland. Edinburgh, printed by Robert Young, Printer to the King's most
excellent Majestie. M.DC.XXXVII. Cum
privilegio." in fol. There appears prefixed a royal proclamation for authorizing the use of it throughout the realm
of Scotland. One of the copies belonging to the University of Edinburgh has
the following MS. inscription :—" Ego
donatus sum Academiæ Edinburgenæ
a Magisterii Candidatis. A.D. 1637."

been recorded by various historians, and are well known. The Magistrates interposed their authority, and with difficulty excluded the most turbulent of the people. The service proceeded, but with much annoyance from without ; and, at the conclusion, the Bishop and Dean, with much ado, escaped the fury of the incensed multitude. In the Greyfriars Church the Bishop of Argyle, who officiated there, experienced a similar treatment. The afternoon service in different churches, by the vigilance of the Magistrates, was performed with much greater tranquillity. But a universal bustle and trepidation prevailed throughout the city. From this imprudent attempt on the part of the King and the Bishops, proceeded those fatal commotions which agitated the nation for many years. The first effect of it was an association of ministers, with many of the nobility, gentry, and most of the burgesses and commons throughout the nation, for the purpose of restoring the Presbyterian mode of worship and church government, as it had been established before the encroachments of the Episcopal hierarchy. Many supplications were presented to the Privy-Council, and also to the King himself, on the part of the Presbyterians ; but the influence of the Bishops and certain courtiers prevented those earnest solicitations from having the desired effect. At length the resolution was taken to renew the Covenant for religion. This new Covenant which was agreed upon, consisted of three parts : 1. The old Covenant, which had been originally subscribed by the late King in 1581, and which was formerly mentioned ; 2. An enumeration of

various Acts of Parliament in support of the Reformed
religion ; 3. A conclusion applicable to the particular
occasion. It is astonishing with what earnestness persons of all ranks entered into this solemn engagement, and hastened to bind themselves to its observance by their oaths and subscriptions. Among those
who strenuously promoted it were the Professors of
the University of Edinburgh, with the exception of
only two of their number, Mr. Robert Rankin and
Mr. John Brown.[1]

1637.
October.
Session LVI.

In October 1637, the classes had as usual assembled
after the vacation, when Mr. Andrew Stevenson undertook the charge of the new Bejan class ; and at the
close of the session, Mr. John Brown's students, thirty-
two in number, being now in the fourth year of their
course, were prepared for receiving the Master's degree

1638.
July 20.
The fiftieth
Class gradu-
ated private-
ly.

on the 20th of July 1638. But though their theses
were distributed, it was thought proper to perform the
ceremony of graduation in a private manner, without
the usual disputation. Mr. Brown, as well as Mr.
Rankin, had by this time incurred the displeasure of
the Covenanters, who were now become very numerous,
and whose influence was sufficient for depriving them
of the countenance of the patrons and of the public.
These two obnoxious Regents, who persisted in their
refusal to take the Covenant, were arraigned before

---

[1] " Edinburgh continues constant.
Mr. Henry [Rollock] and Andrew
[Ramsay], yea, Mr. Robert Blair, and
Mr. James Hamilton, and Mr. John
Livingstone preach there to the people's
heart. Mr. Matthew Weems in the
Canongate, Mr. Forfair [err. for David
Forrester] in North Leith, all the Col-
lege, Principal, Dr. Sharp, Regents,
[and] all the scholars (except Mr. Robert
Rankin and Mr. John Brown, with
some few others with them), have sub-
scribed and sworn."—Baillie's printed
Letters, vol. i. p. 47.

the Town-Council on the 24th of August as persons of whom the greatest part of the nation entertained a most unfavourable opinion.[1] Upon their appearance, in consequence of letters of summons, the Council, at two different meetings, deliberated upon the case, and resolved to take the advice of the Ministers before they pronounced any sentence. On the 5th of September the whole Council, with most of the Ministers, being assembled, they deprived the two delinquents of their offices, alleging, as an extenuation of the violence of this proceeding, that they had been originally elected only during the pleasure of the patrons.

Mr. John Brown and Mr. Robert Rankin deposed.

At another meeting on the 26th of September the Council appointed a day for holding a comparative trial of candidates for supplying the two vacant Professorships, and they ordered programs of invitation to be affixed on the gates of the Colleges of St. Andrews and Glasgow. Aberdeen was omitted, probably because the doctors of that City and University were among the few who had strenuously opposed the Covenant. Four competitors appeared—Mr. James Wiseman, professor of Humanity, and three other Masters of Arts, viz., Duncan Forrester, Patrick Colvill, and Robert Young, the first of whom had taken his degree at St Andrews in 1634, the second at Edinburgh in 1629, and the third at Glasgow in 1638. Mr Andrew Ramsay and Mr. Henry Rollock, ministers, and Mr. Thomas Crawford, then Rector of the High School, were appointed to assist the Principal and the remaining Professors in conducting the trial. Each candi-

A comparative trial for new Professors.

1638. October. Session LVII.

---

[1] Town-Council Records of that date.

date was employed three-quarters of an hour in handling a subject which had been presented to him three days before, and each was required to defend a thesis against three other competitors, who disputed with him severally for half an hour. The Judges, at the close of the examination, decided unanimously in favour of Mr. Wiseman and Mr. Forrester. But, after a conference held with the Town-Council, it was thought expedient that one of the two vacant offices should be supplied by a person of experience, and

1638.
October 26.
Mr. James
Wright
elected the
twenty-fifth,
therefore Mr. James Wright, who, after taking his degree at Edinburgh in the year 1627, had discharged the duty of a Professor of Philosophy at St. Andrews for four years with great applause, was pitched upon ; and being elected in place of Mr. John Brown on the 26th of October, he undertook the charge of the new

1638.
Nov. 10.
and Mr.
James Wise-
man the
twenty-sixth
Professor of
Philosophy.
Bejan class. Mr. Wiseman, in preference to Mr. Forrester, was chosen in place of Mr. Rankin, on the 10th of November, and entered, of course, to the charge of the Magistrand class.

Mr. Wiseman's election having vacated the Professorship of Humanity, the Town-Council on the 14th of November chose their delegates to meet with those from the College of Justice, to be present at a comparative trial previously announced for that day. Two competitors appeared, Mr. Robert Fairly, who had taken his degree in the year 1624, and had been a successful teacher of Latin for many years, and Mr.

Nov. 16.
Mr. Robert
Young
elected
eleventh
Professor of
Humanity.
Robert Young formerly mentioned. The strict trial *ad aperturam libri* was adopted ; and Mr. Young, contrary to expectation, was unanimously preferred

by the Judges, and chosen to succeed Mr. Wiseman as Professor of Humanity on the 16th of the same month.[1]

This year is famous for the General Assembly of the Church which met at Glasgow on the 21st of November. The King's authority for holding this celebrated convention was at last obtained, or rather extorted by the intrepidity and perseverance of the Covenanters. Mr. Alexander Henderson, then minister at Leuchars, and one of the delegates from the Presbytery of St. Andrews, was elected Moderator; and Mr. Archibald Johnston, Advocate, afterwards better known by the appellation of Lord Warriston, was chosen Clerk. Though the Marquis of Hamilton, the King's Commissioner, did everything in his power to control the Assembly, in particular, to prevent all hostile procedure against the Prelates, and to act in every respect conformably to the instructions he had received from the King, yet the reverend court, having found themselves lawfully constituted, proceeded in their own way, without yielding in the least to the Commissioner; which exasperated him so much, that on the 28th of November, the seventh day of their sitting, he dissolved the Assembly in his Majesty's name, and issued a proclamation the next day prohibiting them from all further meeting under pain of treason. Nevertheless, the members continued to sit until the 20th of December, when they finished their business, the principal part of which was the abolition of the High Commission, the Articles of Perth, the Canons, the

Nov. 21.
A General
Assembly
held at Glasgow.

[1] Town-Council Records of that date.

Liturgy, and the whole fabric of Episcopacy, which James and Charles for a course of years had taken so much pains gradually to rear. Mr. John Adamson, Principal of the University of Edinburgh, represented that society in this Assembly. Though the Assembly had invariably expressed the greatest respect for the King, yet his Majesty was extremely displeased with their proceedings, and had, even before their dissolution, formed the rash and ill-advised design of commencing open hostilities against the Covenanters. This was a fatal period, threatening the disturbance of that uninterrupted tranquillity, at least that freedom from war, which the nation had experienced for more than half a century. In a cause such as that in which they were engaged, the Covenanters persuaded themselves that resistance was legal ; and they took the most prudent measures for opposing the force which was preparing against them. In the beginning of May, a powerful fleet which the King had equipped, entered the Firth of Forth, under the command of the Marquis of Hamilton, while Charles in person advanced with a numerous army towards the Border. The country was alarmed. The inhabitants near the sea assembled for the purpose of guarding the coasts against the fleet, and an army took the field under the command of General Leslie, to oppose the King's forces on the Border.

1639.
April 17.
The fifty-first
Class gradu-
ated.

These commotions had accelerated the vacation of the College. And so early as the 17th of April, the Magistrand class, under the charge of Mr. James Wiseman, forty-two in number, were graduated in a private manner in the upper College hall, without the usual disputation, in presence only of the Town-Council, Ministers of the city, and Masters of the College.

After the appearances of hostility that had been exhibited by the King and the Covenanters, it was thought prudent on both sides to come to an accommodation ; and a pacification having been accordingly concluded, the King permitted another General Assembly and a Parliament to meet at Edinburgh, the former on the 6th, and the latter on the 20th of August.

In the following October the College as usual assembled, Mr. James Wiseman taking the charge of the new Bejan class, Mr. James Wright proceeding with the Semi, Mr. Andrew Stevenson with the Bachelor, and Mr. Alexander Hepburn with the Magistrand. _{1639 October Session LVIII}

In December the revenue of the College was augmented by a larger private donation than any that had hitherto been received. Mr. Bartholomew Somerville, the son of Peter Somerville, an opulent burgess and bailie of Edinburgh, being without children, conveyed to the College, for the support of a Professor of Divinity, the sum of 20,000 marks, and also 6000 marks to purchase for his accommodation an adjacent house and garden which belonged to Sir James Skene. _{Somerville's donation,}

About the same time David Mackall, late bailie, bequeathed to the College 1200 marks for the maintenance of two bursars, and also a similar sum for the increase of the Library. _{and Mackall's.}

On the 25th of the same month, Mr. Andrew Stevenson, who had accepted of a call to be minister _{1639. Dec. 27. On the Re-}

signation of
Mr. Andrew
SteVenson,
Mr. Duncan
Forrester
elected
twenty-
seVenth Pro-
fessor of
Philosophy. at Dunbar, resigned his Professorship ; and on the 27th, Mr. Duncan Forrester,[1] who had been much approved of by the judges in a former trial, was elected in his place, and was the twenty-seventh Professor of Philosophy in the University of Edinburgh.

Though hostilities were renewed in the succeeding year on the part of the King against the Covenanters, and the whole nation, particularly the City of Edinburgh, was again alarmed by the threatenings of war, the Town-Council continued to display a laudable zeal for the interest of their College. In a meeting held

1640.
January 8.
Resolution
to chose a
Rector of the
University. on the 8th of January, it was resolved that the office of Rector should be revived and continued annually, and that the person invested with this dignity should have the general inspection of the whole University, and be assisted by six Assessors, selected from the Council of the City, the Ministers, and the Masters of the College.

It was, moreover, ordained that this academical magistrate should preside in public meetings, and on other solemn occasions, and be distinguished by having a silver mace carried before him.[2] And, for ascertaining with greater precision than formerly the nature

---

[1] [Crawford says, " He was son to David Forrester, an honest, pious minister at North Leith,"—who is mentioned in the foot-note to p. 106.]

[2] George Buchanan, a student, was elected to attend the Rector as beadle or macer, with an annual salary of 20 pounds.—Town-Council Records. The Rector, too, was arrayed in a more splendid robe than those of the Principal and Professors. The gown which Mr. Henderson wore as Rector is still preserved in the College chest, and is thus described in a list of some curiosities deposited there : — " Toga D. D. Alexandri Hendersoni Carolo I. Regi à Sacris, et Academiæ quondam Rectoris. Est è panno Cilicino tenuiore, collo verò quadrangulari formâ partibus à fronte replicatis assuto, manicis apertis et promissis, iisque fibulis sericis candatis et ansulis similibus exornatis, undique verò serico villos prætexta."

and extent of his duty, the Town-Council, on this occasion, enacted and authorized a set of regulations and directions to be observed by the new Rector and his successors in office.

These Regulations are as follows :—

" 1. *Imprimo.* The Rector shall wisely consider and carefully observe what things may serve for the good education of the youth, and for the flourishing estate of the College, whether in the rents and buildings, or in ordering of the Masters, Professors, and Students. He shall be the eye of the Council of the town for universal inspection, and as the mouth of the College for giving information and delivering such overtures to the Council as himself and his assessors shall find convenient.

" 2. *Item.* He shall be careful that neither the Principal, Professors, nor Regents, nor any other member of the said College, be deficient in their duty prescribed by the laws and statutes of the College. He shall advise them, and if need be he shall admonish them, but with that respect which is due to their places ; and in case they amend not what he judges amiss, he shall, after the second admonition, make the matter known to the Council of the town.

" 3. *Item.* The Rector and his Assessors shall cognosce and judge of all complaints and debates not proper for the civil nor ecclesiastical jurisdiction, which shall happen to arise amongst any of the prime masters of the College, or amongst the Principal, Professors, or Regents, or any of them ; as also of such complaints and debates, as may arise betwixt any of the students of philosophy, or any of the students of divinity, or betwixt any of these and the students of any other profession, or betwixt any of the students of the professions amongst themselves ; he shall labour to compose them justly and without scandal, but so that it shall be lawful for any of the parties to appeal to the Town-Council.

" 4. *Item.* The Rector shall have in his custody the Matricular of the College, containing the names of all the students of whatsoever profession, who at their entry shall swear and subscribe in his presence, and in presence of the Principal and Regents of the class, if he shall be a student of philosophy, and if he be a student of any other profession, in presence of the Principal and Professor of the said profession, and obedience to the laws and orders of the College, with their fidelity and forwardness for advancing thereof, all the days of their lives; and immediately before they receive the degree, shall appear in the common hall, swear and subscribe the Confession of Faith, as it is prescribed by the late General Assembly held at Edinburgh in the month of August 1639.

"5. *Item.* The Rector shall have a written register of the names of the benefactors, with the expression of their particular beneficence, whether it be in lands, rents, sums of money, books, or any other way of liberality, that there may be preserved that honourable commemoration of them that may be made at such solemn times as shall be thought fit, and that others may be moved to follow their laudable example.

"6. *Item.* The Rector shall receive from the Council a transumpt of the whole rental and sums of money belonging to the said College, subscribed with the hand of the common clerk, that he may ripely advise how far it may extend and be employed for the weal of the College, at the will of the Council.

"7. *Item.* The Rector shall not only be present at the solemn meetings of the College, but also shall be invited by the Preses to begin and go before the rest in all the public disputes of philosophy and divinity. Anent all and sundry which particulars, and every one of them, contained in the articles above written, the said Provost, Bailies, Council, and Deacons of crafts, Patrons of the said College, grant and give, by these presents, to the Rector presently and hereafter to be chosen, their full power and ample commission for doing and exercising the haill particulars contained in the articles above written, in manner therein set down, siclyke and as freely as they might do themselves in all respects."[1]

In pursuance of the Town-Council's resolution, Mr. Alexander Henderson, the well-known moderator of the famous General Assembly held at Glasgow, and who, soon after that Assembly, had been translated from the country parish of Leuchars to be minister of the great church of Edinburgh, was elected Rector of

[1] Town-Council Records, vol. XV. p. 113.

the University for the ensuing year.[1] George Suttie, one of the bailies, James Cochran, dean of guild, Mr. Andrew Ramsay and Mr. Henry Rollock, two of the ministers, Mr. John Adamson, Principal of the College, and Mr. Alexander Hepburn, one of the regents, were chosen as his Assessors.

The Rector's Assessors.

The College now consisted of the following members, viz. :—

Mr. Alexander Henderson, Rector of the University.
Mr. John Adamson, Principal.
Dr. John Sharp, Professor of Divinity.
Mr. James Wiseman,
Mr. James Wright,
Mr. Duncan Forrester, } Professors of Philosophy.
Mr. Alexander Hepburn,
Mr. Robert Young, Professor of Humanity.
Mr. Kenneth Logie, Librarian.

Hitherto the revenues of the College had been under the charge of the Treasurer for the City, but in consequence of the considerable accessions lately made to them, it was thought proper that the College funds should be separated from those of the City, and that a particular treasurer should be appointed to manage them. Accordingly, John Jossie was, on the last day of January, elected College Treasurer, and a Committee

John Jossie elected College Treasurer.

[1] Mr. Henderson was now plainly considered as the most eminent of the Presbyterian Ministers, and was afterwards employed in various important missions. He had already been appointed one of the commissioners to treat with the English about a pacification with the King near the Border in June 1639. On the 9th of that month he was in the Earl of Arundel's tent, where the King was present ; and Lord Loudoun and he were the principal spokesmen in defence of the late transactions in Scotland. He bore a principal share in the debates of the Assembly held in August this year ; and at the opening of the Parliament on the 31st of the same month he preached a sermon on the end, duty, and utility of Magistracy.

appointed to prepare a distinct statement of all that had been destined for the support of the College.[1]

The pacification agreed upon the preceding year between the King and the Covenanters proved but of short duration. Mutual jealousies had continued to prevail, and the unfortunate and ill-advised monarch recurred to his former expedient of drawing the sword against his Scottish subjects. When intelligence was brought of an army being raised in England to invade Scotland, preparation was made for a vigorous resistance. The bustle which the levies occasioned, and particularly the siege of the Castle of Edinburgh by General Leslie, interrupted the studies in the College, and obliged the Professors to conclude the session so early as the 3d of April, on which day the act of graduating Mr. Alexander Hepburn's class, which consisted of thirty-nine students, and composed the fifty-second class since the institution of the College, was performed in a private manner, as had been the case the foregoing year.

1640.
April 3.
The fifty-second Class graduated.

Meanwhile the funds of the College continued to receive considerable additions. Robert Johnston, LL.D., son of a citizen of Edinburgh, and who had lived many

Johnston's legacy for bursars.

---

[1] This Committee in a few days gave in to the Council a particular detail of the College revenues, containing, as recorded by Crawford in his History of the University :—

"1st, The primitive patrimony of the College, consisting of the Archdeaconry of Lothian, being the vicarage and parsonage of Currie.

"The ground-annuals belonging to the Prebendaries of the Kirk of Field, something short of 200 pounds a year.

"The vicarage of the Kirk of Livingstone.

"The teinds of Kirkurd, parsonage and vicarage.

"2d, The benefit of the public mortcloths given by the City, anno 1609."

[The remainder of the Committee's report is here omitted, as the particulars it contains will be found in the list of the Mortifications made to the College from its origin to the beginning of the year 1656, inserted in Appendix.]

years in London, among various legacies bestowed for
public uses in Scotland, bequeathed to the College of
Edinburgh, in which he had been educated, £1000 sterling, to be consigned to the Town-Council for the purpose of purchasing land to produce an annual revenue
of 1000 marks, for maintaining eight bursars, for which
yearly rent the Council afterwards, in October 1641,
gave infeftment on Bonnington Mills.

About the end of May, Alexander Wright, merchant, Wright's donation.
bestowed on the College for augmenting the salaries
of the Professors, the sum of 10,000 marks; and on
the 24th of July, Mr. Alexander Henderson, Rector,
and Mr. Henry Rollock, one of the ministers of the
city, having borrowed from various well-disposed citi-
zens the sum of 21,777 pounds Scots, for the use of Donation of a sum by various citizens.
the public, and having taken a public bond for the
money, they obtained the unanimous consent of the
creditors that the sum should be employed for the use
of the College, and they assigned the bond for that
purpose accordingly.

Immediately after this transaction, Mr. Henderson
set out for Aberdeen, to be present at the General
Assembly which met there on the 28th of the same
month, and sat about ten days, and all the while without any Commissioner from the King. Principal
Adamson was member for the University of Edinburgh in that Assembly, as he had also been in the
two preceding. Mr. Henderson, on his return, was
appointed one of the chaplains to attend the army then
on its march towards England. Soon after he reached
the army he was sent back to Edinburgh, along with the

Earls of Rothes and Loudon and Mr. Archibald Johnston, to endeavour to provide canvas for tents, and a fresh supply of money for the army—a mission which proved very successful. When the King's army was defeated by that of the Scots at Newburn, near Newcastle, and a treaty was held at Rippon, October 1, Mr. Henderson was appointed one of the Commissioners on the part of the Scots; and when the treaty was transferred to London, he went thither also, accompanied by three other ministers, who went in the character of chaplains to the three noblemen who were on the Commission— Mr. Robert Blair, Mr. Robert Baillie, and Mr. George Gillespie. On Sunday the 7th of November, Mr. Henderson and Mr. Blair preached at Darlington. They remained at London till June following, maintained all the time at the expense of the City of London.

1640.
October.
Session
LIX.

Meanwhile the College having again assembled in October after a long vacation, Mr. Alexander Hepburn commenced the session with the new Bejan class, while the other Professors proceeded with the other classes in the usual order.

Mr. James
Wright
resigns.

Mr. James Wright, who had the charge of the Bachelor class, having received a call to be minister at Cockburnspath, resigned his Professorship on the 9th of December. The patrons, considering that two new Regents had been admitted in the course of the two preceding years, were unwilling that a third without experience should be elected within so short a time, and therefore they agreed to invite Mr. Thomas Crawford to return from the office of Rector of the High

School to the College, where he had formerly held the Professorship of Humanity.

He was a man much respected for his talents and learning. For his encouragement they first elected him public Professor of the Mathematics, on the 30th of December, with an annual salary of 600 marks during life ; and on the 6th of January following, he was received as a Regent of Philosophy in place of Mr. Wright, and proceeded with the charge of the Bachelor class.

Mr. Thomas Crawford elected first Public Professor of Mathematics, and also holds with it a Regency in place of J ime Wright.

A legacy of 600 marks having been left by James Dalgleish, citizen,[1] for the use of the public, the Council appointed that sum, together with some arrears of interest upon it, to go to the use of the College, for defraying part of the new mathematical salary.

Dalgleish's legacy

On the 29th of January, Mr. Kenneth Logie, keeper of the Library, having accepted of a call to be minister at Skirling, Mr. Andrew Munro, son of a burgess of Edinburgh, was chosen to succeed him.

On the 15th of July, Mr. Duncan Forrester's class, being the fifty-third, and twenty-eight in number, received the usual degree, after a public examination and disputation in the lower hall, held according to the method originally practised in the College.

1641. July 15. The fifty-third Class graduated

This was the very day on which the Parliament had met, but they agreed to conclude on nothing, but only to sit and prepare business till the arrival of the King. The General Assembly of the Church met this year at St. Andrews on the 20th of the same month, but by general consent was transferred to Edinburgh, where

---

1 [His legacy for the support of three bursars is noticed at p. 126.]

the second session was held on the 27th, when Mr.
Alexander Henderson, newly arrived from England,
was chosen Moderator, to whom Mr. Andrew Fairfoul,
who had been appointed one of the representatives for
the Presbytery of Edinburgh, had yielded his place in
the Assembly, being chosen to sit only in Mr. Henderson's absence. In this Assembly certain overtures
concerning Universities and Colleges were agreed to
be laid before the King and the Parliament.[1] The
King came to Holyroodhouse on the 14th of August,
and next day, being Sunday, he heard Mr. Henderson
preach from Rom. xi. 36 ; and during the remainder
of his stay in Scotland, he was very punctual in his
conformity with the Presbyterian form of worship.
In this Parliament the King at last granted everything
his Presbyterian subjects could wish. Among the
objects of his bounty, Mr. Henderson obtained a gift
of the emoluments of the Dean of the Chapel-Royal,
computed at 4000 marks *per annum*. On the 17th
of November the riding of the Parliament was solemnly
performed, and the King being seated on the throne,
Mr. Henderson prayed, and the business of this last
meeting being over, he concluded with a sermon.
Next morning the King set out for London, leaving
his Scottish subjects a most contented and happy
people.

Among the acts passed by this Parliament, the
Church revenues paid formerly to the Bishops were
ordered to be disposed of chiefly among the Universities. The College of Edinburgh obtained the rents

[1] See Acts, 8vo, p. 98. See also Overture anent Bursars, p. 101.

of the bishoprick and deanery of Edinburgh and of Orkney, but they were found to be greatly impaired by former gifts.

After the vacation of the College, Mr. Duncan Forrester had, in rotation, returned to the charge of a new Bejan class, which, when matriculated on the 20th of December, amounted to the number of eighty-three. Mr. Alexander Hepburn proceeded with the Semi, Mr. James Wiseman with the Bachelor, and Mr. Thomas Crawford with the Magistrand.

October. Session LX.

The Professor of Divinity had hitherto been accustomed to communicate to his students some knowledge of the Hebrew tongue, by giving them a lesson once a week. But it being thought proper that more time should be allotted to that study, and that it would be for the advantage of the College to have a separate Professor of Hebrew and other Oriental languages, the Council gave an invitation to Julius Conradus Otto, a foreigner, of whose skill in that department they had heard a favourable report, to undertake the office. They proposed to take a year's trial of the effect of his learning and labour, and to bestow upon him 1200 marks for his support during that time. He accepted of the offer; and being appointed Professor of Hebrew and Oriental languages on the 26th of January 1642,[1] his course of teaching for the ensuing session was announced by a public program.

1642. Jan. 26. Julius Conradus Otto appointed first Professor of Hebrew.

The College Treasurer on the 25th of February received 1000 marks, being a donation of Mausie Wier, widow of Richard Dobie, late Dean of Guild.

Wier's Donation.

[1] Town-Council Records.

It was employed for the support of a bursar of Divinity.

On the 15th of April, an act of Council was passed for building a new apartment for the Library ; in pursuance of which that part of the fabric which now comprises the Museum and the Humanity class-room was soon after erected.

In July 1642, Mr. Thomas Crawford brought the fifty-fourth class, twenty-five in number, to the public graduation in the lower hall of the College, with the usual solemnity. The Theses printed on this occasion are dedicated to the Earl of Loudon, Chancellor ; and as Mr. Crawford, along with his Regency, held also the office of public Professor of the Mathematies, he added, at the conclusion, several positions, under the title of " Theses Mathematicæ."

Mr. Alexander Henderson still continued to be Rector, and he with Principal Adamson were members of the General Assembly which met this year, 1642, at St. Andrews, on the 27th of July.

Upon the meeting of the College in October, after the usual vacation, Mr. Crawford, in his turn, undertook the charge of the new Bejan class, the number of which, by the Matricular of the College still preserved, appears to have amounted to one hundred, on the 27th of January.

In March, Bailie John Fleming, by advice of the Rector and his Assessors, bestowed the sum of 4000 marks for repairing and augmenting the College buildings. At this time, too, a donation of 500 marks was received, which had been granted in the year 1625 by Sir Robert Denniston of Holland[1] for maintaining a bursar, after being liferented by Christian Gibson, his widow.

This spring, 1643, Mr. Alexander Henderson, Rector, was one of the deputies sent to the King at Oxford, along with the Earl of Loudon, Warriston, and Mr. Barclay, to request him to call his English Parliament, as the best measure for obtaining peace. But the deputation was attended with no success. Mr. Henderson gave an account of their proceedings to the Commission met March 10.[2]

On the 24th of July, Mr. James Wiseman brought the fifty-fifth class, thirty in number, to the Master's degree in the lower hall of the College. On this occasion, after an intermission of thirteen years, the ancient mode of circling the candidates according to their merit and proficiency, was revived, though not without opposition. This arrangement was made on the afternoon previous to the graduation in the upper hall, in presence of a select number of the Town-Council and Ministers, with the Rector and Masters of the College.

1643.
July 24.
The fifty-fifth Class graduated.

The General Assembly met this year at Edinburgh on the 2d of August. Sir Thomas Hope, King's Advocate, was Commissioner, and Mr. Henderson, Moderator. This Assembly was distinguished by a reception given to Sir William Armyn, Sir Harry Vane junior, Mr. Hatcher, and Mr. Darley, Commis-

---

[1] [Sir Robert Dennistoun for thirty years Conservator of the Scots Privileges in the Netherlands. The inscription on his monument in the Greyfriars Churchyard is given in Monteith's Theater of Mortality, 1704.]

[2] See Hume's History of England, near the end of chap. lvi.

sioners from the English Parliament, and Mr. Stephen Marshall, a Presbyterian minister, and Mr. Philip Nye, an Independent from the Assembly of Divines at Westminster. With them the Assembly of this Church agreed upon that mutual Engagement betwixt the two Kingdoms, so well known by the appellation of the Solemn League and Covenant, which the Convention of Estates, met at the same time, sanctioned with their approbation, and which was afterwards approved of also by the English Parliament. This, too, was the Assembly which appointed a deputation of ministers and elders to meet with and to assist the Assembly of Divines at Westminster in their ecclesiastical proceedings. These deputies were Mr. Alexander Henderson, Mr. Robert Douglas, Mr. Samuel Rutherford, Mr. Robert Baillie, and Mr. George Gillespie, Ministers, with John Earl of Cassillis, John Lord Maitland, and Sir Archibald Johnston of Warriston, ruling elders.

Soon after the rising of the Assembly, Lord Maitland, Mr. Henderson, and Mr. Gillespie, with Mr. Hatcher and Mr. Nye, set out for London to get the Solemn League and Covenant ratified there, the other Commissioners remaining till it should be returned.[1]

1643.
October.
Session
LXII.

About the middle of November all the Scots Commissioners reached London, and were introduced to the Assembly at Westminster.[2]

In October, the classes met as usual after the vacation, when the charge of the new Bejan class devolved on Mr. Wiseman, the other classes proceeding in order

---

[1] See Stevenson's History, p. 1093.   [2] See Neall's Puritans, and Stevenson.

under their respective Professors. Mr. Wiseman's students at the matriculation amounted to about the number of eighty.

On the 8th of July, the fifty-sixth class, educated under Mr. Alexander Hepburn, twenty-nine in number, were graduated in a private manner in the upper College hall, without any examination ; and in a few days after, Mr. Hepburn resigned his office, and betook himself to a retired life. 1644. July 8. The fifty-sixth Class graduated, and Mr. Alexander Hepburn resigns his Professorship.

The supplying of the vacant office occasioned a violent dispute for some time. Several members of the Town-Council were disposed to favour the election of Mr. Robert Young, who had been Professor of Humanity during five years. But Sir John Smith, Lord Provost, with the Bailies, several of the ministers, and the Principal, with the rest of the Masters of the College, wishing in the present state of the University to introduce a person of experience, and the Town-Council, who are patrons of the Church of Dumbarney, having agreed to present Mr. Young, who was esteemed an eloquent preacher, to that charge, the vacant Professorship of Philosophy was unanimously offered to Mr. William Tweedie, who had taken his degree at Edinburgh in 1639, and had been a Professor of Philosophy in the old College of St. Andrews with great reputation for four years. He accepted of the offer, and being elected to succeed Mr. Alexander Hepburn on the 16th of October 1644,[1] he entered to the charge of the new Bejan class, and matriculated eighty-two students on the 18th of December, this 1644. October 16. Mr. William Tweedie chosen twenty-eighth Professor of Philosophy.

[1] Town-Council Records, vol. xvi.

Session
LXIII.
being the commencement of the sixty-third session since the institution of the College. The other three Philosophy Regents proceeded with the other classes in their order.

Mr. Robert
Young re-
signs the
Professor-
ship of
Humanity.
Mr. Robert Young having resigned the Professorship of Humanity the same day, candidates for the vacant office were invited by means of public programs. The three following competitors appeared: Mr. James Pillaus, son of a citizen of Edinburgh, Mr. David Kennedy, son of a writer, and Mr. William Crawford, of the family of Fetherhead, in Buchan. The strict method of examination *ad aperturam libri* in Latin and Greek authors was adopted, and the

Nov. 8.
Mr. James
Pillans
elected
twelfth Pro-
fessor of
Humanity.
judges having decided in favour of Mr. Pillans, Principal Adamson appeared in the Town-Council on the 8th of November, and declared him to be the candidate duly elected. The Council admitted the election only during pleasure.[1]

Dalgleish's
three
bursars.
This year, James Dalgleish, formerly mentioned, bequeathed to the College 4000 marks for the maintenance of three bursars.

Margaret
Richardson's
donation.
In December, Margaret Richardson, widow of Mr. John Galloway, paid into the hands of the College Treasurer 500 pounds for the benefit of the College.

Struthers's
donation.
Mr. William Struthers, minister of Edinburgh, had, before his death in 1633, bestowed a donation of 6000 marks to be divided equally betwixt the Colleges of Glasgow and Edinburgh, for maintaining two students

---

[1] Town-Council Records, vol. xvi. [Mr. David Kennedy afterwards became minister of Birsay in Orkney, and Mr. William Crawford minister of a parish in the Merse.—Crawford's History of the University of Edinburgh, p. 149.]

of Divinity in each, reserving the liferent to his wife Elizabeth Robertson, who died in 1641 ; but his will and other documents respecting this gift, came not into the hands of the College Treasurer till this year, 1644.

This year James Barnes, merchant, was elected College Treasurer in place of John Jossie, now preferred to be Treasurer for the City. Jossie had acted in the former capacity for upwards of four years and a half, during which time his services were of the utmost advantage to the College. His great diligence, activity, and zeal, were encouraged and supported by the Town-Council, and by the ministers of the City, particularly Mr. Alexander Henderson, who still continued to hold the office of Rector. This eminent man, who was distinguished for his own literary attainments, was zealous in promoting the cause of learning ; and though the important services which he was called to perform both for the Church and State, in those perilous times in which he lived, particularly during his various missions to England, demanded a great share of his attention, yet he omitted no opportunity of consulting the interest and the credit of the Seminary in which he bore so high a rank. At this time he was attending the Assembly of Divines at Westminster, as one of the Commissioners from the General Assembly of the Church of Scotland. It was chiefly through his influence and persuasion that the revenue of the College and its fabric received so many additions about this time. The sums which were contributed for the increase of the buildings, John Jossie had the merit of seeing faithfully applied to the purpose; and when the money was all expended, that respectable citizen, who well deserves to be commemorated among the benefactors of the College of Edinburgh, made very considerable additions to the work at his own private expense.

He built, in particular, the chamber over the old College gate which fronted the lane leading to the Cowgate, called the College Wynd; and his example was followed, first by John Trotter and Robert Ellis, two of his fellow-citizens, and by Robert Fleming and Lawrence Henderson, two of the bailies, aided by George Suttie, Dean of Guild. William Thomson also, the Town-Clerk, and James Murray, added each of them a chamber, all of which additions were situated where the Anatomical Theatre and Museum now stand. Those which composed the old corner, near the top of the lane called the Horse Wynd, were erected out of a legacy bequeathed by Dr. Robert Johnston, a munificent donor, formerly mentioned, and which had been procured by Mr. Jossie's means. But the most important part of the buildings which he promoted and superintended was the new apartment for the Library,[1] consisting of an arched sunk storey and a principal floor, with a leaden roof, in a direction from west to east, immediately within the line of the present new building, beginning near the centre lobby

[1] This room, in length about — feet, and in breadth about —, after being first the Library, and then a printing office, is now (until one grander and more commodious be erected on the south front of the new building) the Museum for Natural History, with a part of the west end allotted for the Humanity Class. The two rooms above, composing the Natural Philosophy Class, and the additional Library, were reared not many years ago, and the old leaden roof then disposed of.

of the great quadrangle on the north, and extending along so far as the eastern wall of the intended new Chemical Laboratory. This was commenced in the year 1642, in consequence of a legacy of 4000 marks bequeathed by Bailie John Fleming, and a donation put into the hands of Mr. Robert Douglas, one of the ministers of Edinburgh, by a pious matron, Margaret Shoner, Lady Forret, for some public work, and by him employed for this purpose.

But the progress of the buildings was now interrupted, not only by the great expense incurred, but by the disasters which befell the kingdom. The Earl of Montrose, who at first had warmly supported the Covenant, was afterwards gained by the King's caresses to espouse the royal cause. In the preceding year he went to the court at Oxford, after the Scots army had entered England, in order to assist the Parliament of that kingdom; and he secretly obtained from the King a commission to be Captain-General of Scotland. Upon making his appearance in the neighbourhood of the Western Isles, he was joined by the M'Donalds, and by some desperate Irishmen who were assembled there. After this, the progress of Montrose and his victories over the Covenanters, are well known. On the 1st of September, at Tippermuir, near Perth, he defeated a body of troops from Fife with those of Strathearn, assembled in a tumultuary manner, under the command of the Earl of Wemyss. Soon after he was equally successful near Aberdeen, exercising hostilities wherever he went against all who stood for the League and Covenant.

Exploits of Montrose.

In addition to these distresses, the plague had begun to make its appearance in the City of Edinburgh
in the month of October.   But as the infection at first
spread slowly, the meeting of the College, after the
vacation, had not thereby been prevented.

1645.   The General Assembly, which met this year in the
month of January, without a Commissioner, amidst
the urgency of their affairs were not inattentive to the
advancement of learning, but on the 7th of February
passed into an act some Overtures on that subject.

"OVERTURES FOR ADVANCEMENT OF LEARNING, AND GOOD ORDER
IN GRAMMAR SCHOOLS AND COLLEDGES.

"I. That every Grammar School be visited twice in the year by
Visitors, to bee appointed by the Presbytery and Kirk-Session in
Landward Parishes, and by the Town-Council in Burghs, with their
Ministers ; and where Universities are, by the Universities, with
consent always of the patrons of the School, that both the fidelity
and diligence of the Masters, and the proficiency of the Scholars in
Pietie and Learning may appear, and deficiency censured accordingly ;
And that the Visitors see that the Masters be not distracted by
any other employments, which may divert them from their diligent
attendance.

"II. That for the remedy of the great decay of Poesie, and of
ability to make verse, and in respect of the common ignorance of
Prosody, no School Master be admitted to teach a Grammar School,
in Burghs or other considerable Parishes, but such as, after examination, shall be found skilful in the Latin tongue, not only for prose,
but also for verse : And that, after other trials to be made by the
Ministers, and others depute by the Session, town, and parish for
this effect, that he be also approven by the Presbytery.

"III. That neither the Greek Language, nor Logic, nor any part
of Philosophy be taught in any Grammar School, or private place
within this Kingdom to young Scholars, who thereafter are to enter
to any College, unless it be for a preparation to their entry there :
And notwithstanding of any progress, any may pretend to have made

privately in these studies ; yet in the College he shall not enter to any higher class, than that wherein the Greek language is taught, and, being entered, shall proceed orderly through the rest of the Classes, until he finish the ordinary course of four years : Unless, after due trial and examination, he be found equal in learning to the best, or most part of that class to which he desires to ascend, by over-leaping a mid-class, or to the best, or most part of those who are to be graduat, if he supplicate to obtain any degree before the ordinary time.　And also, That there be found other pregnant reasons to move the Faculty of Arts to condescend thereto ; and otherwise, that he be not admitted to the Degree of Master of Arts.

" IIII. That none be admitted to enter a Student of the Greek tongue in any College, unless, after trial, he be found able to make a congruous theme in Latin ; or at least, being admonished of his error, can readily shew how to correct the same.

" V. That none be promoved from an inferior Class of the ordinary course to a superior, unless he be found worthy, and to have sufficiently profited : otherwise, that he be ordained not to ascend with his con-disciples, and, if he be a bursar, that he lose his burse.　And, namely, it is to be required, That those who are taught in Aristotle, be found well instructed in his Text, and be able to repeat in Greek, and understand his whole definitions, divisions, and principal precepts, so far as they have proceeded.

" VI. Because it is a disgrace to Learning, and hindrance to trades and other callings, and an abuse hurtful. to the Public, that such as are ignorant and unworthy, be honoured with a Degree or public testimony of learning ; That, therefore, such trial be taken of students, specially of Magistrands, that those who are found unworthy, be not admitted to the Degree and honour of Masters.

" VII. That none who have entered to one College for trial or study, be admitted to another College without the testimonial of the Masters of that College wherein he entered first, both concerning his literature and dutiful behaviour, so long as he remained there : at least, until the Masters of that College from whence he cometh, be timely advertised, that they may declare if they have anything lawfully to be objected in the contrary.　And that none be admitted, promoved, or receive Degree in any College, who was rejected in another College for his unfitness and unworthiness, or any other cause repugnant to good order ; who leaves the College where he was for eschewing of censure, or chastising for any fault committed by him; or who leaves the College because he was chastised, or for any other grudge or unjust quarrel against his Masters.

"VIII. That none of those who may be lawfully received in one College, after he was in another, be admitted to any other class, but to that wherein he was, or should have been, in the College from whence he came, except upon reasons mentioned in the third article preceding.

"IX. That, at the time of every General Assembly, the Commissioners directed thereto, from all the Universities of this Kingdom, meet and consult together, for the establishment and advancement of piety, learning, and good order in the Schools and Universities, and be careful that a correspondence be kept among the Universities, and, so far as is possible, an Uniformity in doctrine and good order.

"The General Assembly, after serious consideration of the Overtures and Articles above written, Approves the same, and Ordains them to be observed, and to have the strength of an Act and Ordinance of Assembly in all time coming."[1]

1645.
Ainslie's
Legacy.

In February 1645, a legacy of 1250 pounds bequeathed by the late Bailie Andrew Ainslie, for augmenting the stipend of the Professor of Divinity, was delivered by his widow Marion Wilkie to James Barnes the College Treasurer.

April 15.
The fifty-
seventh Class
graduated.

The violence of the plague increased in the spring to such a degree as obliged the College to terminate the session much earlier than usual. On the 15th of April the fifty-seventh class, under Mr. Duncan Forrester, obtained the Master's degree, after a solemn disputation in the great hall. On this occasion there were sixty-six graduates, the greatest number hitherto known in any of the Colleges of Scotland.

Porter's and
Dods's lega-
cies.

During the summer the plague was fatal to two worthy citizens, William Porter, merchant, and

[1] Printed Acts of the General Assembly.

Thomas Dods, plumber, both of whom had bequeathed to the College 100 marks for continuing the building. The College Treasurer received the legacy of the former the ensuing year, and that of the latter in the end of the year 1647.

Montrose, now a Marquis, continued to be successful in the North, having defeated the Parliament's forces at Inverlochie, Auldearn, and Alford ; and having afterwards joined with the Gordons, he obtained that remarkable victory at Kilsyth, on the 15th of August, which seemed to demolish all that the Covenanters had done for eight years, and to give a new turn to the King's affairs in both kingdoms.[1]   But his triumph was of short duration.   Lieutenant-General David Leslie, then in England, was invited into Scotland by the Committee of Estates, and having, with the utmost despatch, united a body of Scots cavalry under his command with the few forces in Scotland who were ready to support him, he surprised Montrose at Philiphaugh, in the Forrest, on the 13th of September, routed him after a gallant resistance, and forced him to fly with precipitation to the mountains.

In October, the usual time for assembling the College, the violence of the plague had greatly abated; but the Professors did not meet till the beginning of November, and as it was not thought advisable even then to convene the students in Edinburgh, it was determined in the Town-Council, on the 19th of that month, that the College for that winter should retire to the town of Linlithgow.

1645.
Nov. 19.
The College to remove to Linlithgow on account of the Plague.

[1] See Hume's History of England, chap. lviii.

Notice of this resolution being publicly intimated, the Principal and five Regents met there in the beginning of December ; and five aisles in the great Church being fitted up, under the inspection of the College Treasurer, for the reception of the Humanity and four Philosophy classes, a considerable number of students immediately resorted thither. The Magistrates and citizens of Linlithgow treated them with great kindness and hospitality ; and the students prosecuted their studies in that place for some months without fear from the plague, and unmolested by the hostilities which still divided the nation ; Mr. Duncan Forrester having the charge of the Bejan class, Mr. William Tweedie the Semi, Mr. James Wiseman the Bachelor, and Mr. Thomas Crawford the Magistrand, Mr. James Pillans being Professor of Humanity.

After repeated deliberation by the Town-Council, the College was at length permitted, about the end of April, to return to Edinburgh, where the students resumed their studies in the usual manner to the end of the session.

Meanwhile, Mr. Andrew Monro, keeper of the Library, being infected by the plague, retired to Perth, where he died of that malady. In the absence of the College and of the Rector, who was still in London, attending the Assembly of Divines at Westminster, a difference arose in the Town-Council about the nomination of a new Librarian. Mr. Thomas Speir, son of a respectable burgess of Edinburgh, was thought by many to have a good claim upon that office. He had taken the Master's degree at the preceding graduation,

1645.
Dec. 1.
The College meets at Linlithgow.
Session LXIV.

1646.
April.
The College returns from Linlithgow.

was grandson to William Little, late Lord Provost of the city, and grand-nephew to Mr. Clement Little, Commissary of Edinburgh, who had given the first beginning to the Library. On the other hand, George Suttie, Dean of Guild, with all his interest, supported his nephew, Mr. Andrew Suttie, a promising young man, born at Forfar, and who had taken his degree in the old College of St. Andrews, also in the year 1644. To avoid all further contest the friends of the candi- ^{Mr. Thomas Speir, and} dates, on the 3d of April,[1] compromised the matter, by ^{Mr. Andrew Suttie elect-} allowing them to hold the office in conjunction, with ^{ed joint-Lib-rarians in} an annual salary of 300 marks each, in lieu of 400 ^{place of Mr. Andrew} ^{Monro, de-} which had been enjoyed by their predecessor. But ^{ceased.} this joint appointment was soon terminated by the lamented death of Mr. Speir, which left Mr. Andrew ^{Mr. Andrew Suttie sole} Suttie sole Librarian, with the former pension of 400 ^{Librarian.} marks.

On the 1st of May, the Town-Council resolved that ^{1646. May 1.} the new room for the Library should be completed ^{The new Library to be} without delay ; and on the 26th of June a bond was ^{completed.} granted by Helen Syme, widow of David Graham, merchant, for 7000 marks, which her late husband ^{Graham's legacy.} had bequeathed for the use of the College by advice of Mr. Alexander Henderson, the Rector, and Mr. Robert Douglas, another minister of the City ; which sum was paid to the College Treasurer on the 17th of November the ensuing year. About this time also a considerable donation was bestowed on the College by ^{Buchanan's donation.} Sir John Buchanan of Buchanan.

On the 30th of July, the fifty-eighth class, educated

---

[1] Town-Council Records of that date.

1646.
July 30.
The fifty-
eighth Class
graduated.
under Mr. Thomas Crawford, forty-six in number, after public trial and solemn disputation, were graduated in the lower hall of the College. The printed Theses on this occasion are dedicated to Sir John Smith, Lord Provost, and the other members of the Town-Council.

The General Assembly, which had met this year on the 3d of June, received a letter from the King, with an excuse for not sending a Commissioner; at the same time, he assured them of his resolution to maintain religion in Scotland as there established, and recommended himself and the distracted state of his kingdoms to their prayers. To this letter the Assembly, on the 18th of June, prepared a short answer; and ordered Mr. Robert Blair, their Moderator, with Mr. Alexander Henderson (who had already been sent down from London to the King), and several other ministers, to wait on his Majesty with this answer, and to present their desires more explicitly than could at that time be expressed in a letter. The King being then with the Scots army at Newcastle, Mr. Henderson was already there, and engaged with his Majesty in that famous controversy respecting Episcopacy and Presbytery, maintained between them by an alternate exchange of papers, which, as they have been frequently printed, are still extant. The King's first paper is dated the 29th of May, and the last, the 3d and the 16th of July. On this occasion the abilities of Charles appear in a very respectable point of view, and the favourers of Prelacy did not fail to boast that his Majesty had evidently gained the superiority over his antagonist. On the other hand, the Presbyterians contended that as their champion drew all his arguments from Holy Writ, while the King's authorities were taken from the Fathers, who were fallible men, and in many instances grossly erroneous, any victory gained by the King over the arguments of his Presbyterian chaplain must have been a triumph over the Word of God. The truth is, that Mr. Henderson's constitution was by this time greatly enfeebled, insomuch that he was under the necessity of leaving unfinished his answer to the King's last paper, and of returning to his native country, where he died on the 19th of August 1646, in the sixty-third year of his age. He was by far the most eminent of all the Scots Presbyterian Ministers who flourished during the troublesome period in which he lived; and their cause suffered an irreparable loss by his death.[1] He had borne the office of Rector of the University of Edinburgh with great lustre about six years, and he never omitted any opportunity of consulting the interest and prosperity of that Society. He was a great benefactor also of the University of St. Andrews, where he had received his education.[2]

The patrons seem to have had in view the establishment of a public table within the College, for the Professors and such of the students as might choose

1646.
Aug. 19.
Death of Mr.
Alexander
Henderson,
Rector

---

[1] See Baillie's Letters, vol. ii. p. 327.
[2] See inscription for his monument, Maitland's History of Edinburgh, p. 194; Acts of Assembly, August 7, 1648; Papers which passed betwixt the King and him at Newcastle, in King Charles the First's Works; Whitlocke; Clarendon; Burnet; Advocates Library Catalogue, Art. Henderson. [For the inscription see Monteith's Theater of Mortality, 1704; Bower (Hist. Univ. vol. i. p. 194) observes, that the copy as given by Maitland is incorrect in several places.]

to avail themselves of an economical institution of that kind. But as this had not yet taken place, and indeed being a plan which never seems to have been adopted, the Town-Council, in the meantime, on the 11th of September this year, resolved to allow each of the Regents one hundred pounds, as an addition to his subsistence.

1646.
Sept. 30.
Patrick
Adam chosen
Janitor.

On the 30th of the same month, Patrick Adam was chosen Janitor of the College, in place of James Marshall, lately deceased.

October.
Session
LXV.

The College having met in October, Mr. Thomas Crawford had the charge of the new Bejan class, amounting at the matriculation to eighty-six students, while Mr. Duncan Forrester proceeded with the Semi, Mr. William Tweedie with the Bachelor, and Mr. James Wiseman with the Magistrand classes.

Nov. 4.
Mr. Andrew
Ramsay
elected Rec-
tor for the
ensuing year.

The Town-Council having resolved to continue the office of Rector, which had been held with great advantage to the College by the late Mr. Henderson, did, on the 4th of November, elect in his place, for the ensuing year, Mr. Andrew Ramsay, oldest minister of the City; the same who had enjoyed the dignity of Rector originally, in conjunction with the Professorship of Divinity, from the year 1620 to the year 1626, when he resigned both offices, upon being appointed to the sole charge of one of the four parishes, into which the City of Edinburgh, from being all in one, was then newly divided. He had acted a distinguished part among the Covenanters, and in particular, had been twice Moderator of the General Assembly. As Rector, he had the same number of Assessors with his immediate predecessor, and a copy of the same instructions was delivered to him.

A meeting was held within the College on the 12th of April 1647, consisting of two of the Bailies, the Dean of Guild, Treasurer, four merchant Councillors, three Deacons, Mr. Andrew Ramsay, Rector, Mr. Robert Douglas, Mr. William Colvill, Mr. Robert Laurie, ministers, Mr. John Adamson, Primar, Dr. John Sharp, Professor of Divinity, and Mr. George Jollie, College Treasurer, when certain salutary regulations for the conduct of the students were enacted.

On the 22d of July, after solemn trial and disputation, in the usual manner, in the public hall of the College, the fifty-ninth class, being in number thirty, educated under Mr. Wiseman, received the degree of M.A.

1647.
July 22.
The fifty-ninth Class graduated.

Among the overtures for the advancement of learning, approved, and enacted by the General Assembly, 1645,[1] it was ordained, that, in the time of every General Assembly, the Commissioners delegated thither from the Universities, should meet and consult for the establishment and advancement of piety, learning, and good order in the Schools and Universities, and be careful that a correspondence be kept among the Universities ; and, so far as is possible, a uniformity in doctrine and good order. Several overtures also were approved of, and ordained by the same Assembly to be observed for the future, respecting Divinity bursars to be maintained at the Universities by the different Presbyteries. The General Assembly, 1646, recommended

[1] Acts, etc. Session XIV. February 7.

to all the Universities to propose the best overtures for the most successful method of teaching Grammar and Philosophy, to be laid before the ensuing Assembly ; and for keeping the Universities pure, and exciting the Professors of Divinity to greater diligence, they are desired to present to the ensuing Assembly their dictates of Divinity; but that part of the overture requiring each Professor in the Universities to bring with him, or send to the General Assembly, a perfect and fair copy of his dictates, to be revised by the Assembly or their Committee, is ordered to remain under consideration till the ensuing Assembly.

In the Assembly, 1647, where Mr. Robert Douglas was Moderator, that famous Confession of Faith composed by the Assembly of Divines at Westminster, with the assistance of Commissioners from the Church of Scotland, received the approbation of the Assembly. It had been previously laid before the Commission of the preceding Assembly, and copies transmitted by them to the several Presbyteries of the Church for their consideration. Mr. Robert Baillie, Professor of Divinity, and afterwards Principal of Glasgow College, one of the Commissioners, had been allowed to come from London to attend the Commission and the General Assembly. He brought along with him the Confession of Faith, delivered it to the Commission, and now also laid it before the General Assembly. On this occasion, that modest, learned, and accomplished man made a short and very appropriate speech, in which he reported the progress of the Westminster Assembly in the great work of a plan of uniformity of religion in the three kingdoms, and concluded with a pathetic encomium on his excellent colleague, Mr. Alexander Henderson, lately dead. This system is still the principal standard of the Church of Scotland next to the Holy Scriptures ; and being since ratified in the Articles of Union between the two kingdoms, must maintain its authority as long as the Presbyterian Church Government established by law remains in Scotland. No person can legally hold an office in any of the Universities who, when judicially required, refuses to subscribe this Confession. The Larger and Shorter Catechisms were not produced, nor approved, till the next Assembly.

In consequence of the enactment of the General Assembly, 1645, Commissioners from the different Universities met at Edinburgh on the 28th of August, and continued their meetings on the 30th and 31st of the same month. Having entered upon the consideration of several circumstances relative to the internal discipline and methods of instruction in their respective societies, and made several remarks and proposals on these subjects, they ordered their Clerk to communicate a copy of the account of their proceedings to each University, and adjourned their meetings till another year.

1647.
August 28. Delegates from all the Universities meet at Edinburgh.

The following is a copy of the Minutes of the proceedings of the Commissioners :—

"*August* 28, 1647.

"Convened in the Lower Council-House these Commissioners from the Universities as follows : Masters Andrew Ramsay, John Adamson, John Strang, Alexander Colvill, Robert Blair, Robert

Baillie, William Douglas, to consult about the affairs of the Universities.

" 1. Mr. Andrew Ramsay is chosen Moderator, and Mr. William Douglas, Clerk.

" 2. It is agreed that there should be a register of the conclusions of our meetings, whereof there shall be four copies, one for each University.

" 3. That our conclusions be communicated to every University, to the end that their Commissioners may come instructed to the next meeting, with power to ratify them in name of their University.

" 4. We did find that the Acts of the Assembly 1645, anent the advancement of learning and students of Divinity, were generally neglected ; for remedy whereof, we opponed that the General Assembly should recommend the visitation of schools, and the sending forth of bursars of Divinity from the several Presbyteries ; and to appoint an account to be craved of the visitors of the Provincial books, anent the observation of these acts in time to come.

" 5. Also, because a great part of the neglect doth lie upon the Universities themselves, we do think meet that the Commissioners, in name of the meeting, do entreat every one their own University to be more careful in the observance of these acts in time coming.

" 6. We find it necessary that the Assembly be entreated to recommend to their Commissioners, who shall attend the next Parliament, to petition the Parliament's ratification of those acts for bursars of Divinity.

" 7. It was thought expedient, after the Parliament's ratification, to urge, if ministers might be moved to entertain at their own charges some bursars of Divinity, if it were only by contributing one mark of the hundred of their stipends yearly.

" 8. It was found expedient to communicate to the General Assembly no more of our University affairs but such as concerned religion, or that had some evident ecclesiastic relation.

" 9. Our next meeting to be on Monday morning in this same place."

" *30th of August.*

" Convened in the Lower Council-House of Edinburgh, Masters Andrew Ramsay, John Adamson, John Strang, Robert Blair, Zachary Boyd, Robert Baillie, and William Douglas.

"Anent Teaching of Grammar.

" 1. We find it necessary that the rudiments be taught in English, as they are now extant.

" 2. We desire that the ' Leges Scholæ et Academiæ Edinburgenæ' be now given or sent to the other three Universities, to be thought upon.

" 3. We find it necessary that Despauterius be interpolated ; and all the Universities recommend the care thereof to Mr. Thomas Crawford ; and the Primar is, in their name, to intimate the same to him.

" 4. It is thought upon if 'Vossii Partitiones Oratoriæ' be not fit to be taught.

" 5. It is thought fit that select parts of poets be taught to scholars, namely, such as are free of obscenity.

" Anent the Teaching of Philosophy.

" 1. That every student subscribe the National Covenant, with the League and Covenant, upon some set day, after the same is explained in English by the Principals and the Logical Professors, besides that explanation which private masters give of it.

" 2. It is found necessary that there be a ' Cursus Philosophicus' drawn up by the four Universities, and printed, to the end that the unprofitable and noxious pains in writing be shunned ; and that each University contribute their travails thereto. And it is to be thought upon against the month of March ensuing, viz.—that St. Andrews take the Metaphysics ; that Glasgow take the Logics ; Aberdeen the Ethics and Mathematics ; and Edinburgh the Physics.

" 3. It is thought that what is found behoveful for the improving of learning in schools and colleges be represented to the Parliament in March next.

" 4. That the Commissioners that come next from the Universities, either to the Commission of the Kirk, Parliament, or Assembly, come instructed to show what course is taken with the students on the Lord's day, viz , what account is taken of their ' Lectiones Sacræ,' and of the Sermons they have heard on the Lord's day.

" 5. It is thought that when students are examined publicly on the ' Black-staine,' before Lammas, and after their return at Michaelmas, that they be examined in some questions of the Catechism.

" 6. That every University provide some good overtures, against the month of March, anent the speedy prosecution of the intended ' Cursus Philosophicus,' and, amongst others of Philosophy, such as Crassotus, Reas, Burgerdicius, Ariaga, Oviedo, etc.

" ANENT TEACHING OF DIVINITY.

" 1. That every Commissioner that comes to the Commission or Parliament in March from Universities, bring with them the order and form of Divinity Professors their teaching ; as also, they are to show what order their schools keep, that further consideration be thereof taken by common consent.

" 2.. That the visitations of the Universities be required from the Assembly and Parliament ; that is, that they renew their last Commissions.

" 3. It is ordained that the Clerk give a copy of the *præmissis* to each University.

" *Sic subscribitur*,

" MR. WILLIAM DOUGLAS."[1]

1647.
October.
Session
LXVI.

In October the sixty-sixth session commenced, when Mr. James Wiseman assembled a new Bejan class, and on the 7th of the ensuing January he matriculated sixty-one students.

Mr. Andrew Suttie, in place of Mr. William Tweedie, elected twenty-ninth Professor of Philosophy.

About this time Mr. William Tweedie seems to have resigned his Regency, and accepted a call to be minister of Slamannan in the presbytery of Linlithgow. Upon this, Mr. Andrew Suttie, keeper of the Library, having been substituted in his place, succeeded to the charge of the Magistrand class this session,[2] while

---

[1] Folio MS. volume belonging to the College of Edinburgh. See also Instructions to the Glasgow Commissioners *penes* the Church of Scotland. Baillie's MSS. vol. iv. p. 69.

[2] The precise dates of Mr. Tweedle's resignation and of Mr. Suttie's election I have not been able to ascertain.

Perhaps a more diligent search in the Town - Council Records, if it were thought of any importance, might discover them. [Mr. Andrew Suttie, keeper of the Library, was elected Regent of Philosophy in place of Mr. William Tweedie resigned, 16th October 1647.—Council Records, vol.

Mr. Thomas Crawford carried forward the Semi, and Mr. Duncan Forrester the Bachelor classes.

The Lord Provost of the City, attended by the same persons who had met in the College in the preceding April, held another meeting there on the 6th of December, where several regulations respecting both Masters and students were enacted. At the same time, Mr. Thomas Crawford, as public Professor of Mathematics, delivered in an account of the method practised by him in teaching that science. And on the 27th of the same month, Mr. Andrew Ramsay was re-elected Rector for the ensuing year, with the usual Council of Assessors.

1647.
Dec. 6.
The Lord Provost, with others, visits the College.

Mr. Andrew Ramsay re-elected Rector.

On the 23d of June 1648, the Town-Council made choice of Dr. Alexander Colvill, Professor of Divinity at St. Andrews, to hold the same office in the College of Edinburgh, in place of Dr. John Sharp lately deceased ; and a deputation was sent to him to announce his election.[1] He expressed his willingness to accept of the charge, and his colleagues consented to part

1648.
June 23.
Dr. Alexander Colvill chosen Professor of Divinity, but the General Assembly refuse to translate him.

xvi. fol. 216.] About ten years afterwards, that is on the 5th of August 1657, we find Mr. William Tweedie elected a Regent in place of Mr. William Forbes deceased ; and he was then minister at Slamannan-muir. The terms of this election, which are rather singular, are specified in the Town-Council Records. It is there stipulated, that, at the end of a course, he is not to commence another without undertaking to finish it, and must give a quarter of a year's notice before he remove. From this it may be inferred, that he had formerly abandoned his office somewhat precipitately, probably in the time of a session, and that the patrons, to prevent the dissipation of the students without the usual form of trial, immediately substituted the Librarian in his place. In Crawford's History of the University of Edinburgh, Mr. William Tweedie, the first chosen Regent of that name, is said to have taken his degree in the year 1639, under which date that name still appears in the graduation book ; by comparing which with another subscription of William Tweedie, which appears in the fifteenth page of the book containing the laws of the Library, and where he subscribes as a Regent in the year 1662, such a similarity appears as leaves little room to doubt of their being the signatures of the same person.

[1] Town-Council Records of that date.

with him.; but the General Assembly, who managed matters of this kind, in the case of ministers, as they pleased, passed an Act refusing to translate Dr. Colvill to the College of Edinburgh.[1]

The King's fate in England was now drawing towards a close, and in Scotland the whole country was in a state of violent agitation. This was chiefly occasioned by the secret "Engagement" for arming Scotland in the King's behalf, which the Earls of Loudon, Lauderdale, and Lanark, had formed with that unfortunate monarch, when they attended him in the Isle of Wight, along with the Commissioners from the English Parliament. When the Articles of this Treaty were divulged in Scotland, and it was found that it imposed no obligation on the King for signing the Covenant, the rigid Presbyterians, supported by the Marquis of Argyll and Johnston of Warriston, were highly exasperated, being determined that the King should be restored on no other terms than those of the Covenant. The more moderate Presbyterians wished to reconcile the interests of Religion and of the Crown, and, by supporting the Presbyterian party in England, to suppress the Sectarian army, and to restore the English Parliament, as well as the King, to their just freedom and authority. The avowed Roy-

---

[1] Index to unprinted Acts of Assembly 1648, Session 29. Baillie's printed Letters (vol. ii. p. 308), where it is said "that the private respects of a very few made him to be fixed to his station." See also p. 342, where it is said, that Dr. Alexander Colvill would not be given to the College of Edinburgh, being "a man demi-malig-nant." In the Appendix to Spottiswood's Hist. (p. 20), it is said, that he had been formerly a Professor at Sedan; that he was learned in the Hebrew; a great textuary, and well seen in Divinity; and that he died about the year 1664.

On the 5th July 1648, Gideon Lithgow was elected Printer to the College.

alists were for re-instating the King, without any limitation or restriction. Of these three parties, the first had the greatest ascendency over the people. The Parliament of Scotland had indeed sanctioned the Engagement, but the Commission of the General Assembly of the Church had declared it to be illegal. Many of the ministers successfully exerted their interest with the people to obstruct the levies ; and the Marquis of Hamilton, who had the principal hand in the Engagement, was under the necessity of marching into England with a raw and deficient force. His design evidently was, not to fulfil the Covenant, but to co-operate with the Royalists in restoring the King unconditionally to the exercise of his former power. But this expedition, conducted as it was by Hamilton with timidity and irresolution, proved entirely unsuccessful. Though the army was superior in number to Cromwell's, it was forced to yield to that victorious general. The Duke of Hamilton himself was taken prisoner, and soon after, by the title of Earl of Cambridge in England, doomed to suffer on the scaffold.

The General Assembly, which met at Edinburgh on the 12th of July, highly approved of the conduct of the Commission. They discovered the same hostility to the Engagement, and proceeded with great rigour against all those within their jurisdiction who either approved of it or did not condemn it. They did not think a Declaration which had been published by the Commission sufficient, but emitted a new one of their own, entitled, "A Declaration concerning the present

Dangers of Religion, especially the unlawful engagement in war against the Kingdom of England; together with many necessary exhortations and directions to all the Members of the Kirk of Scotland." And they passed likewise an " Act for censuring ministers for their silence, and not speaking to the corruptions of the time."[1] The advanced age of the venerable Mr. Andrew Ramsay, formerly Professor of Divinity, and now the third time Rector of the University of Edinburgh, and the respectable abilities of Mr. William Colvill, who was afterwards thought worthy to be Principal of the same seminary, did not protect them on this occasion. Having been convicted either of negligence in condemning, or of avowedly favouring the obnoxious Engagement, the censure of suspension was inflicted on them by this Assembly, and that of deposition by the next.[2]

This Assembly passed also an Act ordaining the Covenant to be taken at the first receiving of the sacrament of the Lord's Supper, and that it should be

[1] See printed Acts of Assembly, 1648. In this Act it is recommended to the Presbyteries and Synods to make special inquiry and trial concerning all the ministers within their bounds, and to threaten with suspension all such as are found too sparing, general, or ambiguous in speaking against prevailing evils, such as profaneness, the defection from the League and Covenant, and the *unlawful* Engagement in war ; and if any continue in the negligence of such applications and reproofs, after due admonition, they are to be cited, and, upon conviction, to be deposed, " for being pleasers of men rather than servants of Christ; for giving themselves to a detestable indifferency or neutrality in the cause of God ; and for defrauding the souls of people, yea, for being highly guilty of the blood of souls, in not giving them warning : much more are such Ministers to be censured with deposition from their ministry who preach for the lawfulness, or pray for the success of the present unlawful Engagement, or that go along with the army themselves, or who subscribe any bands, or take any oaths not approved by the General Assembly or their Commissioners ; or by their counsel, countenance, or approbation, make themselves accessory to the taking of such bands and oaths by others."

[2] Unprinted Acts, Assemblies 1648 and 1649. See Baillie's printed Letters, vol. ii. pp. 282, 283, 289, 311.

received also by all students at their first entry to College.[1] And they renewed the former injunction to Presbyteries for each to maintain a bursar at some one of the Colleges.

Before the conclusion of the session of the College, and while the General Assembly was sitting, the meetings of Commissioners for consulting about the common benefit of all the Universities of the kingdom were renewed. On the 17th of July there appeared within the College of Edinburgh Mr. Samuel Rutherford and Mr. George Wemyss of St. Andrews ; Mr. David Dickson and Mr. Robert Baillie of Glasgow ; Mr. David Lindsay, Mr. William More, and Mr. Patrick Gordon of Aberdeen ; and Mr. John Adamson and Mr. Thomas Crawford of Edinburgh.

"EDINBURGI, IN ACADEMIA JACOBI REGIS,
"17 *Julii* 1648.

" *Sederunt,*—

"From the Universities of St. Andrews, Mr. Samuel Rutherford and Mr. George Wemyss ; of Glasgow, Mr. David Dickson and Mr. Robert Baillie ; of Aberdeen, Mr. David Lindsay, Mr. William More, and Mr. Patrick Gordon ; of Edinburgh, Mr. John Adamson and Mr. Thomas Crawford.

" 1. It is agreed, that all the Universities shall concur with and assist one another, in every common cause, concerning the common weal of all the Universities.

" 2. The former agreement is renewed, that no delinquent in any College shall be received into another College before he give testimony that he hath given satisfaction to the College from which he came.

" 3. It is agreed, that there be required of every student coming from one University to another, a testimonial from the College whence he came, or from the Regent under whom he studied, to be produced within a month after his entry.

---

[1] Printed Acts of Assembly, 1648. Session 31.

" 4. It is agreed, that it be proposed to every University by the Commissioners, that there may be an equal progress in the course of teaching in every class within the whole University."

" Edinburgh, the 19th July 1648.

" Sederunt,—

" From St. Andrews, Mr. Samuel Rutherford, Dr. Alexander Colvill, Mr. James Reid of Pitleithy, and Mr. David Nevay ; from Aberdeen, Mr. David Lindsay, Mr. William More, and Mr. Patrick Gordon ; from Glasgow, Mr. David Dickson and Mr. Robert Baillie ; from Edinburgh, Mr. John Adamson, Mr. Thomas Crawford, Mr. James Wiseman, Mr. Duncan Forrester, and Mr. Andrew Suttie.

" 1. It is agreed, that, at the next meeting, the Commissioners of every University shall produce a note of those things which are taught in every class in their University.

" 2. It is agreed, that, with all convenient diligence, a draught shall be framed of the course of Philosophy to be taught in the Colleges.

" 3. It is agreed, that the draught of the course shall be one for the Colleges.

" 4. It is agreed, that every Regent be tied to prescribe to his scholars all and every part of the said course to be drawn up, and examine the same, with liberty to the Regent to add his own considerations besides, by the advice of the Faculty of the University.

" 5. It is agreed, that every University shall handle and treat the parts allotted to them before ; viz., St. Andrews, the Metaphysics, de Anima, Porphyry, and the Categories, with the prœmial Questiones de Natura Habituum et Logicæ de Universali, etc., and the Rhetoric ; Glasgow, the rest of the Logics ; Aberdeen, the Ethics, Politics, and Economics, with an introduction to the Mathematics ; and Edinburgh, the rest of the Physics.

" 6. That, in the draught of the cursus, the text of Aristotle's Logics and Physics be kept, and shortly anagoged, the textual doubts cleared upon the back of every chapter ; or, in the analysis and commonplaces, handled after the chapters treating of that matter."

" Edinburgh, 24th July 1648.

" Sederunt,—

" From St. Andrews, Mr. George Wemyss ; from Glasgow, Mr. Robert Baillie ; from Aberdeen, Mr. William More and Mr. Patrick

· Gordon ; from Edinburgh, Mr. John Adamson, Mr. Thomas Craw-ford, and Mr. James Wiseman.

" 1. Anent the question proposed by the General Assembly, con-cerning the election of the Commissioners from Universities, by whom and what persons are to be chosen, it is agreed, that they cannot deter-mine at this time, while [until] the old acts of the General Assembly be searched for that effect. Mr. Robert Dalgleish, agent for the Kirk, is appointed to deal earnestly with my Lord Advocate, Mr. David Calderwood and Mr. Andrew Ker to search out of the Re-gisters of the Assembly what hath been practised before, that report may be made to the next General Assembly."

The course of study of the different Universities was then read.

" St. Andrews.

" That diligent students may attain to some measure of know-ledge, not only in the Greek, but Hebrew tongue, and in all the liberal arts necessary to be known by them, and that they may have some insight in all the parts of Aristotle's philosophy,—

" It is appointed that the Regents of Philosophy follow this course in teaching hereafter :—

" In the first year, so soon as the students come to the College, they shall be exercised diligently in translating of English into Latin, and Latin into English, till the month of November, upon the which day, the common Latin theme shall ·be given ; and, the morrow after, they shall begin the Greek grammar, and shall proceed in learning rules and practices of the Greek language till the month of June ; and the remanent time of that year, after the month of June, to be spent in learning the elements of the Hebrew tongue, that at last they may be able to read the elements of Arithmetic, the four species at least.

" That these necessary studies be not neglected, it is ordained that they be examined not only in the knowledge of the Greek, but also in the reading of the Hebrew, and beginnings of Arithmetic.

" In the second year, the scholars, immediately after their meet-ing, shall be exercised in translating Latin into Greek, and Greek into Latin, till the month of November, upon the which day the common Greek theme shall be given ; the next day after they shall begin the ordinary studies of that year at a Logic compend, and proceed in learning of Dialectic, Rhetoric, *Structura Orationis*, with the practice of Logic and Rhetoric.

" In their declamations till the first day of March, at which time they shall begin Porphyry, and proceed to the Categories *de Interpretatione*, and *Priora Analytica*, and upon all these shall sustain examination.

" In the third year, they shall begin the first book of Topics, with which shall be joined in teaching the argument, or compend of the eighth book, and thereafter the Sophist Captions, *Posteriora Analytica*.

" After ending of the Logics, they shall be taught the elements of Geometry, the first two books of Aristotle's Ethics, and five or six chapters of the third book, with the argument or compend of all the rest of the year ; also a compend of Metaphysics shall be taught ; and, last of all, the first and second book of the Arithmetic.

" It is also thought fit, that so much time of the year as may be well spared, be bestowed in the practice of Logic, about *Thema Simplex et Compositum ;* and this exercise to be upon the Saturday.

" In the fourth year shall be taught the other four books of the Arithmetic, the books de Cœlo, the elements of Astronomy and Geography, the books de Ortu et Interitu, the Meteors, some part of the first, with the whole second and third books de Anima ; and, if so much time may be spared, some compend of Anatomy.

" Because the diting of long notes has in time past proved a hindrance, not only to other necessary studies, but also to a knowledge of the text itself, and to the examination of such things as are taught, it is therefore seriously recommended by the Commissioners to the Dean and Faculty of Arts, that the Regents spend not so much time in diting of their notes ; that no new lesson be taught till the former be examined.

" That every student have the text of Aristotle in Greek ; and that the Regent first analyse the text *viva voce*, and thereafter give the sum thereof in writing."

" Courses taught yearly in King's College of Aberdeen.

" The College sitteth down in the beginning of October ; and, for the space of a month, till the students be well convened, both masters and scholars are exercised with repetitions and examinations ; which being done, the courses are begun about the first or second day of November.

" To the first class is taught Clenard with Antesignanus, the greatest part of the New Testament, Basilius M. his epistle, an oration of Isocrates, another of Demosthenes, a book of Homer, Phocylides, some of Nonnus.

" To the second class, Rami Dialectica, Vossii Rhetorica, some elements of Arithmetic, Porphyry, Aristotle, his Categories *de Interpretatione*, and prior Analytics, both text and questions.

" To the third class, the rest of the Logics, two first books of the Ethics, five chapters of the third, with a compend of the particular writes. The first five books of the General Physics, with some elements of Geometry.

" To the fourth class, the books de Cœlo, de Ortu et Interitu, de Anima, de Meteoris, Sphæra Joannis de Sacrobosco, with some beginnings of Geography, and insight in the globes and maps.

" This to be understood ordinarily, and in peaceable times."

" COURSES TAUGHT YEARLY IN THE MARISCHAL COLLEGE AT
" ABERDEEN.

" Unto those of the first class is taught Clenardus, Antesignanus his Grammar ; for orations, two of Demosthenes, one of Isocrates ; for poets, Phocylides, and some portion of Homer, with the whole New Testament.

" Unto the second class, a brief compend of the Logics, the text of Porphyry, and Aristotle's Organon, accurately explained ; the whole questions ordinarily disputed to the end of the demonstrations.

" To the third class, the first two books of Ethics, and the first five chapters of the third text and questions, the first five books of Acroamatics, *Questiones de Compositione continui,* and some of the eight books.

" To the fourth, the books de Cœlo, de Generatione, the Meteors, de Anima, Johannes de Sacrobosco on the Sphere, with some Geometry." [1]

On the 28th of July, Mr. Andrew Suttie brought

1648.
The sixtieth
Class gradu-
ated.

---

[1] [The author refers to a " MS. book in folio, from which to copy the proceedings of the Universities Commissioners in 1647 and 1648. In the absence of that book, extracts are given from Bower's History of the University, vol. i. pp. 239-246.]

the sixtieth class to the usual degree, being in number thirty-five.[1]

Mr. Francis
Adamson,
Librarian.

Mr. Francis Adamson, who succeeded Mr. Suttie as Librarian, was probably chosen about this time ; but I have not been able to ascertain the precise date of his election. He had taken his degree the preceding session under Mr. James Wiseman.

October.
Session
LXVII.

In October the College, as usual, began to meet for the sixty-seventh time, and Mr. Andrew Suttie entered upon the charge of the new Bejan class, which, when fully convened and matriculated, amounted to the number of fifty-two. Mr. James Wiseman proceeded with the Semi, Mr. Thomas Crawford with the Bachelor, and Mr. Duncan Forrester with the Magisstrand classes.

1649.
Mr. Robert
Douglas
chosen
Rector.

On the 1st of January 1649, Mr. Robert Douglas, who, even before the death of Mr. Alexander Henderson, was rising to great eminence among his party, was chosen Rector of the University for the ensuing year, with the usual number of Assessors.

The commencement of this year is a noted era in the history of Great Britain. King Charles the First, after a solemn trial, was condemned to death, and on the 30th of January executed on a public scaffold. The particulars are well known. Oliver Cromwell's influence, supported by the army, immediately upon this event, prevailed in England, and the monarchy there was dissolved. In Scotland, however, Charles

---

[1] The printed Theses of this graduation, if there were any, are not preserved in the College collection. Instead of them are inserted the Theses published this year for the graduation of twenty candidates in St. Leonard's College, St. Andrews, under the tuition of Mr. David Nevay.

the Second, the King's son and successor, then abroad, was immediately proclaimed ; but upon condition " of his good behaviour, and strict observance of the Covenant, and his entertaining no other persons about him but such as were godly men and faithful to that obligation." The insertion of these clauses evidently shows the influence now possessed by the rigid Presbyterians, and their patron, the Marquis of Argyll, whose object had been to prevail with the late King to subscribe the Covenant, and who now, in this their first acknowledgment of the new Sovereign, certainly acted a consistent and laudable part in thus endeavouring to circumscribe his power.

Meanwhile the education in the Colleges was conducted without molestation. On the 5th of March, Mr. Robert Douglas, the Rector, with his council, held a meeting in the College of Edinburgh, and recommended the observation of certain regulations respecting the hours of meeting which had been enacted the 27th of December 1647.[1] And on the 26th of July Mr. Duncan Forrester brought forward the sixty-first class, in number thirty-four, to the Master's degree, after solemn disputation in the public hall ; on which occasion the printed Theses, which furnished the subjects of debate, were dedicated to the Marquis of Argyll.

1649.
July 26. The sixty-first Class graduated.

. In October, after the vacation, the College again assembled, and Mr. Duncan Forrester had the charge of the Bejan class, which at the matriculation on the 11th of the following January, consisted of sixty-

October. Session LXVIII

[1] Town-Council Records of that date.

one students.   The other three Regents proceeded with their classes in the usual order.

1650.
Feb. 16.
Mr. David
Dickson
chosen fifth
Professor of
Divinity.

The Professorship of Divinity, since the death of Dr. John Sharp, had now remained vacant about two years, when on the 16th of February 1650, the Lord Provost, Magistrates, and Council, and the Ministers of Edinburgh, requested the authority of the Commission of the General Assembly, then met, to translate Mr. David Dickson from the Professorship of Divinity in the University of Glasgow to the same office at Edinburgh.   To this the Commission agreed, and ordained Mr. Dickson to remove from Glasgow and take up his residence in Edinburgh before the 1st of April next.[1]

At this time, while the power of Cromwell had not yet extended to Scotland, the following were the members of the College of Edinburgh :—-

1650.
April 1.

Mr. Robert Douglas, Rector of the University.
Mr. John Adamson, Principal.
Mr. David Dickson, Professor of Divinity.
Mr. Duncan Forrester,
Mr. Andrew Suttie,
Mr. James Wiseman,   Regents or Professors of
Mr. Thomas Crawford, also   Philosophy.
  Professor of Mathematics,
Mr. James Pillans, Professor of Humanity.
Mr. Julius Conradus Otto, Professor of Oriental Languages.
Mr. Francis Adamson, Librarian.

Meanwhile, at Breda, where the King then resided, attended by Commissioners from Scotland, a treaty had been set on foot relative to his return to his

[1] Commission Records of February 16, 1650.

ancient kingdom upon the terms of the Covenant. But Charles, with that duplicity and dishonesty of character for which he was afterwards distinguished, carefully concealed his having already encouraged and abetted the Marquis of Montrose in a scheme of invading Scotland. This illustrious adventurer, however, was extremely unfortunate in this new attempt. Having been defeated in the North soon after his landing, he was brought prisoner to Edinburgh, and there executed on the 21st of May, with circumstances of indignity which historians have recorded with an interesting minuteness, and from which his countrymen have derived no honour. After the death of Montrose, the King immediately acquiesced in the proposals of the Scots Commissioners; and having on the 23d of June set sail for Scotland, he landed in the North, but not till after he had signed the Covenant; and on coming ashore, he found himself entirely at the disposal of the zealous Covenanters.

Notwithstanding the agitation which these events, and the approach of fresh hostilities occasioned in the City, the session of the College was carried on almost to the usual period, and on the 15th of July the sixty-second class, under the auspices of Mr. Thomas Crawford, Regent in Philosophy and Professor of Mathematics, received the degree of M.A., being forty-three in number. The ceremony was performed in the public hall, and the Theses were dedicated to Sir James Stewart of Kirkfield, Lord Provost, and to the other magistrates and members of the Town-Council.

July 15.
The sixty-second Class graduated.

On the 16th of August the King emitted his famous Declaration, from Dunfermline, which was entirely conformable to the desire of the strict Presbyterians ; but every article of which he scrupled not afterwards to violate.[1]

Meanwhile, Cromwell, at the head of a great army, had begun his march towards Scotland. Leslie, the Scots General, had entrenched himself in a fortified camp between Leith and Edinburgh, to which place Cromwell soon advanced ; but being much annoyed by that experienced General, without being able to bring him to a general engagement, he was forced to retreat towards Dunbar. Leslie, by his able conduct, reduced him to the utmost extremity ; and historians admit that if he had not been urged by the zeal of the Presbyterian ministers to give immediate battle to Cromwell, the latter with his whole army must have been utterly undone. The battle was fought on the 3d of September. Cromwell obtained a complete victory, and immediately pursued his advantage by taking possession of Edinburgh and Leith ; while the remains of the Scottish army fled to Stirling.[2]

1650.
October.
Session
LXIX.
Held at Kirkaldy in Fife.
While Cromwell was in possession of the city, the Professors of the College found it impracticable to commence their session there as usual in the month of October, but were advised to retire into Fife, and take up their station at Kirkaldy ; to which place a considerable concourse of students resorted. The number

[1] See Appendix to Wodrow's History, vol. i. No. i.
[2] Hume's History of England, chap. lx.

composing the new Bejan class under Mr. Thomas Crawford, if we may judge from the corresponding graduation at the end of their four years' course (for there was no matriculation this session), was very small.

In consequence of the defeat at Dunbar, it became advisable to strengthen the King's party, by admitting of a coalition with those who had favoured Hamilton's Engagement, and even with the Royalists who were usually styled Malignants. Two resolutions were adopted by the Parliament held at Perth, that a profession of repentance on the part of both Engagers and Malignants should be accepted, and that they should be allowed, on this profession, to share in the service and defence of the kingdom. A violent opposition to this indulgence, and to the Commission of the General Assembly which had favoured it, arose, chiefly in the western counties, who entered into a separate association against the Sectaries, and framed a Remonstrance against the King. The nation suffered a new convulsion, and was enfeebled by this new schism betwixt Resolutioners and Remonstrants. In the meantime the King enjoyed greater freedom, and the Parliament agreed to proceed without delay to his coronation ; which was accordingly performed at Scone with great solemnity on the 2d of January, when after an appropriate sermon preached by Mr. Robert Douglas, minister of Edinburgh, and Rector of the University, the Marquis of Argyll set the crown on the King's head.

The classes continued their studies at Kirkaldy till

1651.
May 8.
The sixty-
third Class
graduated,
partly at
Kirkaldy;
the 8th of May 1651, when twelve of the Magistrand class under Mr. James Wiseman, were graduated, and a few days after, thirteen additional, as appears from a certificate extant in the graduation-book,[1] subscribed by Robert Douglas, Rector, Thomas Crawford, James Wiseman, and James Pillans, Professors. In the same certificate mention is made of the candidates having taken both the National Covenant and the Solemn League and Covenant, with the oath of allegiance to the King. It appears likewise, from a note in the

and partly
at Edin-
burgh,
May 20 and
June 13.
same Record, that eleven other students of this class were graduated at Edinburgh by authority of the Principal and the ministers, and recommended by the Rector and Regents,[2] viz., one on the 20th of May, two on the 28th, and the other eight on the 13th of June.

During the winter, the Castle of Edinburgh was betrayed into the hands of Cromwell, who soon subdued the whole country between the Forth and the Clyde. After this, having remained some time in Edinburgh, the Scottish army, with the King, being encamped and strongly fortified at the Torwood, he in vain tried to bring them to an engagement. He then passed over into Fife and came round upon the rear of the Scottish army, who, with the King, instead of waiting for Cromwell's approach, immediately marched into Eng-

---

[1] [Catalogue of the Graduates, p. 71. Edinburgh, 1858. 8vo.]

[2] It was the custom for the Lord Provost, Magistrates, and Council, to give their sanction to every graduation; but on account of the confusion that pre- vailed, no meeting of the Town-Council was held from the 2d of September 1650, till the 5th of December 1651, being fifteen months and three days, till the kingdom was settled under the English power. See Town-Council Records.

land. Cromwell followed; and on the 3d of September 1651, was fought the battle of Worcester, where the King was utterly defeated, and narrowly escaped being taken.

In October the College of Edinburgh was suffered to meet after a long vacation, when Mr. James Wiseman took the charge of the Bejan class, which at the matriculation consisted of fifty-six students, while Mr. Crawford proceeded with the Semis, Mr. Forrester with the Bachelors, and Mr. Suttie with the Magistrands.

1651.
October.
Session
LXX.

It is probable that this year, 1651, died Mr. John Adamson, Principal of the College.[1] He was the son of Henry Adamson, provost of Perth, and had obtained the office of Regent or professor of Philosophy on the resignation of Mr. George Robertson in January 1598 ; the class to the charge of which he succeeded being in the second year of their course. He was then a very young man, and had been graduated the year before. After holding this Professorship till towards the end of the year 1604, he then accepted of a call to be minister of North Berwick ; from thence he was translated to the church of Liberton, and from that was brought to be Principal of the College, to which office he was admitted on the 21st of November 1623. While Mr. Adamson was minister at Liberton, he presided at the famous disputation which was held by the Professors of the College of Edinburgh in the Castle of Stirling,

[1] He was alive May 28, 1651, at which date mention is made of the Principal. —Graduation Book. [From his Confirmed Testament, it appears that Adamson died towards the end of the year 1651.] Mr. Robert Leighton, who succeeded him, was not chosen till January 17, 1653. [See p. 168.]

before King James the Sixth, in the year 1617, being
requested by Mr. Henry Charteris, then Principal of the
College, to appear in his stead upon that occasion. Mr.
Charteris being a man of great modesty, was averse to
speak on such public occasions, though he was a man
of various and profound learning. An account of this
disputation may be collected from Mr. Thomas Crawford's MS. History of the College, and from the publi-
cation entitled " The Muses Welcome," etc., of which
Mr. Adamson was the editor.[1]   He published also
" Εισοδια Musarum Edinensium in Caroli Regis, Musarum Tutani, ingressu in Scotiam, 1633."[2]   And he had
a great share in constructing the different magnificent
shows and pageants exhibited in the City of Edinburgh
on occasion of the King's public entry into that city
when he came to Scotland to be crowned.[3]   Principal
Adamson also published a small Latin Catechism for
the use of students, entitled " Στοιχειωσις Eloquiorum
Dei, sive Methodus Religionis Christianæ Catechetica.
In usum Academiæ Jacobi Regis et Scholarum Edinensium conscripta.   Edinburgi, in Academia Jacobi
Regis, 1637," in 12mo.[4]   He presided over the College about twenty-five years with great reputation.

1652.
April 15.
The sixty-
fourth Class
graduated.
On the 15th of April 1652, Mr. Andrew Suttie
brought his class, which was the sixty-fourth, consisting only of nineteen students, to the Master's degree,

---

1 [A minute account of this Disputation in the presence of King James at
Stirling, is already given : *supra*, pp.
63-71.]

2 [See footnote, p. 98.]

3 See Mr. Thomas Crawford's History
of the College of Edinburgh ; also
Drummond of Hawthornden's Works ;
and Maitland's History of Edinburgh.
[Also *supra*, p. 97.]

4 [Principal Adamson's Latin Catechism was first printed at Edinburgh
in 1627, 12mo. It was dedicated to the
Provost, Magistrates, and Council, who
voted to the author the sum of 400 marks.
—Town-Council Records, June 1627.]

three months earlier than usual, on account of the agitation still prevailing in the City during the arrangement of affairs under the English power. No printed Theses for this graduation appear in the College collection. During the vacation the same degree was conferred on Thomas Tanner of New College, Oxford, on the 1st of June; and on Isaac Chaplyn from Suffolk, Francis Wilcox from Devonshire, and John Davis[1] from Worcestershire, on the 19th of August.

The Town-Council of Edinburgh had not met for upwards of fifteen months. The Provost and several of the members had retired to Stirling immediately after the battle of Dunbar. At last such of the Council as remained held several meetings in the month of December 1651, when they approved of the lists of deacons, and of merchant and trades councillors, which were laid before them, but they put off the new election of Magistrates till the arrival of the English Commissioners who were appointed by the Parliament of England to settle the Scottish affairs. These having accordingly soon after arrived, they gave authority to the citizens to make the election ; which they did, for the ensuing year, on the 5th and 9th days of March 1652.[2]

The Town-Council being thus restored, one of their earliest acts was the election of a Principal of the College, in place of Mr. John Adamson, lately deceased ;[3] and the Council, with the Ministers, being

---

[1] See Calamy's Abridgment of Mr. Baxter's History of his Life and Times, vol. ii. p. 518.

[2] Maitland's History of Edinburgh, p. 89.

[3] Town-Council Records.

met on the 23d of April, a list of candidates was agreed on, in which was included, by majority of votes, Mr. William Colvill, formerly minister of Edinburgh, but who, as was mentioned before, had been deposed by the General Assembly, 1649, on account of his favouring Hamilton's unfortunate Engagement. He was, notwithstanding this circumstance, now elected Principal of the College of Edinburgh, and a letter was sent to him in Holland, where he then was, inviting him to take possession of the office. Nevertheless, this election was soon after set aside, as will appear presently.[1]

1652.
July 23.
Mr. James
Nairne
appointed
Librarian.

On the 23d of July, Mr. James Nairne was appointed keeper of the Library in place of Mr. Adamson, and on the 28th, he took the oath *de fideli administratione*, and gave security.

1652.
October.
Session
LXXI.

In October, the College again assembled ; and Mr. Andrew Suttie, whose turn it was to have the charge of the new class, having died, Mr. James Pillans, who, since the year 1644, had been Professor of Humanity, was,

Novem. 29.
Mr. James
Pillans,
elected
thirtieth
Professor of
Philosophy.

on the 29th of November, elected one of the Professors of Philosophy in his place, and succeeded to the tuition of the Bejan class, in number forty-seven ; the Semi being taught by Mr. James Wiseman, the Bachelor by Mr. Thomas Crawford, and the Magistrand by Mr. Duncan Forrester.

Before the conclusion of the preceding year, the

---

[1] At another meeting of the Town-Council, on the 30th of the same month, where the Regents were present, on the subject of their own salaries, the Provost took the opportunity of asking them if they had any objection against Mr. Colvill's being Principal; to which they answered, that they knew of none, except the difference betwixt him and the Kirk.— Town-Council Records.

greater part of Scotland had submitted to Cromwell's authority; and the nation, after some unsuccessful efforts to oppose General Monk, whom he had left behind him in this country, enjoyed at last considerable tranquillity under the usurpation. About the close of the ensuing year, the military being in reality the sole power which prevailed in the three kingdoms, Cromwell was declared Protector by the council of officers; a title which he was prevailed on, in the year 1656, to retain, rather than assume that of King, and which was then conferred with greater solemnity by a Parliament he had summoned.

Among other arrangements made by the Protector for the government of Scotland, he appointed seven Judges or Commissioners for the Administration of Justice to the people of that country.[1] These discharged the duty of the Courts both of Session and of Justiciary.[2] To a certain number of them, an ample commission was also given by the Parliament of England to place or eject ministers as they thought proper, and to visit and exercise authority over the Universities.[3]

Edward Mosely, one of the judges, having made certain objections to Mr. William Colvill, lately elected Principal, the Town-Council, though satisfied with Mr. Colvill, were obliged to declare the office vacant, that another Principal might be elected more agreeable to the wishes of the Judge; and on the same day, which

1653.
January 17.
The late election of Mr. William Colvill annulled, and Mr. Robert Leighton elected Principal

---

1 [On the 18th of May 1652.]
2 Lord Hailes's Catalogue of the Lords of Session. See a good account of Cromwell's administration in Scotland, in Laing's History of Scotland, vol. i. p. 439.
3 Baillie's Letters and Journals, vol. ii. p. 371.

was the 17th of January 1653, they elected Mr. Robert
Leighton, minister of Newbattle, to be Principal of
their College.   The Ministers refused to vote, as they
had scruples respecting the manner of the call, though
they declared themselves satisfied with the man.   Indeed, however informal the mode of election might
be supposed, a choice more fortunate for the College
could not have been made.   Mr. Leighton was already
distinguished, not only for piety and learning, but for
a gentleness and moderation of character at all times
most amiable and most respectable, but in those days
of violence and faction truly admirable.

He was the eldest son of Alexander Leighton, D.D.,[1]
a native of Scotland, but who had removed to England,
and was the author of two books, "The Looking-Glasse
of the Holy War," and "Zion's Plea against Prelacy,"
for which he suffered severely, being condemned in
the Star-Chamber to be whipped, set upon the pillory,
have his ears cut off, be branded on the face, his nose
slit, pay a fine of £10,000, and be imprisoned for the
remainder of his life.   This sentence was passed upon
him on the 4th of June 1630 ; at which time his son
Robert, being about sixteen years of age, was a
student of Philosophy in the University of Edinburgh under Mr. Robert Rankin, by whom he was
promoted to the degree of M.A., on the 23d of July
1631.   After finishing his academical course, he set
out on foreign travel, and spent some years in France,
where he attained such ease and fluency in the French

[1] [It is a mistake to denote Dr. Alex-   University of Leyden.—See Bannatyne
ander Leighton as D.D. He took his   Miscellany, vol. iii. p. 229.]
degree of Doctor of Medicine in the

language that he spoke it like a native. The study of Divinity had ever been his great and ultimate object. The knowledge of the world which he had acquired, enlarged his elegant mind, without impairing his piety. On his return to Scotland, he passed trials for the holy ministry with great approbation, and was ordained by the Presbyterians minister of Newbattle in the Presbytery of Dalkeith. There he continued for many years in a state of retirement from the bustle of the world, intent upon study, and diligent in the exercise of his pastoral duties. He kept as much as possible aloof from the violence of both the Presbyterian and Episcopal parties; and he lamented the vehemence which characterized the conduct of both, in their procedure respecting the forms of church government. His own education as a Presbyterian, as well as the cruel treatment which his father had endured from the Episcopals of England, countenanced and cordially approved of by Laud, then Bishop of London, seemed to remove him at an infinite distance from all partiality in favour of Prelacy; yet he could not go along with the Covenanters to the utmost extent of their intemperate zeal. He thought that the antipathy of each party against the other was not consistent with the pure spirit of Christianity, according to the dictates of which it was his constant endeavour to regulate his own life. He did not see any model of church-government precisely defined in Holy Scripture, and was of opinion that, under either the Episcopal or Presbyterian form, when purely administered, the true objects of ecclesiastical jurisdic-

tion might be obtained ; but in his own time, and in
his own country, he saw much to blame, not in the
plan or constitution of ecclesiastical judicatories, but
in the violence, intolerance, and unchristian conduct
of many of their members.   When, after the Restoration, he was prevailed on to be a bishop, it was
evident that his accepting of this pre-eminence was
influenced by no ambitious motive, but proceeded
from a fond hope of being more extensively useful,
and that his exertions might have some effect in
reconciling the contending parties to one another ;
for when, after trial, he was entirely disappointed in
this expectation, he relinquished his Episcopal dignity,
and spent the remainder of his life in retirement and
devotion.

He was in the thirty-ninth year of his age, when he
was elected Principal of the University of Edinburgh.
His father, by an order of the Long Parliament, had
recovered his liberty thirteen years before, being in
the seventy-second year of his age, and worn out
with hard imprisonment, poverty, and sickness.[1]
Laud, who had instigated the prosecution against
him, was himself doomed in his turn to suffer, and
had already, on the 10th of January 1645, perished
on the scaffold.

1653.
Jan. 20.
Mr. Leighton
accepts the
office of
Principal.
On the 20th of January 1653, a deputation was
sent to Mr. Leighton, with a letter from the Town-
Council, inviting him to take possession of his new
office.   As the Church of Scotland, of which he was
a minister, continued to be more and more agitated

[1] Neal's History of the Puritans, edit. 1794, vol. ii. p. 336.

and distracted by internal divisions, as well as by the interference of the English power, and as he was still averse from taking any share in its disputes, he considered an Academical life as even more favourable to his views of study and retirement than the charge of a country parish, and therefore was prevailed on to accept of the invitation.

He had not been invested with the office of Principal much longer than a month when Mr. William Colvill, ignorant of what had happened, arrived from Utrecht, with a view to take possession of the same charge. The Town-Council, as some compensation to Mr. Colvill for his disappointment, ordered 2000 marks of vacant salary to be paid to him ;[1] and after the Restoration, when Mr. Leighton accepted of a Bishopric, they recurred to their original choice, and appointed Mr. Colvill to succeed him as Principal of the University of Edinburgh.

The Professorship of Humanity being vacant by the promotion of Mr. James Pillans, Mr. John Wishart, who had taken his degree in the year 1650, under Mr. Thomas Crawford, was, on the 9th of March, elected in his place, probably by the usual number of delegates from the Town-Council, Judges, Advocates, and Writers to the Signet. The election was confirmed in a meeting of the Town-Council on the 11th of the same month.[2]

No new election of a Rector had been made since the year 1651, when Mr. Robert Douglas appears for

Marginal notes: Mr. Colvill returns from Holland, and is disappointed. The Town-Council make some compensation to him. 1653. March 9 Mr. John Wishart elected thirteenth Professor of Humanity.

---

[1] Town-Council Records, February 23, 1653. [It may be added, that Mr. Colvill was admitted one of the ministers of Perth, 1st of February 1655.]
[2] Ibid.

the last time to have been invested with that annual
dignity ; and as the office was still suffered to remain
dormant, the College now consisted of the following
members :—

Mr. Robert Leighton, Principal.
Mr. David Dickson, Professor of Divinity.
Mr. James Pillans,
Mr. James Wiseman,
Mr. Thomas Crawford (also } Regents of Philosophy.
    Professor of Mathematics),
Mr. Duncan Forrester,
Mr. John Wishart, Professor of Humanity.
Mr. Julius Conradus Otto, Professor of Oriental Languages.
Mr. James Nairne, Librarian.

1653.
May.
The sixty-
fifth Class
graduated.

This session was also a short one ; for Mr. Forrester's
class, being the sixty-fifth, and twenty-eight in number, received the usual degree in the month of May ;
among whom was Mr. Thomas Gibson, an Englishman,
whose name appears in the Graduation Book, subscribing a particular *sponsio*, in which he acknowledges his
adherence to the Confession of Faith of the Britannic
churches—that is, of the Assembly of Divines at
Westminster—renounces Popery and Prelacy, and
promises perpetual affection to the University of Edinburgh.[1] This graduation was conducted in a private
manner, in consequence of a petition presented to the
Town-Council by the Magistrates, stating that they
were unable to defray the usual expense attending a

---

[1] At this graduation it is probable
that Mr. Robert Leighton presided as
Principal of the College, and then delivered the first of those Paræneses and
Prayers which are extant in print, and
subjoined to the " Prælectiones Theo-
logicæ," which he delivered to the students of Divinity as Primarius Theologiæ Professor : printed [as a posthumous volume] at London in a small
4to volume in the year 1693.

public graduation ; and also on account of the troubles of the country.[1]

On the 27th of the same month, the Council thought proper that the salary of Mr. David Dickson, Professor of Divinity, should be augmented from 1600 to 2000 marks, as he was called to discharge also the duty of a minister of the city.[2]

1653. May 27. The salary of Mr. David Dickson augmented.

As it was thought expedient this year to summon a General Assembly of the Church against the 20th of July, the Town-Council, on the 14th of that month, held a meeting in the College with the Professors, to which the Ministers also were summoned, but did not attend ; when they elected Mr. Leighton to represent the University in that Assembly. But Mr. Leighton having gone to England during the vacation, as he afterwards frequently used to do, the Council gave a commission to the Professors to choose another member in his place, but protested, at the same time, that this should not be considered as giving up their right to sit and vote at any future election.

At the next meeting of the College in October, after the vacation, we find Mr. John Wishart, who had lately been elected Professor of Humanity, undertaking the charge of the new Bejan class, instead of Mr. Duncan Forrester, who had either died or resigned his office,[3] and that Mr. William Forbes, a young man who had taken his degree at the last graduation, was made Professor of Humanity, in place of Mr. Wishart. Mr. Pillans this session had the charge of the Semi, Mr.

October. Session LXXII. Mr. John Wishart Professor, in place of Mr. Forrester ; and Mr. William Forbes elected fourteenth Professor of Humanity, in place of Mr. Wishart.

---

[1] Town-Council Records, May 6, 1653.

[2] *Ibid.*

[3] [Forrester resigned on account of ill-health, 4th of February 1654.— Town-Council Records.]

Wiseman that of the Bachelor, and Mr. Crawford that of the Magistrand Class.

1654.
The sixty-
sixth Class
graduated. This last-mentioned class being the sixty-sixth since the institution of the University, and which had entered under Mr. Crawford's tuition at Kirkaldy in the end of the year 1650, when the country was in great alarm on account of the approach of Cromwell's army, was graduated this year about the beginning of May, its number being only seventeen. One more was added the 12th of that month, and another the 4th of July.

October.
Session
LXXIII. At the opening of a new session in October, a considerable number of young students seem to have entered to Mr. Crawford's new class, sixty-four names appearing in the list of those who were matriculated, and others being afterwards added.

Before the conclusion of the session, the Town-Council, on the 13th of April 1655, appointed that each student at his entry to the College should contribute a crown, or at the least half-a-crown, for the benefit of the Library; and they likewise ordered particular inquiry to be made concerning the tithes of the parishes of Currie and Kirkurd, being part of the revenue of the Archdeaconry of Lothian, formerly granted to the College.[1]

1655.
March.
Mr. John
Mien, Libra-
rian, in place
of Mr. James
Nairne. About the month of March or April this year, Mr. John Mien was appointed Keeper of the Library in place of Mr. James Nairne. The College mace had been lent for the use of the public, and being produced in the Town-Council on the 7th of March, was, on the

---

[1] Town-Council Records.

23d of May, delivered to Mr. Mien the new Librarian, after being cleaned by John Milne, goldsmith, who received two dollars for his work.[1]

An inventory of the writs belonging to the College having been made out, the Town-Council ordered it, on the 23d of May, to be deposited in the Town's charter-room.

This year Mr. Wiseman's class, being the sixty-seventh, and consisting of thirty-one students, received the usual degree on the 23d of May; which was still considerably sooner than usual, probably owing to the poverty of the country at this time.[2]

1655.
The sixty-seventh
Class graduated.

On the 23d of January 1656, the Council ordered a particular account of the mortifications or donations to the College, and the sums thereof remaining in the Town's hands, to be inserted in the Council Records of this date.[3]

Soon after the commencement of a new session in October, Mr. Wiseman, to whose charge the new Bejan class had fallen in rotation, died; while Mr. Crawford was proceeding with the Semi, Mr. Wishart with the Bachelor, and Mr. Pillaus with the Magistrand class.

October.
Session
LXXIV.

In consequence of a consultation held on the 5th of

---

[1] Town-Council Records.

[2] In the fourth of Mr. Leighton's Paræneses or Exhortations which he delivered to the students at their graduation during the time in which he was Principal, allusion is made to the curtailing of the sessions. " Non est, ut opinor, quod multis urgeam industriam vestram, et assiduum in studiis humanis et philosophicis progressum : in quibus, si quid de solenni curriculo Academico, temporum horum injuria et infelicitas surripuit, id certè lectione sedulâ quamprimùm subsequuturâ reparandum erit : sed etiamsi nil tale contigisset adversi, credo vos non ignorare studiorum illorum in scholis nostris tantum jacta esse fundamenta, quibus plures anni et indefatigata industria plenioris eruditionis ædificium superstruant, quod Divini spiritus accessu Deo in templum consecretur."—P. 210.

[3] See this document in Appendix.

1656.
March 7.
Mr. William
Forbes,
Professor of
Humanity,
elected the
thirty-second
Professor of
Philosophy,
in place of
Mr. Wiseman. March 1656, by a deputation from the Town-Council, with the Principal and Regents, Mr. William Forbes, Professor of Humanity, was elected on the 7th to succeed Mr. Wiseman as Regent of Philosophy, and undertook the charge of the new Bejan class, amounting, when matriculated, to the number of sixty-five students.

April 2.
Proposal to
abolish the
Humanity
class. No record of the students of Humanity had been kept before this time, and therefore their numbers were not known.   But it should seem that the utility of the Professorship of Humanity had begun to be called in question.   For on the 2d of April, the Town-Council appointed two of their number, John Jossie, and Thomas Kincaid, to wait on the Judges, Advo-cates, and Writers, to acquaint them with a proposal to abolish the Humanity class, as prejudicial not only to the Grammar School, but to the College itself, and to employ the salary of the office some other way for the advancement of learning.   It is not easy to dis-cover how an institution so apparently useful could have fallen into such disrepute at this time.   The College of Justice, however, do not seem to have con-curred with the Town-Council in this opinion, but took some time to deliberate upon a subject of such An interim
teacher of
the Hu-
manity class
appointed. importance.   In the meantime, the Council appointed a teacher of the name of John Cruickshanks to be master of the Humanity class till the end of the session.

1656.
The sixty-
eighth Class
graduated. On the 9th of July, Mr. James Pillans's class, being the sixty-eighth, and twenty-three in number, received the degree of M.A., without any printed Theses : none,

at least, for this year are to be found in the collection preserved in the Library ; nor are there indeed any such from the year 1650 till the year 1659.

The Professorship of Hebrew having become vacant by the resignation or death of Julius Conradus Otto, the first Professor, the Town-Council, on the 3d of September, in consequence of a petition of Mr. David Dickson, Professor of Divinity, and of the students of Divinity, elected Mr. Alexander Dickson, minister of Newbattle, to that office, with a salary of £50 sterling per annum. *1656. Septem. 3. Mr. Alexander Dickson elected second Professor of Hebrew.*

At the next meeting of the College in October, Mr. Pillans undertook the care of the new class, the students of which, thirty-two in number, were matriculated on the 2d of November, and subscribed a new *sponsio*, by which they bound themselves to remain attached to the University of Edinburgh, affectionate to one another, free from all concern in any disorder or tumult, ready to check every tendency to discord in their society, not only studious of peace within the University, but of Christian charity everywhere, detesting all mean conversation and profane licentiousness ; understanding this obligation to the practice of wisdom and religion, as well as affection to the seminary where they were bred, to extend not only to the whole time of their course of philosophy, but to the whole course of their life, and acknowledging that if they were found violating this solemn oath, they would deserve to be expelled with disgrace from the University. All this they promised by the grace of God, and with the divine assistance, to perform. *October. Session LXXV.*

1656.
Nov. 14.
Mr. James
M'Gowan
elected
fifteenth
Professor of
Humanity,
in place of
Mr. William
Forbes.
In consequence of a consultation held among the patrons of the Humanity Professorship, on the 3d of October, the proposal of abolishing it was rejected, and a comparative trial appointed to take place on the 14th of November, when Mr. James M'Gowan was the successful candidate, and was elected by the patrons accordingly. The students of Humanity who entered His class matriculated. under his care were the first Humanity class who had been matriculated; and they amounted only to the number of sixteen.

This session Mr. William Forbes proceeded with the Semi class, Mr. Thomas Crawford with the Bachelor, and Mr. John Wishart with the Magistrand.

On the 10th of April 1657, John Nicol, servant to Mr. Leighton, was chosen Janitor, *ad vitam aut culpam*, out of respect for the Principal his master.[1]

1657.
The sixty-
ninth class
graduated.
On the 16th of July same year, Mr. Wishart's class, being the sixty-ninth, and thirty-three in number, received the usual degree.

The Principal, Mr. Robert Leighton, being to set out on a journey to London, the Town-Council, on the 22d of the same month, appointed a committee of their number to consult with him about making application to the Protector for an augmentation of the College revenue, which the Principal undertook to endeavour to procure.

Mr. William Forbes, who about the beginning of the session in October 1653, had been chosen Professor of Humanity, and afterwards Regent of Philosophy, which last office he had held only during two sessions, died

[1] Town-Council Records.

about this time, in whose place the Town-Council, on the 5th of August, again elected Mr. William Tweedie, who had already held one of the Professorships of Philosophy in the College of Edinburgh, from the 16th of October 1644 till about the end of the year 1647, when he resigned, and accepted of a call to be minister at Slamannan Muir in the Presbytery of Linlithgow. He had taught with great reputation first at St. Andrews and afterwards at Edinburgh ; and his resignation, which seems to have been somewhat abrupt, disappointed the patrons and the public in their expectations of his further utility as a Professor. This appears from the particular conditions agreed upon when again he accepted of the office, on the 11th of September, which were, that at the end of a four years' course he should not commence a new one, without undertaking to finish it, and that he should give three months' notice before his removal. Mr. Alexander Dickson, Professor of Hebrew, was the person pitched upon to go to the Presbytery of Linlithgow, on the 19th, to obtain his detachment from his ministerial charge.

1657. August 5. On the death of Mr. William Forbes, Mr. William Tweedie re-elected a Professor of Philosophy.

In October, Mr. John Wishart entered upon a new Bejan class, which, by the matriculation list, appears to have increased to the number of seventy-four. Mr. Pillans carried forward the Semi, Mr. William Tweedie the Bachelor, and the venerable Mr. Thomas Crawford the Magistrand.

October. Session LXXVI.

On the 9th of December, Mr. John Stevenson, keeper of the Library, who had succeeded Mr. John Mein in that charge, but at what precise time is un-

Dec. 9. Mr. John Stevenson, Librarian.

M

certain, was ordered to make two catalogues of the books, one for the Town, and another for the College.[1]

1658.
January.
The Bohe-
mian Pro-
test.

In January 1658, the Bohemian Protest bequeathed to the College by Dr. William Guild, was received, and is still preserved in the Library.[2] It was carefully sent by Katharine Rolland, his widow.[3]

May 19.
Mr. John
Kniland,
Librarian.

On the 19th of May, Mr. John Kniland, who had taken his degree at the preceding graduation, was elected Librarian, in place of Mr. John Stevenson, deceased, on condition of his remaining in the office six years, under the penalty of 1000 marks in case of his withdrawing before that time. It had, as may be supposed, been found very inconvenient that the office had lately passed in rapid succession through so many hands.

On the 30th of June, certain regulations for bursars were adopted by the Town-Council, and inserted in their Records, together with the form of an oath which they should be required to take for the future.

" RULES ANENT BURSARS.

" 1. That it be signified by the Regents to all the present bursars before the ensuing vacance, and be accordingly settled for time to come, that all that are entered to that benefit be present with the first after the vacance ended ; and that if any of them shall be absent at furthest on the 10th of October, without an invincible necessity, clearly certified, abatement shall be made of ———[4], by way of penalty, out of their first quarter's allowance ; and that on the 15th of October, the examination of the said Bursars shall

---

[1] Town-Council Records.
[2] Ibid.
[3] See the old Library Catalogues; Maitland's History of Edinburgh, p.

371; and Shirreff's Life of Guild, p. 74, and note E; 2d edit. p. 85, and note G.
[4] Blank in the original MS.

begin, in order to their testimonials, to be given thereupon, according to their deserving, for the continuance or withdrawing of their respective provisions ; and if any of them shall be absent on the 15th of October, then the abatement for penalty to be ———.[1]

" 2. That new entrants that sute for the benefit of a bursary, do bring with them, or at least before their admission to it, do procure, a sufficient testimonial of their good behaviour and sufficiency from the schoolmaster under whom they learned, and from the minister of the parish.

" 3. That the said entrants do, after due examination by the masters of the College, bring from them a testimonial of their qualification and hopefulness, and present it to the Council of Edinburgh, without which they are not to be admitted to any pension greater or smaller.

" 4. That they have, each quarter, in order to their receiving the quarter's due, a line of testimony of their continuing proficiency and good demeanour, under the hand of the Primar and their own Regent.

" 5. That the testimonials for their first admission to bursaries, as likewise those renewed after their yearly examinations, be subscribed by the Primar and Regents, or all, or two of them at least, who, at their first entry to their several places, ought solemnly to promise to be, to their best discerning, most impartially faithful in giving of the said testimonials.

" 6. That the testimonials, as much as may be, do particularly bear the several degrees of the abilities, and whither commendables, in the students suiting for these places, so as the eminently pregnable wits, being withal diligent and of good behaviour, may be preferred to the best bursaries ; and this more particularly to be regarded in reference to those six to be provided out of the last gift.

" 7. That besides the subscribing the form set down in the common book of matriculation of all students in this College, there may be a particular form of engagement to obedience and good behaviour, and what rules [it] shall be thought fit to specify in it, for all the Bursars to subscribe apart, and that a book be provided for containing the said form and their subscriptions.

" 8. That if any of them, after better expectation, shall, either

---

[1] Blank in the original MS.

by indiligence and non-proficiency, or by any kind of misdemeanour, be found at the close of their course unworthy of their degree, the College do not so much wrong both to the nation and to itself, and to that degree, as to confer it on them, but according to their demerit seclude them from it : which yet will, in a probability, the more rarely fall out, if the former rules for their first admission and after continuance be carefully observed.

" 9. That whosoever hath taken his degree in this College, and shall after put in for one of the provisions appropriated to students in Divinity, it be required of him, besides the common form given to all that have taken the same degree, to bring a particular testimonial from the Primar and Regents of his deserving that favour, as being of an orderly and grave carriage, and a good proficient in his bypast studies ; which, if at all, they will then certainly be best able to give after so long time spent under their discipline, and so many iterated trials of their sufficiency.

" That some of the ministers be spoke withal, for using the like cautions and rules in conferring the allowances given to scholars in this College by the Kirk-Sessions, and that they enact somewhat to that purpose.   Likewise, if there be any others that present to bursaries here they be spoke with, or writ to, to the same effect, and they be desired to return somewhat in writ, testifying their consent to a course, regular and reasonable, and so much tending to the good of church and commonwealth, seeing this kind of scholars that need some help of maintenance, do more generally afterwards apply themselves either to the ministry, or other employments, than those who have larger patrimonies or estates to look to.   And these Orders to be intimated to the College before the time of vacance.

" Follows the Oath or promise of each Bursar, to be administrat to them at their admission :—

" ' I, A.B., now admitted a student in the College of Edinburgh, and to the benefit of a yearly allowance out of the revenues thereof, do solemnly and sincerely promise, as in the sight of God, that I will, through the assistance of his grace, endeavour in my whole conversation to behave myself suitably, not only to my present station and the favour conferred on me therein, but, which is much more, to the high name and calling of a Christian, walking in the fear of God, neither giving evil example to others nor taking it from them, nor familiarly conversing with any persons given to cursing or swearing, or any other vicious practice ; yea, if I know of any such within this College, I will faithfully delate them : nor will I ever involve myself in fightings or jarrings or classical contentions, or any kind of factions and disorderly combinements ; yea, upon the first perceivance of any such thing amongst any persons w$_h$atsome$_v$er under the discipline of this house, I will forthwith discover [it]. Further, that I will do my utmost to preserve the fabric of the College from being wronged, and will be cheerfully ready to do all duties required of me for the service and good thereof, and obedient to the masters of it, in whatsoever they shall reasonably command me, while I am under their charge ; and while I live will bear that grateful affection and respects I owe to this College, and gladly testify it to my power upon all occasions. Further, I declare that if, during the time of my abode in this College, I shall be found disorderly, disobedient, or my carriage any way dissonant to the above mentioned premises, I shall justly be accounted to have forfeited in so doing both the maintenance I enjoy, and whatsoever other favours or privileges I either have or might have expected in this College.'

" The same rules and promise to be extended, so near as can be, to the Bursars of Divinity."[1]

About the end of the same month, the seventieth class, consisting of sixty-four students, was brought by Mr. Thomas Crawford to the usual degree.

1658.
The seventieth Class graduated.

Principal Leighton, during his stay in London the former vacation, had found means to obtain for the College from the Protector a gift of £200 sterling per annum out of the Church lands ; and on the 2d of July he moved, in a meeting of the Town-Council, that the magistrates, ministers, and masters of the College should use their endeavours to procure a locality for that sum. The College-Treasurer was ordered to pay to Mr. Leighton 1000 marks Scots, for defraying his expenses to London.[1]

A gift of £200 sterling per annum obtained from the Protector.

[1] Town-Council Records, vol. xix. p. 315.   [2] Ibid.

At the same meeting the Principal gave in the following complaint to the Council :—1st, That there were suspected houses near the College ; particularly one Mary Kincaid, in the College Wynd, kept an irregular house. 2dly, That the students were not so good proficients in Philosophy as could be wished ; of which the reason was a deficiency in the knowledge of grammar. The Council proposed that Mr. Thomas Crawford should prepare new Rudiments, and be rewarded for his trouble.

1658.
July 30.
The Professor of Divinity's house to be built.

An Act of Council was passed on the 30th of July for building the Professor of Divinity's house, for which a large sum had been bequeathed by Mr. Bartholomew Somerville. It stood very near the corner of the new College, which is now occupied by the house for the Principal, and had a good garden adjoining to it.[1]

As it was found difficult to allocate the Protector's former grant of an annuity of £200, a new signature was obtained from his Highness, specifying the different lands from which this sum was to be got ; and it was given in to the Council on the 20th of August.[2]

Soon after, viz., upon the 3d of September 1658, the Protector died of a fever at his palace of Whitehall. During the time of his Protectorate, Scotland had been governed as a conquered province, but with great lenity, and the country in general, as well as the seats of learning in particular, enjoyed considerable

[1] See the old inscription.
[2] It is probable, as the Protector's death in happened September this year, that the College never obtained any benefit from this grant.

tranquillity and prosperity.[1] On his death, Monk, who had great authority in Scotland, proclaimed Richard Cromwell, Oliver's son, Protector. But Richard being without capacity for holding so high and important an office, was deposed on the 22d of April in the following year.

On the 15th of October 1658, compeared before the Town-Council, Mr. Pillans and Mr. W. Tweedie, Philosophy Regents, with Mr. James M'Gowan, Humanity Regent, who, on account of the state of his health, demitted by delivering a pen into the Provost's hand. The Council of the College was directed to inquire into his condition, and to report as to his deserving charity.[2]

On the same day, Sir James Stewart, Lord Provost, John Marjoribanks, and William Reid, Bailies, David Wilkie, Dean of Guild, William Johnston, Treasurer, John Jossie, John Lauder, John Milne, and James Lawson, were named College Council for the ensuing year. They accepted and took the oath *de fideli administratione;* and the Town-Council appointed their meeting with the Primar, Professors, Regents, and Treasurer of the College, to be each first Tuesday of the month in the afternoon.[3]

The cautioners of the deceased Mr. John Johnston, Librarian, were also appointed to bring in such books as had not yet been brought in.[4]

On the 21st of the same month, offer was made by the Primar, Mr. Robert Leighton, to preach in the

---

[1] See Hume's History of England, chap. lxi.

[2] Town-Council Records.

[3] Town-Council Records.

[4] *Ibid.*

College hall to the scholars, on the Sabbath-day, once in two, three, or four weeks, *per vices*, with the rest of the Professors.[1]

On the 17th of November, report was made to the Town-Council of a meeting held in the College with Judge Mosley, Judge Ker, and Alexander Leslie, Writer to the Signet (Mr. John Nisbet, Advocate, not having compeared), when they chose Mr. Hugh Smith Regent of Humanity in place of Mr. James M'Gowan.

On the 30th of the same month, at a meeting of the Town-Council and Professors held in the College, they appointed the whole writings and papers belonging to the College to be sought out, put into a chest or coffer, and deposited in the charter house or clerk's chamber.[2]

On the same day, Mr. Thomas Crawford was appointed to draw a draught of the great letters to be put upon the board of the Benefactors.[3]

In October, Mr. Thomas Crawford entered upon the charge of a new and numerous class. In the list of those matriculated at the beginning and afterwards there appear 123 names. This probably includes all who entered during the whole course of four years. Such as entered after the first year, either coming from other universities, or found upon examination qualified for being admitted at an advanced period of the course, were called *Supervenientes*. Mr. John Pillans proceeded with the Bachelor, and Mr. William Tweedie with the Magistrand class, in place of Mr. Wil-

---

[1] Town-Council Records.   [2] *Ibid.*   [3] *Ibid.*

liam Forbes, deceased, who had succeeded Mr. James Wiseman in the charge of the Bejan class in March 1656, but did not survive to see them graduated.

Accordingly, Mr. William Tweedie brought the seventy-first class forward to the usual degree of M.A. upon the 14th of July 1659, their number being forty-five. From the printed Theses on this occasion, it appears that the solemnity was performed in the Lady Yester's Church;[1] and the disputation was continued there from eleven o'clock in the morning until the evening.

1659.
July 14.
The seventy-first class graduated.

After the usual vacation, the Bejan class was commenced in October by Mr. Tweedie, who seems already to have acquired great reputation ; for the class was very numerous, the list after the matriculation, which began on the 13th of October, amounting to 123. Mr. Crawford proceeded with the Semi, Mr. Wishart with the Bachelor, and Mr. Pillans with the Magistrand classes.

This formed the year of the restoration of Monarchy to Great Britain. On the 1st of May, General Monk ventured to announce this event to the Parliament of England then convened, where the intelligence was received with the loudest acclamations ; and King Charles the Second having arrived from the Continent, entered London on the 29th of the same month. The Restoration was no less acceptable in Scotland than it was in England ; and men in both kingdoms persuaded themselves that the era of prosperity and happiness had now arrived.

1660.

---

[1] Lady Yester's Church was built about the year 1654.

CHAPTER IV.

FROM THE RESTORATION TO THE REVOLUTION IN 1688.

1660.
The seventy-second Class graduated. ON the 19th of July, the seventy-second class, under the tuition of Mr. James Pillans, was, after solemn dis putation in the Lady Yester's Church, advanced to the degree of M.A., in number forty-four.

In the following October, Mr. Pillans entered upon the tuition of a new Bejan class, in number ninety-four. Mr. Tweedie went forward with the Semi, Mr. Thomas Crawford with the Bachelor, and Mr. John Wishart with the Magistrand classes.

1661.
The seventy-third Class graduated. The seventy-third class, on the 19th of June, under the tuition of Mr. John Wishart, in number fifty, after solemn disputation in Lady Yester's Church, were honoured with the usual degree. On this occasion the printed Theses were dedicated to the Earl of Middleton, the King's Commissioner to the Scottish Parliament.

This year his Majesty was advised to establish Episcopacy in Scotland, though evidently contrary to the inclination of the great body of the people ; and when persons were sought out to be made Bishops, Dr. Robert Leighton, Principal of the College of Edinburgh, being then in London, on his return from Bath, where he had been for the recovery of his health, was prevailed on to accept of the See of Dumblane. He was a man of a singularly pious and respectable char-

,acter, very learned and eloquent, and extremely modest. His character is described in a most favourable manner by Bishop Burnet (in his History of his Own Time, Book II.), who knew him well. He excelled particularly in speaking Latin with great fluency and purity, which fitted him admirably for the public appearances he had to make as the head of a College. Several of his prelections to the students of Divinity, as well as addresses to the candidates at the annual graduations, which are extant in print,[1] do him great honour. He presided over the College of Edinburgh with great prudence and propriety during the greater part of Cromwell's usurpation, but his acceptance of a Bishopric occasioned a vacancy in this office. The patrons of the University now reverted to their former choice, and placed the Rev. Mr. William Colvill at the head of the College, whom they had formerly elected, but superseded before he was installed in the office, in order to make way for Mr. Robert Leighton, now Bishop of Dumblane, and afterwards Archbishop of Glasgow. What was the precise date of Mr. William Colvill's admission as Principal of the College I have not been able to discover,[2] but I find him subscribing the laws of the public Library, along with the Professors, on the 11th December 1662.

In October, Mr. John Wishart began a new Bejan class, eighty-four in number, Mr. Pillans now having the Semi, Mr. Tweedie the Bachelor, and Mr. Thomas Crawford the Magistrand classes.

---

[1] [See *supra*, note, p. 170.]
[2] [Colvill was elected Principal upon Leighton's resignation, 20th March 1662. – Town-Council Records.]

On the 1st of August Mr. Thomas Crawford brought the Magistrand class to the usual degree, forty-four in number. No printed Theses of this graduation appear. Probably Mr. Crawford was excused for not having provided any such on this occasion, on account of his advanced age and long services in the College. This was the last set which he saw graduated, for he died towards the close of this year,[1] after having recently entered to the charge of the Bejan class in the preceding October. Mr. Hugh Smith, Professor of Humanity, was the person who succeeded him in the professorship of Philosophy, but not in that of Mathematics, which Mr. Crawford had likewise held.

On the 29th of October 1662, Mr. Hugh Smith resigned his Regency of Humanity, as he was to enter upon some other charge; and on the 1st of December he was chosen Regent of Philosophy in place of Mr. Thomas Crawford, deceased. The advice of the Principal and Professors was taken on this occasion, which was unanimous in favour of Mr. Smith. Mr. Crawford also on his death-bed had recommended him.[2]

Mr. Crawford was one of the most laborious, successful, and celebrated teachers, who had ever appeared in this University. He had been, first of all, Professor of Humanity, which office he obtained after a very strict comparative trial in the year 1626; he held it only about four years, and then preferred the Rectorship of the High School. From this office he was again translated to the College, and made one of the Professors of Philosophy in place of Mr. James Wright.

[1] [Crawford died "in the moneth, etc. 1662," probably in October.—Register of Confirmed Testaments.]   [2] Town-Council Records.

He was also made public Professor of the Mathematics. Both these offices he held till the time of his death. Notwithstanding his great diligence and fidelity in the discharge of these offices, he found time to draw up a most distinct account of this University from its first foundation in 1581 till the year 1646.[1] It is to be regretted that he did not continue it down to the Restoration, as the papers now to be found do not furnish, by any means, such ample materials as he, if we may judge from what he has written, was possessed of.

After Mr. Crawford's death, Mr. Hugh Smith, his successor in the Philosophy professorship, carried forward the Bejan class, the number of which was 102, Mr. John Wishart the Semi, Mr. James Pillans the Bachelor, and Mr. William Tweedie the Magistrand classes.

On the 5th of December 1662, Mr. Patrick Scougall was chosen Professor of Divinity in place of Mr. David Dickson, who had resigned.

It does not however appear that Mr. Scougall was installed; for, on the 22d of January 1664, the Lord Provost reported in Council that he had written about Mr. Scougall to the Archbishop of St. Andrews, who answered, that he had already provided a higher place in the Church for Mr. Scougall;[2] and therefore the Provost appointed the Council to consider of some other fit person to be Professor of Divinity.

Mr. William Cumming was, by strict comparative trial, chosen to succeed Mr. Hugh Smith in the Pro-

1663.

---

fessorship of Humanity on the 16th of February. So
that after the resignation of Mr. Robert Leighton,
Principal, and the death of Mr. Thomas Crawford,
Professor of Philosophy and of Mathematics, the College
stood as follows :—

> Mr. William Colvill, Principal.
>   (*Vacant.*)   Professor of Divinity.
> Mr. Hugh Smith,
> Mr. John Wishart,
> Mr. James Pillans,   } Professors of Philosophy.
> Mr. William Tweedie,
>   (*Vacant.*)   Professor of Mathematics.
> Mr. Alexander Dickson, Professor of Hebrew.
> Mr. William Cumming, Professor of Humanity.

On the 10th of June 1663, Andrew Anderson was
elected Town and College Printer in place of Gideon
Lithgow.

1663.
The seventy-
fifth Class
graduated.

Mr. William Tweedie graduated the seventy-fifth
class on the 27th of July 1663. The meeting was
held in Lady Yester's Church, and the Theses which
were the subjects of the solemn disputation were
dedicated to John, Earl of Rothes, the King's Commissioner to the Scots Parliament. The number of
the graduates was seventy-one.

On the 11th of September 1663, an Act of Council
was passed declaring the Town's debt due to the
College to be £75,732, 13s. 4d. Scots.

The next Bejan class to which it was Mr. Tweedie's
turn to enter to the charge of, in the following October,
consisted of ninety-two. They were matriculated on
the 14th of next January. Mr. Hugh Smith carried
forward the Semi, Mr. John Wishart the Bachelor, and
Mr. James Pillans the Magistrand classes.

On the 22d of January, the Lord Provost reported about the vacant Professorship of Divinity, etc.[1] He said that he had spoken to Mr. Colvill, Principal, who wished the place to be supplied immediately, and therefore the Provost recommended to the Magistrates to consider of fit persons for the charge. On the same day a meeting was appointed to be held at the College about making exact catalogues of the Library.

1664.
January 22.

On the 27th of January, Mr. William Keith, minister at Udney, was chosen Professor of Divinity, in place of Mr. David Dickson, during the Town's pleasure ; and on the 29th he appeared in Council and accepted.

On the 29th of January it was ordered, that each Magistrand should pay four pounds Scots, and each Bejan 30s. to the Library, instead of a book usually gifted by each. An alphabetical catalogue was to be completed ; also a press catalogue to be made ; and another of all the books as they came in. William Cumming's salary, as Professor of Humanity, was augmented twenty pounds Scots. And on the 15th of July Mr. John Dunlop, present keeper of the Library, by ticket dated September 4, 1662, granted, that he had received from Mr. John Kniland, his predecessor, all the books in the Library.[2]

On the 18th of July, Mr. Pillans's class, consisting of fifty, were graduated, in the usual manner, in Lady Yester's Church ; and after the vacation he began the new Bejan class, consisting of ninety-two students. Mr. William Tweedie having carried on the

1664.
The seventy-sixth Class graduated.

---

[1] See above, December 5, 1662.   [2] Town-Council Records.

Semi to the time of his death in February 1665, was succeeded in this charge by Mr. William Cumming, formerly Professor of Humanity, who now carried on the Semi class, not far advanced in their logic. Mr. Hugh Smith carried forward the Bachelor to the end of the session, and died in August 1665.

On the 24th of August, the alphabetical and press catalogues were produced by Mr. Pillans and Mr. Tweedie; and on the 26th the College Treasurer was appointed to receive the rents for chambers in the College, and for the future to make them be paid per advance.[1]

1665.
Feb. 22.

On the 22d of February 1665, Mr. William Cumming, Regent of Humanity, was elected Regent of Philosophy, in place of Mr. William Tweedie, deceased. On the 1st of March, Sir Andrew Ramsay, Provost, and John Milne, master mason, were appointed to meet with the delegates from the College of Justice, to choose a Professor of Humanity; and on the 10th of the same month Mr. Andrew Ross was chosen.[2]

On the 7th of July, 800 pounds yearly was allowed to Alexander Dickson, who had been Professor of Hebrew since September 3, 1656.

The seventy-seventh Class graduated.

Mr. John Wishart graduated the Magistrand class, consisting of sixty-four, at the conclusion of the session, but no printed Theses appear for this graduation. He had lately been appointed one of the Commissaries of Edinburgh; and he now resigned his charge in the College.

On the 16th of August, Mr. George St. Clair[3] was

---

[1] Town-Council Records.   [2] *Ibid.*   [3] [Or Sinclair.]

elected Regent of Philosophy in place of Hugh Smith deceased, and accepted.

In October next, at the meeting of the classes after the vacation, Mr. Wishart, now a Commissary, at the request of the Town-Council, Principal, and Regents, undertook the charge of the Magistrand class in place of Mr. Hugh Smith, lately deceased, that the College might suffer as little as possible from so great a mortality as had lately happened among its Professors. Mr. Cumming was desired to assemble the new Bejan class ; Mr. Pillans continued with the Semi ; and Mr. Andrew Ross, formerly chosen Professor of Humanity, but now one of the Philosophy Regents,[1] was set over the Bachelor class, which, having been the Semi the former session, had been taught with success a part of the time by Mr. Cumming.

On the 10th of November, the Council agreed that the Lord Provost, present and to come, should be always Rector and Governor of the College.

It was also agreed that Mr. William Colvill, Primar, should be sent for to the Council, and gently reproved for having given greater importance to the Commissioners from the College of Justice, at the choice of a Professor of Humanity, than to the Commissioners from the Town-Council.

On the 6th of December, Thomas Bell was elected Professor of Humanity.

On the 2d of March, 1666, Mr. William Somerville, student of Divinity, son of John Somerville, deacon of

1666.

---

[1] [Mr. Ross was not promoted to be a Regent of Philosophy till the month of November. See notice of Ross in   Notices of Professors of Humanity in a subsequent part of this volume.]

the Skinners, was chosen Librarian, instead of John
Dunlop, resigned.

On the 13th of July, Mr. William Douglas, Advocate, produced to the Town-Council the Earl of
Teviot's testament, wherein he left 8000 marks, with
interest due to him by the town, to be bestowed for
building chambers in the College.

Mr. Commissary Wishart, who, at the request of
the Council, Principal, and Regents, had resumed his
Professorship, brought the seventy-eighth class, as he
had formerly done the seventy-seventh, to the degree,
but at what precise time does not appear; nor are
there any printed Theses for this solemnity extant in
the College collection. The number of the graduates
was fifty-six.

At the opening of the College next October, there
being a vacancy in one of the Professorships of Philosophy, in consequence of Mr. Cumming's having, about
the end of June, accepted an invitation from the
Earl of Argyll to undertake the private tuition of his
son, Lord Lorn, Mr. John Wood was chosen by the
Council from the number of five candidates, and
placed over the new Bejan class. As to the Semi and
the Bachelor classes, Mr. Pillans took the charge of
the one, and Commissary Wishart that of the other;
and Mr. Andrew Ross had that of the Magistrand
class.

On the 9th of October, the Principal and Professors
were summoned by the Town-Council to produce a
certificate under the Bishop's hand, that they had
taken the oath of allegiance and supremacy, and sub-

[margin note] 1666.
The seventy-
eighth Class
graduated.

mitted ·to and owned the Church government established by law.

On the same day, compeared Mr. William Keith,
Professor of Divinity, and produced the Bishop's certificate.

At this time the College stood as follows :—

> Mr. William Colvill, Principal.
> Mr. William Keith, Professor of Divinity.
> Mr. James Pillans,
> Mr. John Wishart,
> Mr. Andrew Ross, } Regents of Philosophy.
> Mr. William Cumming,
> Mr. Thomas Bell, Professor of Humanity.
> Mr. Alexander Dickson, Professor of Hebrew.

On the 4th of January, 1667, was reported to the 1667.
Town-Council a legacy, by Professor William Tweedie,
of 3000 marks to the College. On the same day, the
four Bailies were appointed to go over to the College,
and demand of the Primar and four Regents of Philosophy, the Bishop's certificate, etc., as above ; and
such as should not produce it were to have their places
declared vacant, and their school-doors shut up.

The seventy-ninth class, which had been first assembled by Mr. Tweedie in the month of October
1663, and which, on his death on the 8th of February
1665, had been carried on by Mr. Cumming to the end
of the session, was entered to, in October that year, by
Mr. Andrew Ross, who carried the class forward to the The seventy-
ninth Class
11th of July 1667 ; at which time they received the graduated.
degree without any printed Theses, and in the absence
of their own Professor, who had been taken ill of a

consumption, and died in the succeeding month of
August.   The number of graduates was forty-four.

In place of Mr. Ross, who had taught with great
approbation, Mr. William Paterson was called by the
Council from a Professorship in Marischal College,
Aberdeen, and intrusted with the charge of the new
Bejan class, which assembled in October next,[1] and was
very numerous.   At the matriculation, on February 5,
1668, it consisted of 106.   Mr. John Wood had the
Semi, Mr. James Pillans the Bachelor, and Commissary Wishart the Magistrand classes.

In September 1667, Mr. William Henderson was
chosen Librarian ; and on the 22d of November it
was ordered that no books should be lent out of the
Library without a receipt.

1668.   On the last day of April, 1668, the eightieth class,
The eightieth
Class gradu-   under the tuition of Commissary Wishart, were gra-
ated.
duated in the lower hall of the College ; and the
Theses, on this occasion, which are called "Spicilegia
hæc philosophica raptissimè congesta," were dedicated
to the Right Hon. Andrew Ramsay, Lord Provost, and
the rest of the Town-Council.   The number of the
graduates was sixty-three.

In October, Mr. Wishart entered upon the charge
of a new class, which was very numerous ; for when
they were matriculated, on the 8th of February following, the list amounted to 122.   Mr. William Paterson,
Mr. John Wood, and Mr. James Pillaus, proceeded in
their order with the other classes.

[1] On the 20th of September, 1667,   place of Mr. Andrew Ross, deceased.—
Mr. William Paterson from Aberdeen   Town-Council Records.
was chosen Regent of Philosophy in

Upon the 17th of October, the Rev. Mr. William Colvill, Primar, having called together the Regents into the Bibliothec, after he had laid before them the necessity of a timely reparation of the discipline of the College, which in some things seemed to come short of the ancient Statutes appointed at the foundation, they unanimously concluded upon sixteen Articles; which, upon the 10th of November, a Council being holden, were confirmed by the honourable the patrons of the College.

These Articles are as follows :—

" 1. That whosoever, whether countryman or stranger, should desire to be admitted into the Semi class, not having somewhere been a Bejan before, the Regent of the said class shall not receive him till first the Primar be acquainted, who is to appoint the Magistrand and the Baccalaur Regents to examine him ; and if they find him to have any competent skill in the Greek language, they are to signify the same under their hand, or by word, unto the Semi Regent, who, till then, is declared unfree to receive him into his class. This Article is to stand in force the four subsequent years ; at [the expiration of] which time the honourable patrons and masters of the College may either confirm it anew, or change it, as they shall see cause.

" 2. That in the winter time, the whole scholars shall convene every day before seven in the morning in their respective schools ; the Catalogue immediately after prayer shall be called ; and the absents shall be noted and fined, or otherwise punished, at the discretion of the Regent.

" 3. That in every class the censor write two doubles of the Catalogue, and ascribe to every name the place of residence, that in case of their absence they may be sought after at their quarters or lodgings ; and that one of these Catalogues be given to the Primar, and the other to the respective Regent.

" 4. That the Regents in teaching shall follow, as near as can be, the rules set down in the Statutes, until it seem good unto the visitors appointed by his Majesty, if they see cause, [to appoint] another method of learning and discipline.

" 5. For preventing of tumults at the scholars' entry, that the Hebdomadar shall be present every day at half an hour past six in the morning ; at half an hour past nine in the forenoon ; and, upon the days that the College meets in the afternoon, at half an hour past one.   And if the Hebdomadar have any reasonable business to detain him from the performance of his charge, he shall supply his place by one of his colleagues.

" 6. That none of the scholars in the morning, or at any other time, be permitted to stand within the gate, or to play, or to walk in the higher or lower yard, under the sight of any of the masters.

" 7. That the censors, in their respective classes, observe such as speak Scots, curse, swear, or have any obscene expressions, that the Regent may censure them according to the degree of their offence.

" 8. That in the public disputes of the superior with the inferior class, the superiors shall have the first oration ; and that the subject matter shall not be an opinion contradictory to the other Regent ; but for avoiding contradictions in orations, they may use their liberty of contradiction in the disputes.

" 9. That, before the Laureation, the public Theses to be disputed shall be revised, and cognosced upon by the whole faculty ; and that nothing be suffered to be printed in them that is contrary to faith and good manners.

" 10. That the Regents shall study to be as concise and brief in their dictates as possibly they can, that there may be more time for examination and dispute ; and that, before the dismission in the fore or afternoon, a task be prescribed to be got at home ; and that the next morning the Regent take an account thereof.

" 11. That, in teaching a compend of the Metaphysics, the Regents insist most upon the general part ; and if they teach anything of the special part, de Hypostasi existentia, etc., they do it with all circumspection, retaining the form of sound words, according to the analogy of faith, and shun such expressions as may seem to favour any heresy that oppugns the doctrine of the Holy Trinity.

" 12. For suppression of tumults, for which the College gets a bad report, it is ordained, that none of the scholars stand at the gate, or in the stairs and passages to the classes, and that censors shall be deputed by the respective Regents who shall delate the transgressors, and every one of them shall be fined in two shillings Scots, for the use of the Bibliothec.

" 13. That no scholar be troublesome to another by shouldering or tossing ; for seeing these are the occasions of fighting, whosoever shall be found guilty of tossing, for every time he shall be amerced in four shillings Scots, for the use above mentioned ; and whosoever shall throw snow balls or cast stones, or use the hand ball, shall be liable every time for the same fine.

" 14. That if any shall strike his neighbour, he shall be chastised according to the ancient Statutes of the College, according to the demerit of the fault ; but whosoever shall be head and ringleader in a tumult, shall be extruded and thrust out of the College with disgrace and ignominy.

" 15. That whatsoever scholar shall be deprehended playing, or carelessly walking up and down in any of the courts or yards the time of the meeting in their schools, for every fault he shall be mulcted in a shilling Scots, for the use foresaid.

" 16. That the Janitor at all times, when there is any meeting in the schools, shall stand punctually by the gate, and shall permit none of the scholars to go out without an express command from their proper or respective Regent.

" By the command of the honourable Senate and Patrons of the College, the right Reverend Primar, and the respective Professors and Regents, These Articles were written and inserted in the Register of the College, the last of November 1668,

" By me, W. H., *Bibliothecar.*"[1]

As to the Professor of Mathematics, he was appointed to teach publicly Arithmetic, Geometry, Cosmography, Astronomy, Optics, upon Tuesdays and Fridays, in the afternoon from two to three during the winter season, but after the beginning of March, from three to four ; all the Regents with their respective scholars being present ; at least the Hebdomadar must be present with the scholars.

On the 19th of July 1669, the eighty-first class,

---

[1] [See p. 196 for Henderson's appointment as Librarian.] Register of the University of Edinburgh, MS. in College Library, pp. 54-56.

under the tuition of Mr. James Pillans, were graduated in the public hall of the College; and the Theses were dedicated to Sir Andrew Ramsay of Abbotshall, Lord Provost, and the rest of the Town Council. The number of the graduates was forty-five. In the ensuing October, the Bejan class was assembled by Mr. Pillans; and the number at the matriculation in the following February was seventy. Mr. Wishart, Mr. Paterson, and Mr. Wood, proceeded in their order with the other three classes.

On the 18th of July 1670, the eighty-second class, under the tuition of Mr. John Wood, were graduated in Lady Yester's Church. The Theses, printed in a small 8vo form, are dedicated by Mr. Wood in strains abundantly fulsome to Sir Andrew Ramsay of Abbotshall Knight, Lord Provost of Edinburgh, and to his son, Sir Andrew Ramsay junior, of Waughton, Bass, etc., Knight Baronet. The number of the graduates was fifty-three, and four more were privately graduated at different times. In the following October, the new Bejan class was convened by Mr. Wood, and forty-three were matriculated on the 9th of February next. The other classes were conducted in their order by Mr. Pillans (who matriculated forty-nine supervenients on the 12th February 1671), Mr. Wishart, and Mr. Paterson.

Mr. Paterson graduated the eighty-third class, consisting of fifty, on the 17th of July 1671, in Lady Yester's Church. The Theses were again dedicated to Sir Andrew Ramsay, still Lord Provost, and to the Council. In October, Mr. Paterson assembled

the new Bejan class, which, at the matriculation in
the ensuing March, consisted of seventy-two.   The
other three classes were conducted in their order by
Mr. Wood (who matriculated thirty-six supervenients
in 1672 and 1673), Mr. James Pillans, and Mr. John
Wishart.

On the 27th of January 1672, delegates from the   1672.
different Universities of the kingdom met in the
Library of the College of Edinburgh, to deliberate
about the general concerns of the Universities.   There
appeared from St. Andrews, Dr. Andrew Bruce ; from
Glasgow, Mr. John Tran ; from Aberdeen, Mr. Alexander Middleton ; and from Edinburgh, Mr. William
Colvill and Mr. William Keith.   Mr. Colvill, Primar
of the College of Edinburgh, was chosen Preses, and
Mr. William Henderson, Librarian of the said College,
Clerk.   They agreed—

1. To petition the Lords of the Privy Council to
grant an Act prohibiting all, but the Professors in the
Universities, to convene and teach the youth in this
kingdom, the languages and philosophy taught in the
Universities.

2. That the said delegates, upon obtaining their
petition, shall then consider of the mode of carrying
it into execution.

3. That the Committee of the Council for considering the grievances of the Universities, may report to the
Lords of Council respecting an Act for prohibiting the
several Universities to receive any student coming
from another University, without a certificate from all
the Professors, or at least from the Principal, and

from the particular Master of that College, where he had formerly studied ; and that the same rule be observed relative to the graduation of any student coming from another College and demanding a degree.

4. That none shall be admitted *per saltum* to higher classes without studying the proper time at those previous in order, except foreign students, who upon trial shall be found qualified.

At a subsequent meeting of the same delegates, in the same place, on the 2d of February, Dr. Bruce reported, that the Privy-Council had granted their petition, and had passed an Act accordingly. Whereupon it was resolved :—

1. That each delegate should take an extract of the Act of Council, and have it intimated in the most public meeting of their several societies.

2. To advise with their several Universities about the impropriety of giving the degree to all promiscuously, who have studied philosophy for four years, whether the candidates deserve honour or not.

3. To advise with their constituents about a uniformity of teaching in all the Universities.

4. To propose that some method may be taken to prevent the practice of canvassing for scholars to the several Universities.

5. To consider about the times of convening and dissolving the sessions of the Universities, that there may be a uniformity in these.

6. That the Theses at the graduation be inspected and approved by the respective faculties ; and that the Preses of the Faculty shall signify under his hand,

that there is nothing in them contrary to the true religion and good manners, before they be printed.

7. That the meeting of delegates may, for the future, be on the 2d Tuesday of May, if the Parliament be then sitting. If otherwise, the next meeting to be on the first Tuesday of August next, in the same year 1672.

In July, Commissary Wishart brought the eighty-fourth class to the usual degree, after solemn disputation in Lady Yester's Church. The Theses were dedicated in the most flattering terms to the Duke of Lauderdale, the King's Commissioner for holding the Parliament; and the number who took the degree was fifty-two, fourteen privately, and the others publicly. In October, Mr. Wishart again undertook the tuition of a new class, the number of which, at matriculation on the 18th of March following, was eighty-five. Mr. Paterson, in the Semi, matriculated thirty-one supervenients; Mr. Ward had the Bachelor; and Mr. Pillans the Magistrand class.

1672.
The eighty-
fourth Class
graduated.

The eighty-fifth class, under the tuition of Mr. Pillans, were graduated, some privately, and forty-five publicly, on the 21st of July 1673, patronized by the Lords of Session, to whom the Theses were dedicated; where it is insinuated, that the former splendour of the ceremony at the graduation, had been supported by the countenance and presence of the bench, though, for some time past, it had suffered a considerable diminution.

1673.
The eighty-
fifth Class
graduated.

In October, Mr. Pillans assembled the new Bejan class, which amounted, at the matriculation in next February 25th, to the number of fifty-nine. Mr.

Wishart in the Semi had thirty-two supervenients; Mr. Paterson had the Bachelor; and Mr. John Wood the Magistrand class.

1674.

On the 17th of June 1674, the salary of Mr. William Henderson, Bibliothecar, was augmented from 400 marks to 600 yearly, in consideration of his great diligence.[1]

The eighty-sixth Class graduated.

The eighty-sixth class, under the tuition of Mr. Wood, were graduated on the 27th of July in Lady Yester's Church, in number forty-three. The Theses are printed in small 8vo, and dedicated to Sir Alexander Fraser, Bart., chief physician to the King.

On the 12th of August, the salary of Alexander Dickson, Professor of Hebrew, was reduced from 800 marks to 700. And on the 14th, the Council appointed the College Treasurer to pay to Mr. George Sinclair, Professor of Mathematics, ten pounds sterling as the last year's salary, and 100 marks by way of gratuity.[2]

Next October, Mr. Wood commenced the new Bejan class, thirty-eight in number at the ensuing matriculation in April 1675. Mr. Pillans in the Semi had an accession of twenty-six supervenients. Commissary Wishart had the Bachelor, and Mr. William Paterson the Magistrand class.

This year Mr. James Gregory, a celebrated Professor of Mathematics at St. Andrews, was called by the Town-Council to the same profession in this University; and about the end of November he held his inaugural oration, in a public meeting of the University,

[1] Town-Council Records.   [2] Ibid.

in presence of the Town-Council and many other illustrious and learned hearers.

The eighty-seventh class, under Mr. Paterson, was
graduated on the 19th of July 1675, after solemn disputation in Lady Yester's Church, the Theses being
dedicated to the Right Honourable James Currie, Lord
Provost, and the other members of the Town-Council,
patrons of the University. The number of the graduates was forty-eight. 1675.
The eighty-
seventh Class
graduated.

In October, as usual, Mr. Paterson, in his turn, assembled the new Bejan class, consisting of eighty-
four at the matriculation on the 24th of March 1676.
Mr. Wood proceeded with the Semi, having an accession of seventeen supervenients. Mr. Pillans and Mr.
Wishart in their order had the charge of the Bachelor
and Magistrand classes.

Upon the death of Mr. Colvill, Principal, the Rev.
Mr. Andrew Cant, minister of the College Kirk, was,
on the 29th of September 1675, unanimously chosen,
by the Town-Council, his successor in that office, with
a salary of 2000 marks, and 1600 marks as minister of
the East Kirk of St. Giles, with the house and yards
of former Principals. He held his public inaugural
oration upon the 15th day of November.

On the 3d of November, upon a petition of Mr. John
Young, student, to the Town-Council, he was allowed
by the Council to teach Mathematics in the College,
and a chamber was given him for that purpose, with
a promise of having granted him a reward or honorary
according to his behaviour. And on the 24th, Mr.
Laurence Charteris was chosen Professor of Divinity,

in place of Dr. William Keith, deceased, with a salary of 1600 marks and a house in the College.[1]

On the 15th of December, the salary of Mr. Alexander Dickson, Professor of Hebrew, was augmented by the Town-Council to 1000 marks from 700, to which it had formerly been diminished.[2]

1676.   . On the 26th of January 1676, John Young, teacher of Mathematics, who had taught for the deceased James Gregory, was allowed by the Town-Council 300 marks yearly.

The eighty-eighth Class graduated.   The eighty-eighth class, under Commissary Wishart, were brought to the usual degree, forty-four of them publicly, and nineteen privately ; but it does not appear that there were any printed Theses on this occasion.

In October, Mr. Wishart, still retaining his Professorship along with his office of Commissary, began the new Bejan class, in number forty-four at the ensuing matriculation on the 22d of March.   Mr. William Paterson proceeded with an accession of forty-three supervenients in the Semi ; Mr. Wood had the charge of the Bachelor ; and Mr. Pillans that of the Magistrand class.

On the 10th of November, John Nicol or Nicolson, was deposed by the Town-Council from his office of Janitor, for misbehaviour in resisting the Town-officers, in rescuing some persons taken at a conventicle, and John Brown, merchant, was elected during his good behaviour.[3]

1677.   On the 28th of May 1677, two Acts of the Secret

---

[1] Town-Council Records.   [2] Ibid.   [3] Ibid.

Council were read in the Town-Council ; the one requiring the Professors to take the oath of allegiance
and supremacy, and to own the Episcopal government ; and the other ordaining the students to take
these oaths at their laureation.

On the 1st of August, John Young's salary as Professor of Mathematics was augmented by the Council
from 300 marks to 400.

Mr. Pillans held the graduation of his class, being 1677.
The eighty-
ninth Class
graduated.
the eighty-ninth, on the 3d of August, consisting of
sixty-five candidates ;[1] and the Theses were dedicated
to the Duke of Lauderdale, whose power in Scotland
at this time was enormous.

In October, Mr. Pillans entered on the charge of the
new Bejan class, which, at the matriculation in the
ensuing March, consisted only of thirty-five. Mr.
Wishart in the Semi had an accession of forty-two
supervenients ; Mr. Paterson proceeded with the
Bachelor class ; and Mr. Wood had the charge of the
Magistrand.

The ninetieth class, under the tuition of Mr. Wood, 1678.
The ninetieth
Class gradu-
ated.
were all graduated privately, 1678, at different times,
being only fourteen in number.[2]

These four Professors of Philosophy, Mr. Pillans,
Mr. Wishart, Mr. Paterson, and Mr. Wood, had now

[1] [The Theses, as we learn from the printed copy, were to be disputed on the 3d of August, and the number of the names of the candidates for the degree of Master of Arts, appended to the Theses, is sixty-five. But there was no public laureation this year. The great majority of the students, it would appear, refused to take the oaths, and come under the engagement required of them by the act of the Privy Council just referred to, and therefore did not get their degree. The number who graduated was only twenty-three, and all these were graduated *privately*, except three, who got their degree publicly in Mr. William Paterson's class-room, August 5, 1679. — Record of Laureations.]

[2] [See preceding note.]

been colleagues without interruption since the year 1667, during ten years.

In October 1678, Mr. Wood entered again upon the charge of the new Bejan class, but died on the 22d of March following. Upon which Mr. Gilbert M'Murdo, Professor of Humanity, was chosen in his place, upon the recommendation of his colleagues, on the 2d of April, and proceeded with this new class in the study of the Greek, which they had lately begun. They were matriculated May 1, 1679, in number fifty-seven. In Mr. M'Murdo's place, as Professor of Humanity, Mr. Alexander Cunningham was chosen by comparative trial upon the 14th of the same month.

1679.

Mr. James Pillans had now the charge of the Semi class, with fifteen supervenients; Mr. John Wishart that of the Bachelor; and Mr. William Paterson that of the Magistrand class.

On the 16th of April 1679, Alexander Amedeus, a Florentine, was chosen Professor of Hebrew for a year, with a salary of 600 marks Scots, in place of Mr. Alexander Dickson, who had not given satisfaction to his Majesty's Privy Council as to the engagement.[1]

The ninety-first class, under the tuition of Mr. William Paterson, were graduated on the 5th of August in the public hall of the University. The Theses were dedicated to the Earl of Moray; and the number

The ninety-first Class graduated.

---

[1] Town-Council Records. See Wodrow's History, vol. ii. p. 3 [new edit. vol. iii. p. 3], about the Professors taking oaths. [Dickson refused to subscribe the oaths of allegiance and supremacy, and an engagement that he would submit to and own the government of the church by Archbishops, as then established. He was the only one of the Professors of the College of Edinburgh who refused to do so. He was deprived of his chair by the orders of the Privy-Council.]

of graduates was thirty-seven.[1] In a note at the beginning of the printed Theses, it is said, that about sixty more students, who had attended this class during the whole course of four years, were not inserted in the list, as they were not to be present at the graduation.

Mr. William Paterson resigned his office in the College upon being made Clerk to the Privy-Council, and in his place was chosen, September 19, 1679, Mr. Andrew Massie, formerly a Professor in King's College, Aberdeen, who accordingly entered to the charge of the new Bejan class, of which the number, at the matriculation in April following, was fifty-three. Mr. Gilbert M'Murdo had the Semi class, with an accession of thirty supervenients, matriculated also in April. Mr. Pillans had the Bachelor, and Commissary Wishart the Magistrand.

The ninety-second class, under the charge of Mr. Wishart, were brought to the usual period of graduation by him, in number thirty-nine, but the greater part of them were graduated privately at different times; and the Commissary at last finally resigned his Professorship on the 14th of July 1680.[2] When he had been requested to retain his office in the College, a good many years before, the Principal indulged him with license of absence for certain hours, when his attendance was necessary in the Commissary Court.

1680.
The ninety-second Class graduated.

---

[1] [The number of candidates for the degree of Master of Arts prefixed to the printed Theses is fifty-eight. The class, then, including the sixty mentioned in the next sentence, amounted to 118. Of this number, for the reason assigned in note, p. 207, only thirty-seven obtained the degree of Master of Arts.]

[2] Town-Council Records.

O

In place of Mr. Wishart was chosen by the patrons, on the same 14th of July, Mr. Alexander Cockburn, formerly a Professor in St. Leonard's College, St. Andrews, who undertook the charge of the new Bejan class ; which, being matriculated in May 1681, was in number fifty-one.   Mr. Andrew Massie had the charge of the Semi class, with the accession of fifty-six super-venients, matriculated May 6th.   Mr. M'Murdo had the charge of the Bachelors, and Mr. Pillans that of the Magistrand class.

In December 1680, the students issued the follow-ing advertisement for burning the Pope in effigy :—

"AN ADVERTISEMENT.

" These are to give notice to all Noblemen, Gentlemen, Citizens, and others, That We, the STUDENTS in the ROYAL UNIVERSITY of EDINBURGH (to show our Detestation and Abhorrence of the *Romish Religion*, and Our Zeal and Fervency for the PROTESTANT), Do Resolve to Burn the Effigies of ANTICHRIST, the POPE of ROME, at the Mercat-Cross of *Edinburgh*, the 25 of *December* Instant, pre-cisely at Twelve a-Clock in the Forenoon, (being the Festival of our SAVIOUR'S Nativity) : And since we hate Tumults, as we do Super-stition, we do hereby (under the Pain of Death) Discharge all Plunderers, Robbers, Thieves, Whores, and Bawds, to come within 40 Paces of Our Company, and such as shall be found disobedient to these Our Commands, *Sibi Caveant.*

> " By Our Special Command, ROBERT BROWN, Secretary of State to all Our Theatrical and Extra-literal Divertisements." [1]

On the 23d of February, the Regents being con-

---

[1] Printed copy inserted in a volume of Theses, large folio, belonging to the University of Edinburgh. See about the students burning the Pope in effigy, Wodrow's History, vol. ii. p. 217. See also the Act of Privy-Council passed in consequence of this.—*Ibid.* Appen-dix, No. 72.

vened before the Town-Council, intimation was made to them, that they were to take security from each of the students in their several classes, and from their parents (as is prescribed by the Act of his Majesty's Privy-Council) ; and that the bonds and engagements of the youths were to be inserted in a book, and subscribed by them and their cautioners, before two witnesses, to be kept in the Library by the Librarian, to be seen by his Majesty's Privy-Council, etc.

On the 20th of April, Mr. James Pillans, Regent of Philosophy, being now very old, and having been Professor thirty-seven years, resigned his office in favour of his son-in-law, Mr. Robert Lidderdale, governor to the Laird of Dalmeny, who was chosen in his place.[1]

On the 30th of September, Mr. Alexander Douglas, student of Theology, was elected Professor of Hebrew, in consequence of the removal of Alexander Amedeus, late Professor thereof, his salary to be 600 marks.[2]

The ninety-third class, under the charge of Mr. Pillans, were, after solemn disputation, brought to the usual degree, in number thirty-one.[3] The Theses on this occasion were dedicated to James Duke of Albany and York, etc., afterwards James the Seventh of Scotland and Second of Great Britain.

In October ensuing, Mr. Robert Lidderdale, undertook the charge of the new Bejan class, and on the 18th of April 1682, matriculated fifty students. Mr. Alexander Cockburn proceeded with the Semi, having

1681.
The ninety-third Class graduated.

---

[1] Town-Council Records.
[2] Ibid.
[3] [The names of the candidates for the degree appended to the printed

Theses is thirty-one. The number who were graduated was twenty-three ; and these obtained their degree at different times. Book of Laureations.]

got an accession of thirty-two supervenients. Mr. Massie had the charge of the Bachelor, and Mr. M'Murdo that of the Magistrand.

The ninety-fourth class, under the tuition of Mr. Gilbert M'Murdo, were brought to the usual time for graduation; but, though there were printed Theses, with fifty-two names annexed, prepared for this ceremony, all the candidates seem to have received the degree privately.[1]

In October, Mr. M'Murdo in course entered to the charge of the Bejan class, which, at the matriculation, amounted to fifty-seven in number. Mr. Robert Lidderdale now had the charge of the Semi, with thirty-two supervenients; Mr. Alexander Cockburn that of the Bachelor; and Mr. Andrew Massie that of the Magistrand.

The ninety-fifth class, under the tuition of Mr. Andrew Massie, were brought to the usual time of graduation; and a printed copy of Theses, dedicated to the Earl of Aberdeen, Chancellor of the kingdom, was prepared on this occasion, with the names of eighty-eight candidates. But the graduation seems to have been performed in private, at different times. On and before the 25th of April, ten appear to have taken the degree, after signing the usual *Sponsio;* after which, there is inserted in the graduation-book at full length, the oath of allegiance to King Charles the Second, which is subscribed by about twenty-two, all graduating privately, at different times, from July

---

[1] [Of the fifty-two candidates whose names appear in the printed Theses, only twenty-two obtained their degree. See note, p. 207.]

20, 1683, to March 28, 1689 ;[1] and among them Mr. David Gregory, Professor of Mathematics, and Mr. Robert Henderson, afterwards Librarian.

This year Mr. David Gregory entered upon the profession of Mathematics, with an inaugural oration "De Analyseos Geometricæ progressu et incremento," as successor to his late uncle Mr. James Gregory, who had died, very much regretted, in the year 1675. He was chosen Professor of Mathematics, on the 17th of October. His salary was 1000 pounds, Young seems never to have been Professor, but only teacher authorized by the Town-Council.

On the 26th of October the Rev. Primar and remanent Professors being met in the Bibliothec, for divers weighty reasons, unanimously consented and agreed to alter the diet appointed to Mr. James Gregory (See October 17, 1668), and ordained that Mr. David Gregory, Professor of Mathematics, should read publicly twice a week in the common schools of the College, viz., betwixt the hours of ten and eleven in the forenoon on Monday and Friday, and that from the 1st of December to the last of May each year ; and ordained that all the students in the said College, together with the Masters, at least the Hebdomadar for the time, should be present at the said lessons.[2]

In the beginning of December, Dr. John Strachan was elected Professor of Divinity, in place of the late Mr. Laurence Charteris.

[1] [Thus only thirty-two of the eighty-eight candidates for the degree of Master of Arts obtained that honour.]

[2] Register of the University of Edinburgh, MS. in College Library, p. 59.

In October, Mr. Andrew Massie began a new course with the Bejan class, in number forty-nine. And Mr. Gilbert M'Murdo, who had begun the session with the charge of the Semi class, having died in the month of December, Mr. Herbert Kennedy, January 2, 1684, was elected in his place ; but whether by comparative trial or not does not appear. Of this class the supervenients were twenty-five. Mr. Lidderdale proceeded with the Bachelor, and Mr. Alexander Cockburn with the Magistrand.

1684.

On the 21st of March 1684, the salary of Mr. Alexander Douglas, Professor of Hebrew, was augmented from 600 marks to 1000.

The ninety-
sixth Class
graduated.

The ninety-sixth class, under Mr. Alexander Cockburn, were brought to the usual period for graduation. In the printed Theses, dedicated to the Marquis of Queensberry, Lord Treasurer, there are inserted the names of fifty-one candidates ; but by the graduation book only thirty-two seem to have graduated, and subscribed the oath of allegiance, several of them privately.[1]

In October, Mr. Cockburn entered upon the charge of the new class, which, when matriculated in March, amounted to the number of fifty-six ; Mr. Andrew Massie, in the Semi, had thirty-five supervenients ; Mr. Herbert Kennedy had the charge of the Bachelor ; and Mr. Robert Lidderdale that of the Magistrand.

On the 21st of November, Mr. Robert Henderson was admitted Librarian, probably conjunctly with Mr. William Henderson.

[1] [See note, p. 207.]

On the 6th of February 1685, died King Charles the Second, and was succeeded by his brother, now James the Second, of Great Britain, a prince who, by his bigotry and arbitrary principles, soon after forfeited the throne. The Colleges, not only in England, but also in Scotland, felt their share of his tyrannical influence.

Upon a letter from the Earl of Perth, who was Chancellor, the Town-Council installed Sir Robert Sibbald, Doctor of Physic, in the College, on the 27th of March this year ; and, on the 16th of September following, James Halket and Archibald Pitcairn, Doctors of Physic, were called also by the Council to be Professors of Medicine, that they might unite their endeavours with Sir Robert Sibbald in teaching that science in this University. They had no salary, nor does it appear that they were ever anything but nominal professors. Their efforts, if they ever made any, for founding a medical school, proved unsuccessful. That honour was reserved to others at a later period.

Sir Robert, " who had," says Bishop Burnet,[1] "lived in a course of philosophical virtue, but in great doubts as to revealed religion, was prevailed on by the Earl of Perth to turn Papist, in hopes to find that certainty among them which he could not arrive at upon his own principles." This conversion did not happen till the year 1686. Sibbald, ashamed of his turning Catholic, went some time out of the way, and then returned and recanted.[2]

[1] History of his own Time, folio edit. vol. i. p. 680.
[2] See Sibbald's recantation in Burnet's

History of his own Time, vol. i. p. 680, fol. ; and Fountainhall's Decisions, vol. i. p. 415.

The ninety-seventh class, under the tuition of Mr. Robert Lidderdale, was brought to the usual time of graduation in 1685. In the printed Theses prepared on this occasion, and dedicated to the Duke of Queensberry, the King's Commissioner, there is a list of fifty students ; but from the Graduation-book, in which the oath of allegiance to James the Second is inserted at full length, it does not appear that more than twenty-two took the degree and subscribed the oaths, and that, too, at different times and privately.

The College, soon after its meeting in October, sustained a great loss by the death of Mr. Andrew Cant, the Principal, which happened on the 4th of December. In his place was elected, on the 9th of the same month, Dr. Alexander Monro, Professor of Divinity in the University of St. Andrews, a respectable man, but attached to Episcopacy. He was to have for salary 2000 marks as Principal, and 1600 marks as Minister of the High Kirk.[1]

Mr. Lidderdale, who had begun the Bejan class this year at the usual time, matriculated only twenty-nine students on the 7th of April following ; Mr. Cockburn went on in the Semi with the accession of thirty-two supervenients ; Mr. Massie with the Bachelor ; and Mr. Herbert Kennedy had the charge of the Magistrand class.

On the 31st of March 1686, the Bishop of Edinburgh, Mr. John Paterson, procured himself to be created Chancellor of the College of Edinburgh, by a gift from the King ; which he endeavoured, but

[1] Town-Council Records.

without success, to get ratified in Parliament, June 15, 1686.[1]

The ninety-eighth class, under the care of Mr. Herbert Kennedy, finished their fourth course in 1686 ; and twenty-four out of the fifty, the number which appears in the printed Theses, were graduated privately at different times.[2]

1686.
The ninety-eighth Class graduated.

Mr. Kennedy, in October, entered to the charge of the new Bejan class, which, at the matriculation, the 9th of the following March, consisted of seventy-four.

Mr. Robert Lidderdale having died in October, Mr. Thomas Burnet, formerly a Professor in Marischal College, Aberdeen, was chosen by the Council, on the 15th of that month, to succeed him, and undertook the charge of the Semi class. This Professor was recommended to the patrons by the Earl of Perth, Chancellor, who was a Roman Catholic. Mr. Burnet had distinguished himself the preceding summer by publishing printed Theses, and dedicating them to the Duke of Gordon, in which he asserted the King's absolute power ;[3] and the Magistrates of Edinburgh, Sir Thomas Kennedy being Provost, honoured him with their presence at his introduction into their College.[4] He was suspected of being friendly to Popery ; for which reason most of the parents of the students that were to enter to the second class, which was to be under his charge, were disposed to send them back to the first or Bejan class. But Dr. Monro,

---

[1] See Fountainhall's Decisions, vol. i. pp. 412, 418.

[2] [See Catalogue of the Edinburgh Graduates, p. 128.]

[3] May 26, 1686. See about Burnet's Theses, *Ibid*. vol. i. p. 415.

[4] Fountainhall's Decisions, vol. i. p. 425.

the Principal, supposing the suspicion against Mr.
Burnet to be a calumny, got the Senatus Academicus
to pass an act that all the students formerly under
Mr. Lidderdale should enter under Mr. Burnet, otherwise the College would have been in hazard of wanting an entire class ; and by the exertions chiefly of
the Principal, who in particular prevailed with Bailie
Graham to send his son to the second class, even after
he had entered to the first, Mr. Burnet had twenty
supervenients in his class.[1] Mr. Alexander Cockburn
proceeded with the third class, and Mr. Andrew Massie
with the Magistrand.

1687.   The King had lately granted a commission to fifty
persons, of whom Sir George Lockhart [2] was to be the
president, to visit all the schools and colleges in the
kingdom ; and the members held their first meeting on
the 18th of January 1687. It was then thought that
the intention was to examine into the foundations of
all the colleges, and to place only such persons in them
as were agreeable to the King's system of religion
and government.[3] This is the very year in which the
arbitrary and well-known attempt was made on
Magdalen College, Oxford.[4]

A sub-committee of the new Commission for Visitation met on the 26th of February, and drew up three
overtures to be presented to the Court to be passed
into Acts. 1st, That in their Ethic Dictates the
Regents should instruct the youth in the unlawfulness

---

[1] See Presbyterian Inquisition, pp. 27, 30, etc.

[2] [President of the Court of Session.]

[3] Fountainhall's Decisions, vol. i. p. 144.

[4] Hume's History of England, James II. chap. lxx.

of defensive arms and resistance to the King. 2*d*, That the Regents in all time coming are to be unmarried persons, seeing by the foundations of our colleges in times of Popery they were designed for Churchmen ; and it was a rule and Statute then that they should be unmarried. 3*d*, That no Regent stay above eight years in the University. The last two were to begin at Michaelmas 1688 ; and it was doubted if they were to extend to Bursars and Professors.

There was a bill given in by the College of Edinburgh against these overtures, which put a stop to them.[1] This society then acted with great spirit, and in a manner which did them great honour.

About this time the University of St. Andrews gave in a paper to the Commission of Visitation, containing a " Method of Teaching," drawn up with considerable ability and precision, which, as it will show the notions on that subject then entertained, is here inserted from a copy preserved in the College Library.

" ANENT THE SUBJECT AND METHOD OF TEACHING.

" 1. That, betwixt the day on which the College Table is taken up and that appointed for beginning the next task of that year, these of the first class be exercised in the review of the Latin, by the explaining the authors, and making versions. The rest of the year [to] be chiefly employed in the study of the Greek language, with the practical Arithmetic ; which may be taught by a short lesson in the day, for the two or three last months of that year, and that rather by frequent practices and examples than often repeated rules ; and towards the end of this year, they may also be begun to something of the elements of Geometry, according as their master finds their capacity will allow.

" 2. That, the second year, they be taught a clear and short course

[1] Fountainhall's Decisions, vol. i. p. 551.

of Logics, for explaining the nature and most observable properties of our cogitations ; the ordinary defects and errors of them ; with their remedies ; and particularly the art of reasoning. That, by the time they come to this last part of the Logic course, they be begun, and thence go forward in the elements of Geometry, which, in effect, is true and useful Logic ; and from them is secretly understood the principals and the errors of reasoning. After the Logics, if they be sufficiently short, there will be time for that part of the Métaphysics which have a near affinity with them, viz., the Scholastic explanations of, and disputes about the notion and properties of being, and these common terms of Essence, Existence, Possibility and Impossibility, Relation, Causality, etc., which frequently occur in the Scholastic Philosophy and Divinity ; and therefore something of them may be known.

"3. These of the third year be taught the other part of the Metaphysics concerning the nature and properties of spirits, their distinction from matter, the demonstration of the existence of a Deity, etc. ; for which there is sufficient ground and assistance from what is written in the Meditations of Des Cartes, and the disputes and observations of himself and others thereupon : after that, a short course of Ethics, purged from the Scholastic and Theologic disputes, which are ordinary to be found in these tractates, and reduced from the common principles of natural reason, the nature of human society, the common passions, humours and inclination of mankind, and what experience and observation afford for rectifying the errors of these ; wherein must not be omitted to explain the nature of civil government, the absolute and illimited power of the Supreme Magistrate, and the universal obligation of subjects to obey, and never to resist, his authority. And that, with these short tractates of Metaphysics and Ethics, be completed the elements of Geometry, together with some practices of the Geometry ; which may either be delivered to the students once a week, according to the propositions on which they depend. And this, besides that it would gain time, would also render the speculations more pleasant, and the practices more easy and obvious to the discretion of the master considering the fitness of opportunity, and his scholars' capacity and encouragement : for these Geometrical practices they must necessarily understand the plain Trigonometry, which can be easily taught them in a few days.

" Likewise, if they have timeously begun, and successfully advanced in, the Geometry the second year, so that there be little left to be completed in the third, that the rest they be taught, as much as can be, of the Physics ; for which the Geometry will very much qualify and fit them.

" 4. That, the fourth year, they be taught the rest of the Physics, the history of nature and experiments, together with the Cosmography, Optics, Spherical Trigonometry, and as much of the Mechanics as the time prescribed for their stay that year will allow : And, as to the Mathematics, it is not doubted, that those who in the first two years have got some knowledge of the principles, and see the usefulness, necessity, and pleasure of that science, will apply also themselves to the public professor of it, for making greater progress than is possible in their private schools.

" 5. Because the Greek being a most useful and necessary language, and for that reason made the great part of the first year's task, while as more time is truly required for any perfection in it ; nevertheless, it being generally neglected, throughout the rest of the time of students being at the Colleges, and consequently, what once they learned becomes either entirely forgot or of little purpose ; therefore, throughout the whole three last years, there be a weekly task in the said language, viz., betwixt Friday's night and Monday's morning the master prescribe a portion of some Greek author ; and, if that be a poet, they shall translate and explain it ; if a historian, they shall translate, explain, and give a rational account of that part of the history without book.

" 6. That, for the remembrance and improvement of the Latin language, the several masters appoint frequently, throughout the whole years, solemn exercises and declamations in their private schools ; and this may be done, sometimes, by prescribing to them some of the shortest and most obvious of Cicero's orations, some of these inserted in the histories of Titus Livius, Salust, and other Roman authors, making the students to understand the purpose and humour of such discourse, and causing them to pronounce and declaim them accordingly ; sometimes by prescribing them subjects or orations of their own composition ; and sometimes also appointing them to make orations and discourses in English upon subjects appointed to them, seeing it is not probable that ever they will understand the properties and elegancies of any other language, who are not acquainted with the rhetoric and composure of their own.   The fittest time for these exercises seems to be on the Tuesdays or Thursdays between five and six o'clock at night.

" 7. That, since these private declamations do considerably qualify for more public appearances, therefore there be every Saturday, immediately after divine service in the common schools, some public declamations at which all students and masters within the College shall be present.   And these orations to [be] either by the superior class in the College for the time, and when the exercise has gone through them, that successively it be performed by the next superior class in order ; or that all the three superior classes shall be concerned, one out of every one of them, each Saturday.   Likewise, every one who thus publicly declaims shall have a copy of his oration in a fair and legible hand ; which, after he hath recited, he shall deliver to the Provost or Principal of the College, and, in his necessary absence, to the senior Regent present ; that, after a review of his discourse, he may, some day in the following week, receive censure or commendation, according as the Principal and Regents shall find he deserves.

" 8. That in these actions there shall be no reflection, directly nor indirectly, upon any master, professor, class, or student in the College or University, and that they who transgress in this be exemplarily punished.

" 9. That the examinations in the end of the year (as presently in use) be continued, and exactly performed ; and, for that end, every master, whose scholars are beginning to be examined, shall give in to the Examinators a clear and an exact account of the several things he hath taught and accomplished that year, according to the orders and method prescribed ; and that these shall be the rule and measure for the method and order of examination.

" 10. Likewise, to secure the diligence of students in the vacance, they shall undergo examination, at their return in the beginning of the year, by the Masters in the respective Colleges ; and lest these examinations should turn into a bare custom and form, those who are found insufficient by trial at these occasions, or who shall absent themselves from them, without giving sufficient satisfaction or excuse, shall either be excluded from the degree and honour usual to be conferred on the superior class, or from further progress in the course of his studies in the College, or undergo such censure as the Faculty

he studies in shall think fit, in consideration of his own quality, and
that his defect and fault.

> " Given in by the Masters of the University of St. Andrews
> " to the Lords of the Visitation.   Anno 1687." [1]

The ninety-ninth class, under the charge of Mr.
Andrew Massie, having finished their fourth course,
out of seventy-five candidates who appear in the list in
the printed Theses, dedicated to Sir Thomas Kennedy,
Lord Provost, and the rest of the Council, fifteen were
graduated privately at different times, and twenty-two
publicly on the 9th of July 1687.[2]   The *Sponsio* subscribed on this occasion is more general and short ;
and Dr. Monro, the Principal, was himself suspected
of favouring the King's religion, from the circumstance
that the candidates were required to promise perseverance in the *Christian Religion*, with the omission
of the word *reformed*.   In this way the oath appears
in the Graduation-book in the years 1687 and 1688.

*1687.
The ninety-
ninth Class
graduated.*

Mr. Andrew Massie, in October 1687, entered upon
the charge of the new Bejan class, amounting, at the
matriculation the succeeding March, to sixty-nine.
Mr. Kennedy had the Semi, with twenty-nine Supervenients ; Mr. Thomas Burnet the Bachelor ; and Mr.
Alexander Cockburn the Magistrand.

The hundredth class, under the tuition of Mr. Alexander Cockburn, having finished their course of four
years, there were seventy-one candidates for the degree ;

*1688.
The hun-
dredth Class
graduated.*

---

[1] MS. Papers illustrative of the history and constitution of the University of Edinburgh in College Library,
No. II. p. 161.

[2] [Other two were graduated publicly
on Monday the 11th of July, when those
who had been graduated on Saturday
the 9th, subscribed their names.
Book of Laureations.]

of whom seven received it privately at different times, and thirty-three publicly on the 9th of July 1688. The Theses were dedicated to the Right Honourable Magnus Prince, Lord Provost, and the rest of the Council.

About this time the King granted a signature of confirmation to the University of Edinburgh ; in which, among other things, Sir Magnus Prince, Lord Provost of Edinburgh, with his successors in office, were appointed perpetual Chancellors, a dignity which was understood to be already vested in the Lord Provost ; but the Revolution intervened before this deed was ratified in Parliament. A copy of it is preserved in the College Library.

The College having met again in October, the charge of the new Bejan class fell to Mr. Alexander Cockburn ; but he having died on the 12th of February 1689, Mr. Alexander Cunningham, Professor of Humanity, was chosen, on the 15th of that month, to succeed him. And in place of Mr. Cunningham, Mr. John Drummond, an Episcopal, was chosen Professor of Humanity on the 20th of the same month ; but it does not appear that any comparative trial was held on this occasion.

The end of the year 1688 is famous in the history of Great Britain for the Revolution, in consequence of the abdication of the throne by James the Second, which his bigotry and arbitrary principles rendered him unworthy any longer to fill. This event may be considered as having taken place on the 23d of December ; and soon after, the Prince of Orange with Mary his Consort, were proclaimed King and Queen of England. A Convention of Estates, begun and held in Edinburgh, on the 14th of March, resolved to offer the Crown of Scotland to the same Prince and Princess upon certain conditions, which were soon accepted ; and in the meantime William and Mary were also proclaimed King and Queen of Scotland. This Convention was afterwards converted into a Parliament ; which, among other Acts, passed one appointing a visitation of Schools, Colleges, and Universities, being chap. xvii., 1st Parliament of William and Mary, held at Edinburgh, 25th of April 1690. This produced some important changes in the College of Edinburgh, which shall be mentioned by and by.

In the meantime, Mr. Massie proceeded with the Semi class, with an accession of twelve supervenients ; Mr. Kennedy had the charge of the Bachelors ; and Thomas Burnet that of the Magistrands.

CHAPTER V

FROM THE REVOLUTION TO THE NEW REGULATIONS RESPECTING
THE REGENTS OF PHILOSOPHY IN 1708.

AT the Revolution the Senatus Academicus consisted of the following members :—

> Dr. Alexander Monro, Principal.
> Dr. John Strachan, Professor of Divinity.
> Mr. Alexander Cunningham, ⎫
> Mr. Andrew Massie,   ⎬ Regents or Professors of
> Mr. Herbert Kennedy,   ⎪   Philosophy.
> Mr. Thomas Burnet,   ⎭
> Mr. David Gregory, Professor of Mathematics.
> Mr. John Drummond, Professor of Humanity.
> Mr. Alexander Douglas, Professor of Hebrew.
> Mr. Robert Henderson (probably joint with William), Librarian
>   and Secretary.

1689.
The one-
hundred and
first Class
graduated.

The one-hundred-and-first class, under the tuition
of Mr. Thomas Burnet, being brought towards the
termination of the usual course of four years, twenty-
four of them are all who appear to have taken the
degree, and that privately at different times.

On the meeting of the College again in October,
Mr. Thomas Burnet entered upon the charge of the
new Bejan class, which, at the matriculation of it on
the 31st of the following March, amounted to the
number of forty-seven. Mr. Alexander Cunningham,
of course, had the charge of the Semi class, with forty-
seven supervenients ; Mr. Andrew Massie that of the

Bachelor; and Mr. Herbert Kennedy that of the Magistrand.

On January 3, 1690, Mr. Burnet was ordered by the Faculty to forbear teaching the second Satire of Horace.[1]   1690.

Mr. Herbert Kennedy having brought his class, consisting of sixty, towards the conclusion of their fourth year, five of them were graduated privately, and on the 30th of June twenty-nine publicly, all of whom subscribed the short *Sponsio*, containing allegiance to James the Seventh. One of those who graduated privately received the degree alone on the 21st of July, in presence of the Principal, Mr. Herbert Kennedy, and Mr. John Drummond. Then a *Sponsio* appears in the Graduation-book, including allegiance to William and Mary.[2]   The one-hundred and second Class graduated.

The Parliament had met on the 25th of the preceding April, the Earl of Melvill being Commissioner. In the Act passed for the visitation of Universities, Colleges, and Schools, it is statuted and ordained that no Professor, or other person bearing office in any University or College, shall either be admitted or allowed to continue in the exercise of their functions but such as acknowledge and subscribe the Westminster Confession of Faith, and also swear and subscribe the oath of allegiance to their Majesties, and shall be pious, loyal, and of a peaceable conversation, of good and sufficient literature and abilities, and submitting to the government of the Church established

[1] Register of the University of Edinburgh, p. 23.

[2] [See Catalogue of Edinburgh Graduates, p. 140.]

by law. Visitors are then named and appointed, as may be seen in the Act; and their first meeting is authorized to be at Edinburgh on the 23d day of July 1690, with power to appoint committees and to adjourn. Accordingly a sufficient quorum of them met on that day, and divided themselves into several Committees, one for each University. They met again on the 25th, and drew up certain instructions to be observed by their Committees ; and they appointed those Committees to meet at the respective Universities on the 20th of August.

The following was the Committee for the University of Edinburgh :—Earl of Lothian, Lord Raith, Lord Ruthven, Master of Stair, Lord Mersington, Lord Crosrig, Sir Patrick Hume, Lord Hallcraig, Laird of Pitliver, Sir John Hall, Sir William Hamilton, Mr. Edward Jameson, Mr. Hugh Kennedy, Mr. John Law, Mr. James Kirkton, and Dr. Gilbert Rule, who met accordingly in the upper hall of the College of Edinburgh on the 20th of August, and chose Sir John Hall their Preses. They afterwards adjourned to the 27th of the same month. Having then met, they first proceeded to call before them Dr. Alexander Monro, the Principal of the College. Ten articles of accusation were brought against him, the chief of which were, " that he set up the English Liturgy within the gates of the College; that he was disaffected to the Government both in Church and State ; that at the public laureation or graduation, he sat and publicly heard the Confession of Faith, after it had been approved of in Parliament, ridiculed by Dr. Pitcairne, yea, the existence of God impugned, without any answer or vindication ; that the doctor is addicted to swearing, and neglects the worship of God in his family." The rest were of a frivolous nature. The Principal made a very good defence, considering the shortness of the time allowed him for preparing answers. The Committee, however, were of opinion " that Dr. Alexander Monro, Principal of the College of Edinburgh, should be deprived of his office as Primar there ; and that the said office be declared vacant." When this opinion was reported to the Commissioners on the 25th of September, they found in the following terms :—" The Lords and others of the Commission appointed by Act of Parliament for visitation of Universities, Colleges, and Schools, having this day heard and considered the above-written re-port of the Committee of the College of Edinburgh, anent Dr. Monro, Primar of the College of Edinburgh ; Depositions and other Instructions produced ; and also Doctor Monro being asked, If he was presently willing to swear the Oath of Allegiance to their Majesties King William and Queen Mary, and to sign the same, with the Assurance and the Confession of Faith (which formerly he had offered to sign before the said Com-mittee), and if he would declare his willingness to submit himself to the present Church government as now established ; the said Dr. Monro did judicially in presence of the said Commission, refuse to sign the said Confession of Faith, and to take the said other engagements, required to be done by the said Act of Parliament ; and also did judicially acknowledge his

written answers produced before the Committee ; and did confess he caused remove the pictures of the Reformers out of the Library : Therefore the said Commission approves of the foresaid Committee's Report, and finds the same sufficiently verified and proved ; And hereby deprives the said Doctor Alexander Monro of his place, as Primar of the said College of Edinburgh, and declares the said place vacant. *Sic Subscribitur,*
"CRAWFORD, *P.*"[1]

This sentence was complained of by the Episcopal party as extremely severe ; and the whole particulars of the trial were afterwards published, and stigmatized in terms of reproach, in a pamphlet entitled, " Presbyterian Inquisition, as it was lately practised against the Professors of the College of Edinburgh, August and September 1690, etc. [by Dr. Monro]. Lond. 1691." In 4to, pp. 106.

Dr. John Strachan, Professor of Divinity, was also proceeded against in like manner. The articles of accusation were seven in number, of which the following were the chief :—" That in the New Kirk of Edinburgh, in a public sermon before the Diocesan Synod, he preached reconciliation with the Church of Rome, and openly avowed his holding the doctrine of Consubstantiation : That he was reputed to be an Arminian and Pelagian, and maintained such principles and tenets in the Tron Church : That he set up the English Liturgy : That he was negligent of his duty in instructing the students : That he was dissatisfied

---

[1] Presbyterian Inquisition, p. 46.

with the Government both in Church and State."
Some other things of less moment were also laid
to his charge.   To all these Dr. Strachan gave in
answers expressed with great ability and candour.
The Committee, however, declared it as their opinion,
"that Dr. John Strachan, Professor of Divinity in the
College of Edinburgh, should be deprived of his office
in the said College ; and that the same be declared
vacant." On the 25th of September, the Commission
passed the following sentence against him : "The
Lords, and others of the Commission appointed for
visitation of Colleges and Schools, having heard read,
and considered the above written Report of the Committee for visiting the College of Edinburgh, anent
Dr. John Strachan, Professor of Divinity within the
said College : And the Doctor being called in, and
having heard the written Report read over in his presence, and being asked, If he did acknowledge that
the matters of fact contained in the said Report were
true, he did judicially acknowledge the verity of the
matters of fact therein contained : And also he refused
to swear the Oath of Allegiance, and to sign the same
with the Assurance : And also refused to sign the Confession of Faith, or to declare his submission to the
present Church Government, as now established :
Therefore the said Commission approves of the Report
above written ; and does hereby deprive the said Dr.
John Strachan, Professor of Divinity in the said College, of his said place, as Professor foresaid, and declares the said place to be vacant.

" CRAWFORD, P."[1]

---

[1] Presbyterian Inquisition, p. 85.

This sentence also is stated as extremely severe in the above-mentioned pamphlet, in which are contained many other particulars respecting this case.

Indeed, it is plain that the only true reasons for ejecting both Dr. Monro and Dr. Strachan were, that they were Episcopals and nonjurors. And it would have been more for the credit of the Visitors, if they had rested their procedure entirely on this ground, and had not brought into the account articles of accusation against them without producing either accusers or proof. They removed also at the same time from their respective offices, Mr. Alexander Douglas, Professor of Oriental Languages, Mr. Thomas Burnet, Professor of Philosophy, and Mr. John Drummond, Professor of Humanity; but whether for any other reasons than their refusing to take the oath of allegiance to William and Mary does not appear.

On the 26th of September the same year, the Town-Council elected Dr. Gilbert Rule,[1] one of the ministers of Edinburgh, to succeed Dr. Monro, as Principal of the College; and on the same day Mr. George Campbell, minister of Dumfries, was called by the electors to be Professor of Divinity in place of Dr. John Strachan.[2]

At another meeting held on the 27th of September, the Visitors passed an act statuting and ordaining that " no Regent or master of a class (albeit he hath a presentation thereto), shall be admitted or received in any University or College within this kingdom without a previous trial."

On the 1st of October, the ministers of the city

---

[1] Dr. Rule, though a minister, was M.D. See some account of him in Wodrow's History, vol. ii. p. 126; and in Calamy's Abridgement of Baxter's Life, vol. ii. p. 517.

[2] Town-Council Records.

of Edinburgh approved of both the preceding elections. Mr. Campbell was also called to be one of the ministers of Edinburgh.

On the 10th, the Commissioners sent by the Town-Council to Dumfries regarding Mr. Campbell's election, reported to the Council that the parish of Dumfries objected, and that therefore they had been obliged to appeal to the General Assembly.

On the 14th, Mr. Gilbert Rule accepted, and took the oath *de fideli administratione.* Captain Warrander, Hugh Blair, and two Deacons,[1] were appointed to go over to the College, and install him.

On the 17th, a Committee was named by the Town-Council, viz., Bailie Blackwood, and Deacon Stirling, to meet with the Commissioners of the College of Justice about a Professor of Humanity, in place of Mr. John Drummond deprived.[2]

On the 23d of the same month, after public programs affixed in the usual manner, a comparative trial was appointed to be held for the purpose of supplying the vacancy occasioned by the removal of Mr. Thomas Burnet. Seven candidates appeared.

The subjects of dispute proposed to the candidates, prescribed by advice of the Principal and several of the ministers of the city, were :—

" 1. De primis sciendi principiis.
2. De concursu causæ primæ cum secundis.
3. De bonitate et malitia humanorum actionum.
4. De principiis corporum naturalium.
5. De natura possibilitatis.
6. De natura corporis et spiritus.
7. De motu."

[1] [As members of the Town-Council.] [2] Town-Council Records.

The subjects were assigned by lot, and fell as follows :—1. Mr. John Ross ; 2. Mr. George Hutcheson ; 3. Mr. Robert Graham ; 4. Mr. William Law ; 5. Mr. William Forbes ; 6. Mr. Robert Stuart ; 7. Mr. James Kennedy.

On these subjects the candidates were to give up their Theses to the Principal within the College, on Monday next, at nine o'clock in the morning, that the candidates might interchange them respectively with one another. Each was to make an oration, not exceeding half an hour, on any subject he chose, on Friday thereafter, at two o'clock afternoon in the College ; the first maker of the orations, viz., Mr. John Ross, offering up a short Latin prayer before the orations began.

The public dispute was to begin on Monday come eight days. Certificates of moral character were produced by some of the candidates, and the others promised to produce their certificates to-morrow. The judges preferred Mr. William Law, son of Mr. John Law, minister of Edinburgh, and the Council, on the 7th of November, bestowed on him the office. He took the oath *de fideli administratione,* and the oath of allegiance, and signed the assurance to their Majesties.

On the 5th of November, programs having been affixed, as usual, inviting candidates also to stand a trial for the vacant Professorship of Humanity, four entered their names. Yet, on the 21st of that month, report was made to the Town-Council about a difference between them and the College of Justice respecting the election of a Professor of Humanity, in which the two bodies had a joint right, by virtue of a contract betwixt them. The Council discharged the College Janitor to deliver the keys to any person nominated by the College of Justice, unless he applied to the Council and received his commission from them ; and they appointed Bailie Blackwood and Mr. Henry Ferguson to consult the assessors, and ordained the writs and evidence of this affair to be taken out of the charter-house.[1]

The judges determined in favour of Mr. Laurence Dundas ; and he obtained the office on the 28th of the same month, being admitted and received for five years to come, conform to the contract betwixt the Town-Council and the College of Justice. He accepted, and took the oath *de fideli administratione*, and subscribed the oath of allegiance with the assurance.[2] The vacant professorship of Hebrew was not supplied till February 1694.

After the places declared vacant by the Visitors were, all but the professorship of Hebrew, thus supplied, the Senatus Academicus consisted of the following members :—

Dr. Gilbert Rule, Principal.
Mr. George Campbell, Professor of Divinity.
Mr. Herbert Kennedy,
Mr. William Law,
Mr. Alexander Cunninghame, } Professors of Philosophy.
Mr. Andrew Massie,
Dr. David Gregory, Professor of Mathematics.
Mr. Laurence Dundas, Professor of Humanity.
(*Vacant.*) Professor of Hebrew.

[1] Town-Council Records. [2] *Ibid.*

In October 1690, the College again met. Mr. Kennedy undertook the charge of the Bejan class, consisting, at the matriculation on the 31st of the ensuing March, of forty-seven. Mr. Law carried forward the Semi class, with an accession of thirty-two supervenients; Mr. Cunningham had the Bachelor, and Mr. Massie the Magistrand.

1691.   On the 8th of January 1691, the Rev. Primar, Dr. Rule, had his public inaugural oration; and the laws for the students were read.

It appears that about this time the students had been concerned in various violent and tumultuary proceedings, which induced the Principal and Professors to frame the following engagement against all such practices, which, at a meeting in March 1691, they agreed that the students should be obliged to subscribe :—

"We undersubscribers, students of the College of Edinburgh, do hereby declare and protest our sincere and unfeigned abhorrence and detestation of all tumultuary and disorderly practices, unworthy of scholars, Christians, and gentlemen ; and we do solemnly engage and promise that we shall not be accessory, directly or indirectly, to the continuation of such abusive irregularities ; and particularly, that we shall not wickedly deface and demolish the fabric of the College, either in whole or in part, as being a rude and barbarous enterprize : and furthermore we promise, according to our bounden duty, to perform due obedience to our masters and teachers *in omnibus licitis et honestis*. In witness whereof, we have subscribed these presents at Edinburgh, the —— day of March 1691."[1]

At another meeting on the 8th of October the same year, a paper was drawn up, by which the

---

[1] MS. Papers, illustrative of the History and Constitution of the University of Edinburgh, in College Library, p. 39.

students, upon considering the evil of many bad customs which had crept into their society, were to declare their abhorrence of them, and particularly of the barbarous practice of boxing at the College gate, or elsewhere; that of throwing the ball into the Bejan class,[1] and breaking and demolishing the class-rooms, or any part of the College fabric; and their renouncing for the future all such practices.[2] They were to promise at the same time to behave in the most respectful manner to the Lord Provost, Magistrates, and Council, patrons of the College, and to the Principal and all the Professors. A copy of this paper was given to the Lord Provost on the 10th.

The 103d class, under the tuition of Mr. Massie, being brought forward to the usual time for graduation, fourteen of them took the degree privately at different times, and thirty-two publicly on the 13th of July. No printed Theses appear in the College collection as the subject of disputation for this year. *The one-hundred and third Class graduated.*

In October, after the vacation, Mr. Massie began the new Bejan class, which, at the matriculation in the ensuing March, amounted to fifty-seven; Mr. Kennedy proceeded in the Semi class, with seventy supervenients; Mr. Law had the Bachelor, and Mr. Cunningham the Magistrand.

On the 18th of May 1692, Mr. Patrick Sinclair, son of Mr. John Sinclair, minister of Ormiston, was elected Professor of Hebrew, with 1000 marks Scots salary.[3] *1692.*

On the 3d of June, report was made to the Town-

---

[1] See afterwards, anno 1697.
[2] MS. Papers Illustrative, etc. *ut supra.*   [3] Town-Council Records.

Council of a legacy of 104 books left to the College Library, by Alexander Douglas, late Professor of Hebrew, and also of a legacy of 225 marks Scots, left by him to the College, being a quarter's salary due to him by the College.

On the 15th of September this year, there convened in the College Library the following delegates to consult respecting the general good of the Universities, viz. from Glasgow, Mr. William Dunlop, Principal; from King's College, Aberdeen, Dr. George Middleton, Principal; for Edinburgh, Dr. Gilbert Rule, Primar, and Mr. Andrew Massie, Professor of Philosophy.

Their several commissions being read, after prayer, they chose Dr. Rule to be preses, and Mr. Robert Henderson, Librarian, to be clerk. Dr. Middleton produced an extract of a protest taken by three members of King's College, Aberdeen, viz. Mr. John Moir, civilist, Dr. Patrick Urquhart, medicinar, and Mr. William Black, regent, against the meeting of the correspondents of the Universities, dated the 26th of August 1692, setting forth that Dr. Middleton, at a packed meeting of the College, had obtained a commission for meeting and treating with some other Principals of Universities within this kingdom, for concerting of affairs not known; that King's College has good and wholesome laws, by the foundation and otherwise, whereby it may be properly managed and regulated; that by the laws and acts of Parliament, all conventions and assemblies for treating, consulting, and determining in any matter of state, civil or ecclesiastical, without his Majesty's special license, are

illegal and punishable, as those that unlawfully convocate the King's lieges ; and the convocators holden
and repute as movers of sedition to the breach of the
peace, as is clear from various Acts of Parliament :
and therefore they protest against any such meeting,
or any commission to be given thereto ; and that the
said College and University be noways burdened with
any expense incurred by the said commission, nor in
any ways be liable or subject to any overtures, proposals, or pretended acts that may be made in the
said unwarrantable meeting of Principals ; and they
disown any such meetings, as contrary to the public
laws of this kingdom and privileges of the Universities ; and they further protest, that such as may meet
to consult about any affair relating to the Universities, contrary to their Majesties' command and license,
may be liable, conform to the Acts of Parliament, as
movers of sedition.

At the meeting on the ensuing day, Mr. Dunlop[1] was
appointed to draw up answers to this protest, which
was considered as a very unfair representation of the
nature and design of the delegation. In the meantime the meeting, without waiting any longer for a
Commissioner from the University of St. Andrews, proceeded to the consideration of various particulars
tending to the improvement of the Universities.

"There was an overture proposed for taking some speedy course
to fill up in each University, the public offices of Chancellor, Rector,
Dean of Faculty, etc., and till such time as that be done, the Principals
of the several Colleges should be empowered to supply these offices.

[1] [In Professor Dalzel's MS. it is Dr Middleton by mistake.]

"1. It was agreed that the Principals and Professors of Divinity be careful to put the Synods in mind for obliging their Presbyteries to send bursars of divinity to that profession.

"2. Agreed that the Principals make frequent visitations of the several classes, and particularly take notice how masters teach, explain, and examine their lessons, and how the scholars profit.

"3. Agreed that the Principals take also care that upon the Lord's day the students, after sermons, be instructed in the principles of religion by their particular masters.

"4. Agreed that the several Universities send a copy of their Theses to each other to be laid up in their libraries, that so it may be known what opinions are held by the several professors in the Universities.

"Adjourned to four o'clock this afternoon."

"1. There was then referred to the consideration of the several Universities the reviving of the fifth overture of the sederunt the 30th of August 1647, viz., That when students are examined publicly on the black-stone before Lambas, and after their return at Michaelmas, that they be examined in some questions of the Catechism [see p. 143]; with this alteration, that, instead of the Catechism, they be examined upon the sacred lessons taught them the preceding year.

"2. Referred the reviving of the second, third, fourth, and fifth articles of the sederunt 2d February 1672. [It was agreed that these articles, for which see p. 202, should be adopted.]

"Agreed that the sixth article of the same meeting be revived, viz. [see p. 202].

"Agreed that the third article of the sederunt 17th July 1648 be revived, viz. [see p. 149].

"Agreed that all pedagogues, students of divinity, and whoever besides learn any science or art within the College, and such also as attend them, shall be subject to the discipline of the College, if they transgress the laws of it.

"Adjourned to Monday at ten o'clock."

"19th September 1692.

"The which day, the Principal of Glasgow, to whom it had been recommended, produced a draught of Reasons against the foresaid Protestation; whereupon the meeting came to the following conclusions :—

" The meeting having seen and considered the above Protestation, made by three of the members of the King's College of Aberdeen, against the Commission granted by the College meeting of the said University to Dr. George Middleton, Principal there, do find therein most unjust reflections, not only against Dr. Middleton and the College meeting of that University, but against all the other Universities and their correspondence among themselves ; and that they give a most scandalous and disingenuous representation of the nature and designs of this mutual correspondence, and that for these reasons :—

" 1. Because it doth groundlessly assert, that this meeting of correspondents of the Universities is a meeting of Principals ; whereas it is not a meeting of Principals, but of such members of each University as the Universities, their Faculty and meetings, do think fit to send and commissionate ; who sit in this meeting of correspondents by virtue of their commission, and not as Principals ; nor ever were these meetings constitute of Principals only, nor is this present so.

" 2. It is groundless in asserting that this meeting is illegal and unwarrantable, and in protesting that the keepers of the same may be punished as movers of sedition ; and that because the meetings of the Universities have the uninterrupted practice of the Universities of this kingdom, not only permitted by the Government, but so countenanced from time to time as that their proposals and resolutions have been approven and confirmed by their Majesties' Privy Council, when required ; particularly 1672, as the records of the said meeting can testify.

" 3. Their quotation of diverse Acts of Parliament, and affirming that these meetings for correspondence among the Universities do break the same, the import whereof is no less than unlawful convocating the King's subjects, and moving of sedition, manifest their gross ignorance and calumnious malice, in so far as the true intent of all these acts is to hinder and discharge subjects, without the King's commission or authority, to convocate, so as to take upon them any authority and power, civil or ecclesiastic, and to act as courts and judges, and punishing the contemners of their orders with pains and penalties, and thereby intrude upon the civil or ecclesiastic government established by law, or invalide and raise sedition against the same. Whereas the meeting for correspondence among the Universities never did pretend to be or act as a judicatory

Q

or court, either civil or ecclesiastic ; but each of the four Universities
having by their charters, erections, and laws of the land, not only
power and authority to preserve and put in execution their several
statutes, but in many things relating to the advancement or further-
ance of learning, and the knowledge of the liberal sciences (which is
their province), to add to, amend, and alter the same ; and that
each University may be the better fortified therein by the advice of
others of the same profession, and that the Universities themselves
may keep that amicable and good correspondence as to strengthen one
another's hands, and not encroach upon one another, but may join
together for the mutual help of each other ; [they] have afore, many
years, at set times, met by their Commissioners, for these good and
lawful ends; wherein none of their consultations or conclusions were
binding, unless each University did agree to the same, and who never
acted in a magisterial or authoritative manner.

" 4. It is very calumnious and unreasonable to say that the affairs
to be treated were not known to them, when it was told them that
their present design was to see what was fit to be done for the advancement of learning, and reforming several abuses that in process
of time had crept into the Universities ; and they, or any member of
a University, might very freely have sent their overtures, or any
thing they thought needful to be treated ; and by their instructions
to their Commissioner they might have limited him to determine
nothing without their knowledge ; without which the former meetings
for correspondence did not use to act, nor was there any ground to
think this should at this time.

" 5. Their insinuating that they have such good and wholesome
laws, by which their University may be regulated, should be no
hindrance to them to correspond with other Universities who are
desirous to correspond with them, to communicate these laws unto
them ; but whatever they pretend, none of the other Universities do
think they are arrived at that height of perfection that there can
be no melioration.

" 6. They at length bewray their sordid peevishness, under pretence of saving charges to the University, as if the inconsiderable
charge in meeting with other Universities were enough to hinder
their further promoting of learning, or such joint course as may tend
to the augmenting of the revenues of each of the Universities.

" 7. After all their vain pretences of their loyalty to their Majesties' persons and interests, their zeal for the laws of the land and privileges of Universities, and that those who shall meet at this correspondence be punished as movers of sedition ; let us see that it is *Protestatio contrario facto*, in so far as that [for] three members of a society of eight persons opposing the constant practice of that same University, where they are members, to challenge the meeting of that University they are subject unto and members of, calling them a packed meeting, when so clear a plurality carried the election, and none of them three the heads of the University, doth manifest them to be heinous contemners of the privileges of their own University, to be promoters of sedition there, and a bad example, without precedent, to other Universities ; and how that suits with the laws of the land and loyalty to their Majesties, the world may judge.

" For these and other reasons which might be added, the meeting doth recommend to the head and other members of that College, that they proceed against these three members to censure, conform to the laws, constitution, and customs of that University, unless they give satisfaction to the said College meeting, in as public a manner as they have given the affront ; and it is expected that the Commissioners, who shall come from that University to the next meeting of correspondents, shall bring a report thereof to the same.

" The meeting, considering the overture for filling up the Chancellor's and other offices in the Universities now vacant, thought fit that with all speed and diligence these places should be filled up, according to the different customs and former practices of each University ; and, therefore, that the Lords of their Majesties' Privy Council be supplicate for interposing their authority therein, and that they would allow in the meantime, till that be effectuate, the present heads of the Colleges to supply these vacant offices where it is needful.

" The meeting also thought fit that addresses should be made to the Privy Council for renewing their Act of the date 1st February 1672, relating to the Universities, with this particular addition, that if a student coming from one College to another, shall make it appear to the Principal of the College to which he comes that he hath made application for a testificate, and yet hath got none, nor anything is objected against him by that College, that in that case he may be received.

" The address to the Council for these two particulars is recommended to Dr. Rule and Mr. Massie, who are to acquaint the several Universities timeously with the Council's answer thereanent.

"The conferring the (1st) degree of Bachelors, and (2d), the monthly exercises, are referred to the consideration of the several Universities. (3d), Referred also a paper of proposals anent the manner of teaching Physics and other Sciences, given in by the Primar of the College of Edinburgh, to be set down in the Register.

"Adjourned to the morrow at ten o'clock.

"Which day the meeting thought fit that this correspondence be yearly continued, and that the next meeting shall be in this place the first Thursday of June 1693, by ten o'clock in the forenoon ; and the Preses of the meeting is appointed to acquaint the Colleges of St. Andrews and New Aberdeen with the Diet, and to show them that it was expected they would not have made so light of the advertisement they had for this meeting, and that they would be careful to attend that diet ; as also in case any emergence should fall out, which calls for a meeting of the Universities sooner, the Primar of the College of Edinburgh is hereby empowered to appoint the same, by giving timeous notice to the respective Colleges, of the occasions thereof, that they may come sufficiently instructed for that end.

"To the clerk is ordered to give doubles of what has passed in this meeting to the several Universities."[1]

The one-hundred and fourth Class graduated.

The 104th class, under the tuition of Mr. Cunningham, being now in the last year of their course, and consisting of eighty-eight, thirty-seven were graduated publicly on the 15th of July 1692,[2] in the common hall of the College, and a few more of them privately at different times. The Theses on this occasion were dedicated to Sir Thomas Mure of Thornton, Lord Provost, and the other Magistrates and the Town-Council.

[1] MS. Papers illustrative of the History and Constitution of the University of Edinburgh, No. II. pp. 1-9.

[2] [Forty-four, whose names appear in the printed Theses, as candidates for graduation, did not obtain their degree ; because probably they may have refused to take the required oath of allegiance to King William and Queen Mary.]

Dr. David Gregory having been called to Oxford to be Savilian Professor of Astronomy there, a gratuity of 250 pounds Scots was allowed him by the Town-Council, August 26, 1692, besides his full salary to the time of his removal to Oxford ; and the Council recommended to him to keep a good correspondence with the Masters of the College of Edinburgh.[1]

Mr. James Gregory succeeded his brother David, and at his election the Town-Council erected a constant Professorship of Mathematics.

"EDINBURGH, *September* 23, 1692.

"The which day, the Council taking to their serious consideration how necessary, expedient, and profitable it is for all Colleges and Universities to have the profession of the Mathematics, as well as those of other sciences established therein for the accomplishment and education of youth, and particularly in the art of Navigation (the great ornament of any kingdom or commonwealth): And albeit, the famous College of this City, founded by that mighty and illustrious Prince, King James the Sixth, of ever glorious memory, be furnished with Professors, Principals, Masters, and Regents, both in Divinity, Philosophy, and Humanity, yet never with a constant profession of the Mathematics : And the said Lord Provost, Bailies, Council, and Deacons of Crafts, being informed of the literature, qualifications, and good conversation of Mr. James Gregory, brother-german to Dr. Gregory, present Professor of Astronomy in the University of

[1] Town-Council Records.

Oxford, who is sufficiently qualified to be a Professor of the Mathematics in the said College; and they being most willing and desirous, not only to give him all due encouragement therein for the time, but also to establish and erect the said profession within the said College for ever in time coming: Therefore the said Lord Provost, Bailies, Council, and Deacons of Craftsmen, for themselves and their successors in place and office within the said City, have erected, and hereby erect a profession of the Mathematics, within the said City of Edinburgh, now, and in all time coming, and make, constitute, erect, and appoint the said Mr. James Gregory Professor thereof."[1]

The Council granted him a salary of 900 marks, with promise of more as soon as the Royal Bounty, or new donations would allow; the College revenue at that time not permitting so large a salary to be given him as to Dr. David Gregory.

In October, Mr. Cunningham entered upon the charge of the new Bejan class, consisting at the matriculation of ninety-three. Mr. Massie had the Semi class, with fifty-six supervenients; Mr. Kennedy the Bachelor, and Mr. Law the Magistrand.

1693.   Complaints were made to the Lords of the Privy Council of various tumults and disorders, which had of late happened among the students in the different Universities; upon which they ordered an Act, dated the 9th of March 1693, issued for preventing such for the future, authorizing the Principals and Regents to inflict fines according to the different ranks of the

[1] Town-Council Records.

students, and requiring the Magistrates, in cases of necessity, to support by their authority the sentences of the said Principals and Regents.

"AT EDINBURGH, *the 9th day of March* 1693 *years.*

"The Lords of their Majesties' Privy Council taking to their consideration the tumults and disorders which frequently fall out amongst, and are committed by, the students within the several Colleges and Universities within this kingdom ; and having considered the Report of a Committee of their own number appointed in this matter : The saids Lords, for preventing of any tumults or other disorders within any of the saids Colleges and Universities, Do hereby authorize and empower the several Principals, Regents, and Masters of the saids Colleges respective, in case it shall happen hereafter, any of the students of any of the Colleges above mentioned, to commit, or be guilty of any tumults or other enormous disorder against the quiet and good government of the saids Colleges, to impose and exact fines from such as they shall find guilty, not exceeding the respective rates and proportions after mentioned, viz. :—For a nobleman, or his eldest son, an hundred and fifty pounds Scots ; for noblemen's younger sons, or barons themselves, or their eldest sons, an hundred pounds ; for the younger sons of barons or gentlemen, and for the sons of burgesses, fifty pounds ; and for the sons of craftsmen, or yeomen, fifty marks Scots ; and that by and attour the reparation of damages : And the saids Lords do hereby require and command the Magistrates of the respective Burghs where the saids Colleges are kept, to interpose their authority to the sentence of the saids Masters, and to give them their assistance in executing the same, by imprisonment, if need be : And allows and appoints the sums that shall be exacted for fines, in manner and for the cause above mentioned, to be applied for the use of the several Bibliothecks of the saids Colleges : And the saids Lords having reviewed an Act of Council of the date the 1st day of February 1672, prohibiting one College to receive any scholar from another College, they do restrict the same to such scholars only as have been removed for misdemeanours, or have fled from discipline. —Extracted by me, "DA. MONCRIEFF, *Clk. Sti. Cons.*"[1]

---

[1] Records of Privy-Council.

The 105th class, under the tuition of Mr. Law, being brought towards the conclusion of their course, fifteen of them were graduated privately at different times, and thirty-three of them publicly on the 3d of July. No printed Theses appear in the College collection.

On the 1st of June, in consequence of the adjournment last year, there appeared in the Library the following Commissioners, viz. :—from Glasgow, Mr. Patrick Simson, Dean of Faculty; and for the College of Edinburgh, Dr. Gilbert Rule, Primar, Mr. Herbert Kennedy, and Mr. Andrew Massie, Professors of Philosophy. But as no delegates appeared from the other Universities, they adjourned till next day, when there appeared, besides those already mentioned, viz., from the Old and New Colleges of Aberdeen, Dr. George Middleton, and Mr. Robert Paterson, Principals; Mr. George Fraser, Sub-Principal of King's College; and Mr. George Peacock, Regent, from Marischal's College. They adjourned till Wednesday next, expecting the Commissioner from St. Andrews; but as none appeared on that day but the following delegates formerly mentioned, viz., Dr. Rule, Mr. Paterson, Mr. Fraser, and Mr. Kennedy, they dissolved the meeting.

In October the College met, and Mr. William Law assembled a very numerous Bejan class, consisting at the matriculation in March of 110. Mr. Cunningham had the charge of the Semi class, with thirty-five supervenients : Mr. Massie that of the Bachelor, and Mr. Kennedy that of the Magistrand.

Again, in the month of December, the Privy Council found it necessary to re-enact their former order respecting tumults, and to cause it to be made more generally known, by having it printed and published, at the market crosses of Edinburgh, Old and New Aberdeen, St. Andrews, and Glasgow, and read in the public halls of all the Universities, and printed copies affixed upon the gates of the Universities and Colleges.

On the 1st of December, an Act was passed by the Town-Council as to the application of 1000 pounds Scots, mortified by Bailie Penman, for a bursar.

On the 26th of January, several members of the Town-Council moved that it were necessary that a Professor of Hebrew should be authorized in the College. The Council, before giving answer, recommended to the Principal and Professor of Divinity, and the Ministers of the City, to recommend a fit and qualified person.[1]

On the 29th of January, Mr. Alexander Cunningham was suspended from his office as Regent by the Council, in consequence of a complaint by James Grant, second son of the Laird of Grant, and on the Report of the Committee appointed to take trial of the said complaint. The Council recommended to the Principal to take care of his class during the suspension. The notoriety of his crime was taken into their consideration.[2]

On the 2d of February, Mr. Alexander Rule, student of Divinity, on the recommendation of the Principal, Professor of Divinity, and Ministers, who had taken trial of him, was elected Professor of Hebrew, in place of Mr. Alexander Douglas, who had been removed by

1694.

---

[1] Town-Council Records.   [2] Ibid.

the Visitors for refusing to take the oath of allegiance. On the 21st of the same month he was appointed to hold his inaugural oration ; and he was ordered to give his lessons on Mondays and Fridays.[1]

This year, 1694, King William, by a deed of gift, dated February 28, as will afterwards be mentioned,[2] bestowed a perpetual annuity of £300 per annum out of the Bishops' rents, of which £100 was appropriated for a salary to a Regius Professor of Divinity and Ecclesiastical History. The first Regius Professor introduced about this time into the College by a commission from the King, was Mr. John Cumming.[3] He began a course of public lectures on Church History, and continued them regularly till his death, which happened in the year 1714.

The one hundred and sixth Class graduated.

The 106th class, under the tuition of Mr. Kennedy, were brought to the conclusion of their fourth year. Twenty-one of them took the degree privately at differcut times, and forty-one of them publicly, on the 9th of July. No Theses for this graduation appear in the College collection.[4]

In October, Mr. Kennedy began the new Bejan class, of whom there were sixty at the matriculation, on the 13th of February. Mr. Law in the Semi class had seventy-eight supervenients ; Mr. Alexander Cunningham had the Bachelors, and Mr. Andrew Massie the Magistrands.

[1] Town-Council Records.

[3] [There is, however, no evidence that Cumming obtained his commission till the year 1702. He qualified before the Magistrates on 10th November that year.—Town-Council Records.]

[2] See *infra*, pp. 256, 271.

[4] [The Theses were printed ; and forty-two, whose names appear in the list of candidates for graduation inserted in the Theses, did not obtain their degree. See p. 244, note 2.]

It would seem that the Commission for visitation of schools and Colleges had been so dilatory, as to allow the appointed time for their meeting to elapse. The Privy-Council therefore issued an order, dated the 13th of December 1694, ordering a meeting in January 1695. Accordingly, in consequence of such a meeting, we find that on the 28th of that month a Committee of their number had prepared several acts and overtures to be submitted to the consideration of the Commission.

They recommended :—

" 1. That the Professor of the Greek tongue be fixed to that class, there being far fewer eminent in the knowledge of that language than in Philosophy ; and that nothing be taught that year but Greek.

" 2. That in the Semi the Logics be taught, without mixture of what concerns Metaphysics ; and that therewithal the common terms, notions, and axioms be taught.

" 3. That in the third class the Ethics, general and special, the practice of Oratory, and also the general Physics be taught.

" 4. That in the fourth class there be taught the special Physics and the Pneumatologia.

" 5. It is also the opinion of the Committee that the Hebdomadar be obliged to lie within the College the time of his office, and that he visit the students in their chambers every morning at six of the clock, and every evening at nine of the clock.

" 6. That all Masters and Regents, and also the students in the several Universities and Colleges within this kingdom, be obliged to wear constantly gowns the time of the sitting of the Colleges ; and the Regents or Masters shall be obliged to wear black gowns, and the students red gowns, that thereby the students may be discouraged from vageing or vice.

" 7. That, at the time of the laureation, the students be strictly and exactly examined by the Principals and Regents ; and that at their promotion there be distinction made by the Masters of some of the pregnant spirits in the class, who are to [be] called by their names in order before the rest of the class ; and that none receive degrees but those who are qualified.

" 8. That in time coming no person be admitted a Professor or Regent in any University or College within this kingdom, to have the government of students, unless they be of the age of twenty-one years complete at least.

" 9. As also, that the Masters and Regents of all Colleges and Universities within this kingdom do begin the teaching of their course for the subsequent year upon the first lawful day of November, and to continue teaching until the last day of June thereafter, except the Regent of the Magistrand class, who is to continue teaching until the first day of May yearly.

" 10. As also, that it should be enacted, that no student shall be hereafter admitted into any College, who has been any former years studying in any other College, unless he produce sufficient testificates of his good behaviour, signed by his Regent, or the Principal of the College where he last studied, and which testificates they shall be obliged to grant when required, unless they can give very pregnant reasons for their refusing ; and if the Masters, being required, shall refuse to give the saids testificates without just cause, then it shall be leasom to any College, to which the student applies, to receive him, without obliging him to produce the said testificate.

" 11. And also, that in time coming the students shall not spend their time in writing their courses of Philosophy in their class, but in place thereof, that there be a printed course thought upon ; and to that end, that timeous intimation be made to the Professors and Regents or Masters of the haill Universities and Colleges within this kingdom, to send two of their number from every College to Edinburgh, the last Wednesday of July next to come, and sufficiently instructed, to meet with these of the Commission of Parliament, appointed for visitation of Universities, Colleges, and Schools, and to advise and consult with them, what method shall be fallen upon for writing and printing an uniform course of Philosophy, to be hereafter taught in all the Colleges.

" 12. As also, that when the Commissioners from the several Colleges meet the last Wednesday of July next, that they then take to their consideration how expedient it will be for the haill Colleges to meet by their delegates every year, and report their opinion, with the reasons for the same, to the general meeting of the Commission or their Committee.

" 13. It is also the opinion of the Committee, that the several classes in the Colleges, when they first enter and convene, be all publicly examined in the common hall by the Principal and haill Regents of the College, who shall all be obliged to convene for the said examinations.

" 14. That all Bursars be strictly examined every year ; and that such as do not duly attend, and make sufficient proficiency in their studies, be turned out of their bursaries.

" 15. That every year the Regents of the said several classes be obliged to teach their students some rudiments of the Mathematics, with their course yearly.

" 16. That it be recommended to the Principal, Professor, and Regents, to receive none into the Colleges, but upon strict trial of their proficiency in the Latin and Greek tongues respective.

" 17. The Committee are of opinion, that, until there be a printed course of Philosophy composed, the Regents shall be obliged yearly to produce and show, in the beginning of the year, to the Principal or Dean of Faculty of the College, the dictates that he is to teach his students the year following ; and that these dictates are and shall be subject and liable to the amendments and correction of the Principal and Faculty of the College.

" That, at the yearly laureation in the respective Colleges, there be honourable mention made of the founders and benefactors by public recital."[1]

On the 29th of January 1695, the Faculty ordered that Mr. Campbell and Mr. Law should attend the Commission of Parliament for visitation of Universities, the — day of July, as their representatives.[2]

On the 1st of February, James Sutherland, Master of the Physic Garden, was elected by the Town-Council Professor of Botany in the College, with all emoluments, profits, and casualties, and the former pension of £20 sterling annually was allowed him.[3]

---

[1] MS. Papers Illustrative of the History and Constitution of the University of Edinburgh, in the College Library, No. II. p. 153.

[2] Register of the University of Edinburgh, in the College Library, p. 33.

[3] [On the 8th of September 1676, the Town-Council, "considering the use-

In the act it is said that " the Physic Garden is in great reputation, both in England and foreign nations, by the great care and knowledge of the said Mr. James." He had "been at great pains and expenses in bringing foreign plants and seeds, and making several divisions, hedges, and improvements in the said garden."[1]

On the 17th of April, an Act was passed by the Town-Council, appointing Mr. William Henderson, father of Mr. Robert, at that time Librarian, to officiate in the Library for his son, till the son should finish the catalogues.[2]

The one hundred and seventh Class graduated.

The 107th class, under Mr. Massie, were brought to the conclusion of their course ; nineteen of them graduated privately at different times, and thirty-nine publicly on the 13th of July.[3]

It was a favourite object with the Commission of Visitation to bring all the Universities to adopt a uniform method of teaching the different parts of Philosophy ; and therefore, at a meeting held on the 1st of August 1695, they passed the following Act :—

fulness and necessity of encouragement of the art of botany and planting of medicinal herbs, and that it were fit for the better flourishing of the Colleges that the said profession be joined to the other professions, . . . appointed a yearly salary of £20 sterling, to be paid to Mr. John Sutherland, present botanist, who professes the said art, . . . and, upon the considerations foresaid, unites, annexes, and adjoins the said profession to the rest of the liberal sciences taught in the College, and recommends the Treasurer of the College to provide a convenient room in the College, for keeping books and seeds relating to the said profession."—Town Council Records. It was not, however, till the period specified in the text that Sutherland became properly Professor of Botany in the College.]

[1] Town-Council Records.

[2] On the 14th of August following, Mr. Robert Henderson gave in two Catalogues of the Library.—*Ibid*.

[3] [Thirty-one, whose names appear in the printed Theses as candidates for graduation, did not obtain their degree. See p. 244, note 2.]

" The Commission of Parliament for visiting Universities, Colleges, and Schools, having met with the delegates sent from the several Colleges, and heard them both *scripto* and *viva voce* anent an uniform printed course of Philosophy, to be hereafter taught, Do statute, enact, and ordain, that the ordinary custom of dictating and writing of notes in the classes be discharged from and after the month of October 1696 ; and ordain, that in place thereof, there be a printed course or system of Philosophy composed, to be taught in all the Colleges. And the Commission appoints the Faculties of Philosophy in the several Colleges to compile the said system ; and for that end ordains the said Faculty of every College to meet and convene, and to appoint one or more of the Regents of the said Faculty to compile that part of the course appointed for each College's share ; and ordains the person or persons so to be appointed, to perform and do the work that the Faculty lays upon them ; and if they refuse or fail in the performance thereof, the Commission declares, he or they shall *ipso facto* be exauctorat and deprived of their office. And farther, the Commission appoints the said system or course of Philosophy, to be composed by the Faculties of the several Colleges, conform to the division following, viz. : That the Logics and general Metaphysics be composed by the two Colleges of St. Andrews, and the general and special Ethics by the College of Glasgow ; the general and special Physics by the two Colleges of Aberdeen, and the Pneumatics or special Metaphysics by the College of Edinburgh : And appoints the Faculty of each of the said Colleges to give in a scheme of what points and articles they are to treat of in each of their parts of the said work, to the Commission of Parliament, or their Committee, against the first Wednesday of October next ; and appoints the several Colleges to keep a correspondence amongst themselves during their writing of their several parts of the said work ; and that they send parcels of their writings to each College, that the same may be revised ; and that each of the said Colleges be assistant to others, for the better carrying on of the said work. And the Commission appoints a general meeting of the haill Colleges by their delegates, to be at Edinburgh, the first Wednesday of July next to come, at which time they are to revise the whole system and course of Philosophy ; which is hereby appointed to be in readiness against the said day : And that they present the same to the said Commission of Parliament, that the same may be approven, and put to the press against the first day of August thereafter. And the Commission recommends to the Faculties of the several Colleges, that they be exact and diligent in composing the said system, for the nation's and their own credit, with as much succinctness as can be ; and for their encouragement, the Commission declares they will write to the Secretary of State to interpose with his Majesty, that he would be pleased to give a gratification of £50 sterling to each College at the completing of the said work."[1]

On the 28th of August 1695, Mr. Hugh Linn, College Treasurer, produced before the Town-Council the mortification granted by his Majesty, dated at Kensington, the 28th February 1693-4,[2] whereby his Majesty mortified and disponed £300 sterling to the College of Edinburgh, for the maintenance of a Professor of Theology, by and attour the present Professor established there, who was to have £100 sterling of the said sum yearly, together with twenty bursars of Divinity, who were to have £10 sterling each yearly, to be presented by his Majesty or the Lords of Treasury ; which sum of £300 sterling his Majesty appointed to be paid to the College Treasurer and his successors, by the Lords of Treasury and his Majesty's collectors, out of the Bishops' rents, and that termly, beginning the first term's payment at the term of Whitsunday 1694.[3]

On the 10th of August, the Faculty of the University "assigned to Mr. Law to draw up that part of Philosophy which was appointed by the Committee of Parliament for Edinburgh College, viz., the Pneu-

---

[1] MS. Papers illustrative of the History and Constitution of the University of Edinburgh, No. II. p. 139.

[2] See notice of this Royal Grant, *supra*, p. 250.

[3] Town-Council Records.

maties, in order to a printed course to be established in the Universities."

On the 8th of October, the Faculty appointed " that Mr. Law be exempted from the Hebdomadar's work and the public examinations for this year, upon the consideration of his being appointed to compose a part of the course of Philosophy that is to be printed," viz., the Pneumatics. On the same day the Faculty also ordered, " that the Act of the Privy-Council against tumults be read in all the classes the first week of November next."

On the 19th of November, an Act of Faculty was passed against cursing, swearing, and profane speeches. " The Faculty considering how frequent cursing, swearing, and profane speeches, are among students, therefore they appoint that such as are found guilty shall be liable for sixpence, *toties quoties ;* and if it be found that any are habitually guilty they shall be extruded the College."[1]

On the 26th of November, an Act of Faculty was passed against drunkenness and frequenting taverns. " The Faculty, considering how odious the sin of drunkenness is, especially in students, and how indecent it is for such, who should be bred up in religion and learning, to haunt taverns or alehouses, therefore they do strictly forbid and inhibit the students of this University under their charge to go into any alehouse or tavern without a sufficient cause, which is to be judged of by the Rev. Primar or their respective Regents ; and if the cause be not found relevant, they

[1] Register of the University of Edinburgh, in College Library, p. 34.

R

are to be fined as follows, viz. :—Each for the first fault a sixpence, for the second a shilling, the third in eighteenpence, or to be augmented at the discretion of their respective Regents ; and if any be found drunk, he shall pay three pounds Scots, *toties quoties*, and if often found so, to be extruded."[1]

On the 18th of December 1695, the degree of Doctor of the Civil Law was conferred on Mr. Joseph Brown, an Englishman, being the first doctor's degree upon record given by the University of Edinburgh. Dr. Brown, on his return to England, remitted for the Library a donation of £15 sterling.

On the 9th of August 1695, the Town-Council appointed a comparative trial to be held in the College, in the usual manner, on the 10th of September, for supplying the place of Mr. Alexander Cunningham, Professor of Philosophy, who had demitted. Three candidates entered their names, of whom Mr. William Scott, who had studied under Mr. Thomas Burnet in 1688, but was not graduated till September 3, 1695, was judged to be the fittest, and the office was conferred upon him the 16th day of the same month.

In October, when the College met, Mr. Scott entered upon the charge of the Bejan class, the number of which, at the matriculation on the 2d of February 1696, amounted to sixty-six. Mr. Herbert Kennedy, in the Semi class, had forty-six supervenients ; Mr. Law went on with the Bachelors ; and Mr. John Row, a professor from St. Andrews, who had succeeded upon

[1] Register of the University of Edinburgh, in College Library, p. 31.

the deprivation of Mr. Andrew Massie,[1] went on with the Magistrand class.

On the 18th of February 1696, the Faculty of the University met, and received from St. Andrews the General and Special Physics composed at Aberdeen, to be revised against a certain day, with a promise that they are to send the notes and remarks upon them by St. Andrews.

1696.

On the 20th of June, Mr. Herbert Kennedy, Mr. Law, and Mr. Row, Regents, were appointed to attend the diets of the Commission of Parliament for visiting Universities, in consequence of a letter from Mr. Hamilton, Clerk to the said Commission.[2]

The 108th class, now under the tuition of Mr. John Row, was brought to the conclusion of the course; of whom fourteen were graduated privately, at different times, and thirty-seven publicly, on the 13th of July.

The one hundred and eighth Class graduated.

On the 15th of the same month, the delegates from the different Universities having been called before the Visitors, were interrogated respecting the progress they had made in preparing the different parts of the course of Philosophy. They produced all the different parts, and gave them in to the meeting. Upon this they were ordered to receive them all again, and carry them back to the different Colleges from whence they had been brought, to be revised, etc.[3]

In October 1696, Mr. John Row entered upon the

---

[1] [Row was elected August 9, 1695, in place of Massie, who had been deprived. —Town-Council Records.]

[2] Register of the University of Edinburgh, p. 35.

[3] MS. Papers, illustrative of the History and Constitution of the University of Edinburgh, in College Library, No. II. p. 145.

charge of the Bejan class, in number seventy-four, at the matriculation, February 9, 1697. Mr. Scott proceeded with the Semi class, with forty-two supervenients ; Mr. Kennedy had the Bachelor, and Mr. Law the Magistrand.

1697.
The one
hundred and
ninth Class
graduated.

The 109th class, under the tuition of Mr. William Law, being brought towards the conclusion of their four years' course, twenty-three of them were graduated privately, and fifty-eight publicly, on the 28th of June 1697. No printed theses appear.

As to the custom of the students of the Semi class throwing a foot-ball into the Bejan class on the 10th of March, to prevent its renewal, the students of the Semi class this year subscribed the following document :—

" We, undersubscribers, students in the Semi class of the College of Edinburgh, being fully persuaded that the custom of throwing a foot-ball into the Bejan class upon the 10th of March yearly hath been the occasion of much disorder and confusion in the said College, and being earnestly entreated by our Regent to give this public testimony of our willingness to have this abominable custom for ever banished the College : Therefore, we hereby solemnly declare and own our dislike of the same, and that it may effectually appear, we hereby bind ourselves, that we in no manner of way, either directly or indirectly, shall contribute to the keeping up of the foresaid custom, or attempt the throwing in of the said ball on the 10th of March ensuing, or at any other time hereafter, while we are students in the said College ; and if any of our number shall offer, notwithstanding of this our solemn declaration and engagement, to throw in the said ball, we do hereby renounce them for our comrades for ever, and declare them unworthy of the name of students and gentlemen, and give them freely up to the Faculty of the College, whom we hereby earnestly entreat to banish and extrude from their society such infamous and unworthy members ; and in testimony of the sincerity of this our declaration, we are willing and consent that the same should remain amongst the records of this College.—In witness whereof, we have signed these presents at the College of Edinburgh, the third day of March 1697 years."

This document has appended to it 121 signatures.[1]

Though the several Universities and Colleges had been employed in drawing up a uniform system of Philosophy, ever since this was enjoined by the Commission of Visitation in their Act of the 2d of August 1695, yet the different parts of that system could not be brought forward in a sufficiently correct state so soon as the Commission had appointed. First drafts, however, of these different parts had been circulated among the several Universities and Colleges, and written observations made upon them had been laid before the delegates from the Colleges, at their meetings at Edinburgh this year.

In the above-mentioned Act, the Commission had appointed that the Logics and General Metaphysics should be composed by the two Colleges of St. Andrews; the General and Special Ethics by the College of Glasgow; the General and Special Physics by the two Colleges of Aberdeen; and the Pneumatics or Special Metaphysics by the College of Edinburgh.

On the 12th of March 1697, "the Faculty received from the University of St. Andrews their observations on that part of the course of Philosophy composed by Aberdeen, together with the Tractatus Anatomicus composed by Aberdeen." On the 9th of April, they "received from St. Andrews the Glasgow Ethics, to be revised by the Faculty." Particular posts were

[1] MS. Papers, illustrative of the History and Constitution of the University of Edinburgh, in College Library, No. I. p. 63.

allotted to Messrs. Law, Kennedy, Row, Dundas, and Scott. On the 14th of May the Faculty "received the St. Andrews animadversions on the Glasgow Ethics." And on the 1st of July they "appointed Mr. Law and Mr. Row to attend the Committee of Commission of Parliament for visiting Universities."[1]

Various meetings were held by the delegates in the months of July and August this year for considering the remarks and animadversions transmitted from different Colleges, previous to their delivering the different parts of the system in a correct form to the Commission of Visitation.

These original animadversions by the separate Colleges, with the observations made upon them by the delegates from all the Colleges met at Edinburgh, are preserved among the papers of the University of Edinburgh, and form a curious collection, from which might be gathered a pretty good notion of what sort of science was understood and taught in the Colleges of Scotland at that time. Among the MSS. of the same College is likewise preserved the original of the Special Physics, as transmitted by the King's College, Aberdeen, and drawn up by Mr. William Black,[2] a member of that Society.

The animadversions upon this performance made by the Faculty of Arts of the University of St. Andrews are expressed with great severity; which drew answers of the same sort from the author. These were all laid before a meeting of the delegates on the 16th of

---

[1] Register of the University of Edinburgh, in College Library, pp. 35, 36.

[2] Black was the master of Ruddiman. — See Chalmers's Life of Ruddiman.

August 1697 ; whose opinion upon them is also preserved. As a specimen of this opinion we may quote the paragraphs upon the 20th and 30th animadversions.

20th. "One part of the delegates are of opinion that Newton's hypothesis of the ebbing and flowing of the sea should be insert, or a reason given why it is not ; and the other part think there is no need to make any mention of it. And the author gives this reason why he has omitted it,—because neither he nor any he has conversed with on the subject do so fully understand what Newton does write thereon as they can make it intelligible to the young students, for whose sake this tractate is chiefly designed. And the delegates do not find that the author has anywhere promised to examine all the celebrated opinions on this subject, as this observe does allege."

30th. "From this remark the delegates took occasion to consider the difficulty proponed by the author in the tractate against Newton's opinion of the Earth's being seventeen Gallic miles higher at the equator than at the poles ; and judging it a real difficulty, some of the delegates were of opinion, that it might be proper to take the opinion of the most knowing mathematicians in the nation anent this particular. But others thought this not needful, and thinking the arguments proposed against Newton valid, do refer this whole matter to the Commission."[1]

The Special Physics of King's College, Aberdeen, are the only branch of the intended system to be found in

[1] MS. Papers illustrative of the History and Constitution of the University of Edinburgh, in College Library, No. II. pp. 92, 93.

the Library of the University of Edinburgh. Perhaps the other parts may still be preserved in some of the other Colleges.

On the 29th of January 1697, in the Court of Session, Philiphaugh reported Mr. Andrew Massie against the town of Edinburgh, for reducing the decreet, whereby they had deprived him of being one of the Philosophy Regents in the College of Edinburgh. The Lords, on account of some informality on the part of the town, reponed Mr. Massie against the decreet, and allowed him to be farther heard before the Ordinary anent his repossession and damages in lying out of his place.[1] In the debate betwixt Row and Scott, which of the two should cede his place to make room for Massie's re-entry, the Lords ordained Mr. Scott to cede.[2]

In October 1697, Mr. William Law entered upon the charge of the new Bejan class, the number of which at the matriculation amounted to seventy-seven; Mr. John Row proceeded in the Semi, with fifty-seven supervenients; Mr. William Scott in the Bachelor; and Mr. Herbert Kennedy in the Magistrand.

1698.
The one
hundred and
tenth Class
graduated.

The 110th class, under the tuition of Mr. Herbert Kennedy, was brought to the conclusion of the course in July 1698, forty-five of them having graduated privately at different times.

By an Act passed on the 3d of January 1698, the Commission for Visitation appointed copies of the St. Andrews Logics and Metaphysics to each of the Col-

[1] See Fountainhall's Decisions, vol. i. p. 761.　　[2] Ibid. vol. i. p. 787.

leges, and ordained the same to be dictated and taught this year to the students.   They also ordained the Masters of the Colleges of Glasgow, Aberdeen, and Edinburgh, to finish the several parts of Philosophy composed by them with all expedition, and that each College teach that course or system composed by themselves, and which had been produced before the Commission in the preceding July, according as the same was ordered to be corrected and amended by the delegates from the Colleges.   They also ordered the Colleges to return to the Clerk of the Commission the observations made by the several Colleges upon each part of Philosophy, also the observations made by the delegates from the several Universities, when they met jointly together at Edinburgh in the preceding July and August, that the observations may be considered by the Commission, and determined upon by them ; and further, that they send a copy of the system of Philosophy composed by each College, corrected and amended conformable to the said observations, to the Clerk of the Commission, to be considered by the Commission or their Committee ; and this to be done with all expedition.

On the 31st of January 1698, it was ordered by the Commission of Visitation, that intimation be made to the Principal and Professors of the College of Edinburgh, that they must produce against the ensuing Monday the Pneumatics, Logic, or Special Metaphysics, composed by them, corrected and amended, as formerly appointed ; and that they have seven copies thereof complete in readiness against that day, viz., the 7th of

February next, to be transmitted to the several Universities and Colleges, under pain of being declared contemners of the authority of the Commission, and deprivation of their offices. And it is recommended to the Magistrates of Edinburgh, Patrons of the College, and to the College Treasurer, to advance money for defraying the expense of copying the said Course of Philosophy.

On the 25th of March 1698, Mr. Andrew Massie was, upon petition, reponed to his office by the Town-Council (after being "stopped and hindered for more than two years"), in the room of Mr. Herbert Kennedy deceased, whose classes he succeeded to. He states that it was "through a misfortune, which he did heartily regret."

On the 13th of April, an Act of Council was passed allowing Mr. Robert Henderson thirty pounds sterling, over and above his salary, for his great trouble in making catalogues of the Library. He says, that he had gone abroad to visit the state of other libraries. His father had officiated for him during his absence.[1]

On the 12th of December 1698, the Commission of Parliament ordered their Clerk to communicate to the several Colleges that they are to teach the same course of Philosophy which they were enjoined to have taught the preceding year, with power, if long or prolix, to abridge it. And the Masters of the several Colleges are required to send the first copies of the courses composed by them before they were amended, and to which the observations relate, that the same may be

[1] Town-Council Records.

considered by the Committee, in order to their better despatching the report they are to make to the Commission concerning them.

In October 1698, Mr. Herbert Kennedy, whose turn it was to begin the Bejan class, being dead, Mr. Andrew Massie entered upon the charge of the new Bejan class, which at the matriculation, February 23, 1699, were in number forty-seven. Mr. William Law proceeded in the Semi class, with an accession of eighty-five supervenients; Mr. John Row proceeded with the Bachelors; and Mr. William Scott, who was to have ceded for the re-entry of Mr. Massie, retained his place in consequence of the death of Mr. Herbert Kennedy.

On the 4th of June 1699, the Faculty enacted that each graduate, when he received his degree, should subscribe an obligation never to take any degree inferior to that of M.A. in any other University or College; and they appointed Monday the 26th for the Laureation. 1699

The 111th class, under the tuition of Mr. William Scott, was brought to the conclusion of their course in June this year, of whom twenty-seven were graduated privately, and forty-three publicly, the 23d and 24th of that month.[1] The one hundred and eleventh Class graduated.

On the 10th of October, the Faculty appointed that

---

[1] Arnot, in his History of Edinburgh, p. 158, anno 1698, on the margin says that, " at a public graduation of students, at which the Magistrates, in their formalities, attended, the Professor of Philosophy pronounced a harangue in favour of that settlement on the Isthmus of Darien, the legality of which, against all other pretenders, was maintained in their printed theses." This could not be the graduation June 1698, as that was a private one. That of 1697 and this of 1699 were public; but of these there are no printed theses in the College collection. Mr. Arnot does not mention where he got this anecdote. It is, however, extremely probable.

every student who should enter to the study of Divinity, should have a certificate of his education, and receiving the degree of M.A. from the College where he had been taught.

On the 27th of November this year, "the Commission of Parliament appointed for visitation of Universities, Colleges, and Schools, having considered some propositions produced before them, which they are informed are vented among students, and contained in some books made use of by them, and having considered a Report of a Committee of their number thereanent, the Commission finds that there are some of these Propositions so manifestly false and pernicious, that they hereby enjoin the Masters of the Colleges to watch over their scholars, that they do not own nor argue for them, and that the Masters confute them, and restrain their scholars from such books as vent them, such as :—

" 1. Mundum vel materiam esse ab æterno.

" 2. Rationem nostram, seu philosophiam esse Scripturæ Interpretem seu Regulam, secundum quam de veritate in divinis est judicandum.

" 3. Rationem prudentis esse Primam Regulam morum.

" Secondly, There are others of the said Propositions presented to the Commission, which are not so manifestly absurd as the former, yet being generally disapproven by the Reformed and Popish divines, the Commission appoints that the same may be forborne, and discharges the Masters to teach them, which are as follows :—

" 1. Spiritus esse nullibi.

" 2. Animæ essentiam in actuali cogitatione esse positam.

" 3. Spirituum purorum finitorum (id est) Angelorum existentiam, non posse, nisi ex Scriptura, probari.

" 4· De omnibus est dubitandum, vel assensum esse tantisper suspendendum, in ordine ad veritatem cognoscendam.

" 5. Claram nostram et distinctam cognitionem esse veritatis optimum criterium.

" 6. Brutis non competere sensationes sed esse mera automata.

" 7. Animam humanam fieri ex traduce.

" Thirdly, The Commission finds that there are some of the said Propositions which, at first hearing, are offensive, and in their full latitude may be false, that yet with restriction and limitation may be passed ; yet the Commission enjoyns that either these be not taught or cautiously explained, such as :—

" 1. Rerum essentias esse æternas.

" 2. Dari propositiones (quarum uterque terminus est Creatura) æternæ veritatis.

" 3. Rerum possibilitatem esse iis intrinsecam ab æterno.

" 4. Animæ esse essentiale quod semper actu cogitet.

" 5. Dari felicitatem naturalem, eamque consistere in actione virtutis.

" 6. Natura nos esse aptos ad virtutem, eamque agendo comparari.

" And generally the Commission does discharge all

Propositions to be taught which are *contra fidem et bonos mores.*"[1]

The Commission for Visitation still continued their meetings, but complained, that the Committee formerly named for revising the intended Philosophical course had made small progress in that work ; and that it was difficult to get them to meet. They ordained (27th of November 1699), that the Principals of the several Universities and Colleges go through the whole system, copies of which were now in every University ; and that they compendize the said course, and make their remarks thereon ; and that they all meet at Edinburgh the 21st of May 1700, and bring with them their several remarks and observations ; and that at that time they go through the same jointly, with all possible exactness, and have a report of the whole work ready to be presented to the Commission against their first meeting in June next, under pain of censure for neglect and contempt.

In October 1699, after the usual vacation, Mr. William Scott entered upon the charge of a new Bejan class, of which the number matriculated on the 15th of February following amounted to seventy-seven. Mr. Massie proceeded with the Semi class, with an accession of thirty supervenients ; Mr. Law had the Bachelors, and Mr. Row the Magistrand class.

1700.   On the 31st of January 1700, Mr. George Meldrum, minister of Edinburgh, was chosen member of the

[1] MS. Papers illustrative of the History and Constitution of the University of Edinburgh, in College Library, No. II. p. 143. Entitled on the back : "Order anent some erroneous propositions, 1699."

General Assembly for the College by the Magistrates and Professors met together in Council.[1]

The 112th class, under the tuition of Mr. John Row, being in their fourth year, were graduated, nineteen of them privately, and thirty-four publicly, so early as the 30th of April.

The one hundred and twelfth Class graduated

On the 12th of June, " the Council taking into their consideration that the deceased Mr. William Dunlop, Principal of the College of Glasgow, was at considerable pains and expenses in procuring from his Majesty the gift of twelve hundred pounds sterling yearly, out of the Bishops' rents, to the use of the four Universities of this Kingdom;[2] of which sum three hundred pounds sterling was, by the said gift, granted to the University of this city ; and that the said Mr. William Dunlop did, while in life, and now Mr. Alexander Dunlop, his son, does claim a certain sum of money from the good town, as their part of the expenses disbursed by the said. defunct in obtaining the said gift : Therefore the Council appoint and assign to be granted to the said Mr. Alexander Dunlop by the Town Council one hundred pounds sterling."[3]

On the 16th of August, the Commission of Visitation "having taken into their consideration that it would conduce much to the better learning, and for the improvement of the study of the Greek tongue, that the teacher thereof in the first of the four classes in use for Greek and Philosophy in each University and

[1] Town-Council Records.
[2] [Mr. Dunlop had been in London on this business.]
[3] Town-Council Records.

College were fixed and not ambulatory, as now he is, do therefore, for hereafter appoint and ordain, that the said teacher of the Greek tongue be fixed, and continue still to teach the same in the said first class, to all that come to learn under him from year to year, as constant master of the said Greek language, which he is hereby appointed to begin to teach, at and after the first day of November, through the whole year, until the rising of his class by the ordinary vacation ; so that, in all that space, he is only to teach the Greek Grammar and proper Greek authors, without teaching so much as any *structura syllogismi*, or anything else belonging to the course of Philosophy, which is only to be commenced the next year thereafter ; and this act and ordinance to take effect after the first day of November next : Likeas, for the better encouragement of the said fixed teacher of the said Greek, it is hereby appointed, that no scholar bred at school in Scotland, and not foreign-bred, shall be admitted to learn the Philosophy, or any part of the course thereof, in any of the said Colleges and Universities, unless that he have learned the Greek, at least for the ordinary year, under the said fixed Greek master, and report an authentic certificate thereon ; and this provision to take effect for and after the year 1701, and no sooner."[1]

The office of a Regent having become vacant by the resignation of Mr. Row, a program was published, inviting candidates to a comparative trial for the vacant chair on the 12th of November 1700.

[1] MS. Papers illustrative of the History and Constitution of the University of Edinburgh, in College Library, No. II.

November 12, 1700.—Sederunt at the College, the Magistrates and Council, with the Principal and Professors, Principal Rule, Mr. George Campbell, Mr. Andrew Massie, Mr. William Scott, Mr. William Law, Mr. Laurence Dundas, Mr. James Gregory, and Mr. Alexander Rule ; and the Ministers, Mr. William Crighton, Mr. James Webster, Mr. George Hamilton, Mr. John Hamilton, Mr. George Andrews.

The candidates who appeared for a disputation for the place of Mr. John Row, were Mr. William Hog, son to the deceased William Hog, merchant-burgess of Edinburgh ; Mr. Charles Erskine, brother-german to the Laird of Alva ; Kenneth Campbell, servant to the Earl of Argyll ; and John Beaton, servant to the Laird of Culloden junior.

Lots having been drawn by the candidates for the subjects of debate, the lots fell as follows :—No. 5, De Motu, to Mr. Beaton ; No. 6, De Prima Moralitatis Regulæ, to Mr. Hog ; No. 8, De Materiæ Divisibilitate, to Mr. Erskine ; No. 9, De Brutorum Perceptione, to Mr. Campbell. The candidates were enjoined to have ready an exegesis upon an ode of Pindar, prescribed by the Principal against that day eight days, for a trial of their skill in Greek.

Thursday thereafter was appointed for the public dispute ; and, in order thereto, the candidates were to interchange their theses on Saturday next. The candidate who got the first lot, was to say prayers in Latin at the opening of the disputation.[1]

Mr. Charles Erskine (who became Lord Advocate,[2]

---

[1] Town-Council Records. [2 See p. 295.]

and afterwards Lord Justice-Clerk) was preferred at this trial; and, on the 26th of February 1701, he obtained the office. He entered to the charge of the new Bejan class, the number of which, at the matriculation on the 20th of May 1701, amounted to thirty; Mr. Scott went on in the Semi, with sixty-one supervenients; Mr. Massie with the Bachelors; and Mr. Law with the Magistrands.

1701.

On the 24th of January 1701, some additional laws for the College, concerning the students, given in to the Town-Council by the Principal and Professors, having been considered, were approved of by the Council; and the Librarian was ordered to insert them with the other laws of the College.

ADDITIONAL LAWS FOR THE COLLEGE.

" 1. The College meetings begin with October.

" 2. In the winter session, the students are to meet in their classes every day before seven in the morning; and after prayer the rolls are called. Absents are to be marked, and fined at the Regent's pleasure. No student, therefore, at such a time or any other appointed for meeting, may walk idly in the courts, or be present at any game, viz., the hand-ball, billiards, or bowls, and the like, under the penalty of threepence for the first and second time, and the double for the third, to be exacted of each student transgressing.

" 3. On the Lord's day the students are to convene in their classes presently after sermons, to be exercised in their sacred lessons.

" 4. The Censor of each class is to write two rolls of names, and to affix to each student's name his residence, that, if any withdraw, inquiry may be made at his landlord's. One of the rolls is for the Primar's use; the other for the Regent's use.

" 5. None may do or speak wickedly, wrongfully, or obscenely, or nasty and obscene talk. Such, therefore, as profane God's sacred name and vent horrid oaths, or nasty and obscene talk, are to pay sixpence the first time, and thereafter to be severely chastised.

" 6. All students are to carry respectfully towards the Professors, and to obey their injunctions. Those who transgress, are to be fined, first in a penny, and after in twopence.

" 7. Students are obliged to discourse always in Latin ; as also to speak modestly, chastely, courteously, and in no manner uncivilly or [to be] quarrelsome, but to entertain good, profitable, and pious conferences. Those who transgress, especially such as speak English within the college, are liable the first time in a penny ; thereafter in twopence.

" 8. All are to be diligent and painful in their studies, neither must any interrupt another, by entering into his class or chamber, or curiously hearken or listen at doors or windows except the Censors.

" 9. None may absent from the College, or go out of it, without his Regent's license.

" 10. Neither may any go out of the class without leave of the Regent or of the Censor in his absence ; and he who goes out by permission is presently to return, for upon no account is he to tarry. Those who transgress are amerced in twopence.

" 11. Every one is to show good example to others by his piety, goodness, modesty, and diligence in learning, as becomes a disciple of Christ.

" 12. Let none molest another by word, gesture, or deed, or any way wrong or reproach another ; otherwise to be fined at pleasure.

" 13. Let all strife, reproaches, and what is dishonest, be removed.

" 14. Every one is obliged to warn those who either loiter, or do anything blameable, in a friendly way, as becomes a Christian ; and if the person thus admonished do not amend, he is to mark and delate him.

" 15. None may in word or deed avenge himself when wronged or reproached, but is to complain to the Primar or the Master of the student offending. Those who transgress shall be fined at discretion.

" 16. None may irreverently pass by, behold, or bespeak persons of respect, but in good manners set off their college education.

" 17. Let none in public behave himself otherwise than gravely, modestly, as becomes students of good letters.

" 18. Let all shun bad company, as a corrupting plague.

" 19. None may carry sword, gun, and dagger, and such arms, or forfeit threepence.

" 20. None in the evening may walk the streets.

" 21. Let none throw at glass windows, spoil or abuse the walls, seats, forms, desks, pulpits, or whatever is included in the College, by breaking or violent usage ; but let all things be preserved entire and clean.

" 22. The Censors are to be faithful in their duty, to admonish delinquents, and delate them. And if any of them act negligently or remissly, in concealing another's fault, he shall find, to his great dishonour, to have transferred the same to himself ; for he will be liable to that fine which the fault concealed deserved. And if any shall threaten, or do harm to, the Censor in doing his office, he shall pay sixpence, *toties quoties*.

" 23. Those who transgress any way shall be chastised accordingly.

" 24. Those who are arraigned guilty of rebellion, sedition, or tumults, and ringleaders of any such notable wickedness, are first of all obnoxious to the fines and punishments denounced by his Majesty's Privy Council, and thereafter are to be extruded and cast out of the College.

" 25. None may stand at the gate any time, or forfeit fourpence ; neither use unhandsomely, uncivilly, or toss those who enter or pass, or incur the fine of sixpence ; nor may any play or walk in view of the Professors, otherwise he will be fined arbitrarily.

" 26. Let none throw stones or snow-balls, or incur a fine at pleasure.

" 27. Let none in the classes or passages way-lay or lay-wait any who pass, or forfeit a sixpence.

" 28. The Principal and Masters being informed that the most destructive custom of playing at dice (owing its rise to infamous bankrupts) has lately crept into the College, and knowing what hazard and mischief this portends to studies, piety, and good manners, therefore they strictly discharge students to use cards, dice, raffling, or any such games of lottery, and enact, that whoever is guilty and convicted of these unlawful games, he shall pay half-a-crown the first time, then a crown, the third time a crown and a half, for the use of the Library ; and if, thereafter, the said person convicted and fined cannot be reduced nor reformed, he is to be extruded with disgrace, as one lost and incorrigible, and a corrupter of the youth.

" 29. None may enter taverns, ale-houses, or incur an arbitrary fine.

" 30. Those who neglect to go to church shall forfeit sixpence each time.

" 31. The Censors of each class are carefully to mark those that speak English, or who curse, swear, or talk smutty or obscene [language], or any way contravene the laws foresaid, that so they may be punished according to the offence given." [1]

The 113th class, under Mr. Law, being now in their fourth year, twenty-seven of them were graduated privately, and fifty-three publicly, on the 29th of April 1701.

The one hundred and thirteenth Class graduated.

In October the College, as usual, met, when Mr. Law entered upon the charge of the new Bejan class, amounting, at the matriculation, February 20, 1702, to ninety-two. Mr. Charles Erskine proceeded in the Semi class, having received forty-two supervenients. Mr. William Scott had the charge of the Bachelors, and Mr. Massie that of the Magistrands.

On the 24th of December 1701, the Council, with advice of the ministers, elected the Rev. Mr. George Meldrum, minister of the Tron Church, to be Professor of Divinity, in place of Mr. George Campbell deceased, but he was not installed till the 13th of October 1702. [2]

On the 26th of December 1701, Mr. Alexander Rule resigned the Professorship of Hebrew and other Oriental languages ; and the place was not supplied till the 6th of November 1702, when the Council elected Mr. John Goodall, with an annual salary of 500 marks.

---

[1] Register of the University of Edinburgh, pp. 16-18.
[2] See Wodrow's History, vol. i. p. 149.

King William died on the 8th of March 1702, in
the fifty-second year of his age, and was succeeded by
Queen Anne. He was one of the most considerable
benefactors of the College of Edinburgh, having, in
the year 1694, granted a fund of £300 per annum
out of the Bishops' rents, etc.[1]

On the 8th of May, report was made to the Town-
Council concerning the Theological Library, begun
and collected by the late Reverend George Campbell,
Professor of Divinity, and that all the books and
donations were found to be distinctly recorded in a
book.[2]

The 114th class, under the charge of Mr. Massie,
being now in the fourth year of their course, twelve
of them were graduated privately, and twenty-six
publicly, on the 28th of April.

In October 1702, at the usual meeting of the
College, Mr. Massie undertook the charge of the new
Bejan class, in number twenty-five at the matriculation, February 25, 1703. Mr. Law had the Semi
class, with seventy-eight supervenients ; Mr. Erskine
the Bachelors ; and Mr. Scott the Magistrands.

On the 4th of November, the Town-Council having
considered that the several funds and donations mortified to the College had been far short of the payment
of former salaries settled upon the Principal, Masters,
and Professors of the College, and that, to supply this
deficiency, considerable sums had been paid out of
the good Town's common-good yearly, the Council,

The one
hundred and
fourteenth
Class gra-
duated.

---

[1] See *supra*, p. 250.

[2] Town-Council Records. [The Theo-   the Students in the Divinity Hall, is
logical Library, chiefly for the use of   still kept up within the College.]

therefore, fixed and settled 1600 marks of yearly salary on the Principal in all time coming, to be paid quarterly by the College-Treasurer.[1]

The 115th class, under Mr. William Scott, being now in the fourth year of their course, the graduation, by permission of the Faculty, was authorized by the following act to be entirely private :— *The one hundred and fifteenth Class graduated. 1703.*

" The Faculty of Philosophy within the University of Edinburgh, taking into their consideration the reasons offered by Mr. Scott why his Magistrand class should be privately graduated, and being fully satisfied with the same, Do unanimously, according to their undoubted right, contained in the charter of erection, and their constant and uninterrupted custom in such cases, appoint the said class to be laureated privately upon the last Tuesday of April next, being the 27th day of the said month.—Signed by order, and in presence of the Faculty, by Robert Henderson, Clerk, January 20, 1703."

The Professors having, by this act, claimed to themselves the powers of an independent faculty, and virtually set aside the authority of the Town-Council over the management of the internal affairs of the College, this gave great offence to the Town-Council. The Lord Provost, therefore, proposed a visitation of the College. This visitation took place in the Library, on the 15th of February 1703.

Sederunt (on that day),—the Lord Provost, Hugh Cunningham, etc., with the Assessors, viz., Sir James Stewart, Lord Advocate, and Sir Gilbert Elliot, and

---

[1] Town-Council Records.

the following ministers, Mr. William Crighton, Mr. David Blair, Mr. Thomas Wilkie, Mr. John Moncrieff, Mr. James Webster, Mr. George Andrew, Mr. James Hart, and Mr. Robert Sandilands.

The Masters of the College being called for, there compeared Mr. George Meldrum, Mr. Andrew Massie, Mr. William Law, Mr. William Scott, Mr. Charles Erskine, Mr. Laurence Dundas, Mr. James Gregory, Mr. John Goodall, and Mr. John Cumming.

The Lord Provost ordered the laws given by the Town-Council of Edinburgh, 1628, to be read, and that paragraph of the laws anent the visitation of the College, was read accordingly. Thereafter the act of the Town-Council, 1663, anent the visitation of the College was read.

The Provost complained that he had seen an unwarrantable act of the Masters of the College, viz., the Professors of Philosophy, Humanity, Mathematics, and Church History, wherein they asserted themselves a Faculty empowered by a charter of erection, and appointed Mr. William Scott's Magistrand class to be privately graduated this year; and desired the pretended act to be read.

This the Lord Advocate advised to be deferred at that time, as, after conference with the Masters, he found them willing to pass from that act, and to take up and withdraw their protest anent the electing of a commissioner from the College to the General Assembly; and that they would apply to their patrons to know the time and place, way and manner, how the laureation should be made this year; and he said that he would wait on any committee of the Council, and make such overtures as might regulate such matters in time coming, to the honour of the Council as patrons, and advantage of the Masters, with their due dependence upon the Council.

Bailie Blackwood approved of the Lord Advocate's proposal, but thought the Council would not be satisfied unless the Masters not only passed from their pretended act, but owned that it wanted all manner of foundation. Dean of Guild Brown also approved of what the Lord Advocate proposed, but desired that the Masters should be interrogated if they themselves agreed to what had been proposed. Upon this the Lord Provost asked them all separately, and they all severally assented, and the Lord Advocate undertook to extend the matter in writing.

Then follows the Act of Visitation :—

" The Lord Provost, Bailies, and Council of Edinburgh, being convened in Council at the foresaid Visitation held within the College of Edinburgh, taking into their consideration the charter granted to the good town by King James the Sixth of happy memory, upon the 14th day of August 1582, empowering the good town to found schools and colleges within their precincts, in manner therein provided, with power to the Magistrates and Council thereof to build houses and schools for all manner of professors and sciences, as grammar, humanity, languages, theology, philosophy, medicine, laws, or for whatever other liberal science ; and to elect, input, and output masters, as they shall think fit, inhibiting all other schools and professions within the said burgh ; as the said charter more fully bears : And that, conform thereto, and ever since the erecting of the said College, the Magistrates and Council have had and exercised the only and full government of the said College, by electing, inputting, and outputting masters and professors, prescribing and appointing laws, rules and statutes, for direction of the said masters and professors and their scholars ; and generally for ordering and regulating all things belonging to the discipline and police of the said College, and due administration thereof ; as also in choosing a commissioner to the Assemblies of this Kirk in behalf of the said College, as the records of the good town seen, revised, and considered, do particularly and fully testify : Notwithstanding whereof, the Masters of the said College, taking upon them of late to meet by themselves as an independent Faculty of the said College, did on the 20th of January last make the following act—[The act is given before, p. 279] : As also that some of the said Masters did lately claim a power to themselves, separately from the Magistrates and Town-Council, to elect a commissioner to the ensuing General Assembly, and in the face of the Town-Council protested for the same : Therefore, the said Lord Provost, Bailies, and Council being met upon the foresaid occasion, in the said Visitation with the Ministers of Edinburgh thereunto called, Did declare their just dissatisfaction with the foresaid act and proceedings of the said Masters, as being unwarrantable and unprecedented.   But it having been proposed, for the more peaceable and more happy composure of those differences, that the said Masters should, in presence of the Magistrates and Town-Council, with the said Ministers convened in manner foresaid, pass from their said act, as unwarrantable, and submit themselves entirely to the Magistrates and Town-Council, to order the foresaid laureation as to time, place, and manner, as the Council should think fit ; as also to take up, and withdraw their said protest taken anent the electing a commissioner for the Assembly : And that a committee of the Town-Council might be appointed for revising the laws of the College prescribed to them by the Town-Council, and for making such other laws, after our hearing of the said Masters, as may be thought proper to prevent the like mistakes in time coming, for the weal and benefit of the College : And the said Masters, to wit, the Professors of Philosophy, Humanity, Mathematics, and Church History, being all present, and particularly interrogated, if they agreed to the said proposals, and they having each of them for himself, and all of them together, declared their assent, the said Magistrates and Town-Council, with advice of the said Ministers, declared their acceptance of the foresaid proposal and agreement, and that they would appoint a committee with their first convenience for the ends above expressed.   And they ordained this act to be drawn up, and extended upon the whole premisses, and recorded in the books of Council, relating to the College, *ad futuram rei memoriam.—Sic subscribitur,*

"HUGH CUNNINGHAM, *Provost.*"[1]

On the 5th of March, the Town-Council appointed Mr. Scott's class to be publicly graduated, the consideration of the time, place, and manner being deferred until the next Council day. On the 12th of the same month they appointed the public laureation to be kept in the common hall of the College upon the first Tuesday of May next. But, *pro hac vice*, they allowed a private graduation, on the petition of Mr. Scott, " showing, that it having pleased the Council some time ago, by their act, to appoint the Magistrand class to be publicly graduated upon the 4th day of May instant, in obedience thereto the petitioner duly intimated the same to his scholars present, but most of them being gone before the said act and intimation thereof, so through the want of intelligence, and other causes, many of the scholars were not returned from the country upon the said 4th instant, and other insuperable difficulties falling in the way of a public graduation in this juncture, the same could not be performed, craving, therefore, the Council to allow the said class to be graduated privately, *pro hac vice.*"[2]

On the same day the Council passed an act ordering diplomas or testificates to the graduates, to have the town's seal appended to them in a white iron box. The Primar with three or four of the Regents were to sign the diploma, and the Librarian was not to exact above four pounds Scots, and was to be easy to poor

[1] Town-Council Records.
[2] [See Catalogue of the Graduates, pp. 172-174.]

scholars. In the formula used at the graduation, honourable mention was ordered to be made of the Town-Council, the patrons.[1]

The office of Principal of the College having become vacant by the death of Dr. Gilbert Rule, it was offered to Mr. William Carstairs, a distinguished Presbyterian clergyman, who had been the confidential friend of King William; and he was prevailed with by his friends to accept it.[2] He was elected by the Council May 12, 1703 ; and, on the 19th, he appeared in Council, and took the oath of allegiance to Queen Anne, and subscribed the same with the assurance. His inauguration was appointed to take place on the 3d of June ; and instructions were ordered to be delivered to him by the Lord Provost as to " the office of the Principal of the College," as laid down in " The Discipline of the College of Edinburgh," appointed and ordained December 3, 1628.

On the 3d of September, the Lord Provost produced before the Town-Council an abbreviate of the acts anent the College ; which being read, together with an Act of Parliament ratifying the rights of the College, they ordained the said abbreviate to be recorded.[3]

On the 8th of September, Bailie Hugh Linn produced at the Council-table a Catalogue of the College Library, which was delivered by the Council to the clerks, to be kept by them for their use.

On the 22d of October, by an act of the Town-

---

[1] Town-Council Records.

[2] See his Life, by Rev. Dr. Joseph M'Cormick, prefixed to Carstairs's State Papers, etc. Edinb. 1774, 4to.

[3] [This abbreviate is printed in Bower's History of the University of Edinburgh, vol. ii. pp. 395-405.]

Council, the Regents' salaries were stopped till they had extracted or taken out their acts of admission (which they had never done), and produced them to the Council.

On the same day an act was passed, requiring the College, all Professors of Theology, Philosophy, Languages, and Humanity, and other masters and members thereof whatsoever, to conform themselves to and obey the laws and regulations, according to the constitution and statutes thereof.

In October 1703, Mr. Scott entered upon the charge of the new Bejan class, in number eighty, as matriculated, February 23, 1704. Mr. Robert Stewart, son of Sir Thomas Stewart of Coltness, who was, with the advice of the ministers, elected on the 22d of October 1703, in consequence of the resignation of Mr. Massie, took the charge of the Semis; Mr. Law had that of the Bachelors; and Mr. Erskine that of the Magistrands.

On the 10th of November, Mr. John Goodall, Professor of Hebrew, had his salary augmented 200 marks.

On the 24th of the same month, the Town-clerks were ordered by the Town-Council to keep a separate register for bursars, and particularly to record the Queen's bursars.[1]

The 116th class, under the charge of Mr. Charles Erskine, being in the fourth year of their course, fourteen of them graduated privately, and twenty-five publicly, May 12, 1704.

1704.
The one hundred and sixteenth Class graduated.

On the 17th of May this year, the Town-Council

---

[1] Town-Council Records.

having taken into consideration that the good order
and discipline of the College were much decayed, and
that the power and authority of the Regents were not
duly regarded by many of the scholars, whence disorders were committed which exceedingly reflected upon
the government of the College—the Council, therefore,
appointed the Magistrates to meet with the Ministers
and the Principal, who was now in the beginning of
his office, to consult and advise about proper methods
for restoring order and discipline.

On the 16th of June, the Town-Council passed the
following act anent the College records :—

" The Lord Provost reported that he was informed that the book
containing the Laws made by the Town-Council of Edinburgh, for
governing both masters and scholars in the College, wanted a date,
and the act of Council prefixed to the said laws, in the records of
the Town-Council, warranting the recording of the said laws in that
book ; and that it had several leaves battered together, with many
other notable blemishes, unworthy of a record of so ancient a
College : Therefore called the Bibliothecar to produce the said book,
that the Magistrates, Ministers, and Town-Council might be satisfied
of the truth thereof ; and, accordingly, the said book was produced
and inspected in presence of the Lord Provost, Magistrates, Ministers,
Town-Council, and whole Masters of the College ; and to the
Council and Ministers' great surprise, the following faults were
found in the said book :—

" 1. It is observed that the book begins with the laws of the College,
yet without any date or act of Council of their patrons, authorizing
the said laws, as is prefixed to the original copy in the town's records.

" 2. In the 13th, 19th, and 25th pages, the leaves are battered
together ; which renders the pretended record suspect, and of no
authority.

" 3. In the 18th page, it is observed that the word *faculty* is
then first assumed, and without warrant, or any former practice, insert
in October 1686 : And although the College had been now 100

years standing before the said time, no record bears the word 'faculty :' And, in the said meeting in October 1686, there is no person named at the pretended faculty, but the Reverend Primar, Doctor Monro, and that only interlined.

"4. In the said 18th page, there is an interval from October 1686 to January 1690 years, of any pretended faculty, and even at that time, the haill names of professors present are only interlined.

"5. The said page, January 1691 years, the Reverend and worthy Doctor Rule is said to have a prelection as Primar, without mentioning any other present, and he is insert only R. Doctor Rule, and that also interlined.

"6. The word 'faculty' is again mentioned in p. 18, in the year 1691, and several times thereafter, so that there has been about five years betwixt the first and second times mentioning the word 'faculty,' which they had presumptuously assumed to themselves.

"7. In p. 19, the worthy and famous Mr. George Campbell is so little noticed at his first appearance in the said book, that he is only designed R. Mr. Campbell, Professor, giving no account how he came to that office.

"8. In p. 27, it is observed, from this pretended record, that there has been no meeting of the Professors from July 1697 to June 1699 ; and from October 1699 there have been no sederunts until January 1703, at which time the Professors of Philosophy, Mathematics, and Humanity, also assumed to themselves the name of a Faculty of Philosophy, and by an act declared their undoubted right, and their constant uninterrupted custom of appointing Laureations; which act was solemnly condemned as unwarrantable and unprecedented, by a visitation of the College, as recorded the 15th day of February 1703 years. And there are a great many other gross informalities in the said book, unbecoming any society.

"And it being overtured, that the Lord Provost might name a committee, to the effect the said book might be fairly transumed, and more regularly written, it was unanimously consented to by the Magistrates and Town-Council, and also the advice of the said reverend Ministers, that the Lord Provost, at the Council-table, should name a committee to the effect foresaid. To which the Reverend Principal, in name of Mr. William Law, Mr. William Scott, and Mr. Robert Stewart, Professors of Philosophy, and Mr. Laurence Dundas, Professor of Humanity, craved liberty to represent, that in respect the said book had been long in their possession, as one of the College records, and for their exoneration, at the hands of the Commission for Visitation of Schools and Colleges, to whom the said book was once produced : Therefore he himself in their name, and with all submission to the Magistrates and Town-Council, their honourable patrons, desired the clerk, for their vindication, might mark, it was not with their will the book was delivered up. To which it was replied, that the true reason why the overture was agreed to [was], that the faults and blemishes foresaid, with many others not named, might be duly regulated in manner as is above. And it was also craved, that the clerk might mark this answer, lest the said book hereafter might be either represented or pretended to have been a more formal record than truly it is now found to be."

On the same day a memoir being presented to the Council, containing several complaints against the masters and students of the College, the same was read, and ordained to be recorded, and a copy to be delivered to the Principal, whereof the tenor follows:—

" 1. That neither the Professors of Philosophy nor the students keep the hours and diets appointed by the statutes, neither on the week nor Sabbath days, which is the occasion of great disorder.

" 2. That the speaking of English, and not Latin, is become customary ; and cursing and swearing are too ordinary without any due punishment.

" 3. That the fabric of the College is greatly damnified by students playing at rackets and hand-balls, and many other abuses committed at the public meetings and solemnities of the College.

" 4. The neighbourhood of the College is daily molested by the students, and the grammar-school exceedingly disturbed, so that it is given as one of the chief [reasons] of the great decay thereof.

" 5. That the best chambers in the College, which were usually possessed by children of noblemen, and other persons of quality, and were mortified for students allenarly, and paid a considerable rent to the College, are now otherwise inhabited.

" 6. That the College gates are so frequently kept open, in the very time and hours of meeting in the classes, and the duty and office of Hebdomadar is much neglected; which is the cause of many disorders.

" 7. That a great many books are lent out, and kept out of the Library, contrary to the laws thereof, which ought to be subscribed by all the Professors in the College.

" 8. That the rules anent bursars be renewed, and that they be examined anent the discipline and order of the College, and what progress they make in the College."

Thereafter there was presented to the Council a long report anent the Library ; which being read, the Council declared that they would, at their next sederunt, in the ordinary Council-house, appoint a committee to consider the complaints in the said memoir, together with the book containing the laws made by the Town-Council of Edinburgh for governing both masters and scholars belonging to the College, in order to prepare a report of the whole matter, to be laid before the Council.

On the 21st of June, a committee of the Council, with Mr. Carstairs, Principal, and Mr. George Meldrum, Professor of Divinity, was appointed to consider the above complaints, together with the report anent the Library, and the book containing the laws of the College, and to report.

On the 28th of June, 2000 marks were allowed the Principal, so long as he has no charge in the city.

On the 5th of September 1704, the Council continned the laws of the College, as they were approved of by the Council in the year 1601, to be observed in the meantime, and ordained the Bibliothecar to record the laws in the large book appointed for that end. Having considered the additional laws given in by the Masters of the College,[1] the Council again approved thereof, and ordained the Bibliothecar to record the same among the laws of the College. They appointed the Masters to subscribe the laws of the Library, as they had been subscribed from the year 1636 to the year 1650, when the practice of subscription was interrupted till the year 1662. They ordered the College treasurer to pay Mr. Robert Henderson, Bibliothecar, five pounds sterling, on his recording the laws; and they delayed the consideration of the answers given in by the Professors of Philosophy to the grievances and complaints against the College.

In October, Mr. Erskine began the Bejan class, and thirty-six matriculated in March 1705. Mr. Scott, with thirty supervenients, went forward with the Semi class; Mr. Robert Stewart with the Bachelors; and Mr. William Law with the Magistrands.

On the 29th of November, the Town-Council appointed the book belonging to the College of Edin-

---

[1] [See these laws at p. 274.]

burgh, entitled, "Register of the University of Edinburgh," to be put up in the charter-house, and ordained their clerk to write at the end of it, that the same was condemned, as informal, and many ways vitiated, in terms of the act of Council, June 16th, bypast. At the same meeting, the Bibliothecar was ordered to pursue all who had borrowed books out of the Library, and had not returned them ; and the Professors were certified that if they did not return what books they had borrowed, the Council would order their salaries to be stopped till they did so.[1]

The 117th class, under the charge of Mr. William Law, being in the fourth year of their course, ten of them received the usual degree privately, and on the 9th of April thirty-five of them publicly ; on which occasion the printing of Theses, which seems to have been omitted for a considerable number of years, was revived.[2] A copy of what was printed on this occasion is preserved in the College collection, dedicated to Sir Patrick Johnston, Knight, Lord Provost, and to the rest of the Town-Council. By a list of students prefixed, it appears that the Magistrand class on this occasion consisted of 110.

1705. The one hundred and seventeenth Class graduated.

On the 29th of August, Robert Elliot, surgeon, was allowed by the Town-Council fifteen pounds sterling yearly for teaching Anatomy.

" EDINBURGH, 29*th August* 1705.

" The which day, anent the petition given in by Robert Elliot, chirurgeon-apothecary, burgess of Edinburgh, showing that where it being the practice of the best regulated cities to give encouragement

[1] Town-Council Records.
[2] [The Theses, however, for the year 1704, were printed.]

to the professing and teaching of liberal arts and sciences for the education of youth, to the great benefit and advantage of the place ; and the petitioner, by an act of the incorporation of the chirurgeon-apothecaries of this city, [was] unanimously elected their public dis-sector of anatomy, the petitioner was of intention to make a public profession and teaching thereof for instructing of youth, to serve her Majesty's lieges both at home and abroad, in her armies and fleets, which he hoped, by the blessing of God, would be a means in saving much money to the nation, expended in teaching anatomy in foreign places, beside the preventing of many dangers and inconveniences to which youth were exposed in their travels to other countries ; and the petitioner finding this undertaking will prove expensive, and cannot be done without suitable encouragement, has therefore laid the matter before the Council, who have been always ready to give encouragement to such undertakings ; and therefore craved the Council to consider the premises, and to remit to a committee of their number to hear and receive what proposals the petitioner had to make for setting up of the said profession, and to report, as the petition bears : Which being considered by the Council, they remitted the consideration of the same to a committee of their own number, who accordingly reported that they, having considered the above petition, were of opinion that the profession of anatomy was very necessary and useful to this nation, and might be very helpful to the youth that follow that art, and might prevent much needless expense spent by them abroad : And in regard the petitioner was, by the incorporation of the chirurgeons, unanimously chosen for that effect, therefore the committee were of opinion that the petitioner should have an yearly allowance of what sum the Council should think fit, towards the encouragement and defraying his charges and expenses thereanent, with this express provision and condition, that the peti-tioner take exact notice and inspection of the order and condition of the rarities of the College ; and that an exact inventory be made of the same, and given in to the Council ; and also to keep the said rarities in good order and condition, during the said allowance, as the report under the hands of the committee bears : Which being considered by the Council, they, with the extraordinary deacons, approved thereof ; and for the petitioner's encouragement to go on in the said profession, they allow the petitioner fifteen pounds ster-ling of yearly salary . . . during the Council's pleasure."[1] . . .

[1] Town-Council Records.

In October, Mr. Law began the new Bejan class, and he matriculated sixty-six. Mr. Erskine proceeded in the Semi class, having eighteen supervenients ; Mr. Scott with the Bachelors ; and Mr. Robert Stewart with the Magistrands.

On the 14th of May this year, Mr. David Cockburn, A.M., received the degree of M.D., the first medical degree on record conferred by the College of Edinburgh. The ceremony was performed by Principal Carstairs, attended by Mr. William Law, Mr. William Scott, Mr. Charles Erskine, and Mr. Robert Stewart, Professors of Philosophy, Mr. Laurence Dundas, Professor of Humanity, and Mr. John Goodall, Professor of Hebrew, the candidate having subscribed a very particular form of oath, adapted to the nature of the degree. It was an abridged form of Hippocrates's oath.[1]

The 118th class, under the charge of Mr. Robert Stewart, being now in their fourth year, twenty of them were graduated privately, at different times, on and after the 28th of February 1706.

1706.
The one hundred and eighteenth Class graduated.

On the 11th of September, Mr. Alexander Rule, formerly Professor of Hebrew, son of the late Dr. Rule, Principal, obtained a pension of fifty marks quarterly, in consequence of his having resigned, and in consideration of his circumstances.[2]

In October 1706, Mr. Robert Stewart having entered on the charge of the new Bejan class, he matriculated only eighteen on the 26th of February 1707.

---

[1] *Vid.* Hippocrat. Opera, edit. Lugd. Bat. 1665. Gr. Lat. vol. i. p. 42.
[2] Town-Council Records.

Mr. Law went on with the Semi class, having forty-six supervenients ; Mr. Erskine had the Bachelors ; and Mr. Scott the Magistrands.

The 119th class, under the tuition of Mr. William Scott, being now in the fourth year of their course, eight of them were graduated privately, at different times, and twenty publicly, on the 7th of April 1707.

By a deed of Queen Anne, dated February 11, 1707,[1] a Professorship of Public Law, and of the Law of Nature and Nations, was instituted in favour of Mr. Charles Erskine, one of the Regents or Professors of Philosophy. The fund appointed for a salary to this new Professor was £150 per annum, obtained by sinking fifteen of King William's twenty Divinity Bursaries ; a scandalous job, which ought not to have been consented to by her Majesty's ministers, and which was resisted by the patrons and the Principal and Professors of the University. In the deed itself, the pretext for sinking the bursaries is stated to have been the ceasing of the original reason for founding them ; which is alleged to have been to encourage young men to enter upon the study of Theology, that the great number of vacancies in the churches at that time might be supplied with learned and able pastors ; an object which, it is pretended, had been obtained by the time of the institution of this Professorship ; and that therefore this last institution was likely to prove more beneficial to the public. The argument in both cases has been by the event proved equally fallacious, for the institution has hitherto been of

---

[1] Privy Seal English Records, in the Register Office, vol. vi. folio 180.

almost no advantage to the public ; and a most useful society, lately established for the benefits of the sons of the clergy, has proved how advantageous the bursaries still would have been if they had existed.

On the 21st of May 1707, Bailie John Cleghorn produced to the Town-Council an extract from the treasurer's books of his protest taken at Holyrood-house, on that day, in conjunction with Bailie William Baird, Treasurer, and Mr. George Meldrum, Professor of Divinity, for his interest, for themselves, and in name of the Magistrates, in presence of the Lord High Commissioner, James Duke of Queensberry, and Lords Commissioners of her Majesty's Treasury and Exche-quer : That the passing of a signature in favour of Mr. Charles Erskine, one of the Regents of the Col-lege, as Professor of Law, for £150 sterling of yearly salary, as a part of the fund of £200 sterling, morti-fied by the late King William, out of the late Bishops' rents, for maintenance of twenty bursars in the said College, with all that has followed, or may follow there-upon, should not in the least prejudge a former gift granted by the late King William, perpetually mor-tifying the said sum of £200 sterling, for the mainten-ance of the said twenty bursars ; which protestation the Lord High Commissioner, and Lords of her Majesty's Treasury and Exchequer, admitted. Whereupon they took instruments in the hands of Sir James Mackenzie, Clerk of her Majesty's Treasury and Exchequer.[1]

Mr. Erskine was no doubt a man of ability ; but instead of doing the duty of his new office, and for

---

[1] Town-Council Records.

which he had resigned his Regency of Philosophy, he took this opportunity to make the tour of Europe ; and on his return, having devoted himself to the practice of the law, he rose to be her Majesty's Advocate, and afterwards Lord Justice-Clerk. He held the Professorship till he became Lord Advocate in the year 1734, and then resigned it. Soon after the erection of this office, Mr. Erskine had interest to obtain another grant from her Majesty Queen Anne, allocating the payment of the salary upon the rents of the See of Edinburgh, by which means it became payable in grain, and therefore often amounts to an annual sum far beyond that of the original intention of £150, and is by much the most lucrative salary in the University of Edinburgh.

When Mr. Erskine, on the 17th of October 1707, resigned his Professorship of Philosophy, Mr. Colin Drummond, son of the late Adam Drummond of Megginsh, was elected in his place, but not by comparative trial, as we learn from the Town-Council Records.

On the petition of Mr. Drummond, that he might be chosen to succeed to this charge, the Town-Council recommended to the Principal and Masters, with some of the ministers, to take trial of his qualifications, and to report. And, on the 24th of October, the Town-Council, considering their undoubted power, with the advice of the ministers of the city, to appoint Professors and Masters, to input and output the same within the College of Edinburgh, did, upon report of the qualifications of the above Colin Drummond, appoint him Regent in place of Mr. Erskine, with all emoluments, fees, and profits. He compeared and accepted, made oath *de fideli administratione;* promised to observe and obey all the laws and constitutions of the College already made, or to be made, and to submit to the Magistrates and Council ; and took the oath of allegiance, and subscribed it, with the assurance, to her Majesty Queen Anne.[1]

In October, at the meeting of the College, Mr. Scott entered upon the charge of the new Bejan class, of which the number at matriculation amounted to fifty. Mr. Stewart with seventeen supervenients proceeded in the Semi class ; Mr. Law in the Bachelor ; and Mr. Colin Drummond, who had succeeded Mr. Erskine, took the charge of the Magistrand class.

On the 7th of November 1707, Mr. Charles Erskine "appeared in Council, and produced a gift under the Privy-seal making and constituting him her Majesty's Professor of Public Law, Law of Nature and Nations, in the College of Edinburgh, and therefore craved the Council would call the Principal and Masters of the College and install him in the said office, and administer to him the oath of allegiance, to be subscribed by him with the assurance, and also the oath *de fideli,* and to use the haill other order for qualifying him according to law."

The Lord Provost, in name of the Council, refused, as they had already protested in Exchequer against the passing of the said gift, because it contained a disposition to the sum of £150 sterling, payable yearly to him out of the sum of £200 sterling, mortified by the

---

[1] Town-Council Records.

late King William's letters to the College of Edinburgh for the maintenance of twenty bursars of theology.

Mr. Erskine "protested, that he might possess and enjoy the said profession and yearly salary with all other profits, emoluments, and dignity competent thereto, sicklike as if he had been actually qualified thereto, and admitted in manner forsaid, and for all cost, skaith, damage, and expenses he may happen to sustain by and through the Magistrates and Town-Council their refusing to qualify and admit him, as said is ; and thereupon asked and took instruments in the hands of the Town-Clerk ; and further protested that this his protest be recorded in the Town-Council's books, for the better verification of the premises."[1]

1708.
The one
hundred and
twentieth
Class gra-
duated.
The 120th class, under the tuition of Mr. Colin Drummond, being in the fourth year of their course, seventeen of them were graduated at different times.

In June this year, at the rising of the College, the Senatus Academicus stood as follows :—

Mr. William Carstairs, Principal.

Mr. George Meldrum, Professor of Divinity.

Mr. John Cumming, Regius Professor of Divinity and Ecclesiastical History.

Mr. William Law,
Mr. William Scott,   } Regents or Professors of
Mr. Robert Stewart,   }   Philosophy.
Mr. Colin Drummond,

Mr. Laurence Dundas, Professor of Humanity.

Mr. James Gregory, Professor of Mathematics.

Mr. John Goodall, Professor of Oriental Languages.

Mr. Charles Erskine, Regius Professor of Public Law, and Law of Nature and Nations.

[1] Town-Council Records.

This was the year in which the new regulations for the teaching of Greek and Philosophy took place ; which were ratified by an act of the Town-Council, patrons of the University, of date the 16th of June 1708. It was enacted for the future,—

" 1. That all the parts of Philosophy should be taught in two years, as they are in the most famous Universities abroad.

" 2. That, as a consequence of this article, there be but two Philosophy classes in the College, to be taught by two of the four present Professors of Philosophy.

" 3. That in the first of these classes the students be taught Logic and Metaphysics ; and in the last a compend of Ethics and Natural Philosophy.

" 4. Because there are many useful things belonging to the Pneumatics and Moral Philosophy which the two Professors, in the present method of teaching classes, cannot overtake, therefore it is proposed that one of the two remaining Professors shall be appointed to teach these two parts of Philosophy more fully, at such times as the students are not obliged to be in their classes. And because he has not the charge of a class, he may have public lessons of Philosophy in the common hall, where all the students may be present at such times as shall be most convenient.

" 5. That there shall be a fixed Professor of Greek, but so that neither he nor his successors shall, upon any pretence whatsoever, endeavour to hinder the admission of students into the Philosophy classes in the usual manner, although they have not been taught Greek by him.

" 6. And in regard the present Professors have

given a proof of their qualifications in all the parts both of Philosophy and Greek, therefore when any of these four Professors' places becomes vacant, the remaining Professors of these now in places, allenarly, shall have the offer of the vacancy according to their standing; and when one chooses it the rest shall, in the like manner, be allowed to succeed him."[1]

In consequence of these regulations the four Regents, without waiting for a vacancy, were prevailed with to make the following arrangement:—Mr. William Law, at that time oldest Professor in the University, and who was esteemed peculiarly qualified to teach Moral Philosophy, agreed to restrict and limit himself to that department; Mr. William Scott confined himself to the Greek; Mr. Robert Stewart to the Natural Philosophy; and Mr. Colin Drummond to the Logic.

But as it was understood that the Professor of Moral Philosophy was to give only public lectures, and consequently to receive no honoraries from his students, the patrons thought proper that he should have £50 of additional salary. This was therefore expressed in his new commission. But as, according to the old plan of teaching, Mr. Law at this time had the charge of a class who had just completed the third year of their course, he was authorized, likewise, in his new commission, to continue his charge through the fourth or Magistrand year, previous to the commencement of the new mode of teaching; and 500 marks additional were ordered to be paid him yearly from October 1709, till the sum of £50 should be provided.

A new commission was likewise granted to Mr.

[1] Register of the University of Edinburgh, p. 60; Town-Council Records.

William Scott to be Professor of Greek, in terms of the above regulations; his teaching of that language to commence in October 1709.

On the 24th of June, at a meeting of the Town-Council in the College high common-hall, present also the Professors Law, Scott, Stewart, Drummond, Dundas, and Goodall; Bailie Archibald Cockburn and the College Committee were appointed to inquire what books were lent out of the Library or were wanting, and to report to the Council betwixt that date and the 10th of July next. Meanwhile the Bibliothecar was appointed to furnish the committee with the receipts of the books lent, and to mark what books might probably be recovered, and what not. The Council for the future prohibited the Library-Keeper to lend books to any but the Professors, and such students as produced an order for the particular books they were to borrow under their own Professor's hands, to be returned within three months. The Professors were recommended not to borrow any books out of the Library, but for their own use.

The Library-Keeper was also ordained from time to time to give notice to the College treasurer against the masters who were transgressors hereof, that the payment of their salaries might be stopped accordingly. An exact alphabetical catalogue was wanted, which the Library-Keeper was ordered to prepare some years ago. The Council now peremptorily enjoined him to prepare the same betwixt that date and the 1st of January 1710, under pain of deprivation. No manuscript, under any pretence whatsoever, was to be lent.

The Council also enacted that no bursar should be admitted till first tried by the Professors. Humanity bursars were to be tried by the Professor of Greek, and bursars of Greek were to be tried by the Professor of Humanity. And as now, according to the new method of teaching, there were only two Philosophy classes, the bursars were to be obliged, with respect to the two first years, to spend one in the Humanity class, and the other in the Greek, and none was to have a bursary who had not stayed a year in each of these classes, and none was to enjoy his bursary longer than he was a student in one of the classes of the College : And in regard Hector Foord's mortification required of the bursars on it five years' attendance, and that they should enter the Humanity class, they were to be obliged to study two years in one of the two lower classes. The Council further ordained that all bursars, after they had begun their Philosophy studies, should attend the Professor of Hebrew's lessons ; also bursars of Divinity ; and that none should be admitted bursars of Divinity until they procured the Professor of Hebrew's certificate that they attended his lessons.[1]

On the 30th of July, the Council considering that, agreeably to an act dated September 11, 1706, the sum of fifty marks Scots quarterly, allowed to Mr. Alexander Rule, late Professor of Hebrew, was payable for his use to Bailie Archibald Rule, who is now in a dying condition, appointed this sum, in time coming, during the Council's pleasure, to be paid to

1 Town-Council Records.

David Kennedy, writer in Edinburgh, for the said Mr. Alexander's use.[1]

In October 1708, the College having met, Mr. Drummond had the charge of the new Bejan class for this course on the old plan; Mr. William Scott the Semi class; Mr. Robert Stewart the Bachelor; and Mr. Law the Magistrand.

About this time the salaries of many of the Professors being still extremely small, amounting to no more than 400 marks each, *i.e.*, £22, 4s. 5⅓d., yearly, paid by the town to four of the number, and £50 to the Professor of Moral Philosophy, who had no other emolument; Principal Carstairs, from a disinterested regard to the society of which he was the head, used his interest with Queen Anne, and obtained from her Majesty a donation of £250 sterling yearly, to make additional salaries to those Professors who were worst provided; and the distribution of this fund being committed to himself, he divided it into seven equal parts, to make an addition of £30 annually. These were the Professors of Humanity, Greek, Logic, Natural Philosophy, and Moral Philosophy, Mathematics, and Hebrew; Mr. Gregory having had from his first admission till that time £50 of salary from the town, and the Professor of Hebrew the same sum. This fund, which is commonly called Queen Anne's Bounty, was, during the remainder of her reign, paid out of the Post Office, but has been ever since put upon the Civil List.[2]

---

[1] Town-Council Records.   [2] Mr. Mackie's Account.

CHAPTER VI.

1709. ON the 10th of June, the Town-Council subscribed, in name of the town, the sum of fifty pounds sterling for procuring instruments and machines necessary for confirming and illustrating by experiments the truths advanced in the Mathematics and Natural Philosophy within the University, as proposed by the Principal and Professors.[1]

On the 17th of August, Mr. William Hamilton, minister of Cramond, was elected Professor of Divinity, in place of Mr. George Meldrum. As it was ordained by the Town-Council that he should have no ministerial charge, " the said office, when in conjunction with the ministerial charge, being too great a burden for one person," the Council, for his greater encouragement, fixed upon him 2000 marks Scots of yearly salary, being 400 marks more than former Professors enjoyed, with the house in the College formerly possessed by Mr. Meldrum.[2]

The one hundred and twenty-first Class graduated. The 121st class having, now in their fourth year, under the charge of Mr. Law, forty-three, including four Englishmen, received the degree of A.M. at dif-

---

[1] Town Council Records.   [2] *Ibid.*

ferent times ; of whom Mr. Edmund Calamy, minister of the gospel at London, after subscribing the Westminster Confession of Faith, received also the degree of D.D. Six more were made Masters of Arts on the 20th of October this year. The taking the degree of A.M. for the future became much more irregular.

On the 28th of October, Mr. William Hamilton, who had been chosen Professor of Divinity, without any other charge, accepted of the said office in presence of the Town-Council, took the oath *de fideli administratione*, the oath of allegiance to her Majesty Queen Anne, and subscribed the same with the assurance, promising at the same time to subject himself in all things to the regulation of the patrons of the College. The Principal reported that the said Professor had likewise qualified himself by subscribing the Confession of Faith before the Presbytery of Edinburgh.[1]

On the same day, after reading the laws and constitutions of the College, the Lord Provost, Rector of the said College, interrogated the Principal if they were observed. The Principal answered, that they were observed in so far as it was thought proper for the greater convenience and better improvement of learning.[2]

The Librarian was asked about the Alphabetical Catalogue. He said that he had made considerable progress in it, and would complete it with all possible diligence. The Provost again recommended to him that it might be finished against the time prescribed

---

[1] Town-Council Records. [2] *Ibid.*

in the act of the 24th of June 1708, and that under the penalties contained therein.[1]

1709-1710. In October 1709, the College having met, the teaching was conducted upon the new plan, and the classes matriculated in the following order :—

1. The Humanity class was matriculated for the first time, under Professor Laurence Dundas, in number seventy, March 1, 1710.

2. The Bejan or Greek class, under Professor William Scott, in number fifty-four, March 1, 1710.

3. The Semi or Logic class, under Professor Colin Drummond, in number forty-one.

4. The Magistrand or Natural Philosophy class, under Professor Robert Stewart, in number forty-six.

The Moral Philosophy class was not matriculated, being a gratis class.

The one hundred and twenty-second Class graduated. This year, thirty-two students took the degree of A.M. privately, and at different times.

In the year 1710, the Senatus Academicus stood as follows :—

Mr. William Carstairs, Principal.

Mr. William Hamilton, Professor of Divinity.

Mr. John Cumming, Regius Professor of Divinity and Ecclesiastical History.

Mr. Laurence Dundas, Professor of Humanity.

Mr. William Scott, Professor of Greek.

Mr. Colin Drummond, Professor of Logic.

Mr. Robert Stewart, Professor of Natural Philosophy.

Mr. William Law, Professor of Moral Philosophy.

Mr. James Gregory, Professor of Mathematics.

Mr. John Goodall, Professor of Oriental Languages.

Mr. Charles Erskine, Regius Professor of Public Law and the Law of Nature and Nations.

[1] Town-Council Records.

In October the College, as usual, assembled, and at the matriculation of the classes the number were as follows :—

1. The Humanity class, Mr. Laurence Dundas, Professor, in number sixty-five, February 20, 1711.

2. The Greek class, Mr. William Scott, Professor, in number fifty-two, February 21, 1711.

3. The Logic class, Mr. Colin Drummond, Professor, in number fifty-six, February 21, 1711.

4. The Natural Philosophy class, Mr. Robert Stewart, Professor, in number fifty.

The students in each of these classes are to be considered as different, and therefore the number of students of Humanity, Greek, and Philosophy, was in all 223 this year.

The hours of assembling these classes, if we may judge from what was the custom long after, were eight in the morning and eleven in the forenoon, and three times in the week, one o'clock afternoon. The Professors of Humanity and Greek had each of them a separate hour for his private class, for carrying on such students as chose to attend them in the knowledge of Latin and Greek. The hour for the former is supposed to have been nine in the morning, and that for the latter ten. The Professors of Mathematics, and of Moral Philosophy, gave their instructions to whatever students from the other classes chose to attend them ; the former receiving fees, the latter none. But as some students might probably attend the Mathematics, who were at no other class in the College, and about forty might attend the stated classes

who did not matriculate, the number of students, ex-
elusive of students of Divinity (of whose number there
is, at this time, no record), attending the College this
year might be about 270 or 280 ; a number by no
means equal to what had been known on many former
years. Indeed, about the time of the Union of the
Kingdoms, and for many years after, the College does
not seem to have been in so flourishing a condition as
it was in formerly, and now is ; the reason of which
was the removal of the Scottish Parliament, and of the
immediate patronage of the people in power, etc.

On the 18th of October 1710, the Town-Council,
patrons of the University, having taken into consideration the great utility of a public teacher of the Civil
Law in their College, and that, for want of such, young
gentlemen disposed to that study were obliged to go
abroad to foreign Universities, therefore they resolved
to elect Mr. James Craig, Advocate, of whose qualifications for the office they were fully assured, Professor
of the Civil Law in the College of Edinburgh, but
without a salary in the meantime, till a fund should
in some way be provided for that purpose; and Mr.
Craig accepted of the office on this condition.

On the 28th of December, same year, the Rev. Mr.
Jonathan Harley received the degree of M.D., having
been examined and recommended as duly qualified by
Dr. Matthew St. Clair, President, Dr. David Mitchell,
Dr. David Dickson, and Dr. James Forrest, Fellows of
the Royal College of Physicians, Edinburgh. He was
the second doctor of physic created by the University
of Edinburgh.

In 1711, the degree A.M. was conferred on three privately, and on eleven publicly. On the 6th of April, Benjamin Avery, A.M., an Englishman, had the degree of LL.D. publicly conferred on him.

On the 2d of January 1712, Mr. George Preston, apothecary and burgess of Edinburgh, was elected Professor of Botany in the College, and Master of the Physic Garden of the city, in place of the deceased Charles Preston, Doctor of Medicine; the Council "allowing him the sum of ten pounds sterling of yearly salary, for his encouragement, to carry on the said profession of Botany, and cultivate the said garden; and to keep correspondents for procuring plants and seeds from foreign countries; and with the burden always of the payment of forty pounds Scots to the treasurer of the Trinity Hospital for the said garden, as formerly."[1]

On the 10th of September, the Town-Council ordered the College treasurer to pay to George Preston an additional salary of ten pounds sterling, on condition that he should build a green-house in the Physic Garden.

"EDINBURGH, *September* 10, 1712.

"The which day the Council, with the extraordinary deacons, upon a petition given in by George Preston, Botanist and Intendant of the Physic Garden, showing that he had been at considerable charges in putting the garden in good order, and in laying two new syvers for draining of the ground that was much ruined with underwater, and in laying of new ground above these syvers and other parts of the garden, for the better improving of the plants, besides considerable charges in adding of new plants that were wanting, and that he would be at yet more considerable charges in bringing of

[1] Town-Council Records.

new plants out of foreign countries, and was of intention to build a green-house, which was most necessary for preserving of foreign and tender plants and trees, and that his present salary was so very mean that he could not proceed in so great an undertaking unless he were enabled thereto by some allowance from the honourable Magistrates and Council, patrons of the said garden ; which being considered by the Council, they remitted the consideration thereof to a committee of their number, who reported that they, having considered the said petition, were of opinion that the Council, for encouragement of so good and useful an undertaking, should add to the petitioner's former salary ten pounds sterling yearly, to be paid by the College treasurer, upon this general condition, that he should build the green-house above mentioned, and likewise keep the College garden in good order, and to that effect, to recommend to the College treasurer to deliver to the petitioner the keys of the said garden, and put him in possession, as the report under the hands of the committee more fully bears :   Which being considered by the Council, they, with the extraordinary deacons, approved of the said report, and allowed to the petitioner ten pounds sterling of additional salary by and attour the present salary in use to be paid to him, and appointed the present College treasurer, and his successors in office, to pay the same to him termly, commencing the said additional salary from Lammas last, beginning the first term's payment at Candlemas next, and thenceforth termly in time coming, during the Council's pleasure ; whereanent thir presents shall be a warrant." [1]

In October the College again convened, and—

1. Professor Laurence Dundas matriculated in the Humanity class, February 25, 1712, sixty students.

2. Professor William Scott in the Greek class, February 27, seventy students.

3. Professor Colin Drummond in the Logic class, February 29, forty-five students.

4. Professor Robert Stewart in the Natural Philosophy class, February 23 and 29, fifty students.

[1] Town-Council Records.

At different times fifteen students received the de- The one hundred and twenty-fourth Class graduated. 1712-13. gree of A.M. privately, two of whom in their absence.

In October the College again met, and—

1. Mr. Laurence Dundas, on the 18th of February 1713, matriculated fifty-seven students of Humanity.

2. Mr. William Scott, February the 20th, thirty-two students of Greek.

3. Mr. Colin Drummond, February the 23d, forty-six students of Logic.

4. Mr. Robert Stewart, February the 23d, forty-four students of Philosophy.

On the 24th of February, 1713, four received the The one hundred and twenty-fifth Class graduated. degree of A.M. privately; and on the 9th of April, ten publicly in the common hall, after the Principal had delivered a discourse, " De Sacræ Scripturæ necessitate, interpretatione et utilitate." On the 16th of June, four more were graduated publicly, one of them having defended a theses. Edward Leeds was first created A.M. then LL.D. on the 30th of July publicly.

On the 1st of April, same year, Mr. Goodall, Professor of Hebrew, was allowed by the Council the use of the four rooms in the College lying on the northwest corner, near the top of the Horse Wynd, for the space of four years after Whitsunday next, upon his obliging himself to repair the said four rooms at his own charges, and to leave them in a good condition at the expiration of the said years. On the 8th of the same month, the place of Andrew M'Lellan, Janitor, was declared vacant by the Council, and James Seton was chosen in his place, burdened, as Mr. M'Lellan had been, with 300 pounds Scots, to Elizabeth Black-adder.[1]

On the 1st of July, the Council passed an act taking off from Mr. William Hamilton, Professor of Divinity, the restraint of their act, August 17, 1709, and allowing him to be chosen a minister of Edinburgh, and his salary in that case to be 1600 marks yearly instead of 2000.[2]

Charles Melvill, being in England, obtained the degree of M.D., on the 26th of August, in consequence of an ample recommendation.

On the 9th of December 1713, the Town-Council wishing to introduce the study of Physic as a branch of education into their College, which they were entitled to do from the original charter granted to them by King James the Sixth, elected James Crawford, M.D., to be Professor of Chemistry and Medicine, but without a salary ; and they allotted him two apartments within the College for teaching these sciences.

1713-14. On the meeting of the College in October—

1. Mr Laurence Dundas matriculated fifty-five students of Humanity, February 26, 1714.

2. Mr. William Scott, forty-six students of Greek, March 1.

3. Mr. Colin Drummond, thirty-nine students of Logic, March 3.

4. Mr. Robert Stewart, forty-three students of Natural Philosophy.

The one hundred and twenty-sixth Class graduated. This session fifteen students received the degree of A.M. privately, and nine publicly.

[1] Town-Council Records.　　　[2] *Ibid.*

On the 5th of May, George Warrender of Lochend, Lord Provost of Edinburgh, presented to the Town-Council a letter from Robert Brown in Zamose, in Poland, addressed to the Provost and Council, dated July 14, 1713, mortifying £500 sterling for two Protestant students at the College of Edinburgh, the one to be a Scottish student, and the other a Polish, who were to receive the ordinary interest allowed by law yearly for their maintenance and education at the said College. Lord Arnistoun, and Mr. Michael Allan, merchant in Edinburgh, were to be conjunct with the Town-Council in the direction thereof. In case the interest yielded six per cent. there would be £30 per annum. Two fifth parts were to be allowed to the one student to be born in Scotland, and of the surname of Brown, but if none of that name appeared, to any other whom the Council, Lord Arnistoun, and Mr. Allan should think fit. The other student, who was to be born a Pole, was to have three-fifths of the said stock ; and in order to enjoy it, he behoved to be provided with a sufficient testimony and recommendation from the Synod of the Protestant Polish ministers in Poland, " and then by the consent and recommendation of the elders of my countrymen, Protestant burgesses of this city [Zamose], to your worthy selves or your successors." The student was to enjoy the bursary until he had finished his studies at the College, as is usual in such cases. The principal sum was paid by Mr. Allan to the College Treasurer.[1]

1 Town-Council Records.

On the 1st of August 1714, Queen Anne expired, and George the First succeeded.

In that year, Mr. John Cumming, Regius Professor of Divinity and Ecclesiastical History, dying, was succeeded by Mr. William Dunlop, a celebrated preacher in 1715.

1714-1715. On the meeting of the College in October 1714—

1. Mr. Laurence Dundas matriculated sixty-six students of Humanity, February 28.

2. Mr. William Scott, fifty-eight students of Greek, March 2.

3. Mr. Colin Drummond, thirty-four students of Logic, March 2.

4. Mr. Robert Stewart, only ten students of Philosophy.

The one hundred and twenty-seventh Class graduated. 1715-1716.

This session fifteen students received the degree of A.M., all privately.

On the 4th of March 1715, the Town-Council, having met with the Principal and Professors of the College in the Council-Chamber, elected Mr. William Hamilton, Professor of Divinity, member of next General Assembly. On the same day, it was agreed that Mr. William Dunlop should be received into the College as second Professor of Divinity, on his Majesty King George the First's presentation.[1]

The Rebellion prevailed in Scotland at this time, particularly in Lothian in the month of October, which, no doubt, was unfavourable to the assembling of the College.

November 13, the rebels surrendered at Preston.

[1] Town-Council Records.

On the same day the battle of Dunblane was fought. Not long after, the Pretender landed in Scotland, but was soon obliged to re-embark and make his escape, and the rebellion was soon quelled.

On the meeting of the College in October 1715—

1. Mr. Laurence Dundas matriculated fifty-two students of Humanity, February 28.

2. Mr. William Scott, forty-five students of Greek, March 2.

3. Mr. Colin Drummond, thirty-eight students of Logic, March 2.

4. Mr. Robert Stewart did not matriculate.

This session eight students received the degree of A.M., all privately. *The one hundred and twenty-eighth Class graduated.*

Mr. William Carstairs, Principal, having died on the 28th of December 1715, the patrons, on the 1st of June 1716, elected the Reverend Mr. William Wishart in his stead, and a copy of the instructions, usually given to the Principal, was ordered to be ready to be delivered to him at his inauguration.

The Senatus Academicus now stood as follows :—

> The Rev. Mr. William Wishart, Principal.
> Mr. William Hamilton, Professor of Divinity.
> Mr. William Dunlop, Regius Professor of Divinity and Ecclesiastical History.
> Mr. Laurence Dundas, Professor of Humanity.
> Mr. William Scott, Professor of Greek.
> Mr. Colin Drummond, Professor of Logic.
> Mr. Robert Stewart, Professor of Natural Philosophy.
> Mr. William Law, Professor of Moral Philosophy.
> Mr. James Gregory, Professor of Mathematics.
> Mr. John Goodall, Professor of Oriental Languages.

Mr. Charles Erskine, Regius Professor of Public Law and
   Law of Nature and Nations.
Mr. James Craig, Professor of Civil Law.
Dr. James Crawford, Professor of Chemistry and Medicine.

On the 24th of August 1716, bond was granted by
the Town-Council to James Laing, merchant, College
treasurer, for 20,600 pounds Scots, expressing, that
considering that they had authorized the said James
Laing to uplift 20,600 pounds of the stock due to the
College by the Town, from Sir William Johnston and
others, undertakers to pay the good Town's debts, and
to lend the same to the good Town, for paying part of
a debt contracted by the said good Town for the extraordinary expenses the Town had been put to in forti-
fying the City during the late rebellion, and for the
levies of men raised for defence thereof ; which sum
was contained in the following College bonds granted
by the good Town :—

1. A bond (of date June 4, 1675) for 2000 pounds
Scots, mortified by William Tweedie, late Regent ; of
which the annual rent was payable to the Professor of
Humanity, over and above his salary.

2. A bond for 1800 pounds Scots, being Dr. Robert
Leighton's mortification (of date September 30, 1685),
for a bursar of Divinity.

3. A bond for 1200 pounds Scots, mortified by
John Penman, Bailie, for a bursar.

4. A bond for 4000 pounds Scots, mortified by
James Nairn for two Divinity bursars.

5. A bond for 6000 pounds Scots, granted to Sir
Donald Bain of Tulloch, in prosecution of a mortification

for John Bain of Pitcarlie, for three bursars of Divinity, to be presented by the said Sir Donald Bain, and his heirs succeeding him in the estate of Tulloch.

6. A bond for 1000 pounds Scots, mortified by Sir Patrick Hepburn of Blackcastle, for a Philosophy bursar, to be presented by Sir Colin Campbell of Arbuchell, and Sir Patrick Aikenhead, and their heirs, *per vices.*

7. A bond for 1533 pounds, 6 shillings, and 8 pence, Scots, mortified by James Pringle of Torwoodlee, for a Divinity bursar, or Philosophy, to be presented by him and his heirs.

8. A bond of 3066 pounds Scots, granted to the Presbytery of Dunbar, for two bursars, which was left by Thomas Bryson, sometime bailie in Dunbar, to be presented by the said Presbytery.[1]

The College having met as usual in October— 1716-1717

1. Mr. Laurence Dundas, in February 1717, matriculated seventy-five students of Humanity.

2. Mr. William Scott, March 1, fifty-three students of Greek.

3. Mr. Colin Drummond, in March and April, sixty-nine students of Logic.

4. Mr. Robert Stewart matriculated no students of Natural Philosophy.

This session only five students received the degree of A.M. Oliver Horsman, from England, received the degree of LL.D., and James Dalgleish and John Quincy that of M.D. John Quincy was recommended by the celebrated Dr. Mead, and also Dr. Brown of London.

The one hundred and twenty-ninth Class graduated.

[1] Town-Council Records.

In October, the classes having met, there was matriculated—

1. By Mr. Laurence Dundas, on the 26th of February, seventy-seven students of Humanity.

2. By Mr. William Scott, February 28, fifty-four students of Greek.

3. By Mr. Colin Drummond, February, seventy-one students of Logic.

4. By Mr. Robert Stewart no matriculation.

The one hundred and thirtieth Class graduated.

This session, eighteen students received the degree of A.M., and all privately.

1718-1719. On the 21st of May 1718, the treasurer reported to the Town-Council that the accountant had revised the acts of Council concerning the College funds, in order to make up a just rental. It was found that the particular mortifications in the act of Council, dated January 23, 1656, extended to 73,400 pounds Scots, but the act itself only mentioned 71,000 pounds Scots, of which last sum only, the town had paid interest to the College; and seeing several of the sums mentioned in the said act were mortified for the College in general, and that the College funds applicable towards the maintenance of the fabric were insufficient : Therefore the sum of £200 sterling, in which the particulars of the said act of Council exceed the sum therein mentioned, together with the interest thereof being accumulated into the principal sum of 10,986 pounds Scots, should be added to the College funds, and a bond granted therefor to the College treasurer, and the interest thereof appropriated, in all time coming, towards the maintenance of the fabric : Which being considered by the Council, they approved of the said report, and ordained bond to be granted to James Lang, merchant, present College treasurer, for the said sum of 10,986 pounds, the interest whereof to be applied towards the maintenance of the fabric of the said College.

In October, the classes having met, there were matriculated—

1. By Mr. Laurence Dundas, 25th February, fifty-three students of Humanity.

2. By Mr. William Scott, February 26, sixty students of Greek.

3. By Mr. Colin Drummond, February 27, forty-eight students of Logic.

4. By Mr. Robert Stewart, February 25, thirty-one students of Natural Philosophy.

This session, eighteen students received the degree of A.M., and four the degree of M.D.

The one hundred and thirty-first Class graduated.

It had been the custom since the Revolution, in electing a member to represent the University in the General Assembly, for the Principal and Professors to meet with the Town-Council, and to make the election together. But in the year 1719, the Principal and Professors, having reason to suspect that the Council did not mean to summon them to attend for that purpose, met by themselves and elected Mr. William Hamilton, Professor of Divinity. At last, however, they were summoned to attend the Council; but next day they were informed that the meeting was adjourned to that day se'nnight. At the time appointed for the adjourned meeting, the Principal, with almost all the

Professors, went to a tavern near the Council-chamber; but after waiting there more than an hour, they were acquainted by two of the Magistrates that the Council was to make no election. Wishing still to promote peace and good agreement, the College sent two of their number to the Lord Provost, the day before the sitting of the Assembly, to entreat him to call a meeting of Council, assuring him that they were willing to withdraw their own commission and unite with their patrons in a new election, hoping that the General Assembly would overlook the informality as to the time of election ; but all this was to no purpose. The Professors therefore gave in a commission, signed by themselves, to the clerk of the Assembly. But on the meeting of the Assembly, the Lord Provost protested against this commission as invalid, because the election had not been made with the assistance of the Town-Council, as had been formerly the custom. The Assembly, however, thought proper to sustain the commission.

The College had long thought the mode of electing their member of Assembly, in conjunction with the Town-Council, an improper and unnecessary practice, and had only consented to it for the sake of preserving a good understanding with their patrons. Principal Rule always, and Mr. Carstairs several times, declared that their going to the Council should not be interpreted as a giving up of their privilege, and in the interval betwixt the death of Dr. Rule and the instalment of Principal Carstairs, Mr. Meldrum, Professor of Divinity, spoke in Council to the same pur-

pose. In the year 1702, one of the Professors entered
a protest against the Town-Council's interfering in
electing a member of Assembly for the College, to
which all the Professors except one adhered; and some
of them never went afterwards to the Council. Sir
Robert Chiesley, when Provost, went to the College,
with some of the Magistrates only, and in conjunction
with the Principal and Professors, elected the Commissioner to the Assembly.

Perhaps the proper mode would be for the Lord
Provost alone, as Chancellor of the University, to preside in person on this, or any other public occasion,
within the College, if he chose to come. The whole
Town-Council are the undoubted patrons of the University; but it seems inconsistent with the nature of
a University, that they should on any occasion sit
with the Principal and Professors in an academical
capacity. They have the power of choosing a Rector,
which they formerly used to exercise, though they
have long laid it aside; but while they do not choose
to send a Rector, the Principal of the College is understood to possess the power of that academical officer.
That the Provost should appear occasionally within
the College, in the high character of Chancellor, and
preside in College meetings, would not detract from
the dignity of the University, but rather add to it.
But the sending for the Principal and Professors, and
making them sit in their academical capacity along
with the Town-Council, is what the patrons themselves
should have no desire to do. They are the guardians
of the dignity of their own University; the more

X

dignified the body of which they are the patrons, the more splendid is that patronage ; and the Magistrates will be found to consult their own interest, as well as that of the public, when they consult the dignity of their College.

This right of interfering with the College in the choice of their member of Assembly, was asserted by the Council, and still questioned by the College, till the Assembly, in the year 1723, passed an act declaring the right to be only in the Professors, Principal, Regents, Masters, and others bearing office in the University ; that is to say, the Chancellor, Rector, and Dean of Faculty, if any such there be, exclusive of all others.[1]

1719-1720.   On the 21st of August 1719, a pension of fifty marks Scots, quarterly, was ordered by the Town-Council to be paid to Margaret, widow of Mr. John Goodall, late Professor of Hebrew, out of respect to his memory, and in regard of her numerous family and indigent condition. They, at the same time, restricted the yearly salary of the office of Professor of Hebrew, which was formerly 900 marks Scots, to 700.

The Professorship of Oriental Languages having become vacant by the death of Mr. Goodall, Dr. James Crawford (still retaining the titular Professorship of

---

[1] Act VI. Assembly 1723.—A printed paper on the subject, designated " The Case of the University of Edinburgh considered with respect to their right of choosing a Member to the General Assembly," was given in to the Clerk of the General Assembly, and distri- buted among the members, May 14, 1723, by Commissary Campbell, agent for the town, and his nephew. This paper is preserved in MS. Papers Illustrative of the History and Constitution of the University of Edinburgh, in College Library, No. I. p. 95.

Chemistry and Medicine) was on the same day elected successor to Mr. Goodall.

On the 28th of August, an Act was passed by the Town-Council, by which all Professors and Masters were declared to hold their office for the future only during the Council's pleasure.

At the same meeting, the patrons thought proper to establish a new Professorship, viz., that of Universal Civil History ; and Mr. Charles Mackie was the first elected Professor, with a temporary salary of £50 per annum, to expire at the commencement of the progatives of the duty on ale, which the patrons had a near prospect of obtaining from Parliament.

" EDINBURGH, *August* 28, 1719.

" The which day, the Council, considering the great advantages that arise to the nation from the encouragement of learning, by the establishment of such professions in our College, as enable our youth to study with equal advantages at home as they do abroad, and considering the advantages that arise to this City, in particular, from the reputation that the Professors of the liberal Arts and Sciences have justly acquired to themselves in the said College, and that a profession of Universal History is extremely necessary to complete the same, this profession being very much esteemed, and the most attended of any one profession at all the Universities abroad, and yet nowhere set up in any of our Colleges in Scotland ; and considering that the expense with which the setting up thereof must be attended, make it necessary for the Council to favour it in its infancy by giving a reasonable encouragement to any well-qualified person whom they shall happen to choose to be Professor thereof ; and considering, that although the Town's revenue cannot afford the continuance of this allowance after the 1st of July 1723, at which time the petty port customs are declared by an Act of George the First to cease, they agree, that a Professor of Universal History be established in the College of this City, and that, to enable the Professor thereof in some measure to defray the expense it must be attended with at its first setting up, he have a salary of fifty pounds sterling per annum, commencing from Martinmas next, and to continue till the said 1st of July 1723 years, and no longer.

"The same day the Council . . . nominated and elected Mr. Charles Mackie to be Professor of Universal History in the College of this City during the Council's pleasure, and allowed to him the sum of fifty pounds sterling money yearly, commencing from Martinmas next, and to continue till the first day of July 1723 years, and appointed Mr. George Drummond, present Treasurer, and his successors in office, to pay the same accordingly out of the said petty port customs, during the Council's pleasure, as said is ; and the said Mr. Charles Mackie, compearing, accepted of his office, and made oath *de fideli administratione*, and qualified himself by taking the oath of allegiance, and subscribed the same with the assurance to his Majesty King George."[1]

On the same day that Mr. Mackie was elected Professor of Universal Civil History, Mr. James Gregory, Professor of Mathematics, obtained from the patrons an additional salary of 600 marks Scots, which had been formerly granted to his brother, Dr. David, his immediate predecessor, but had been withheld from him till this time. This sum, with his original salary of £50, and the £30 of Queen Anne's bounty, formerly mentioned, made the Mathematical salary the largest in the College, except that of the Professor of Public Law. The salary of Dr. James Crawford, Professor of Hebrew, was also augmented from 700 marks to 900.

On the meeting of the College in October, there were matriculated by—

1. Mr. Laurence Dundas, February 25, fifty-four students of Humanity.

2. Mr. William Scott, February 26, forty students of Greek.

[1] Town-Council Records.

3. Mr. Colin Drummond, forty-four students of Logic.

4. Mr. Robert Stewart, March 22, forty students of Philosophy.

This session twenty students took the degree of A.M., and one that of M.D.

On the 26th of October, the Town-Council passed an act, disallowing the present Professors of Divinity and Church History, or any other Professor in the College, from being ministers of Edinburgh in time coming, and appointed the draught of an act to be brought in hereupon, rescinding the Council's act July 1, 1713, contrary to the said resolution, to be laid before the Magistrates· and Council, for their approbation.

A full account of this matter is given in an act of the Town-Council passed on the 2d of November following.

The one h^{u}ndred and thirty-second Class graduated. 1720-1721.

"EDINBURGH, *November* 2, 1720.

"The which day, the Council, with the extraordinary deacons, taking to their consideration the weight and importance of a ministerial charge in this City, and also of a Professorship of Divinity or History in the College thereof, and being fully satisfied and convinced, not only from the nature of the things, and from the universal practice of all well governed Colleges and cities, that the office of a Minister and Professor cannot be discharged, in a suitable manner, by one person at one and the same time ; and having likewise observed, that the few instances of contrary practices, in their said College, have rather arisen from necessity than choice, Do hereby statute and ordain, that henceforth, and in all time coming, no person who is a minister of the Gospel, and in the actual exercise of his ministry in this City, shall be by us, or our successors in office, elected, and admitted Professor of Divinity or History in the said College, unless, previous to his admission, he demit his ministerial charge, not to be re-assumed during his continuance in his office of Professor, and all future commissions to the said Professors shall bear a clause, by which they shall be voided, and become null, in the event of any Professor becoming a minister of this City : And do hereby declare, that they will not, directly or indirectly, consent to, nor concur in the leeting or calling of any person to be a minister of this City, who is at the same time a Professor of Divinity or Church History in their said College, unless he previously resign and demit his Professorship, declaring always, as it is hereby declared, that nothing herein contained shall be construed to extend to the office of Principal of their said College." [1]

The College having met as usual in October, there were matriculated by—

1. Mr. Laurence Dundas, March 29, forty-five students of humanity.

2. Mr. William Scott, March 31, fifty-four students of Greek.

3. Mr. Colin Drummond, April 3, fifty-four students of Logic.

4. Mr. Robert Stewart, no students of Natural Philosophy.

The one hundred and thirty-third Class graduated.

This session fourteen students took the degree of A.M., and one that of M.D.

Mr. William Dunlop, Regius Professor of Ecclesiastical History, died in the year 1720, and Mr. Matthew Crawford, minister of Inchinnon, obtained the office from the Crown in 1721. Mr. Crawford was admitted November 15, 1721, having been introduced by Bailie Drummond, Bailie Lindsay, and others of the Town-Council.[2] The Commission is dated at St. James's. June 16, 1721.

---

[1] Town-Council Records.
[2] [Mr. Crawford held this Professor-

ship till his death, which took place some fifteen years after. His class, it

After the meeting of the College again in October, 1721-1722. there were matriculated by—

1. Mr. Laurence Dundas, no matriculation this session.

2. By Mr. William Scott, February 27, forty-six students of Greek.

3. By Mr. Colin Drummond, March 30, forty-seven students of Logic.

4. By Mr. Robert Stewart, January 11, only five students of Philosophy.

This session twenty-six students were made A.M., and one M.D. The one hundred and thirty-fourth Class graduated.

In October, the College having again met, there were 1722-1723. matriculated by—

1. Mr. Laurence Dundas, no matriculation.

2. Mr. William Scott, February 27 and March 1, sixty-three students of Greek.

3. Mr. Colin Drummond, April 5, thirteen supervenients, as they are called in the album.

4. Mr. Robert Stewart, no matriculation.

This session twenty-eight students received the degree of A.M. ; one that of M.D. ; and another, viz., George Oswald, an alumnus of this University, and then M.D. of the University of Rheims, was admitted, *ad eundem*.   One, viz., Halford Cotton, A.M., Presbyter of the Church of England, received the degree of LL.D. The one hundred and thirty-fifth Class graduated.

---

appears, was not well attended. " He has £100," says Wodrow, writing March 1731, " and really does nothing for it. He will give no private colledges [*i.e.*, private examinations and instructions after lecture] but for money, and nobody comes to him. His public prelections are not frequented ; he will not have six or seven hearers, they say." —Wodrow's Analecta, vol. iv. p. 212.]

In 1722, the patrons erected a Professorship of the Scots or Municipal Law in this University, of which they chose, November 28, Mr. Alexander Bayne of Revas, Advocate, the first Professor for teaching the same, and qualifying Writers to the Signet. On the same day, Mr. Charles Mackie, who had been elected Professor of Universal Civil History, was also elected Professor of the History of Scotland in particular, and of Greek, Roman, and British Antiquities.

A salary was provided for Mr. Bayne in the manner immediately to be mentioned.

In the year 1723, the City of Edinburgh obtained a renewal of their duty of two pennies Scots on each pint of ale brewed and sold within the City, with an extension to the four adjacent parishes ;[1] and this gift, by Act of Parliament, was burdened with a salary of £100 sterling yearly, to the three following Professors, viz., Civil Law, History, and Scots Law. And because Mr. Mackie had, for some years, given lectures to his students, not only on Universal History, but likewise on Roman Antiquities, for the benefit of students of the Roman or Civil Law, he was designed in the Act of Parliament Professor of Universal Civil History, and of Greek and Roman Antiquities.

Though these three first Professors of Civil Law, Scots Law, and History were elected simply by the Town-Council, the patrons of the University, yet when their salaries were provided by this Act of Parliament, it was there also enacted, that when, in time coming, a vacancy should happen in any of these three offices,

[1] See Arnot, p. 520.

it should be supplied by the Faculty of Advocates presenting a leet of two candidates to the Town-Council, of whom the Council is limited to make choice of one.

The Senatus Academicus, in the year 1723, stood as follows :—

> Mr. William Wishart, Principal.
> Mr. William Hamilton, Professor of Divinity.
> Mr. Matthew Crawford, Regius Professor of Divinity and Ecclesiastical History.
> Mr. Laurence Dundas, Professor of Humanity.
> Mr. William Scott, Professor of Greek.
> Mr. Colin Drummond, Professor of Logic.
> Mr. Robert Stewart, Professor of Natural Philosophy.
> Mr. William Law, Professor of Moral Philosophy.
> Mr. James Gregory, Professor of Mathematics.
> Dr. James Crawford, Professor of Chemistry and Medicine, also of Oriental Languages.
> Mr. Charles Erskine, Regius Professor of Public Law.
> Mr. James Craig, Professor of the Civil Law.
> Mr. Charles Mackie, Professor of Civil History, and Greek and Roman Antiquities.
> Mr. Alexander Bayne, Professor of Scots Law.]

On the 28th of March 1723, the Town-Council, with the Professors of the College, in a very full meeting, chose the Principal, Mr. William Wishart, to represent the College in the ensuing General Assembly. Mr. Robert Henderson, Librarian, having been examined whether he had made the alphabetical catalogue of the books of the College Library, conform to the appointment of the Council, answered, that he was going on in the said work, and had made considerable progress therein. A committee was appointed to examine

1723-1724.

about this, and to report. Thereafter the laws of the College were read, and the consideration of them adjourned till next meeting.[1]

On the 1st of November 1723, the Council appointed the Professors and students to be accommodated with seats in Lady Yester's Church.

In October the classes as usual met, and there were matriculated by—

1. Mr. Laurence Dundas's class not matriculated.

2. Mr. William Scott, February 27, forty-four students of Greek.

3. Mr. Colin Drummond, March 27, twenty-two supervenients, as they are called in the album.

4. Mr. Robert Stewart's class not matriculated.

The one hundred and thirty-sixth Class graduated. This session thirty-four students obtained the degree of A.M., and four that of M.D., of which last was John Moubray, A.M., in the University of Wittemberg, where he had also obtained the degree of M.D., and had afterwards been admitted, *ad eundem,* in the Universities of Padua and of Leyden.[2]

---

[1] Town-Council Records.

[2] [Here Professor Dalzel's History of the University of Edinburgh abruptly closes. It was evidently his intention to bring it down to his own time.

It appears also to have been a part of his plan to subjoin brief biographical memorials of the Professors in the various chairs. This part of his plan he has only partially executed. He has given a list of the Principals, Rectors, and Professors of Divinity, without entering into biographical detail. He has, however, written notices of the Professors of Mathematics down to his own time; an account of the Library and Librarians down to the year 1747 ; and notices of the Professors of Humanity down to the year 1741. These parts of the work now follow.]

PRINCIPALS OF THE UNIVERSITY.

1. MR. ROBERT ROLLOCK, elected February 9, 1585-6 ; died February 8, 1599.

2. MR. HENRY CHARTERIS, elected February 14, 1598-9 ; resigned March 20, 1620.

3. MR. PATRICK SANDS, elected March 20, 1620 ; resigned August 1622.

4. MR. RORERT BOYD, elected October 18, 1622 ; removed January 31, 1623.

5. MR. JOHN ADAMSON, elected November 21, 1623. I find his name as Principal in 1649, and May 20, 1650.

6. MR. WILLIAM COLVILL, elected April 23, 1652. His election set aside. See p. 165.

7. MR. ROBERT LEIGHTON, afterwards Bishop of Dunblane and Archbishop of Glasgow, elected January 17, 1653 ; resigned   1662.

8. MR. WILLIAM COLVILL, again elected March 20, 1662. His name appears in 1662, 1663, 1670, 1672.

9. DR. ANDREW CANT, elected September 29, 1675. Holds his inaugural oration November 15, 1675. Died December 4, 1685.

10. DR. ALEXANDER MONRO, formerly Professor of Divinity at St. Andrews, elected Principal, December 9, 1685. Removed by the Visitors for refusing to take the oaths to King William and Queen Mary, September 25, 1690.

11. DR. GILBERT RULE, one of the ministers of Edinburgh, chosen Principal, September 26, 1690 ; died in 1701.

12. MR. WILLIAM CARSTAIRS, elected May 12, 1703 ; died December 28, 1715.

13. MR. WILLIAM WISHART, one of the ministers of Edinburgh, elected Principal, June 1, 1716 ; died June 1729.

14. MR. WILLIAM HAMILTON, Professor of Divinity, elected Principal, February 16, 1732 ; died November 1732.

15. MR. JAMES SMITH, Professor of Divinity, elected Principal, July 18, 1733 ; died August 1736.

16. DR. WILLIAM WISHART, elected Principal, November 20, 1737 ; died May 12, 1753.

17. DR. JOHN GOWDIE, Professor of Divinity, elected Principal, February 6, 1754 ; died February 19, 1762.

18. DR. WILLIAM ROBERTSON, one of the ministers of Edinburgh, elected Principal, March 10, 1762 ; admitted November 10, following ; died June 11, 1793.

19. DR. GEORGE BAIRD, joint Professor of Hebrew, and one of the ministers of Edinburgh, elected Principal, July 3, 1793 ; admitted September 11, following.

RECTORS OF THE UNIVERSITY.

1. [JOHN JOHNSTOUN, brother to the Laird of Elphinstoun, appointed " to have the oversight and government of the affairs of the College, lately founded and erected by the guid toun," February 11, 1586-7.]

2. MR. ANDREW RAMSAY, one of the ministers of Edinburgh, elected March 20, 1620.

3. MR. ALEXANDER MORISON of Prestongrange, a Lord of Session, chosen Rector, January 5, 1627.

4. MR. ALEXANDER HENDERSON, minister of the Great Kirk of Edinburgh, chosen Rector, January 8, 1640, for the ensuing years. A beadle was appointed to carry a silver mace before him.[1] Died, August 19, 1646.[2]

5. MR. ANDREW RAMSAY,. one of the ministers of Edinburgh, again elected Rector, November 4, 1646 ; re-elected the next two years.

6. MR. ROBERT DOUGLAS, one of the ministers of Edinburgh, elected Rector, January 1, 1649.

[The Provost of Edinburgh, present and to come, to be Rector and Governor of the College in all time coming, November 10, 1665.]

---

[1] Maitland's History of Edinburgh, p. 195. [2] See Chalmers's Life of Ruddiman, p. 222.

PROFESSORS OF DIVINITY IN THE UNIVERSITY.

1. MR ROBERT ROLLOCK, elected August 27, 1587.

2. MR. HENRY CHARTERIS, elected February 14, 1599; resigned, March 20, 1620.

3. MR. ANDREW RAMSAY, elected March 20, 1620; resigned March 8, 1626.

4. MR. HENRY CHARTERIS, formerly Principal, was translated from the North Kirk of Leith, and again admitted Professor of Divinity, April 19, 1727; died in the summer of 1629.

5. MR. JAMES FAIRLY, minister at South Leith, elected July 24, 1629; resigned August 1630.

6. JOHN SHARPE, D.D., and formerly Professor in the College of Die in Dauphiny in France, elected November 17, 1630.

7. DR. ALEXANDER COLVILL, a Professor in St. Andrews, elected, June 23, 1648, in place of Dr. Sharp, deceased, but not admitted. See page 146.

8. MR. SAMUEL RUTHERFORD, elected June 27, 1649. Did not accept.

9. MR. DAVID DICKSON, elected, February 16, 1650; demitted 1662; died in December same year.

10. MR. PATRICK SCOUGALL, elected December 5, 1662. Did not accept.

11. MR. WILLIAM KEITH, elected January 27, 1664; died, November 18, 1675.

12. MR. LAURENCE CHARTERIS, elected November 24, 1675 ; demitted in 1681.

13. MR. JOHN MENZIES, elected June 21, 1682. Did not accept.

14. DR. JOHN STRACHAN, elected March 21, 1683. Deprived by the Visitors for refusing to take the oaths to William and Mary, September 25, 1690.

15. MR. GEORGE CAMPBELL, minister of Dumfries, chosen in place of Dr. Strachan, September 26, 1690 ; died in the autumn of 1701.

16. MR. GEORGE MELDRUM, one of the ministers of Edinburgh, elected December 24, 1701, in place of Mr. George Campbell, deceased.

17. MR. WILLIAM HAMILTON, minister of Cramond, elected August 17, 1709.

18. MR. JAMES SMITH, one of the ministers of Edinburgh, succeeded Mr. William Hamilton, February 16, 1732.

PROFESSORS OF MATHEMATICS IN THE UNIVERSITY.

THERE was no Professor of Mathematics in the College of Edinburgh till 1620, when, upon some new arrangement in the College, which proved to be but temporary, Mr. ANDREW YOUNG, who had been chosen one of the Professors or Regents of Philosophy in the year 1601, was also made public Professor of the Mathematics.[1] Whether he ever taught a separate mathematical class does not appear. He held the office but a short time, having died in the year 1623. He had been a Professor at Aberdeen two years previous to his coming to Edinburgh.

Mr. Andrew Young, first Professor.

He had no successor in the Professorship of Mathematics till the year 1640, when the Town-Council invited Mr. THOMAS CRAWFORD, then Rector of the High School, to hold that office. He was a man of great learning, and had formerly been Professor of Humanity in the College; a situation which he obtained on the 29th of March 1626, after a very strict comparative trial. But a vacancy having happened in the Rectorship of the High School by the death of Mr. John Ray, in the month of February 1630, he preferred that office to the other in the College. In the year 1640, the Council, with the Rector of the University (an office

Mr. Thomas Crawford, second Professor, 1640.

---

[1] Mr. Young's salary as Regent was 150 marks, and he had as much as Professor of Mathematics.

then held by the famous Mr. Alexander Henderson, but which has now been dormant for many years), considering that, the two preceding years, two Regents or Professors of Philosophy had been recently admitted, and being unwilling to introduce a third inexperienced one within so short a period, they offered a public Professorship of the Mathematics to Mr. Thomas Crawford, to be held by him in conjunction with one of the four Professorships of Philosophy, with a salary for life of 600 marks per annum. Upon this he returned to the College, and undertook the duty of both these offices, which he discharged with great fidelity and reputation for many years, and till the time of his death, which happened on the 30th of March 1662.

Previous to this election of Mr. Crawford, Mathematies as well as Greek had been considered as a part of the philosophical course of four years, and were taught by the four Regents or Professors of Philosophy. As Professor of Mathematics, it is probable that Mr. Crawford did no more than give public lectures twice a week to all of the students who chose to attend.[1] The principal part of his duty was that of one of the four ordinary Professors of Philosophy. As such, he commenced with the charge of the class of Bachelors, or the class which was entering to the third year of their course, left in that state by his predecessor, Mr. James Wright ; and the second year afterwards he

---

[1] This at least was the case with Mr. James Gregory, Professor of Mathematics first at St. Andrews in the year 1670, and afterwards at Edinburgh in the year 1674; as appears by a letter of his in the Biographia Britannica, first edition, vol. iv. p. 2361. It likewise appears that he gave private lessons.

brought them to the usual degree of Master of Arts. It is remarkable that in the Theses which he printed at this graduation, and which are dedicated to John Earl of Loudon, Chancellor of Scotland, he has subjoined a few positions, under the title of "Theses Mathematicæ;" a practice which he followed in all the copies of Theses which remain of graduations afterwards conducted by him. In the titles of these Theses he takes the appellation of Professor of Mathematics, of which he seems to have been very fond. In an imperfect record preserved in the College Library, entitled " Tabulæ petentium et adeuntium Professiones publicas in Academiâ Jacobi Regis Edinburgenâ, post ineuntem annum 1663," Mr. Thomas Crawford is denominated " a grammarian and philosopher, likewise profoundly skilled in theology, and a man of the greatest piety and integrity."

Nothing of his composition appears in print except the short Theses already mentioned; but to him we owe a distinct account of the College of Edinburgh from its foundation in 1581 till the year 1646. Of this there is a copy in the Advocates Library, in the handwriting of Mr. Matthew Crawford, Regius Professor of Divinity and Church History; as appears from a docquet at the conclusion, bearing that the original from which this was taken belonged to Mr. Laurence Dundas, Professor of Humanity, who had lent it to Mr. Matthew Crawford. It is probable that this original is in the possession of Sir Thomas, now Lord Dundas, whose father, the late Sir Laurence Dundas, Bart., of Kerse, was a nephew or near relation of the above Professor Laurence Dundas, and inherited not only his name, but a considerable part of his fortune. Another copy of this history, in the handwriting of Mr. William Henderson, Librarian, belongs to the College Library, and bears in the title to have been given in to Mungo Wood, City Treasurer, the 15th of January 1673.[1]

There are extant also in the Advocates Library some MS. Notes on Virgil, composed by Mr. Thomas Crawford ; and there is a poem of his, in Latin, in " Εισοδια Musarum Edinensium in Caroli Regis ingressu in Scotiam," 1633.

After the death of Mr. Thomas Crawford in 1662, the Professorship of Mathematics remained dormant till the year 1674, when the Town-Council invited the famous Mr. JAMES GREGORY, Professor of Mathematics at St. Andrews, to take upon him the same office in the College of Edinburgh, which he accepted ; and in the beginning of November of that year he entered upon his new charge by delivering an inaugural oration before the patrons of the University, and a great number of illustrious and learned auditors.

1674.

Mr. James Gregory, F.R S., third Professor.

This celebrated person, who at a very early period of life showed a great genius for geometrical studies, for which his family, both before and since his time, have been greatly distinguished, soon attracted the notice of the greatest mathematicians of the age, New-

---

[1] [Crawford's History of the University was printed by Dr. Andrew Duncan, Sen., at Edinburgh, 1808, 8vo. Another posthumous work of Craw- ford's, entitled, " Notes and Observations on Mr. George Buchanan's History of Scotland," appeared at Edinburgh, 1708, 12mo.]

ton, Huygens, Halley, Wallis, and others, by his ingenious publications. He had travelled to London, and afterwards to Padua; at which last place he resided for some years, and cultivated his favourite science with the greatest success. Having returned to his native country, he was elected Professor of Mathematics in the University of St. Andrews about the year 1668, which office he held about six years previous to his removal to Edinburgh. In a minute account of his Life in the Biographia Britannica, it is said that he died in his Professorship at St. Andrews, which was all the preferment he ever obtained. But this is a mistake; for he had held the Professorship of Mathematics at Edinburgh for nearly a year, when, in October 1675, being employed in showing the satellites of Jupiter through a telescope to some of his pupils, he was suddenly struck with total blindness, and died a few days after, at the early age of thirty-seven.[1] It is said of him in the life in the Biographia Britannica already mentioned, " that in the Mathematical Sciences he discovered a genius superior to most, and not much, if at all, unequal to the best of his time. This," it is added, " happened to be in the interval between Des Cartes and Sir Isaac Newton ; when having the advantage of those improvements that had been made by the former, he struck a considerable part of that dawning light into the sublimer geometry, or geometry of curves, which preceded the rising of the latter."

No successor to Mr. James Gregory in the Mathe-

---

[1] See a life [by Lord Woodhouselee] of the late Dr. John Gregory, lately published, and prefixed to his Works. [Edinb., 1796, 4 vols., small 8vo.]

matical chair at Edinburgh was appointed till towards
the end of the year 1683, when the Town-Council 1683.
elected his nephew, MR. DAVID GREGORY, to supply David Gre-
gory, M.D.,
F.R.S.,
his place.   This is the same Mathematician who was fourth Pro-
fessor.
afterwards so celebrated, that, when the Savilian Professorship of Astronomy at Oxford became vacant by
the resignation of Dr. Bernard in the year 1691, he
proved the successful candidate for that office, though
the famous Halley was his competitor.   When he succeeded his uncle at Edinburgh, he was only twenty-
three years of age ; but very soon after this, he published his first work, " Exercitatio Geometrica de
Dimensione Figurarum," etc.   Edinburgh, 1684, 4to.

He was born at Aberdeen on the 24th of June 1661,
where he received the early parts of his education.
He completed his studies at Edinburgh, and took his
Master's degree there, but not till after he was Professor of Mathematics, when we find him obtaining
that honour on the 27th of November 1683, in a private manner, at the same time subscribing the oath of
allegiance to King Charles II., with the addition of
M.P. to his name.[1]   On the 10th of December the
same year, he delivered his inaugural oration, " De
Analyseos Geometricæ progressu et incrementis."[2]

Mr. David Gregory had discharged the duties of his
office in the College of Edinburgh with great fidelity
and approbation for seven years, when he was called
to be Savilian Professor of Astronomy at Oxford.
Upon that occasion he was first received into Baliol
College, then admitted, *ad eundem*, as Master of Arts,

[1] See Graduation Book.   [2] See Tabulæ Petentium, etc., p. 14.

in that University, on the 8th of February 1691, and afterwards created M.D. on the 18th of the same month.

Dr. David Gregory had the honour of being the first who introduced the Newtonian Philosophy into the University of Edinburgh. Mr. Whiston, in Memoirs of his own Life, says, "that he was greatly excited to the study of Sir Isaac Newton's wonderful discoveries in his Principia,[1] by a paper of Dr. Gregory's, when he was Professor in Scotland, wherein he had given the most prodigious commendations to that work, as not only right in all things, but in a manner the effect of a plainly divine genius, and had already caused several of his scholars to keep acts, as we call them, upon several branches of the Newtonian Philosophy, while we at Cambridge, poor wretches, were ignominiously studying the fictitious hypotheses of the Cartesian."[2]

1692.
Mr. James Gregory, second of that name, the fifth Professor.

In the month of September 1692, MR. JAMES GREGORY, the brother of Dr. David, and likewise an eminent Mathematician, was next elected, and was the fifth Professor of Mathematics in the College of Edinburgh. He continued in this office till the year 1725, when, his great age and infirmities rendering him incapable of teaching, he resigned ; and by the particular recommendation of Sir Isaac Newton, who wrote a letter to the Magistrates of Edinburgh on that occasion, on the 3d of November, Mr. Colin M'Laurin,

---

[1] [Newton's Principia was first Published in 1687.]

[2] Biographia Britannica, vol. iv. p. 2366. A more particular account (Prof. Dalzel adds) of David Gregory's genius and writings to be here introduced.

then Professor of Mathematics in the Marischal College, Aberdeen, was elected as joint Professor with Gregory.

MR. COLIN M'LAURIN was thus introduced into this University at the same time with his particular friend Dr. Alexander Monro, Professor of Anatomy, in November 1725,[1] and was sixth Professor of Mathematics.[2] He died in June 1746, at the age of forty-eight, and was succeeded by

1725.
Mr. Colin M'Laurin, F.R.S., sixth Professor.

DR. MATTHEW STEWART, minister of Roseneath, who was elected Professor of Mathematics on the 2d of September 1747.[3]

1747.
Dr. Matthew Stewart, F.R.S., Edinburgh, seventh Professor.

He remained in this office till the year 1775, when, being very infirm, he resigned, and was re-elected, June 14, in conjunction with his only son, MR. DUGALD STEWART, who had been his assistant for two or three sessions before, and proved himself worthy to succeed so eminent a father.

Mr. Dugald Stewart, F.R.S., Edinburgh, eighth Professor.

Dr. Matthew Stewart[4] died on the 23d of January

---

[1] [Dr. Monro was introduced as Professor of Anatomy nearly six years before this, namely, in January 1720. (Town-Council Records.) Professor Dalzel has fallen into this mistake, by following, as other biographers have done, Murdoch's account of Mr. M'Laurin.]

[2] See a particular account of his Life and Writings, prefixed to his "Account of Sir Isaac Newton's Philosophical Discoveries; in four books. Published from the Author's Manuscript Papers, by Patrick Murdoch, M.A., and F.R.S., London. Printed for the Author's children, 1748." 4to. See also his Son's Works lately published.

[3] Of this eminent Geometer and his Writings, see Mr. Playfair's account in Transactions of the Royal Society, Edinburgh, vol. i. ["If it be confessed," says Mr. Playfair, "that Dr. Stewart rated in any respect too high the merit of the ancient Geometry, this may well be excused in the man whom it had conducted to the discovery of the *General Theorems*, to the *solution of* KEPLER'S *Problem*, and to an accurate determination of the *sun's disturbing force.* His great modesty made him ascribe to the method he used that success which he owed to his own abilities."]

[4] [After the appointment of his son Professor Stewart retired into privacy, living mostly at his country seat in Ayrshire.]

1785, at the age of sixty-eight, and Mr. Dugald Stewart, now sole Professor, continued in the office, of which he had discharged the duties with the greatest success, no longer than till the month of May in the same year 1785, when, on the resignation of Dr. Adam Ferguson, Professor of Moral Philosophy, he preferred this last office, as being more suited to his taste, though less lucrative than the Professorship of Mathematics.

1785.
Mr. John
Playfair,
ninth Pro-
fessor.

Mr. Stewart being admitted Professor of Moral Philosophy, on the 20th of May 1785, MR. JOHN PLAYFAIR, whose learning, and particularly whose mathematical abilities were well known, was elected Professor of Mathematics, in conjunction with Dr. Ferguson, and received into the College on the 21st of June following. The sole purpose of Dr. Ferguson's joint election with Mr. Playfair, was to give him a right to a salary, as an equivalent for that which Mr. Stewart now enjoyed, and which Mr. Playfair was not to be entitled to till Dr. Ferguson's death.[1]

[1] The salary of this office was at first 600 marks. There is a tradition that it was augmented to its present state, by way of favour to Dr. David Gregory, by the Council, because he took their side on a particular occasion in opposition to his colleagues. Mr. Dugald Stewart had this anecdote from his father. At present it is the best in the College, except that of the Law of Nature and Nations.

THE LIBRARY.

In the year 1580, Mr. Clement Little, Advocate, 1580. and one of the Commissaries of Edinburgh, bequeathed his library,[1] consisting of about 300 volumes, for the use of the citizens of Edinburgh. At that time this was considered as a very valuable collection. These books were at first deposited in a gallery belonging to Mr. James Lawson, which was a part of the lodgings appropriated to the accommodation of the ministers of Edinburgh, and situated on the spot where the Parliament House was afterwards built. Mr. Lawson was a strenuous promoter of the scheme of erecting a College in Edinburgh, which was at last accomplished in the year 1582 ;[2] but the Presbyterian interest having soon after declined, and the Councils of the Earl of Arran prevailing, several of the Presbyterian ministers were forced into exile, among whom was Mr. Lawson, who died at London in the year

---

[1] The deed of conveyance of these books to the Town-Council of Edinburgh, with a catalogue of them subjoined, is still extant in the College collection, written on vellum, in a beautiful hand. See Appendix.

[2] [It was not till the year 1582 that the Town-Council succeeded in recovering the legacy of 8000 marks bequeathed by Robert Reid, Bishop of Orkney, about the year 1558, for the endowment of a College at Edinburgh.—See p. 2. Here it may be noted that Bishop Reid died at Dieppe in the autumn of the year 1558, when returning to Scotland from his attendance on the marriage of Queen Mary with the Dauphin of France. This we learn from a letter which Mary wrote to her mother, the Queen Dowager of Scotland, dated September 16, 1558, in which she says : "Madame, Dieu a voulu que les embassadeurs qui vont presentement vers vous estant a mi chemin, ayent este reponses jusques a Diepe, la ou ils sont tous malades, et Monsieur d'Orcenay mort."—Miscellany of the Maitland Club, vol. i. p. 243.]

1584, much regretted by all his friends.   The Town-
Council, however, persevered in their attention to the
interest of the College; and, in particular, they caused
Mr. Clement Little's donation of books to be removed
from Mr. Lawson's house to the College, and delivered
to the care of Professor, afterwards Principal Rollock.

Such was the commencement of the College Library,
which continued to increase rapidly, not only by donations from those who annually received the degree of
A.M., but by the munificence of many well-disposed
citizens and others, who contributed considerable sums
of money, as well as books, for that purpose.

1626.   In the year 1626, it was found necessary to remove
the books from the small apartment which they first
occupied in the College, and to place them in the high
public hall, until a more commodious receptacle should
be provided for them.   Hitherto the charge of the
Library had devolved on the Principals of the College;
but Mr. John Adamson, at that time Principal, finding
the complete discharge of the office of Librarian now
becoming too laborious, particularly as the large windows of the hall were in such a state as to expose the
books to some injury from the weather, the Council,
December 26, allowed him 180 marks per annum for
employing an assistant or servant to attend to the
state of the volumes, and for purchasing coals to
counteract the bad effect of the damp air.

It was at length found that the Library would be
more generally useful, if instead of the Principal, who
could not be supposed to give the necessary attendance, a Librarian should be appointed, who might

attend regularly at certain stated hours for the accommodation of those who should be admitted to the use of the books, agreeably to certain laws and regulations. Accordingly, in the year 1635, MR. KENNETH LOGIE, son to Mr. James Logie, Advocate, was chosen Keeper of the Library, with an annual salary of 400 marks, and the addition of some occasional perquisites. He had been recommended to this employment from the successful assistance he had given to the Principal in arranging the books in presses, and in making catalogues of them. The method adopted at this time answered all the necessary purposes of accommodation as long as the books remained in the higher hall.[1] Mr. Logie held the office of Librarian till the year 1641, when he accepted of a call to be minister of Skirling.

1635.
April 22.
Mr. Kenneth
Logie, first
Librarian.

In his place, on the 29th of January 1641, was chosen MR. ANDREW MONRO, son of Mr. John Monro, burgess of Edinburgh; and in the month of April 1642, an act was passed for building a new apartment for the Library. For this work Bailie John Fleming left 4000 marks.

1641.
January 29.
Mr. Andrew
Monro,
second
Librarian.

This is the room which is at present called the Museum, where the Professor of Natural History also gives his lectures, and part of which, at the west end, is the class for the Professor of Humanity. It runs along within the new parallel College inner quadrangle, to the Chemical Laboratory, and the house of the Professor of Chemistry; and must be demolished

[1] What is here called the higher hall is the very room in which the Library is at present [1799] accommodated. [But all the College buildings here described by Professor Dalzel, as appropriated to the Museum and Library, are now removed.]

in the progress of the new buildings. The sunk storey was intended for a printing-house ; and the building was at first covered with a flat leaden roof, and remained so till about the year 1766, when the leaden roof was taken off, and an upper storey added, which being divided into two rooms, the one serves as a class-room for the Professor of Natural Philosophy, the other as an addition to the present Library.

The books were removed from the higher hall, and deposited in this new room upon its being completed. This continued to be the Library for many years ; and the higher hall, which is now again the Library, was the room for the meetings of the Professors ; and sometimes the graduations were performed in it. How it was again made use of for the Library room will be seen afterwards.

Mr. Andrew Monro, Keeper of the Library, died in the year 1645, of the plague,[1] which then prevailed ; and which had forced the Professors and students to retire to the town of Linlithgow to avoid the infection. In their absence, the Town-Council had some difference among themselves about a successor to Mr. Momo. There were two candidates for the office. The one was MR. THOMAS SPEIR, son of a respectable burgess of Edinburgh, and who had taken the Master's degree the preceding August. He was the grandson of Provost William Little, who had been very friendly to the College, and grandnephew to Mr. Clement Little, who had given a beginning to the Library. The other

---

[1] [" Retiring to Perth, having been seized of the pestilence before his departure from Edinburgh, he died there-of."—Crawford's History of the University of Edinburgh, p. 159.]

candidate was MR. ANDREW SUTTIE, nephew to Mr. George Suttie, Dean of Guild, a promising young man, born in the town of Forfar, and who had taken the Master's degree at St. Andrews in the year 1644. Both candidates had considerable interest with the patrons ; and to avoid all further contention, it was agreed that the two should be conjoined in the office ; and that each of them should have 300 marks salary, instead of the 400, which the sole Librarian had enjoyed. However, Mr. Speir did not long survive his election, having died soon after of a consumption, much regretted ; and Mr. Suttie became sole Librarian, and returned to the former salary of 400 marks.[1]

The fourth Librarian was MR FRANCIS ADAMSON, who was chosen about 1648. (See p. 154.)

The fifth Librarian was MR. JAMES NAIRNE, who was chosen July 23, 1652. (See p. 164.)

The sixth Librarian was MR. JOHN MIEN, who was chosen about March or April 1655. (See p. 172.)

The seventh Librarian was MR. JOHN STEVENSON who was elected December 9, 1657. (See p. 177.)

The eighth Librarian was MR. JOHN KNILAND, who was elected May 19, 1658, in place of Mr. John Stevenson, deceased. (See p. 178.)

The ninth Librarian was MR. JOHN DUNLOP. (See p. 191.)

Marginal note: 1645. Mr. Thomas Speir and Mr. Andrew Suttie, joint Librarians. The former dies soon after his election, and leaves Mr. Andrew Suttie sole, and the third Librarian.

---

[1] [The names of the next seven Librarians, omitted in Professor Dalzel's MS., are supplied from the preceding history. The following extract from the Council Register would seem, however, to show that some uncertainty prevails regarding Nairne's successor :—

"28th December 1653.—Mr. John Stevensone admitted Keiper of the Bibliotheque of the Colledge of this Burgh, in place of Mr. James Nairne, lait keiper thairof, demitted, with the yearlie feall of 400 merks."]

The tenth Librarian was MR. WILLIAM SOMERVILLE, who was chosen March 2, 1666, in place of Mr. John Dunlop, resigned.[1] (See p. 193.)

1667.
Mr. William
Henderson,
eleventh
Librarian.

The eleventh Librarian was MR. WILLIAM HENDER-. SON, who was elected in the year 1667, and who seems to have discharged the duties of the office with great diligence. His handwriting appears in several of the books and registers preserved in the Library. In particular, during the time of his holding the office, he kept an exact account of the books and other donations presented to the College, with the names of the donors ; this is preceded by a very distinct catalogue of the benefactors of the College from its foundation to the year 1679. The history of the College, from its beginning to the year 1646, as collected from the MSS. of Mr. Thomas Crawford, is very abstractly copied in the handwriting of Mr. Henderson. He acted as Secretary also to the University, and had the charge of the graduation book, where his writing is to be observed for a considerable series of years. The graduation book is the most curious and valuable record in the College.[2] It is to be regretted that Mr. Henderson did not keep regular minutes of the meetings of the Senatus Academicus, for he was very

[1] I have found a note on the back of an old catalogue, in the handwriting of Mr. Robert Henderson, son and successor to Mr. William, bearing that certain books were given in by Mr. John Dunlop's brother as belonging to the Library ; and on the same page mention is made of certain other books wanting in Mr. Dunlop's time. [As to these books, there is the following minute in the Records of the Town-

Council :—" *Edinburgh, July* 17, 1668. — The Council appoints that 100 marks, detained in the College Treasurer's hand the time of Mr. John Dunlop, late Bibliothecarius, his decease, for the books that were then amissing, be given in by the Treasurer to the Primar to be expended upon books."]

[2] [See the volume already mentioned, "The Catalogue of Graduates, etc." Edinb., 1858, 8vo.]

distinct and accurate. This method, however, was not adopted till the year 1733. He was clerk to several meetings of delegates from the different Universities of Scotland, and the minutes he wrote of their proceedings have been preserved, and are curious.

In the year 1636, soon after Mr. Kenneth Logie was appointed Librarian, certain regulations were drawn up, to be observed by those who should have the privilege of reading books in the Library. By these it was ordained, that no person should enter the Library without permission of the Keeper, or go out without his knowledge : that none but those who were regularly admitted, and who had taken a solemn promise to submit to the regulations, should have the privilege of reading the books : that none should touch any of the books but such as were delivered to him by the Keeper : that none be allowed to carry out a book : that none shall mark any book, either with ink or by doubling down the leaves : that if any one happen inadvertently to stain a book, he shall immediately inform the Librarian, according to whose judgment he is to repair the damage to the Library : that none shall be permitted to read by candle-light, or to carry a book near the fire : that the hours for reading, while the College is open, shall be every day, except Sundays, from ten o'clock till twelve, and in the afternoon, from two till four in winter ; in summer, the same, and likewise, from seven in the morning till nine : that upon a signal given at nine, at twelve, and at four in the afternoon, all shall immediately depart from the Library : that no person shall read aloud, nor disturb others in the time of reading ; and if he has occasion to speak to another, it shall be by whispering : that whatever book any one has got after coming into the Library, he may, if he please, retain till the signal of quitting the room be given ; and no one shall be allowed to seize a book in the possession of another.[1]

Every one accordingly, before he could have the use of the Library, was required to come under a solemn obligation to obey these laws.

Upon the 12th of December 1636, for the first time these conditions were agreed to, and subscribed by the Principal and Professors, and several others, in presence of James Cochrane, Andrew Ainslie, and Charles Hamilton, Bailies of Edinburgh, and Sir John Sinclair, Dean of Guild, and James Roughead, Treasurer, with certain others of the Council.

The next day ten more entered, and subscribed before the Principal, and Mr. Andrew Stevenson, Professor of Philosophy ; and this practice of entering and subscribing in presence of the Principal, and one or more Professors, or of one or two or more Professors, prevailed till the 20th of May 1650, on which day Mr. Robert Burnet appears as the last who subscribed and was admitted (the Principal and Professor Duncan Forrester being present), previous to an interruption of several years.

It is to be observed, that there was an interval with respect to admitting any person to the privilege of

---

[1] See these laws in the book kept for admitting *cives* of the Library.

the Library, betwixt the 6th of May 1642, till the 22d of March 1644. As the act was passed for building the new room in April 1642, it is probable that this interruption was occasioned by the removing of the books into their new situation ; where they continued till about the year 1753.

The interval in the regular admission of persons to the use of the Library, and the obliging them to subscribe the laws—which interval commenced in the year 1650—continued till about the end of the year 1662, that is, during the time of Cromwell's usurpation, and for some time after his death, till the Restoration, and towards the last years that Principal Adamson was at the head of the College, and during all the time that Mr. Robert Leighton was Principal. But in Principal Colvill's time there is a note inserted in the Admission book, bearing, that the Principal and Professors caused the laudable custom by which persons admitted to the privilege of reading books in the Library were obliged to subscribe the usual laws, and which had been intermitted for many years on account of the war, to be revived on the 11th of December 1662 ; and they themselves subscribed on that day, viz. :—

William Colvill, Principal.
William Keith, Professor of Divinity.
Alexander Dickson, Professor of Hebrew.
William Tweedie,
James Pillans,
John Wishart,
Hugh Smith,
} Professors of Philosophy.

Z

Also,—

William Cumming, Professor of Humanity, on the 28th
February 1663.

And afterwards,—

Thomas Bell, and

William Henderson, Librarian.[1]

1684.
Mr. Robert
Henderson,
Librarian.

Mr. William Henderson discharged the office of sole Librarian till 1684, when his son, MR. ROBERT HENDERSON, was elected on the 21st of November, either in conjunction with him, or his sole successor, though more probably in the former way.

Mr. Robert Henderson continued in office as Librarian till the 25th of March 1747, a period of sixty-two years, much longer than any of his predecessors, or than any Professor had ever continued in the College of Edinburgh. He had received an academical education, as appears from his having taken the degree of A.M. on the 28th of November 1683. When Mr. John Drummond, Professor of Humanity, was deprived of that office by the Parliamentary Visitors on the 25th of September 1690, Mr. Henderson appeared, as one of the candidates to succeed him, at the comparative trial held on the 5th of November the same year. There were four other candidates, one of whom, Mr. Laurence Dundas, proved successful.

[1] See the Book.

PROFESSORS OF HUMANITY.

IN the year 1590, in consequence of a consultation held between the Lords of Session and the Town-Council of Edinburgh, a contract was entered into, by which it was stipulated that the Lords of Session in the first place, the Town-Council in the second, and the Faculty of Advocates and Clerks to the Signet in the third, should contribute, each of the three parties, 1000 pounds Scots, making up the sum of 3000 pounds, for which the Town-Council obliged themselves to pay 300 pounds per annum for maintaining a Professor of Laws. In consequence of this agreement Mr. Adam Newton, Advocate, began to give lectures in the College publicly on the Latin language, or, as it was called, Humanity, probably with a view to prepare the students for the study of the Civil Law. But having entered upon his office without a due attention to the Town-Council, who are the general patrons of the University, and supposing, as it should seem, that the authority of the other contracting parties was sufficient, he was, on the 19th of June 1594, prohibited to teach in the College, after having given lectures for three years. In his stead was substituted, by consent of all the parties, Sir Adrian Damman, a native of Denmark, and then resident at the Court of Scotland, as orator and agent for the estates of the Low Countries. This Professor likewise gave lectures only on Humanity, making no mention of Law ; and having held the office till the year 1597, he then resigned.   Upon this the three parties entered into a new contract, whereby it was agreed that the annual interest of 2000 pounds of the stock should be employed for maintaining six bursars or scholars ; 50 marks being at that time thought sufficient for a provision to each bursar ; and the annuity arising from the remaining 1000 pounds was allotted as a salary for a private Professor of Humanity ; the other four Regents or Professors of Philosophy having at that time no more salary than 100 pounds per annum each.   It was agreed, at the same time, that this Professor of Humanity should be elected by six delegates, whereof two should be for the Lords of Session, two for the Town-Council, one for the Faculty of Advocates, and one for the Writers to the Signet, using the advice of the Principal of the College.

1597.
December.
Mr. John
Ray, first
Professor of
Humanity.

MR. JOHN RAY, a native of Angus, a person well advanced in life, who had great experience in teaching privately, and who was esteemed well skilled in the Latin tongue,[1] was, on the 28th of December 1597, unanimously chosen, and was the first Professor of Humanity in the University of Edinburgh.   He not only taught a private class, but frequently gave lectures on Humanity publicly.   After he had held the office in

---

[1] [" He had been employed in divers private charges before his coming to the College, and thereby well seen in Humanity ; and at that time he was in the family of Mr. Alexander Guthrie, Town-Clerk, attending his son."— Crawford's History of the University of Edinburgh, p. 41.]

the University for upwards of ten years, upon the resignation of Mr. Alexander Hume, Rector of the High
School of Edinburgh,[1] he preferred that charge to the
Professorship of Humanity in the College, and was
translated thither in October 1606, where he continued till his death, which took place in February
1630; almost twenty-four years.[2]

MR. BLASE COLT, son of Mr. Oliver Colt, Advocate, 1606. Mr. Blase Colt, second Professor.
a young man greatly distinguished for his knowledge
not only of the Latin, but the Greek tongue, was
elected Professor of Humanity, instead of Mr. John
Ray, by the Lords of Session, Town-Council, Advocates and Writers to the Signet, on the 5th of December 1606. He died in the year 1611, much
regretted, being greatly esteemed for his learning and
the politeness of his manners, and was succeeded by
his eldest brother,

MR. OLIVER COLT, Advocate, who, after many 1611. Mr. Oliver Colt, third Professor.
years practice of the Law, to which he had been bred,
became wearied of that profession, and was unanimously chosen Professor of Humanity in place of his
younger brother. But he did not long continue in
that office. Having studied Divinity, he received a
call to be minister of Holyrood-house, and resigned

---

[1] [Hume had been Rector of the High School "ten years, with great commen- dation of the truly learned." — Craw- ford's History of the University of Edinburgh, p. 64. See also Dr. Ste- ven's History of the High School of Edinburgh.]

[2] [See p. 93; also Crawford's History of the University of Edinburgh, p. 117.

William Drummond of Hawthorn- den, who had studied under Ray, wrote

a "tribute to the memory of his much- loving and beloved master." The fol- lowing are the concluding lines :—

"Bright RAY of learning, which so clear didst stream,
Farewell, soul which so many souls did frame.
Many Olympiades about shall come,
Ere earth like thee another can entomb."

--Drummond's Poems, Maitland Club edition, p. 400.]

his Professorship in the month of November of the same year 1611.

1611.
Mr. Robert
Burnet,
fourth Pro-
fessor.

MR. RORERT BURNET, son to Burnet of Barns in Tweeddale, was, by comparative trial, elected to succeed Mr. Oliver Colt. His only competitor was Galbraith, son of Valentine Galbraith, burgess of Edinburgh ; and the candidates appearing to the judges to be equally well qualified, the affair was decided by lot, in consequence of which Mr. Burnet was preferred. How long he held the office does not appear, but he was succeeded by—

Mr. Andrew
Stevenson,
fifth Pro-
fessor.

MR. ANDREW STEVENSON, son to a burgess of Edinburgh of the same name, who had, in the year 1611, been chosen, by comparative trial, Regent or Professor of Philosophy in place of Mr. Andrew Young, who was afflicted by a disease that threatened to be very lingering. But he obtained the office upon condition that he should retire, in case Mr. Young should recover his health ; and Mr. Young having actually recovered, resumed his office accordingly. Mr. Stevenson, who retired for some time, afterwards succeeded Mr. Burnet in the Professorship of Humanity, which office he held at the time of Mr. Young's death in the year 1623 ; and then he succeeded him again, after an interval of twelve years, as one of the Professors of Philosophy, which occasioned a vacancy in the Professorship of Humanity.

1623.
Mr. Samuel
Rutherford,
sixth Pro-
fessor.

MR. SAMUEL RUTHERFORD having stood a comparative trial, was preferred to the office of Professor of Humanity in the year 1623,—the same year in which the celebrated Mr. John Adamson was chosen

Principal of the College. He held the Professorship only till about the end of the year 1625, when he found it prudent to resign.

Mr. Thomas Crawford, after a very strict comparative trial, next obtained, on the 29th of March 1626, this office, which he held till the death of Mr. John Ray, Rector of the High School, and formerly Professor of Humanity in the College, in February 1630; and then the Council elected him successor to Mr. Ray in the charge of the High School, from whence he was again translated to the College, where he held the offices of Regent in Philosophy, and also Professor of Mathematics, with great reputation for many years.

1626.
Mr. Thomas Crawford, seventh Professor.

Mr. John Armour was, by comparative trial, chosen, on the 12th of March 1630, to succeed Mr. Crawford in the Professorship of Humanity; which he held till the month of December 1633, when he was called to a Professorship of Philosophy at St. Andrews.

1630.
Mr. John Armour, eighth Professor.

Mr. Alexander Gibson, the son of a Writer, was next chosen, being favoured by the Episcopal faction, which had then become very powerful, and preferred by them to another candidate, Mr. Archibald Newton, son to a burgess of Edinburgh, who was known to be of far superior ability to the successful candidate. Mr. Gibson was elected to the office on the 21st of December 1633. But, in October 1636, to the surprise of his friends, he accepted of a call to be master of the grammar-school of the Canongate.

1633.
Mr. Alexander Gibson, ninth Profe'ss'or.

Mr. James Wiseman, master of the grammar-school at Linlithgow, offered himself as a candidate to suc-

1636.
Nov. 11.
Mr. James
Wiseman,
tenth Pro-
fessor.

cecd to the vacant Professorship of Humanity ; and, there being no competitor, he was admitted to that office on the 11th of November 1636 ; which again became vacant on the 10th of November 1638, Mr. Wiseman having been then appointed one of the Professors of Philosophy.

1638.
Nov. 14.
Mr. Robert
Young,
eleventh
fessor.

MR. ROBERT YOUNG,[1] who had attained the degree of Master of Arts at Glasgow, was next chosen, after a comparative trial, Professor of Humanity, on the 16th of November 1638. After holding the office for five years, being esteemed an eloquent preacher, he was presented by the Town-Council to the church of Dumbarney, in the year 1644.

1644.
Mr. James
Pillans,
twelfth
Professor.

MR. JAMES PILLANS, son of a citizen of Edinburgh, after a strict comparative trial, was chosen to succeed Mr. Robert Young, and was Professor of Humanity till November 29th in the year 1652, when he was chosen one of the four Philosophy Professors, in the room of Mr. Andrew Suttie.

1653.
Mr. John
Wishart,
thirteenth
Professor.

MR. JOHN WISHART was elected Professor of Humanity on the 9th of March 1653, in place of Mr. James Pillaus chosen a Regent of Philosophy ; but he probably held the office no longer than about the end of the session ; for, in October of this same year, we find by the College Register that he had the charge of the Bejan class in place of Mr. Duncan Forrester.

1654.
Mr. William
Forbes,
fourteenth
Professor.

MR. WILLIAM FORBES was chosen to succeed Mr. John Wishart, probably about the beginning of the year[2] 1654 ; and, on the 7th of March 1656, he was

[1] [" Son to Mr. Andrew Young, late minister at Abercorn."—Crawford's History of the University, p. 134.]

[2] [March 1st. Town-Council Records.]

appointed Regent of Philosophy in place of Mr. James Wiseman deceased. The office of Professor of Humanity being thus vacant, the Town-Council, upon the 2d of April 1656, appointed Mr. John Jossie and Mr. Thomas Kincaid to wait on the College of Justice, joint patrons with them of this Professorship, and inform them that several persons had suggested the propriety of taking this opportunity of abolishing the office of Professor of Humanity, as prejudicial not only to the grammar-school but to the College itself ; and they proposed that the salary should be applied to some other purpose for the advancement of learning. But it should seem that the College of Justice were not of this opinion ; for we find that the Town-Council, on the 11th of the same month, received and admitted Mr. John Cruickshanks to be Master of the Humanity class till the beginning of the ensuing August, when the session was to conclude ; and, on the 3d of the ensuing October, a consultation was held by the Town-Council and College of Justice about the Humanity class, the result of which was a resolution to hold a comparative trial for a new Professor.

MR. JAMES M'GOWAN, in consequence of being most approved by the judges in the comparative trial, was, on the 14th of November, elected, and was the fifteenth Professor of Humanity in the College of Edinburgh. But he remained in the office only for about two years ; for, on the 15th of October 1658, he appeared before the Town-Council, attended by Mr. James Pillans and Mr. William Tweedie, two of the Philosophy Regents, and, on account of sickness, re-

1656.
Mr. James M'Gowan, fifteenth Professor.

signed his office, by delivering a pen into the hand of the Provost. On the 17th of November, a report was made to the Town-Council that their Commissioners had met in the College, with Judge Mosley and Judge Ker, and Alexander Nisbet, W.S. (Mr. John Nisbet, Advocate, being absent), and had chosen Mr. Hugh Smith Professor of Humanity.

1658.
Mr. Hugh
Smith,
sixteenth
Professor.

MR. HUGH SMITH was chosen, November 17, 1658, in place of Mr. James M'Gown resigned, but not by comparative trial. He held the Professorship of Humanity till the 29th of October 1662, when he resigned ; and on the 1st of December he was elected by the Council to succeed the celebrated Mr. Thomas Crawford as one of the Professors of Philosophy, upon an ample and honourable recommendation by his colleagues. He did not, however, survive this last choice three years, having died of a hectic fever about the middle of August 1665.

. 1663.
Mr. William
Cumming,
seventeenth
Professor.

MR. WILLIAM CUMMING was chosen to succeed Mr. Hugh Smith, after a very strict comparative trial, on the 16th of February 1663, and was the seventeenth Professor of Humanity. A particular account of this trial, expressed in elegant Latin, is preserved in an imperfect record extant in the public Library, entitled " Tabulæ petentium et adeuntium Professiones publicas in Academiâ Jacobi Regis Edinburgenâ, post incuntem annum Domini 1663." And, as it shows the form of proceeding adopted also in other cases of this kind, it may be considered as a piece of curious information. It is in substance as follows :—

" Upon notice being given of a vacancy in the Professorship of Humanity to the College of Justice, who (in consequence of the original contract entered into with the Town-Council, vesting in them two-thirds of the patronage of this office) are concerned in supplying such a vacancy, they delegated four of their number, according to the different ranks of which their body consists ; and the Town-Council also delegated two out of their own number. On this occasion the two named by the Lords of Session were Sir James Robertoun of Bedley, and Sir David Nevoy of Reidy, knights ; by the Town-Council, Robert Sandilands, Dean of Guild, and John Milne, chief of the King's masons ; by the Faculty of Advocates, Mr. John Ellis, their Dean ; and by the Writers, Mr. William Sharp, Keeper of the Signet. These six delegates, after consulting together, appointed a meeting to be held on the 1st of January 1663, in the upper hall of the University. There, in presence of the Lord Provost and others of the Town-Council, who appeared in right of their general patronage of the University, for the interest of the City and University, after prayer, according to custom, the forementioned judges first inquired of the Rev. Mr. William Colvill, Principal of the College, concerning the usual style and manner of substituting a Professor of Humanity. Upon this he desired the Regents who, from frequent practice, were well acquainted with all these circumstances, to give a distinct and candid account of them. After this the judges, with the approbation of the Lord Provost, ordained that by a program to be affixed, as soon as possible, in all the cities being seats of Universities in this kingdom, and in all the Universities themselves, notice should be given to all who were skilled in Philology, that the Professorship thereof in this place, now vacant, would most certainly be conferred on the person who, after producing proper certificates of his character by those acquainted with him, and submitting to the trial prescribed by the judges against the 9th of February next, should obtain their highest approbation in point of erudition and moral character. Copies of the program were undertaken to be sent to Aberdeen by the Lord Provost; to Glasgow by Lord Bedley; and to St. Andrews by Mr. Sharp; which was done by them accordingly.

"On the 9th of February, in the place appointed, appeared seven young men, and declared themselves candidates for the vacant office, upon the terms proposed; and wrote down their names, not in any particular order, but as each happened to stand nearest, as follows :—

1. Mr. Robert Baron.	5. Mr. John Law.
2. Mr. William Turner.	3. Mr. William Cumming.
7. Mr. Thomas Bell.	6. Mr. Robert Hume.
	4. Mr. Humphrey Galbraith.

"The candidates being then ordered to withdraw into the Library, the judges agreed that on the 12th of the same month, in the lower hall of the University, the said candidates should be required, by way of public exhibition of their skill in polite literature (without prejudice of the private examination afterwards to be enjoined), in presence of all the patrons of such literature to be convened thither by program, to illustrate in a short and perspicuous Latin paraphrase, with apt observations, the prologue to the Satires of Persius, each of them being allowed one half-hour by the glass and no more. The candidates being called back, the Rev. Principal stated to them the whole method and rules of the future examination ; and upon their assenting to the proposals, they were commanded to decide by lot the order in which they were to.be called upon at the examination ; and the lots happened according to the figures prefixed as above to their names ; after which this meeting was closed with prayer.

"On the 12th of February all the candidates appeared, except Mr. Bell, who was detained by the death of his father, a respectable citizen. On this account, his examination, at his own request, was put off till the 16th of the same month. Robert Hume, likewise, who had waited his turn for three hours and a half, being taken suddenly ill, obtained the same favour with Mr. Bell.

"On the 16th, accordingly, Hume first, and then Bell, performed the public exercise prescribed to the candidates. Upon this, the meeting being dismissed, the Lord Provost, with the judges, the Principal, and several of the Council and ministers of the city, the Regents, with the seven candidates, went up by themselves into the upper hall. Then the candidates, conducted by one of the Regents, were desired to retire into the Library, from whence, after consultation held among the judges, each, according to the order formerly

decided by lot, was introduced separately by the Regent; when a private exercise was prescribed to them,
first of Latin, consisting of a passage of Apuleius, to be
turned into Scots; and then of Greek, consisting of a
passage of Isocrates, to be turned into Latin.   When
each in order had performed this task, they were all
desired to return to the Library.   Then, after deliberation among the judges for the purpose of ascertaining
the most meritorious candidate, it was agreed that
they should all at once be summoned again into the
hall; and that the thanks of the meeting should be
given to them in polite terms by the Principal, for
the great ardour they had displayed in the cause of
elegant literature; and that he should assure them that
each of them deserved to fill an academical chair, but
as there was only one vacant, one of them only could
have it; and that the judges had thought fit to declare
in favour of Mr. William Cumming, on account of his
possessing somewhat of superiority to the other candidates in point of years and experience; and that they
had no doubt but he would prove an ornament to the
profession which he had thus obtained."

Mr. Cumming, however, remained in this office only
about two years; for, on the 22d of February 1665,
he was elected Professor of Philosophy, in place of
Mr. William Tweedie, who had died on the 8th day
of the same month; and after discharging the duties
of this last Professorship no longer than towards the
conclusion of the session, he accepted an invitation
from the Earl of Argyle, about the end of June, to
undertake the education of his eldest son, the Lord Lorn.

Mr. Andrew Ross was the next who obtained the Professorship of Humanity, having been successful in a comparative trial with another candidate, whose name was Kirkwood. He was chosen March 10, 1665, but continued in the office no longer than to the month of November of the same year 1665, when he was promoted to a vacant Professorship of Philosophy; an office which he filled only for two years, having died in August 1667.

1665.
Mr. Andrew Ross, eighteenth Professor.

Mr. Thomas Bell, who had been one of seven candidates when Mr. William Cumming proved successful, appeared again to contend for this office, with four new candidates, whose names were George Landells, Robert M'Clellan, William Gulon, and Gasper Kellie. The judges hesitated for some time betwixt Mr. Bell and Mr. M'Clellan. At last, in respect that Mr. Bell had appeared to very great advantage on the former trial, and was on this occasion fully equal to his competitor, and had, besides, the advantage of him in point of age, they determined unanimously in his favour. He was accordingly elected, December 6, 1665. Having discharged the duties of this office for ten years with great reputation, he died about the end of February 1676.

1665.
Dec. 6.
Mr. Thomas Bell, nineteenth Professor.

Mr. Gilbert M'Murdo succeeded Mr. Bell, in consequence of being found superior to four other candidates who contended with him on this occasion, on the 3d day of April 1676, and was the eighteenth Professor. He remained in this station till the death of Mr. John Wood, Professor of Philosophy, which happened on the 22d of March 1679, and was on the 2d

1676.
Mr. Gilbert M'Murdo, twentieth Professor.

of April chosen Mr. Wood's successor by the Town-Council, upon the recommendation of his colleagues. He continued Professor of Philosophy till the time of his death, which happened in the year 1683.

1679.
Mr. Alexander Cunningham,
twenty-first
Professor.
MR. ALEXANDER CUNNINGHAM having proved successful in a competition with Mr. Robert Monteith, the only other candidate who stood upon this occasion, was admitted to the Professorship of Humanity in April 1679, and was the 21st Professor. Having taught Humanity with great applause about ten years, he was then made one of the Professors of Philosophy in consequence of the death of Mr. Alexander Cockburn.

1689.
Mr. John Drummond,
twenty-second
Professor.
MR. JOHN DRUMMOND was chosen, by the delegates appointed by the patrons to fill up this office, on the 20th of February 1689 ; but on the 25th of September the following year he was deposed by the Visitors of the University, for refusing to take the oaths of allegiance to King William and Queen Mary ; upon which a new election was held by comparative trial.

1690.
Mr. Laurence Dundas,
twenty-third
Professor.
MR. LAURENCE DUNDAS, upon the trial which was held on the 5th of November 1690, was preferred to other three competitors ; and, on the 28th of the same month, he was invested with the office of Professor of Humanity. After the year 1708, when a new arrangement took place respecting the mode of teaching Greek and Philosophy, it was agreed that the students of the Humanity class should be matriculated in the same manner with those of Greek and Philosophy, which had not formerly been the practice. Accordingly, Mr. Dundas's class, which had convened in October 1709, was matriculated on the 1st of March 1710; on which

occasion sixty-nine students of Humanity entered their names in the Album. Before this period there is no record extant of the numbers of students of Humanity attending this University. In the class commencing in October 1716, and matriculated on the 26th of February 1717, there appear seventy-seven names in the list, which seems to be the most numerous class ever taught by Mr. Laurence Dundas. It may be supposed, however, that several were absent on this occasion; which was probably the case then, as well as now, at the matriculation.

Mr. Dundas taught with great reputation till the year 1727, when he resigned.[1] He died near the end of the year 1734. He had acquired a considerable fortune; and, among other legacies, he bequeathed 9000 marks Scots, as a perpetual fund for educating three bursars. The deed of Mortification appears in the Records of the University for the 26th of May 1735.

MR. ADAM WATT was elected Professor of Humanity in the year 1727, in place of Mr. Laurence Dundas, who had resigned; and he was the twenty-fourth Professor. He taught till the time of his death, which happened in March 1734.

1727. Mr. Adam Watt, twenty-fourth Professor

MR. JOHN KER, formerly Professor of Greek in King's College, Aberdeen,[2] being elected by the usual

1734. Mr. John Ker, twenty-fifth Professor.

---

[1] [Dundas gave in his resignation, after having taught the class for the long period of thirty-seven years, in favour of Adam Watt, son of his old friend, the City clerk of Edinburgh.]

[2] [Ker had previously been one of the classical Masters in the High School of Edinburgh. He was the author of "Donaides," and other works. His Latin version of the "Canticum Solomonis," Edinb. 1727, small 8vo, is included in Lauder's collection, entitled "Poetarum Scotorum Musæ Sacræ," Edinb. 1739, 2 vols. 8vo.]

delegates from the College of Justice and Town-Council, to succeed Mr. Adam Watt, deceased, was, by the Lord Provost in person, attended by several of the Magistrates, presented to the Senatus Academicus on the 4th of October 1734. He taught till the time of his death, which happened on the 19th of November 1741 ; and, at a meeting of the Senatus Academicus, held on the 20th, his son was desired to teach the class till it should be otherwise supplied.

1741.
Mr. George
Stuart,
twenty-
sixth Pro-
fessor. MR. GEORGE STUART having been elected by the usual delegates Professor of Humanity, in place of Mr. Ker, deceased, and Mr. Robert Hunter having been elected by the Town-Council Professor of Greek, they were both on the same day, being the 17th of December 1741, introduced into the Senatus Academicus, by the College Bailie, the Dean of Guild, and several of the Council ; but before their commissions were read, the Rev. Dr. William Wishart, Principal, in his own name and in that of his colleagues, signified to the deputies from the Council, that, whereas it had been the constant custom, that before the presenting any persons elected to such offices in this University, the Professors were required to take trial of them, and make a report to the Magistrates and Council of their sufficiency ; this having been omitted in the present case, the Masters of the University had, by themselves, considered the qualifications of these gentlemen, and were content to receive and admit them to the respective offices, not only on account of other evidences they had of their qualifications, but particularly as Mr. Hunter was in the practice of teaching Greek suc-

cessfully, and Mr. Stuart had been in the like practice of teaching Latin ; but that they found it incumbent upon them to insist that this should be no precedent in prejudice of their right of trying persons chosen to the like offices in time coming, and rejecting any who upon such trial should be found insufficient.   After this, the commissions being read, they were received and admitted to their respective offices, by the Senatus Academicus, in the usual manner.

APPENDIX.

I.

ELEGIAC VERSES TO THE MEMORY OF PRINCIPAL
ROLLOCK.—(Page 39.)

THE authors of these verses, written all in Latin, except one copy in
Greek by Mr. Henry Charteris, were,—Mr. Robert Pont, minister
of St. Cuthbert's Church, Edinburgh; Mr. Alexander Ruthven,
brother to the Earl of Gowrie; Sir Adrian Damman of Bysterveldt,
who had taught Humanity for several years in the College; Mr.
Thomas Craig; Mr. John Johnstone; Mr. Henry Charteris, Rol-
lock's successor; Mr. William Craig, Professor of Philosophy; Mr.
John Adamson, afterwards Principal; Mr. David Barclay; Mr. John
Ray, Professor of Humanity; Mr. George Greir; Mr. William Arthur;
Mr. Thomas Bellenden; Mr. John Scott; Mr. Nathaniel Udward;
Mr. George Douglas; Mr. David Hume; Mr. Alexander Hume;
and Mr. Hercules Rollock. These verses are subjoined to the
Latin Account of Rollock's Life and Death, written by Mr. George
Robertson, Professor of Philosophy, and afterwards one of the
ministers of Edinburgh. [It has the following title: "Vitæ et
mortis D. Roberti Rolloci Scoti narratio. Scripta per Georgium
Robertsonum. Adjectis in eundem quorundam Epitaphiis. Edinburgi, apud Henricum Charteris, 1599." 12mo.] The verses
themselves are certainly not inferior to any of the kind composed
by scholars in other countries of Europe at that period, which was
the age of modern Latin Poetry. Buchanan, who had died the
very year before Rollock began to teach in the College of Edinburgh, had been styled, by the universal suffrage of the learned,
"Poetarum sui seculi facilè princeps." As Robertson's Account
of Rollock's Life and Death is now extremely scarce, I shall
subjoin a specimen of these verses :—

DE me, deque meo meruit tua fratre voluntas,
De te verum index ut moriente loquar.

Nobiscum hunc orbem donec, Rolloce, tenebas,
Mortales inter Numinis instar eras.
Morte (quod optabas) idem nunc additus astris,
Implebis merita laude superstes humum.

M. A. Ruthvenus.

Ρολλώκον δείνησιν ἀτασθαλίῃσι λύθεντα,
Σώματος ἧδ' αἴνους εὐθὺς ἀφεντα πόνους
Οὐλύμπον δ' ἀναβαντα Θέου βούλησις ἀνωγεν
Αἴεν τῷ Χριστῷ συμβασιλευέμεναι.
Ἄστρα γὰρ ὤφλησαν βαίνειν ἐπὶ δύσβατα, πίστις,
Εὐσέβιη, κόσμος, παντοδαπαι, τ' ἀρεταί.
Καὶ προτερὸν γ' ἵκειν εἰς οὐράνον ἔπρεπ' ἀληθοῦς
Ἄλλους παιδεύσανθ' ἀγνα κέλευθα πατεῖν.

Henricus Charterisius.

Aliud.

Dum vitam ambiret, toto vivebat in orbe
Rollocus, solis qua micat igne globus.
Vidit et ingemuit, non hæc mea vita, nec orbis
Jure, inquit, civem me ferat esse suum.
Vita mihi est Christus, cœlum est mea patria, cunctæ
Res mundi mihi sunt stercora, damna, nihil.
Audiit hos gemitus summa qui spectat ab arce :
Ergo veni in patriam, mox ait, ergo veni.
Jam jam adeunda tibi est fulgentis regia cœli ;
Ut vita optata sic potiaris ovans.

Aliud.

Quæris viator tumulus iste quem tegat ?
Nemo referre posset hoc plenè tibi.
Audire verbo si tamen verum cupis ?
Operta virtus omnis hoc cippo jacet.

Henricus Charterisius.

M. A. Ruthvenus, the author of the first of these pieces, was Mr. Alexander Ruthven, third son to the first, and brother to the second Earl of Gowrie. The mention made of his brother's obligation to Rollock, as well as his own, is a proof of this, as they both studied at the College of Edinburgh, and took the Master's degree ; the Earl on the 12th of August 1593, in Mr. Ferme's class ; and Alexander on the 29th of July 1598, in Mr. Charteris's class. M. prefixed to his name is for " Magister," which then only those who took the degree were called.

[It is surprising that Professor Dalzel should have overlooked a manuscript volume in the University Library which contains a Life of Rollock, evidently prepared for the press by his colleague, Henry Charteris, who succeeded him as Principal. It is added to a Commentary on the First Epistle of Peter, by Rollock, revised and completed by Charteris in 1627. It also includes the elegiac verses above mentioned, with the exception of the lines quoted by Alexander Ruthven, which, no doubt, were purposely omitted, but with additional verses by Mr. Robert Boyd, Mr. William Hart, Mr. George Thomson, Mr. John Douglas, Mr. James Coldin, Mr. Adam Abernethy, and Mr. Andrew Melville. This Life was first printed in 1826, for the Bannatyne Club, as the sequel to a reprint of Robertson's *Narratio*, 1599, along with the complete series of these elegiac verses. The Life by Charteris was again printed, with a translation by Mr. W. M. Gunn, in the first volume of Rollock's Select Works, 1849, 8vo, for the Wodrow Society.]

II.

The Printed Theses of the Regents and Students of Philosophy.

[Professor Dalzel frequently refers to the Philosophical Theses, which were printed before the day fixed for the graduation of Masters of Arts. No complete series of these Theses exists; and the earliest one that has been discovered is that for the year 1596. In 1599 and subsequent years, the names of the candidates, as well as of the presiding Regent, are affixed, with a dedication to the Provost and Magistrates of Edinburgh, or to some person of distinction. Till 1632, these Theses were printed in quarto, with the exception of two in small folio. Some of the following years have not been met with; but from 1641 till the close of the seventeenth century, the form usually adopted (known as broadsides, from being printed only on one side of the leaf) was a folio sheet in small type, and in two or more columns. The quarto size was again resumed, for a few years, before the change in the course of study, which took place in 1708, when the custom of public disputations for the honour of A.M. was laid aside; although occasionally persons ambitious of distinction prepared a separate philosophical dissertation on some subject of Philosophy, which was printed in the same quarto form.

From the Register of Laureations, mentioned at page 17, by Professor Dalzel, compared with the names which appear in the various printed Theses alluded to, the Editor of this work prepared " A Catalogue of the Graduates in the Faculties of Arts, Divinity, and Law, of the University of Edinburgh, since its Foundation.   Edinburgh: 1858."   8vo.   It may be added, that a similar Catalogue of the Edinburgh Graduates in Medicine, from the institution of the Medical Faculty in 1726, had previously been printed.   As each candidate was required to submit a dissertation on some particular topic, and being uniformly printed in an octavo size (excepting the earlier ones), the collection, during the course of upwards of 130 years, forms a most voluminous series.   The subject of each Thesis is specified in the printed lists of the Medical Graduates.]

III.

The Discipline of the College of Edinburgh, December 3, 1628: Wherein is contained the Offices and Duties of the Professors, Masters, Scholars, Bursars, and Servants, as it has been observed many years ago.—(Page 91.)

The Order of the First Year.

In the beginning of October the entrant students to the discipline of the College are exercised in Latin authors, chiefly in Cicero, and turning of Scots into Latin and Latin into Scots; and the Regent is to examine these versions both in the etymology, construction, and in the right writing of them, until the Primar give and examine a common theme.

The common theme being examined, Clenard's Greek Grammar is continually taught, in which, when they come to the annotations on the nouns, the practice of the rules is joined with the Grammar out of some part of the New Testament.   Then are taught the first and second orations of Isocrates, and also one or two others of the same author, and of the poets, Phocilides, the first book of Hesiod, with some books of Homer.

About the middle of May are taught Ramus's Logics, and with the Logics, some Latin themes to be turned into Greek, and some in Greek to be turned into Latin.

What they hear at the beginning out of the New Testament, the first oration of Isocrates and Phocilides, or the first book of Hesiod, they commit to memory ; and what is taught during the week they repeat on the Saturday mornings with a clear voice in the Master's audience ; on that same day they dispute betwixt ten and twelve o'clock. On the morning of the Lord's day the Catechism is taught.

The Order of the Second Year.

From the beginning of October they are exercised in repeating those things which were taught in the former year ; and near the end of October they are examined on the same.

The examinations being ended, they are examined in themes and versions, until the Greek theme be taught by the Primar ; which uses to be taught the day after the common theme (foresaid) is given.

After the Greek theme is taught Talæus' Rhetoric with Cassander, or the like, together with Apthonius's Progymnasmata. Afterwards they make orations to exercise their style in Logic and Rhetoric.

In the beginning of January Aristotle's Organon is begun to be taught, beginning at Porphyry's Isagoge ; and in that year are taught the books of the Categories on the Interpretation of the Prior Analytics, the first, second, and eight of the Topics, and the two books of Sophistics.

In the end of the year is taught a compend of Arithmetic.

On the Saturday they dispute on-Logic theses in their private schools. But on the first Saturday of May, at three o'clock in the afternoon, they begin to have orations in public ; and they have each days appointed, until all of them have declaimed before the end of the year.

On the Lord's day, in the morning, the Regent goes on in the explication of the Catechism.

The Order of the Third Class.

In the beginning of the third year, they repeat what was taught in the former year, until the examinations.

After the examinations, the Regent teaches his scholars the Hebrew Grammar, and exercises them in Logical analysis and Rhetoric, in what authors he thinks best, until a public examination of their progress in analysis is made by the Primar ; which usually takes place the day after the Greek theme (foresaid) is given and examined.

The trial of their ability in analysis being made, the Regent goes on to teach his scholars the two books of the Posteriores in the Logics, and then teaches the first, second, the half of the third, the fifth and sixth books of the Ethics, afterwards the five first books of the Acroamatics (or general Physics), and teaches a short compend of the three last.

In the end of the year the anatomy of the human body is described.

On the Saturdays they dispute in their private schools on theses which the Regent prescribes out of those things which they have heard.

On the Lord's day, some commonplace of Divinity is taught.

The Order of the Fourth Class.

In the beginning of the fourth year, after the vacation, all those things which were formerly learned are repeated, until the two inferior classes be examined.

The examinations being ended, they begin the books de Cœlo (*i.e.*, concerning the heavens), and the Regent teaches the first book, the greater part of the second and fourth; which being perfected, the Sphere of John de Sacrobosco is taught, with some theorems of the planets, to the fourth chapter; as also the more notable constellations are shown in the book, in the Celestial Globe, and in the heavens.

Then are taught most exactly the books de Ortu (*i.e.*, of generation), and the books de Meteoris, as much as sufficeth. Then are taught the three books de Anima (*i.e.*, concerning the soul).

In the beginning of May they begin to repeat all those things learned in the Logics and Philosophy.

In the time of the repetitions Hunter's Cosmography is taught; and afterwards they are exercised in disputing, chiefly on the theses, which they are publicly to defend at the laureation.

On the Lord's day, in the morning, they are exercised in commonplaces of Theology, and on the most necessary controversies.

The Bachelors, after they have learned in the third year the first four chapters of the first book de Demonstratione, convene in the Magistrand school at five o'clock at night, and there dispute with the Magistrands, every one of them having a Magistrand for his antagonist, the choice being made by the Regents, who likewise prescribe the matter of disputation, and so they exercise themselves till six.

In like manner, upon the Saturdays from ten o'clock, all the three superior classes dispute in the public schools; the Magistrands first give the theses, then the Bachelors, and thirdly, the Semies; and so by turns in circle. These public disputations are begun so soon as the Semies have learned Porphyry's Isagoge, from whence the matter of disputation is taken.

These disputations are continued until the examination of the Magistrands.

The Order of the Humanity Class.

In this class are taught classic and historical authors, orators, poets. They translate themes out of Latin into Scots and from Scots into Latin. They are also sometimes exercised in making of verses. In the morning they repeat their task in the Grammar, and also Talæus' Rhetoric uses to be taught, both for the precepts and the illustrious examples.

The University being dismissed, and the Magistrands laureat, they learn somewhat of the Greek, that they may learn to decline and conjugate, and so they are exercised to the month of September.

On the Lord's day they learn the Catechism; on the Saturdays some of Buchanan's psalms are taught; and an account of their prelections is rendered upon Monday morning.

The vacation being ended, they are examined by the Regents both in those things they have learned, and in those things which they have added by their own private studies.

The Order of the Examinations.

The first class is examined by three Regents, whereof one examineth the prose, another the poesy, the third the Logics; and not only do they use to make trial of those things which were taught, but also of those things which every one has added by his own proper and private studies.

The second class likewise is examined by three Regents of those things which were learned the former year. The first examinator makes a trial of each in Porphyry's Isagoge and the Categories; the second in the book de Interpretatione and the prior Analytics; the third in the Topics and Sophistics.

This examination being ended, the highest class undergoes examination of all those things which they have formerly learned in Aristotle. Every one of them is examined by each of the three

Regents of the inferior classes. After this order, the first Regent makes trial, in the first place, in the common parts of Logic ; the second, in the posterior Analytics ; the third, in the Topics and Sophistical Captions. In the next place, the first Regent makes trial in the two books of general Physics ; the second, in the other three books ; and the third, in the Ethics.

In the end of the year they are again examined before the Laureation by the four Regents, the Regent of the Humanity class being joined to the former three. And each of the four Regents examines each student twice. In the first place, the first of the four Regents examines on the common part of the Logics ; the second, on the books de Demonstratione ; the third, on the Topics and Sophistics ; and the fourth, on the Ethics. The second time, the first makes examination on the common part of the Physics ; the second, on the books de Cœlo (*i.e.*, concerning the heavens), and the Sphere ; the third, on de Ortu (*i.e.*, concerning the generation or original of all things), and of the Meteors ; and the fourth, de Anima (*i.e.*, concerning the soul).

Before the examination of the Magistrands, the Town-Council is pre-admonished by the Primar, that they may send some grave men with the Rector, who, together with the Primar, shall take an oath of every one of the examinators, *de fideli administratione*, and that, without respect of persons, they shall assign to every one his deserved degree of honour in the public laureation ; and who shall bind the Magistrands also by an oath, that each of them shall be content with that degree and place to which he shall be appointed by the Primar and Examinators ; with this certification, that he who carries himself stubbornly and forwardly, and betrays any outrageous passion of mind, shall be immediately thrust out with ignominy, and shall not be permitted to enter the public solemnity, nor shall be laureat.

The Time of Convening after the Vacation.

They return to the College after the vacation in the beginning of October.

The Office of Primar.

The vacation being ended, the Primar calls the Regents to him, that, without delay, they may return to their office and trust, and that, with common consent, they may advise and deliberate upon those things that are most advantageous or conducible to the good

of the University; what is to be renewed; and what is further to
be appointed for preserving the order and discipline thereof.

It is his part, not only immediately after the vacation, but also
at all other times needful, to call the Regents together, that by their
mutual counsel they may restore or add vigour to the practice of
those things which are fallen out of use, or may appoint new things
which they find requisite for the better discipline of the College;
of which the Primar is to let the Council know, that it may be
further approven and confirmed. It is his office also to admonish
the bursars, janitor, and all others belonging to the University, of
their duties.

To take heed to the College, to see that the scholars be diligently
exercised, and to visit the schools as often as there is need. If any
of the scholars is guilty of obstinacy or rebellion against his Master
or Regent, the Primar is so to correct and chastise him, that reverence and respect may from thence be bred in others.

He ought to take care that grievous and scandalous faults be
punished, in the public schools, before the Regents and all the
scholars.

At the public meeting of all the scholars at six o'clock at night,
or four o'clock in the summer in the afternoon, the Primar makes
public prayers unto God.

Upon the fourth day of the week, which is called Wednesday,
at three o'clock in the afternoon, upon the tolling of the bell, the
scholars convene in the common hall; and there, after a sacred
lesson, wherein the scholars are instructed to pious duties, the
censors are examined anent the order which has been observed in
every class and by every scholar in the week preceding, and that
according to the prescriptions of their duties; and new censors are
appointed.

The Primar takes care, also, that all entrants be matriculated, and
each at his matriculation shall solemnly vow and promise obedience
to the discipline of the College, and to all the Regents or Masters.

THE OFFICE OF THE PROFESSOR OF THEOLOGY.

The Professor of Theology must teach the students the right
method of learning Theology; what they should read first, or at the
beginning, and what is necessary afterwards; and in all things which
they should chiefly exercise themselves in. He shall teach publicly
on the Tuesday and Friday, betwixt eleven and twelve in the forenoon; and he shall be present on the Monday at an exercise in

Scots of the students in Theology.   On the Thursdays he shall take
care that one of the students make trial privately in Latin upon
some head of Theology, both by teaching and by sustaining theses;
the Professor himself, in the meanwhile, moderating in the disputations.

It belongs also to the Professor of Theology to teach something
of the Hebrew tongue.

The Offices or Duties of the Regents and Hebdomadar.

The Regents, when by humble prayer they have committed themselves and their scholars unto God, respectively teach those things
which are to be taught; and then take care that the scholars in
their several sections confer amongst themselves concerning those
things which have been taught.

If they have not taught sufficiently in the morning, they proceed
further at ten o'clock; and the rest of the time the scholars confer
in their several sections or dispute.

In the afternoon they attend their scholars, that they may confer
or dispute till four o'clock, and then they examine until six; but on
days designed for play or recreation, the scholars go out to the fields
at two o'clock, and return at four; and from that time are examined
till six.   But in summer they confer on these things which were
taught till three; and from three till four they are examined by the
Regent; and from four to six they recreat themselves in the fields.

On the Saturday, each of the Regents attends the disputations in
his own class; in the winter, from seven o'clock in the morning,
and in the summer, from six till nine; and, in like manner, from
ten o'clock in the forenoon till twelve.   But in the public disputations of the three classes, the Regents, each in his turn, moderate at
the disputations in the public schools.   In the afternoon, they either
teach or dispute, as it shall seem fit to the Regent, and as the
Statutes of the College appoint.

On the Lord's day, the private lessons being ended, at the second
bell, they go to the church, four of the Regents going before, and
the Hebdomadar follows behind.   Sermon being ended, and the
assembly dismissed, in the afternoon they return in order, as they
went, to their respective schools, where the Regents take an account
of the sermons, and of their morning lessons.

The students being dismissed, the Regents convene at five o'clock
in the Hebdomadar's chamber, that each may report what disorder he
has seen in the preceding week, that it may be timeously amended,

and that they may incite and stir up one another mutually to their duty, and that they may by all means endeavour to reclaim the scholars from disorder, and provoke them to the study of piety and good learning.

All the scholars, by turns, execute the office of Hebdomadar, whose duty it is,—

1. To take care that at the public meetings there be no confusion or disorder ; and, in like manner, that at the dismission the scholars may get out without trouble and disorder.

2. That, at every hour appointed for meeting, they, immediately after the bell, go and visit the classes, and that they take care that all the scholars fall readily and cheerfully to their studies.

3. That, upon play-days, they attend the students to the fields, and wait upon them in the fields, and bring them all back in company to their schools, and give the names of the absents in every class written by the censors to their respective Regents.

4. To be present at the public lessons, where all the scholars ought to be present, and to observe and to delate those who misbehave themselves.

5. To call the Regents to him at five o'clock at night, upon the Lord's day, and to relate to them what fault he has observed in any class or scholar, that it may be corrected by the Regent; and, if there be any need of the Primar, to signify it unto him, that, by the mutual counsel of the Masters, any damage which, by bad example, may redound to the College, may be quickly prevented.

6. That also, in the Primar's absence, he may, at the dismission of the College, make prayers unto God. It is incumbent on the Regents to be always intent upon their duty, but chiefly that none be absent in the time of public prayers, nor from a public oration, nor from the public account required of the order and discipline.

Not one of the Regents may absent himself from the College a day, without leave asked or given of the Primar; and that not one of them be absent two days, without liberty granted by the Town-Council; and that, in the time of his absence, he provide one in his place to attend and teach his class. But it is to be provided, that no Regent depute the teaching of his scholars to any who read notes out of a book, neither in his own presence nor absence. Regard also is to be had that all the Regents behave themselves with all reverence and observance towards the Primar; for he is set over them by the Town-Council.

The Duties of the Bursars.

To ring the bell at the appointed hours.

To make clean the stairs which carry up to the schools, from dirt and dust with a pedle and besom.

The hours of convening are six o'clock in the morning in the winter, and five in the summer, beginning with May till the vacation ; at ten o'clock in the forenoon, and at half-two in the afternoon ; at which times and hours it is the bursar's part to ring the bell, and two of them are commanded to attend these duties every week.

The Duties of the Janitor, translated out of the Old Statutes.

The Janitor ought to wait at the gates continually.

To open and lock the schools at the appointed hours.

To close the gate of the College at ten o'clock at night, and to open it timeously in the morning.

To set up a lantern with candles in the porch, and in both the trances, higher and lower.

To sweep the schools three times every week.

To keep the close clean.

To see that no damage or harm be done to the fabric of the College, and if anything be broken or spoiled, to give immediate notice to the Primar and Masters, that it may be timeously repaired at the expenses of the guilty, and that they may be punished.

The Duties of the Scholars.

Upon the Lord's day, at seven o'clock in the morning, every one shall be present in his respective class for hearing of the sacred lessons taught.

At the second bell, with beseeming gravity and modesty, they shall go to the church, and there they shall with all seriousness and reverence employ themselves in prayers, praises, and in hearing sermons ; and the church being dismissed in the afternoon, they shall return in good order with the Regents to the College, that they may give an account of the public sermons, and of their morning lessons.

Upon the Wednesdays, at three o'clock in the afternoon, the bell being rung, with great modesty and gravity, they shall convene in the common hall for receiving a sacred lesson, and for giving an account of their manners and behaviour.

In like manner, they shall exercise becoming modesty, at their meetings for evening prayers; all noise and tumult and disorder being banished away.

In the morning, as every one shall enter the school, let him, as a humble supplicant, adore the Lord; nor may he attempt or begin any study, until he have first implored or begged for grace and divine aid in private.

In the winter, let all and every one be present in the schools at six o'clock in the morning; in the summer, at five o'clock; and there continue in hearing their lessons till nine, and in writing the same; and let them confer and repeat the things heard and written with their condisciples, appointed by the Regent, in the distribution of the class in sections for that purpose.

In like manner, from ten o'clock to twelve, they confer, repeat, and dispute as long as it is permitted them to cease from their public prelections. And also, at half-past one o'clock, let them be present, confer, and give an account unto their Masters (excepting the hours distinat for play).

Upon the Saturdays, from three o'clock in the afternoon, it is lawful for them to take the play from their schools; and upon Tuesdays and Thursdays, from mid-day to four o'clock in the winter; but let it be from four o'clock in the afternoon in the summer. Neither may they play at any other time but when it shall seem good to the Regents, and that for the relaxation of the mind, and the health and exercise of the body; but let none of them, in the meanwhile, walk upon the streets, nor, as idle spectators, stand in the highways or narrow passages. Neither must any of them, at any time, go in to blind ale-houses, cellars or cooks houses, nor to taverns.

Upon the Saturdays mornings all the classes are to dispute, every one of them in their proper school.

From the beginning of February until the 1st of July, the Magistrands are to dispute with the Bachelors in the Magistrand class; and antagonists, fitly chosen by the Regents, shall by turns, night by night, from five o'clock till six, propound matters of disputation.

From the middle of January until the second Saturday of July, three classes of the students of Philosophy shall dispute in the common hall upon theses propounded by every class, time about, in the presence of three Regents, each of them moderating at the disputations by turns. This shall be from ten o'clock till twelve. But the rest of the classes shall every Saturday, for that time, repeat, dispute, and hear their prelections.

Besides the books for their ordinary learning, let none of them be without a Latin New Testament, a Catechism and a Psalm Book in Scots.

If any act, or speak impiously, injuriously, and obscenely, he must not be permitted to pass without punishment. Whoever, therefore, profanes the holy name of God, whoever pours forth curses and execrations, whoever talks rotten, filthy, and obscene speeches, let them be severely chastised.

Let every scholar carry himself reverently to every one of the Masters, and give obedience with all submission to their admoni- tions.

Let all their discourses everywhere be in Latin; and let them be honest, chaste, modest, generous, not contentious, but discreet and pious, nor about any subject or matter but what is good and honest.

Let every one be diligent and laborious in his studies.

Let none interrupt the studies of his neighbours.

Let none enter the classes or chambers of others.

Neither let any one, out of curiosity, stand and listen at the doors of others, except censors.

Let none be absent from the College without liberty first obtained from the Regent; neither should any go out without the College gate, except his Regent grant him liberty to do so.

Let no censor presume to move out of his own class without leave from his Regent; but in his Regent's absence he must in no case go out till his return. Any who obtain liberty to go out, let him return without delay; for upon no pretext whatsoever must any be suffered to play the truant.

Let every one, as becomes a disciple of Christ, show himself a pattern to his condisciples of piety, goodness, modesty, and diligence in his studies.

None must provoke or give offence to his neighbour in word, deed, or behaviour; neither must any offer to wrong or reproach his neighbour.

Let all scoldings, revilings, and reproachful language be utterly banished from all and every one of the students.

If any shall see his neighbour idle, or doing anything against his duty, let him, as becomes a good Christian, give him a friendly and brotherly admonition; and if, so admonished, he do not repent and amend, let him mark and delate him.

Let none take upon him to revenge himself, either by word or deed, when he is reproached or wronged in any manner of way by another; but let him complain of the wrong done him, either to the Primar, or the Regent of the scholar who has done the offence.

Let none in a rude or unreverent manner pass by, speak, or look to those that are worthy of respect, such as magistrates, ministers of the gospel, aged men, or others eminent for learning, virtue, or authority.

Let none otherwise behave himself in public, but as it becomes the students of good learning, that is, gravely, modestly, and reverently.

Let every one flee the company and familiar conversation with wicked persons as a pest.

Let none carry a sword or dagger about him.

Let none walk by night upon the public streets.

Extra secessum recrementis excipiendis destinatum nemo vel alvi fæces deponito vel urinam redito.

Let none break, deface, or any way spoil the glass windows, walls, forms, seats, pulpits, or any other thing within the precincts of the College, but let them keep all things light, neat, and sound.

Let the censors be faithful in the discharge of their trust, by admonishing offenders, and delating them, as is required.

Let him be punished who is anywise faulty, according to the nature of his offence.

Let them be extruded, or thrust out of the College with disgrace, who shall be found to be authors or ringleaders of rebellion or sedition, or who shall be convicted of any notable or heinous crime.[1]

IV.

MORTIFICATIONS TO THE COLLEGE, AND THE SUMS THEREOF RESTAND IN THE TOWN'S HANDS.—(Page 173.)

"The 23d January 1656. . . . The Provost, Bailies, and Council, having perused the haill Council books, Town's compts, and writs, since the foundation of the College, and made the most narrow search that can be, at the sight of the Regents and present Treasurer of the College, they find that the Provost, Bailies, and

---

[1] Register of the University of Edinburgh, pp. 39-53.

Council, and the Treasurers of this burgh, have received, from the persons underwritten, the particular sums of money aftermentioned, mortified to the College of this burgh, converted to their own use, and for the which they are debtors, as follows :—

" 1. From the Lords of Session, Provost, Bailies, and Council of this burgh, and from the Advocates, Writers to the Signet, and Clerks of Session, the sum of three thousand pounds for entertaining of a Master of Humanity and six bursars within the said College, conform to the contract passed betwixt the said parties thereanent, and actit in December 1597.

" 2. Item, Received from umquhile James Bannatyne, the sum of 100 marks, for the use of the College, conform to an act of Council, dated the 19th July 1598.

" 3. Item, Received from the heirs of the deceased William Cowper, tailor, the sum of 100 marks, to help to entertain a student within the College, conform to an act of Council, dated the 23d December 1607.

" 4. Item, From the Ministers and Kirk-Session of Edinburgh, 8100 pounds, to be employed for the annual rent of 1000 marks, for the sustentation of the Masters and Regents of the College, conform to an act of Council, dated the last of September 1608.

" 5. Item, Received by Thomas Speir, treasurer, from the Lord Lindsay, for demitting the benefice of Haddingtoun again by the town in his favour, anno 1609, 1333 lib. 6s. 8d.

" 6. Item, Received from Charles Sheirar the sum of 1000 marks, whereof 500 marks [to be] employed for the College, for entertaining of the Regents, conform to an act of Council, dated the penult. day of July 1617 ; for the which the Council are debtors ; and the other 500 marks for the hospital.

" 7. Item, Received from Isobel Allan, relict of the deceased David Alexander, merchant, in name of her three daughters, executors to the defunct, the sum of 200 marks, conform to an act of Council, dated the 4th March 1617.

" 8. Item, Received from Hew Wright, merchant, the right of assignation to the sum of 1000 marks, due to him by the Lady Broughtoun, and her cautioners, the annual rent whereof to be paid to himself, during his lifetime, and, after his decease, to be employed for sustentation of a Professor of Divinity within the said College, conform to an act of Council, dated the penult. of December 1618.

" 9. Item, Received from Alexander Stobo, messenger, 300 marks money, for sustentation of a Professor of Divinity in the said

College, reserving his own liferent thereof, conform to an act of Council, dated the 15th January 1619.

" 10. Item, Received from Mr. Samuel Johnstoun, for the executors of the deceased Archibald Johnstoun, merchant, the sum of 1000 marks, left in legacy, to be employed upon profit, for maintenance of bursars and students in the said College, conform to an act of Council, of the date the 28th May 1619.

" 11. Item, Received from Sir William Nisbet of Dean, the sum of 1100 pounds ; for which they are obliged to pay 100 pounds yearly for sustentation of a Professor of Divinity within the said College, conform to two acts of Council, the one dated the 2d of June 1619, and the other dated the 20th of April 1621.

" 12. Item, Received from Gilbert Hay, executor, confirmit to umquhile James Young, and Barbara Robertson his spouse, the sum of 100 marks, to be employed upon profit, for the use of two poor [scholars] in the College, for their help two years before they be made Masters, conform to an act of Council, dated 21st July 1619.

" 13. Item, Received from the heirs of William Rig, the sum of 625 marks, for payment of an yearly annual rent of threescore two marks and ane half, for help to entertain a Professor of Divinity within the said College, conform to an Act of Council, dated the 23rd August 1620.

" 14. Item, From Thomas Spier, the sum of 1000 marks, to be employed for the maintenance of a Professor of Divinity within the said College, conform to an act of Council, dated 3d January 1621.

" 15. Item, From the · executors of umquhile John Lawtie, Apothecar, the sum of 100 pounds, ordaining to buy books therewith, conform to an act of Council, 19th July 1622.

" 16. Item, Received from the executors of umquhile Mr. Walter Balcanquhal, the sum of 1100 marks, towards the maintenance of a Professor of Divinity within the said College, conform to an act of Council, dated the 30th of August 1622.

" 17. Item, Received from Isobel Brown, relict of the deceased John Mason, merchant, the sum of 300 marks money, to the use of a Professor of Divinity within the said College, conform to an act of Council, dated the 29th of October 1622.

" 18. Item, Received from the executors of umquhile Margaret Stewart, the sum of 300 marks, to be employed to the use of the College, conform to an act of Council, dated the 10th day of December 1623.

" 19. Item, Received from the executors of umquhile James Ainslie, the sum of 500 marks, to be employed for the maintenance of a Professor of Divinity within the said College, conform to an act of Council, dated the 16th of January 1624.

" 20. Item, Received by George Suttie, treasurer, from Margaret Zuill, 500 marks, 23d June 1624.

" 21· Item, Received by George Suttie, treasurer, by James Murray, master of work for Michael Findlay, anno 1624, 320 lib.

" 22· Item, Received by George Suttie, treasurer, from Margaret Cowper, relict of James Mestertoun, 9th November 1625, for bursars, 333 lib. 6s. 8d.

" 23. Item, Left in legacy by umquhile Hew Wright, the sum of 500 marks, towards the sustentation of a bursar at the College of this burgh, conform to an act of Council, dated the 5th of January 1626.

" 24· Item, Received from Charles Sheirar, the sum of 1000 marks, to be employed upon annual rent, to be paid to himself during his lifetime, and, after his decease, to John Sheirar, his kinsman, and, after his decease, to be employed for help to entertain a Professor of Divinity within the said College, conform to an act of Council, dated the 29th December 1630.

" 25· Item, Received from the executors of the deceased John Byres of Coattis, the sum of 300 marks, to be employed to the use of the College, conform to an act of Council, dated the 18th of January 1632.

" 26. Item, Received from the heirs of umquhile Patrick Gillies [or Ellis] elder, and Patrick Gillies younger, the sum of 1000[1] marks, to be employed for sustaining of a Professor of Divinity within the said College, conform to an act of Council, dated the 19th of February 1634.

" 27. Item, Received from the executors of umquhile Thomas Muir, the sum of 100 marks, for help of maintenance of two bursars at the said College, conform to an act of Council, dated the 6th of January 1636.

" Which haill particular sums before mentioned are contained in the before specified act of Council, dated the 3d day of April 1640.

" 28. Item, Received by John Fleming, treasurer, for Mr. Bartlie Sommerville, portioner of Sauchtounhall, the sum of 26,000 marks, upon the town's band, to be employed upon annual rent, in manner following :—20,000 marks thereof for entertainment of a Professor of

---

[1] " Extending, with some by-run annuals, to 1300 marks." –Crawford's Hist. of the University, p. 125.

Divinity within the said College, and 6000 marks thereof for building of a house to the Professor, ordaining the sum to be lent to Sir
William Dick, upon band, for annual rent, conform to an act of Council of the date the 17th December 1639; which sum of 26,000 marks
was employed in the hands of the said Sir William Dick, and his
band thereof delivered to John Jossie, treasurer of the College, to be
used according to the said act; and the said John Jossie charged
therewith, and the annual rent thereof in his accounts, conform to
an act of Council of the 1st of May 1640; of the which sum 20,000
marks afterwards came into the town's hands, partly by purchasing
of the King's Warke of Leith from the said Sir William, and
allowing 1600 marks thereof, in his own hand, and partly by paying
of John Marjoribank's debt, and assigning to him 4000 marks of the
said sum, and giving bands to the College in place thereof, conform
to the act of Council, of —————,[1] and 7th of January 1653.

" 29. Item, Received from Sir William Dick, 1000 pounds sterling, due by him to Mr. Robert Johnstoun, Esquire, and left in
legacy by the defunct to the College of this burgh for entertaining
of eight poor scholars therein, upon the town's security of the payment of 1000 marks, by year, to the said College, to be upliftit
furth of the milns at Bonnington, conform to the acts of Council of
the 26th of February 1640, and 13th of October 1641.

" 30. Item, There is adebtit, awand by the good town to the said
College, the sum of 1200 marks, left in legacy by umquhile David
Mackall, for entertaining of two bursars at the said College, and payable by the good town out of the first and readiest of the sums due
by the good town, to the said umquhile David, conform to the acts
of Council of the 18th December 1639, and 28th November 1640.

" 31. Item, There is adebtit, awand by the good town to the said
College, by band, the sum of 5000 marks, of the equal half of
11,771 marks, assigned by umquhile Alexander Wright to the College, conform to the acts of Council of the 1st of May 1640, and
8th December 1641.

" 32. Item, There was left by umquhile James Dalgleish to the
good town, 7000 marks, by act of Council, 1st January 1640, received the 25th December 1640 by the Town-Treasurer, and converted to the use of the College ; for the which the good town are
debtors to the College, conform to an act of Council of the penult.
of December 1640.

" 33. And sicklyke, there is mortified to the College by the said

---

[1] Blank in the Records.

umquhile James Dalgleish, the sum of 4000 marks, to be employed upon annual rent, for entertainment of three bursars of Divinity in the said College ; of the which sum the town became debtors to the College be band in 2640 marks, bearing annual rent and precept of payment; and John Jossie, treasurer of the College, received the rest, conform to an act of Council of the 24th of May 1644.

" 34. Item, There was left to the College of this burgh, by um-quhile Mr. William Struthers, one of the ministers thereof, the sum of 3000 marks, conform to an act of Council, 3d January 1645; which was received by Andrew Brysonne, treasurer, and the town's security given for payment of the annual rent thereof to the College, conform to the mortification and acts of Council, the 4th of January and 8th of February 1654 : Which sum of 3000 marks being received by the town-treasurers, with the bygone annual rents thereof, at Martinmas last, extending to the sum of 2000 marks, extends in the haill principal and annual rents to the sum of 5000 marks, whereof the good town are proper debtors to the College.

" 35· Item, Received by John Jossie, treasurer of this burgh, from John Buchanan of that ilk, the sum of 9000 marks, to be bestowed upon bursars, and the keepers of the libraries within the College of Edinburgh, St. Andrews, Aberdeen, and Glasgow, conform to an act of Council, 24th July 1646; which sum of 9000 marks, and annual rents thereof to Lammas 1650, extending in haill to 7560 lib., was afterward convented wholly to the use of the College of this burgh, for training of able spirits, after the laureation, in the studies of Divinity ; which act contains the sum of 3000 marks, awand by Dame Marie Stewart, Countess of Marr, and other 3000 marks deponed in the hands of the ministers of Dumbarton, and medlit with by the Provost, Bailies, and Council or Kirk-Session thereof, with the benefit of patronage of the sums dotted to the College of St. Andrews, conform to an act of Council of the 5th of November 1649, which was never received as yet by the Council of Edinburgh.

" 36. Item, There was left in legacy to the said College, by um-quhile Sir Thomas Hope of Craighall, the sum of 1000 pounds Scots, the annual rent whereof, with the yearly maill of these two chalmers he built there, was allotted for entertaining of two bursars; which thousand pound was discharged to Sir John Hope, in respect paid to the Council by Sir James Stewart and Robert Lockhart. And the Council became debtors to the College of the same, conform to an act of Council of the 7th of January 1653.

" 37. Item, There was assigned by umquhile Alexander Wright to the Provost, Bailies, and Council, several sums of money, to the uses contained in the assignation ; and in special, the sum of 3399 pounds, 19s. 4d. of principal, due by Mr. Gilbert Mowat, and his cautioners, for the which there was new band given by the said Mr. Gilbert, his son, and their cautioners, to the treasurers of the Kirk and College, equally betwixt them, conform to an act of Council of the 24th of August 1642. Likeas, the. Council being adebtit to Robert Murray certain sums of money, they assigned the haill sum to the said Robert, in satisfaction of their debt to him *pro tanto ;* whereof the College part, in principal and annual rent, extends to 2381 lib. ; and became debtors to the College for payment thereof, conform to an act of Council of the 14th of March 1655.

" 38. Item, There was left in legacy to the College of this burgh, by Isobel Richiesone, relict of umquhile William Little, merchant, the sum of 8000 pounds ; and the Council being debtors to the said Isobel in the sum of 1107 lib. 16s. 8d., the legacy was defalked of the said sum, the superplus paid unto her executors ; and the Council became debtors to the College for the legacy of 8000 lib., conform to an act of Council of the 14th of December 1655.

" 39. Item, More received by the present treasurer of this burgh from John Lawder, present treasurer of the College, the sum of 202 lib. 6s. 8d.

" All which sums of money, mortified to the College since the very first foundation of the said College to this day, conform to the several acts of Council above mentioned, do extend in the whole to the sum of threescore eleven thousand pounds Scots money.   71,000 lib.

" The Provost, Bailies, and Council, finding that the foresaid sum is a very considerable part of the stock mortified to the College, as said is, and that they are bound in duty and conscience to pay annual rent for the same, for defraying of the burdens thereof : Therefore, ordains the treasurers of this burgh, present and to come, to pay to the treasurer of the College, and his successors in his office, yearly, in all time coming, the ordinary annual rent of the foresaid stock of 71,000 lib." [1]

[1] Town-Council Records, vol. xix. pp. 87-91.

V.

EXTRACTS FROM THE EDINBURGH TOWN-COUNCIL RECORDS
RELATING TO THE UNIVERSITY, FROM AUGUST 12, 1724,
TO MAY 9, 1779.—(Page 330.)

VOL. L

12*th August* 1724.—The Council, considering that they are
vested with a power of instituting professions of all liberal arts and
sciences in their College; and considering how much it would be
for the advantage of the city and kingdom, that all parts of medicine were taught here; and considering that the Institutes and
Practice of Medicine have not been professed or taught as yet in
the College: Therefore they institute the foresaid profession, and
elect Dr. William Porterfield, Professor of the Institutes and Practice of Medicine in this College.

11*th November*.—A memorial given in to the Town-Council by
Messrs. Rutherford, St. Clair, Plummer, and Innes, showing, that
these gentlemen, having purchased a house for a chemical laboratory, adjoining to the College garden, formerly let to Mr. George
Preston, and finding that the garden, neglected by Mr. Preston,
had for some years lain in disorder, desired of the honourable the Town-Council, that they might be allowed the use of
that ground for the better carrying on their design of furnishing
the apothecary shops with chemical medicines, and instructing the
students of medicine in that part of the science. They hoped the
Council would the more readily comply with their request, in regard
that the ground formerly allotted for the use of medicine would
still be employed in nursing and propagating such plants as were
necessary for the improvement of chemistry in this place. Beg
to have it on the same terms Mr. Preston had it before; or they
were willing to be at the charge of dressing and keeping it, provided the Council allowed them to have a grant of the ground for
ten years. Lease of the ground granted them as they petitioned.

18*th August* 1725.—Mr. Laurence Dundas to have those rooms
which he at present possesses within the College for life, and to be
allowed the dignity of a Professor, even though he should demit,
and still a vote among the Professors.

8th September.—Bailie Alexander Simpson reported, that he had intimated to Mr. Robert Henderson, Bibliothecar, to attend a committee appointed August 25th last; but since that time, he has gone to the country, and cannot be got. Bailie Simpson to write to him, informing him, that if he do not attend the committee betwixt and the next Council day, the Council will declare the office void, and appoint another Library-Keeper.

VOL. LI.

20th October.—Mr. Alexander Monro, Professor of Anatomy, upon petition, obtains a theatre in the College for public dissections, for teaching Anatomy.

3d November.—On petition of Mr. James Gregory, Professor of Mathematics, the Council agree to elect Mr. Colin M'Laurin, Professor of Mathematics in Marischall College, Aberdeen, joint with him. Great commendation of the profession of Mathematics in this College; of Mr. Gregory; and Mr. M'Laurin, who was recommended by very great men, and even by Sir Isaac Newton, who offered to contribute £20 per annum to assist in providing for him a salary, but the Council declined the generous offer. Mr. Gregory to enjoy his salary of £83, 6s. 8d. sterling, to go to his children for seven years from the date of Martinmas next, in case of his death. £50 sterling annually to Mr. M'Laurin, in addition to his students' fees.

9th February 1726.—Mr. Joseph Gibson, upon petition, appointed City Professor of Midwifery, but without fee or salary.

14th September.—Mr. Charles Mackie, Professor of Universal History, to have a chamber in the College free of rent.

15th December.—Provost Drummond, with the Council, a full meeting, met in the College, with Mr. William Wishart, Principal; Mr. William Hamilton, Professor of Divinity; Mr. Matthew Crawford, Professor of Church History; Mr. William Law, Professor of Moral Philosophy; Mr. Laurence Dundas, Professor of Humanity; Mr. James Gregory, Professor of Mathematics; Mr. William Scott, Professor of Greek; Mr. Charles Erskine, Professor of Law; Mr. Robert Stewart, Professor of Philosophy; Mr. Colin Drummond, Professor of Philosophy; Mr. James Crawford, Professor of Hebrew; Mr. James Craig, Mr. Charles Mackie, Mr. Alexander Bayne, Law Professors; Mr. Colin M'Laurin, Professor of Mathematics; Mr. Alexander Monro, Professor of Anatomy; Mr. Andrew Sinclair,

Mr. Andrew Plummer, Mr. John Innes, and Mr. John Rutherford, Professors of Chemistry.

Which day the Council, considering that the by-laws, rules, and regulations made about the administration and government of the University, ought to be revised and examined : Likewise, that it ought to be inquired into, how far such by-laws, rules, and regulations have been complied with, and whether the same, or any part thereof, ought to be continued or altered : As also, that the state of the Library, and conduct of the keeper thereof, with respect to his executing and discharging that office, ought to be inquired into : RESOLVED, that a committee be appointed for that purpose, to meet immediately, and to have power to adjourn, and to call for persons, papers, and records, necessary to their performing the matters to them committed, and to report, with an opinion : And, accordingly, the Council appointed Bailie James Nimmo, John Ferguson, Patrick Lindsay, Dean Guild, David Flint, old Treasurer, Allan Whiteford, Merchant Councillor, John Lauder, Trades' Councillor, William Cant, Convener, John Kirkwood, chirurgeon, and David Mitchell, goldsmith, as a committee.

Same day, the Lord Provost adjourned the meeting till Tuesday January 3, next, at two o'clock, and appointed the whole Council, with the Masters and Professors, to attend that diet in this place.

3d January 1727.—In the College Bailie Nimmo reported from the committee, anent the College affairs, that they had made some progress in the affairs committed to them, and desired leave to sit again. Which being considered by the Council, they appointed the said committee to meet frequently, and to prepare a report, with their opinion, against the 7th of February next. The committee having desired that a deputation from the Professors and Masters may be appointed, to confer with them touching the affairs to them committed, the Reverend Principal reported, that they had named Mr. Hamilton, Mr. Law, Mr. Scott, Mr. Stewart, Mr. Drummond, Mr. Mackie, Mr. Erskine, Mr. M'Laurin, Mr. Monro, Mr. Plummer, and Mr. Sinclair. Council adjourned to the 7th February.

10th February.—Council adjourned their meeting in the College on Tuesday next, till the 2d Tuesday of March, and appointed the Principal and Masters to be acquainted therewith.

28th July.—On examining the College Treasurer's accounts from Martinmas 1724 to Whitsunday 1726, found his receipts, including former arrears, £2050, 5s. 1⅝d. sterling ; his payments

£2158, 7s. 10d. sterling, whereby it appears that his payments exceed his receipts in £108, 2s. 8⅙d. sterling.

23d November.—Delegates appointed to meet with delegates from the College of Justice, to consider Mr. Laurence Dundas's proposal to resign in favour of Adam Watt, second son of Adam Watt, town-clerk of this city. The town delegates authorized to give their voice in favour of Mr. Watt, provided he be found qualified.

5th January 1728.—Patrick Lindsay, Dean of Guild, reports that Mr. Adam Watt was, by the delegates from the Lords of Session, the Advocates, the Writers to the Signet, and the Town-Council, unanimously elected Professor of Humanity.

3d April.—Two Polish students, Valdislaus Boweits and Gabriel Brenia Sheroski, appointed to receive £10 sterling out of the interest of the mortification of Robert Brown, merchant in Zamose in Poland.

14th May—Bailie Thomas Fenton reported, that he was informed that the Masters and Professors of the College had presumed to meet as a Faculty, and to do certain deeds, particularly to draw up and sign a protest to be given in to the Assembly, in the cause of Mr. John Simson, Professor of Divinity in the College of Glasgow. The Council find, that if this was the case, it was unwarrantable and illegal; and if the foresaid protest be presented to the Assembly, the Council authorize and appoint Bailie Fenton to give in to the Assembly a protest against such a proceeding as illegal without the Council's sanction.

VOL. LII.

28th August.—Mr Adam Watt, Professor of Humanity, to possess Mr. Dundas's chambers when the latter has no more use for them.

12th February 1729.—Council appoint the College Treasurer to pay to Valdislaus Boweits, a Polish student of divinity, £15 sterling out of the bygone annual rents due on mortification of the late Robert Brown, merchant in Zamose, in Poland. James Nimmo, Dean of Guild, to write a letter to the consistory of Zamose anent bygone annual rents, and to report.

Council appoint Mr. William Hamilton, Professor of Divinity, Mr. Charles Erskine, Advocate, his Majesty's Solicitor, and Mr. Colin Drummond, Professor of Philosophy, to meet on Monday next, at two o'clock afternoon, in the common hall of the College, in presence of the ministers of the city, to take trial of the qualifications of Mr. William Scott, junior, for teaching of Greek : Against which Bailie Thomas Fenton, old Provost, protested, and gave in protest in writing, bearing, that it is irregular and precipitant to appoint examinators for a Professor of Greek in the College of Edinburgh when there is no vacancy ; and, also, that to proceed to the trial of a Professor of Ethics in the said College in a private way, is contrary to a standing law and act of Council, August 9, 1694, and *that* before any visitation of the College be made by the Council, as patrons ; with a resolution to amend errors and irregularities that have of late crept in amongst the Professors.

Therefore, and for several other weighty reasons, too notour to the Council, and all the inhabitants of this city, he protests—1. Against the Council's proceeding to appoint examinators for the trial of a Professor of Greek in the College of Edinburgh, there being no vacancy ; and as this procedure is inconsistent. 2. Against appointing any private examination of a Professor as contrary to the above act, August 9, 1694, which appoints the publicly affixing of programs upon all the College gates of Scotland, that men of learning may appear, and gain the office by merit ; and as public learning hath already suffered by certain persons being admitted to be Masters of the College in a clandestine way, and contrary to the said act, wisely made. 3. Against any Professor of Ethics being appointed, till after a visitation for reformation of abuses there practised, to the dishonour of the Council and discouragement of learning. 4. Against giving any greater salary to the Professor of Ethics than to the other Regents of Philosophy, considering the low state of the public funds of the city.

To this Bailies James Flint, Archibald M'Coull, and Mr. James Davidson, City Treasurer, gave answers as follows in behalf of the Council :—

That Mr. William Scott was by a former act already preferred to the profession of Ethics, if he should choose, on Mr. Law's death, which has intervened, and he has already given proof of his qualifications.

The act of Council, August 9, 1694, has gone into disuse ; and indeed public trials, from experience, have been found not to answer—on the contrary, to have been attended with bad effects, which is so obvious to all, that it is unnecessary to mention instances ; and the Council, no doubt, have power to rescind that regulation of anno 1694.

There is no good reason why the town should delay the supplying these offices till after a visitation, with which it has no connexion. The Council may visit the College when they please. There is a salary annexed to the Professorship of Ethics, which ought neither to be diminished nor augmented but on good grounds; and no reason appears for diminishing it.

26th February.—The Provost reports that the examinators had found Mr. William Scott, junior, son of Mr. William Scott, Professor of Greek, qualified. Mr. William Scott, senior, Professor of Greek, represents, that as he had right to be Professor of Ethics, if he chose, on Mr. Law's death, by virtue of an act of the Town-Council (see below under January 30, 1730), he accordingly chose to be so.

Thomas Fenton, old Provost, upon this, gives in a draft of an act to the Council, in which he proposes that Professors, in all time coming, should be fixed and settled during the Council's pleasure only; which is put to the vote, and rejected by the Council, who proceed to confirm Mr. Scott senior's election as Professor of Ethics, and elect Mr. Scott, junior, Professor of Greek, both *ad vitam aut culpam.*

Same day.—Dr. John Rutherford, Andrew St. Clair, Andrew Plummer, and John Innes, who were formerly restricted, so that only two of them could vote in the Senatus Academicus, allowed all to vote. This in answer to their humble petition.

9th July.—College Treasurer to pay to the heirs of Principal Wishart £10 sterling in full payment of all repairs done by him to his lodging.

19th November.—Lists of bursars in the town's gift to be given in to the Lord Provost.

College Treasurer not to undertake any work without an order of Council.

30th January 1730.—Upon the representation of Mr. Colin Drummond, Professor of Philosophy, he is chosen Professor of Greek, in place of Mr. William Scott, junior, deceased, in virtue of the act of Council, June 16, 1708; which was to the effect, that when any vacancy should happen, the remaining Professors, or those then in places, should have the offer of the vacancy, according to their standing. Mr. Robert Stewart declining to accept of this vacancy, Mr. Drummond humbly represented to the honourable Council that, as he had by the above act the liberty to choose the said office, he made choice of it. The Council agree that the office of Professor of Logic and Metaphysics should be declared vacant ; but that, as the said Mr. Colin Drummond has so far advanced in teaching that class for this season, he should continue therein until the next session ; and that the person to be elected Professor of Logic and Metaphysics should carry on the teaching of the Greek class till that period, at which time the several Professors are to begin and open their several professions.

At the same time, it is declared that it shall be lawful for any student to enter to the Semi class, or any superior class, although he was not a Bejan, or taught Greek by Mr. Colin Drummond. Mr. Drummond's acceptance of the Professorship of Greek not to impair his position, by degree of seniority or otherwise, among the Professors of Philosophy, but he and his successors in office and profession to be numbered and placed amongst the Professors of Philosophy according to their admission.

5th February.—At a meeting of the Town-Council with the Professors, to deliberate about a Professor of Logic and Metaphysics, they agree upon a comparative trial. A Latin discourse, prescribed to the candidates, on " The Origin, Cause, and Remedy of Error ; " and the candidates, after their discourses are over, to be at liberty to make reflections on one another's discourses, which the authors may defend *viva voce.* Each of the candidates also to be tried on Greek ; and the Faculty shall appoint any one of their number to take this trial. No one discourse to exceed three-quarters of an hour. The trial to be taken on Monday, the 23d instant, and to begin at nine o'clock forenoon in the common hall. This to be intimated to Mr. Robert Hamilton, Mr. James Balfour, Mr. John Stevenson, Mr. Thomas Johnston, and Mr. John Lees. That the meeting shall be opened and constituted by prayer, in Latin, by the Professor of Divinity.

25th February.—The Council, taking into consideration the opinion of the Professors of the College upon the late comparative trial, taken by appointment of the Council, and in presence of the members and ministers of Edinburgh, unanimously elected Mr. John Stevenson,[1] governor to Lord Bargenie, to be Professor of Logic

---

[1] [Stevenson's appointment to this chair gave a powerful impulse to the cause of literature in Scotland. His course of rhetoric consisted simply in the observations which he made on Aristotle's Poetics and Longinus's Essay on the Sublime, in the course of reading them with his students, for he did not deliver formal lectures. His illustrations he drew not only from the rhetorical and critical works of Cicero, Quintilian, and Horace, but from modern authors, prose and poetical, including French, quoting, however, most

and Metaphysics, with all fees, profits, emoluments, and privileges; and the said Mr. John, by his acceptation hereof, promises to observe the laws and constitutions of the College, and to submit himself to the Magistrates and Council, conform to the foundation of said College in their favours.

VOL. LIII.

6*th January* 1731.—A room in the College granted to the academy for drawing.

24*th February.*—A warrant for College Treasurer to sell two lodgings in Niddry's Wynd, belonging to the College.

9*th June.*—College Treasurer to make out a list of bursars, and to inform the Council two months before any vacancy happen.

3*d November.*—John Drysdale, lawful son of the deceased John Drysdale, minister of Kirkaldy, a bursar on Dalgleish's mortification, in the gift of the town.

VOL. LIV.

9*th February* 1732.—College Treasurer prohibited from undertaking any work in the College above 20 pounds Scots, without laying the same before the Council.

16*th February.*—Mr. William Hamilton, Professor of Divinity, elected Principal, in place of the deceased Mr. William Wishart.[1]

---

largely from the English classics. In the more proper business of his class, while giving a general history of scholastic logic, which he taught was no fit instrument for the discovery of truth, he delivered lectures on Locke's Essay on the Human Understanding, using as his text-book Bishop Wynne's abridgment of that work. Speculations, such as those contained in that essay, were then almost wholly unknown in our Scottish Universities, and were little appreciated even in England.—Bower's Hist. of the Univ. of Edinburgh, vol. ii. pp. 269-281.]

[1] [Principal William Wishart, whose father was minister of Kinneil (now united to Borrowstounness), in Linlithgowshire, was first minister of South Leith, from which he was translated to the Tron Church, Edinburgh. He was the author of Theologia, or Discourses of God, in 2 vols. Edinburgh, 1716.

Writing of Wishart's successor in May 1730, nine months before the election, Wodrow says, "Dr. Hamilton has taught Divinity now twenty or twenty-one years, and is weary of the toil; and the Principal's post is an easy post for him, now that he is aged, and turned sixty."—(Analecta, vol. iv. p. 138.) From several passages in the Analecta, it appears that Hamilton's orthodoxy was suspected. He enjoyed his new dignity only one year.]

And Mr. James Smith, minister of Edinburgh,[1] elected Professor of Divinity, but must resign his charge as minister.

15th March.—Appoint Robert Manderston, present College Treasurer, to receive by inventory from Mr. William Hog, late College Treasurer, all the writs in his custody belonging to the College.

19th April.—Patrick Crokat elected Janitor, in place of James Seton deceased, burdened with five pounds sterling per annum, to Anna Campbell, relict of Alexander Somerville, writer, burgess.

26th July.—Mr. William Dawson, minister at Newcastle-upon-Tyne, chosen Professor of Hebrew and Oriental Languages, in place of Dr. James Crawford,[2] deceased, with 600 pounds Scots of yearly salary. *N.B.*—About this time a great many repairs were made in the College.

30th August.—Mr. William Hog, late College Treasurer, his accounts audited and approven, from Martinmas 1729 to Candlemas 1732.—Receipts, £3135, 18s. 5⅝d. sterling; payments, £3128, 3s. 2⅝d. sterling; balance due by him, £7, 15s. 3d. sterling.

15th November.—Mr. George Sinclair and Mr. Charles Anstruther, Advocates, from the Faculty of Advocates, delivered to the Magistrates and Council a leet of two, one of whom to be chosen Professor of Civil Law in the College by the Council, in terms of Act of Parliament, 9 George I., viz.:—Mr. Thomas Dundas, who had 119 votes of the Faculty, and Mr. John Erskine, who had 82. The Council chose Mr. Thomas Dundas,[3] in place of Mr. James Craig, deceased; and he appeared in Council, and qualified himself by swearing the oath *de fideli administratione*, and the oath of allegiance, and signing the same with the assurance to King George II., and subscribed the oath in the Council's Act, 10th September 1718.

14th February 1733.—William Dawson, Professor of Hebrew, allowed the possession of that house in the College presently possessed by Margaret Piggot, relict of Mr. John Goodall.

18th July.—Mr. James Smith, Professor of Divinity,[4] elected Principal, in place of Mr. William Hamilton, deceased; and Mr.

---

[1] [Mr. Smith had been recently translated from Cramond to Edinburgh.]

[2] ["March 1731. Dr. James Crawford, Professor of the Hebrew tongue at Edinburgh—a man of piety, of excellent solid sense, but a recluse, modest man—died in the end of February, or the beginning of this month."—Wodrow's Analecta, vol. iv. p. 212.]

[3] [Dundas was afterwards Sheriff-depute of Kirkcudbright.]

[4] [Smith held the office only three years.]

John Gowdie, one of the ministers of Edinburgh, elected Professor of Divinity.[1]

19*th December.*—Report of all the chambers in the College. The rental of those that pay amounts to about £30 sterling. *N.B.*—This shows the state of the College apartments at that time.

VOL. LV.

9*th January* 1734.—Mr. William Scott, Professor of Ethics, gives in a letter, bearing that he is so indisposed by a bad state of health as to be unfit for his office, and requesting that John Pringle, junior, Professor of Medicine, may be joined with him as a colleague. The Council resolve to take the opinion of the other Professors respecting Dr. Pringle's fitness.

Wednesday, 13th February.—Dr. Pringle to deliver a discourse, in the common hall on Tuesday next, upon Ethics and Moral Philosophy, and the ministers to be called to give their avisamentum, Tuesday next, afternoon.

Wednesday, 20th February.—The Provost reports that Dr. Pringle's discourse had been highly approved by all the learned audience, and that the ministers thought him most fit. Dr. Pringle[2] therefore unanimously chosen Professor of Ethics, jointly with Mr. William Scott, the full salary to be enjoyed by Mr. Scott during all the days of his life; and Dr. Pringle to have the said salary in case he survive Mr. Scott, only from and after the time of Mr. Scott's decease.

27*th February.*—Dr. Pringle accepts the office, and takes the oaths, etc.

22*d May.*—The roof of the Library to be repaired.

19*th June.*—Commissioners appointed to meet with delegates from the College of Justice, to choose a Professor of Humanity, in place of Adam Watt, deceased.

24*th July.*—John Drysdale, son to the deceased Mr. John Drysdale, minister of the gospel at Kirkaldy, received Divinity bursar on Ramsay's Mortification.

[1] [Gowdie or Goldie had been recently translated from Earlston to Edinburgh. In the Theological Chair he used as his text-book Benedicti Picteti Theologia Christiana. He died on the 19th of February 1762, in the eightieth year of his age.—See Morren's Annals of the General Assembly, vol. i. pp. 319, 320.]

[2] [Dr., afterwards Sir John Pringle, Bart., had taken his degree of M.D. at Leyden, on the 20th of July 1730; and returning to Scotland, he practised as a physician in Edinburgh.]

11*th September.*—A petition of Colin Drummond about the teaching of Greek (*N.B.*—This in the College Records); and act thereanent. This act superseded, January 15, 1735.

2*d October.*—Mr. John Ker, Professor of Greek, Aberdeen, chosen Professor of Humanity by the delegates.

16*th October.*—Weneslaus Radose, a Polish bursar, in the College, to receive a quarter's payment on Robert Brown's Mortification.

11*th November.*—" A petition from Mr. Colin Drummond, Professor of Greek in the College, having been read and remitted to a proper committee, the committee this day reported, that they having duly considered the said petition, with the extract of the Act of Parliamentary visitation therein referred to, dated the 16th of August 1700, were of opinion that it might contribute much to the advancement of learning, and to the encouragement of this University, that said act of visitation were duly observed, and particularly that part of it for the encouragement of public Universities, by a due discouragement of private and clandestine teaching, whereby it is enacted, that no scholar bred at the schools in Scotland, and not foreign bred, should be admitted to learn philosophy, or any part of the course thereof, in any of the Colleges of Scotland, unless he had learned the Greek, at least for the ordinary year, under the fixed Greek Master. The committee were of opinion that the foresaid act should be duly observed in all time coming; but, being informed that the foresaid act of visitation had not hitherto been observed in the University of Glasgow, that it may be prejudicial to this University to put the said act in full execution, unless the same were duly observed in Glasgow; and that therefore this act should not take place until the University of Glasgow bound themselves to the punctual observation of the same. The Council approved of the said report, and enacted that the said Parliamentary visitation shall be put to due execution in the University of this city so soon as the same is done in the University of Glasgow; and till such time as the said act shall take place in both the said Universities, appointed all students entering to the Semi class to undergo an examination upon the Greek in presence of the Greek Professor: Also appointed, that no scholar from any private school within this city or its liberty shall be allowed to enter to the Philosophy classes, unless he has been a year under a fixed Professor of Greek, and this to take place at the sitting down of the sessions in October first: And statute and ordain, that none shall have a title to the degree of Master of Arts, except such as, after their first year's reading of Greek, either under any teacher not within the liberties of this city (until the Parliamentary act of visitation take place), or under our, or any other fixed Professor of Greek, shall attend our Professor of Greek his private lectures, for their further improvement in that language, for at least another year, so long as he continues to give the same five days in the week; and he is hereby obliged not to take an honorary from any scholar above twice, which shall entitle all to attend such private lectures as many sessions as they please : And further ordain, that none be enrolled students of Divinity but such as have got the degree of Master of Arts, and report a certificate thereof to the Professor of Divinity."

15*th January* 1735.—" Having considered a representation of the Principal and Professors of the College, with answers thereto made by Mr. Drummond, Professor of Greek, and having heard the opinion of a Committee, to whom the same was referred, the Council resolved that the matters mentioned in the said representation and answers, be taken into consideration, at the visitation which is appointed to be held in the College upon the 27th instant; meantime did supersede the effect and execution of the act of Council therein specified, in favours of Mr. Drummond, dated the 11th of September last."

15*th January* 1735.—Mr. John Ker, Professor of Humanity, to have possession of the two rooms in the College that were lately in the possession of the deceased Mr. Laurence Dundas, and that during the Council's pleasure.

VOL. LVI.

15*th August.*—Report of committee about teaching Greek. See September 10, *infra.*

29*th August.*—Mr. Robert Henderson, Library-keeper, to give in an account of the present state of the Library, and of what catalogues of the books he has made out.

10*th September.*—The above order renewed, and that Mr. Henderson give strict attendance in the Library, and admit Mr. William Lauder to inspect the presses and shelves.

Upon the report of committee about teaching Greek, the Council agreed to put the Professorship of Greek on the same footing with the Professors of Greek in other Colleges in Scotland; and that the Professors of Greek and Philosophy begin the business of their respective professions on the 20th of November yearly, and, after that date, to interfere no more in teaching the business of the other Professors.

15th October.—Intimation of this act to be made to the Principal and Professors.

3d December.—Professor Bayne to have a chamber in the College.

17th December.—Mr. George Abercrombie, Advocate, on the King's presentation, to be admitted Professor of Public Law and Law of Nature and Nations in place of Mr. William Kirkpatrick, Advocate, bearing date September 5, last. The Magistrates agree to the admission, but protest against its prejudging their right as patrons.

26th December.—Alexander Carlyle,[1] son to Mr. William Carlyle, minister at Prestonpans, preferred to a Bursary of Philosophy on Hector Ford of Branxton's Mortification. The same rescinded February 18, 1736, as the holder was not qualified according to the Mortification, and a Bursary of Philosophy granted him on Dr. Robert Johnston's Mortification.

21st January 1736.—Mr. Monro, Professor of Anatomy, upon a petition from him, allowed a room in the College, during the Council's pleasure, and that for teaching his private sessions only.

VOL. LVII.

28th July.—Dr. Pringle's rooms in the College to be repaired.

10th November.—Dr. William Wishart, minister of a dissenting congregation in London, elected Principal[2] in place of Mr. James Smith, deceased.

17th November.—College committee to order Mr. Robert Henderson to deliver in a catalogue of the books and other things under his care.

8th December.—Bursars to extract their acts; and all grants of bursaries which shall hereafter be made and granted, and shall not be extracted and duly intimated to the College Treasurer, or his successors, within the space of thirty-one days next after the same shall be given, shall be void.

---

[1] [Dr. Alexander Carlyle, afterwards minister of Inveresk, and whose recently published Autobiography has excited so much attention.]

[Dr. William Wishart was the son of the former Principal of the same name. For some reason not explained, he was not installed until the 9th of November the year following. About fifteen or sixteen months after his installation, he became minister of New Greyfriars' Church. — See Morren's Annals, vol. i. pp. 309-315.]

13th *July* 1737.—Upon a leet of two from the Advocates, viz.,
Mr. John Erskine, senior, and Mr. James Balfour, the Magistrates
and Council elect the said John Erskine[1] Professor of Scots Law,
in place of Mr. Andrew Bayne, deceased. Salary £100 sterling.
Erskine compeared, and qualified himself by swearing and signing
the oath *de fideli administratione*—the oath appointed to be taken
by every person who obtained any lucrative office of this city by the
Council's act, dated September 10, 1718,—the oaths of allegiance
and abjuration, and by signing the assurance to his Majesty, King
George the Second.

9th *November.*—Dr, William Wishart appeared in Council, and
took the usual oaths. Installed this day, and a copy of the regulations and instructions, usually given to his predecessors, to be
delivered to him.

7th *December.*—A Commission from the King to Mr. Patrick
Cumming, one of the ministers of the city,[2] to be Professor of
Ecclesiastical History in place of Mr. Matthew Crawford, was read.
Resolved that he be admitted, under the protest, that his admission
should not prejudice the Council's right to the patronage of the
College.

31st *March* 1738.—Dr. Charles Alston[3] elected Professor of
Medicine and Botany.

10th *May.*—Tack of the Physic garden in the College, granted
rent free for twelve years from Martinmas 1738, to Drs. Rutherford, Sinclair, and Plummer, Professors of Medicine.

[1] [From Erskine's high reputation, the class of Scots Law was now attended by a greater number of students than formerly. His text-book for several years was Mackenzie's Institutions; but about the year 1752 he published a text-book of his own. He taught Scots Law in the University twenty-eight years. His Institute of the Law of Scotland, which is still considered a standard book on the subject, was not published till after his death in 1773. He was the father of the celebrated Dr. John Erskine, one of the ministers of the Greyfriars' Church, Edinburgh.]

[2] [Cumming had recently been trans- lated from Lochmaben to Edinburgh.

He gave lectures upon Jo. Alphonsi Turretini Compendium Historiæ Eccle- siasticæ. He died on the 1st of April 1776, in the eighty-first year of his age. —See Morren's Annals, vol. i. pp. 319- 324, and vol. ii. p. 391.]

[3] [Alston, who was King's Botanist for Scotland, was elected in the room of Mr. George Preston, who had been long superannuated. He was Professor twenty-two years; and during that period he regularly delivered two courses of lectures every year, one on Botany in summer, and the other on *Materia Medica* in winter. He died on the 22d of November 1760, in the seventy- seventh year of his age.]

26th July.—Colin Drummond resigns his Professorship of Greek to be joined with Mr. Robert Law, son to the deceased Mr. William Law of Elvingston, late Professor of Moral Philosophy, on condition that he enjoy his salary during his life, and be allowed to teach students of Chirurgery, Anatomy, or Medicine such Greek books as relate to their business only.

Previous notice had been given, namely, by an act of Council, July 19, to the Principal and Professors and Ministers to attend in the Burgh room, on Tuesday following, at three o'clock afternoon, the trial of Mr. Robert Law's qualifications for teaching Greek. The examinators declared themselves satisfied with Mr. Robert Law's qualifications. Mr. Drummond and he are therefore elected conjunct Professors of Greek.

VOL. LX.

14th December 1739.—Mr. Robert Smith, surgeon, elected Professor of Midwifery in the College, on the death of Joseph Gibson, Professor thereof in the city, but without a salary.[1]

VOL. LXI.

18th March 1741.—A bond by the city to Patrick Manderston, College Treasurer, and his successors in office, to and for the use of the said College, pursuant to the Council's act, February 11th last, containing the accumulated sum of £11,451, 12s. 2⅔d. sterling, bearing annual rent, from and after Candlemas last, with £2000 sterling of liquidate penalty, was brought in, and read, and signed, and ordered to be registered in the Burgh Court Books.

VOL. LXII.

17th November.—College Treasurer's account from Lammas 1739 to Lammas last 1741, with the account of mortcloth dues.—His charge, inclusive of £23, 2s. 4d. sterling, of former arrears, amounts to £2192, 11s. 5d.; and his discharge extends to £1853, 0s. $8\frac{11}{12}$d.; balance due by him, £339, 10s. $8\frac{1}{12}$d.

9th December.—On the death of Mr. Robert Law,[2] joint Professor

---

[1] [Smith's commission was ampler than that of his predecessor; it constituted him a member of the Senate. He held this Professorship 17 years.]

[2] [Law taught only three sessions, when he was prematurely cut off by consumption.]

of Greek, Mr. Colin Drummond resigns, on condition he may retain the salary upon a new election, and be on the same footing he was with Mr. Law.

Mr. Robert Hunter elected, as he had given sufficient proof of his qualifications by teaching Greek privately within this city, for several years, with great success and applause. He qualifies. Only the fees granted to Mr. Hunter; the salary annexed to the office being reserved for Mr. Drummond.

The Humanity class being vacant by the death of Mr. John Ker, two candidates having appeared, Mr. Foulis and Mr. George Stewart, the Council agree, previous to the choice of their delegates, that the Principal and Professors take trial of the knowledge of these two candidates in the Greek and Latin languages, and report.

11*th December.*—The trial not yet being taken, a majority of the Council agree now to choose their delegates, viz., Bailie Mark Sandilands, and Walter Boswell, Deacon of the Hammermen. The delegates instructed to insist on a trial of the candidates, before all the delegates, and ordered to give their votes for the best qualified, according to the signed report of the examinators.

16*th December.*—An extract of the election of Mr. George Stewart to be Professor of Humanity produced, bearing that the delegates had met in the Advocates' Library, December 11, 1741, viz., Lord Justice-Clerk; Lord Minto; Mr. James Graham of Airth, Dean of Faculty; Mr. Alexander M'Millan, Deputy-Keeper of the Signet; and the two from the Town-Council as above. The Town-Council delegates insisted on a trial; and the two candidates attending informed them that each believed the other sufficiently qualified, and therefore insisted not on a trial, but submitted themselves to the delegates; who accordingly proceeded to the election. The two Lords of Session, and two delegates for the Council, voted for Mr. Stewart, and the rest for Mr. Foulis. Whereupon all the delegates declared that Mr. Stewart was duly elected, and appointed Mr. Ruddiman, their clerk, to give out extracts to all having interest. The Council appoint Mr. Stewart to be admitted.

3*d February* 1742.—Reported by Bailie Mark Sandilands and his committee, that they were of opinion that the proper place for building the observatory in the College is at the back of the house formerly possessed by Mr. John Ker; that therefore Mr. M'Laurin should have possession of the said house, and what more of the adjacent rooms he may have occasion for, he paying the ordinary rent for the said rooms.

10th February.—Mr. Robert Hunter allowed to possess seven rooms in the College rent free, upon condition of his laying out £50 sterling of his own money in repairing the said rooms ; and if he die before five years, that then £10 sterling yearly shall be paid to his heirs, for the remainder of that time.

VOL. LXIII.

17th March.—Room in the College possessed by Mr. John Murdoch, French teacher, to be given to Mr. George Stewart, during the pleasure of the Council.

25th August.—Memorial from Mr. Robert Stewart,[1] Professor of Natural Philosophy, read in Council, setting forth, that he had been above thirty-eight years a member of the University, and was now old, and requesting that his son, Dr. John Stewart, might be conjunct Professor with him ; and stating that Dr. Stewart had given proof of his abilities, by teaching a good part of the last session, to the general satisfaction of all the students, and was amply recommended by those Professors of the College whose subjects were most nearly connected with that of Natural Philosophy. These recommendations read. Signed,—Colin Drummond, Gr. L. et Phil. P. ; Charles Alston, M. et Bot. P. ; Colin M'Laurin, Math. P. ; Alexander Monro, Anat. P. ; Andrew Plummer, Med. P. ; Jo. Rutherford, Med. P. Professors and ministers to take trial of him in the lower Council house on Tuesday first.

1st September.—Report of the Examinators, who were the Principal and Professors of the College, in presence of some of the Town-Council and some of the ministers of the city. The examination took place, August 31. Report favourable to Dr. John Stewart. Also produced the avisamentum of the ministers who attended the examination, in favour of the said Dr. John Stewart. Wherefore he and his father, Mr. Robert, are chosen joint Professors of Natural Philosophy, the salary being reserved to Mr. Robert, and the other emoluments to Dr. John, during their joint lives, and it

---

[1] [Professor Robert Stewart was the youngest son of Sir Thomas Stewart of Coltness, Bart. He appears at first to have taught the Cartesian philosophy, in which he had been educated ; a system of philosophy very different from that into which Mr. Colin M'Laurin, who contemporaneously occupied the Mathematical Chair, initiated his class. But for a considerable number of years, during the latter period of his Professorship, having renounced, as untenable, the Cartesian theories, he taught the Newtonian system. He followed Keill's Introduction, Hydrostatics and Pneumatics, and adopted as his text-book, Gregory's Optics, Astronomy, etc.]

being declared that they are to have but one voice in the Faculty of Professors, and that *per vices*. They qualify.

24th November.—College treasurer's accounts from Lammas 1741 to Michaelmas 1742. His charge, including £81, 7s. 0⅔d. of former arrears, and £339, 10s. 8d., the balance due by Patrick Manderston, last College treasurer, amounts to £1335, 15s. 7⅓d. sterling; and his discharge, inclusive of £542, 9s. 8d. of arrears, amounts to £1518, 2s. 0⅔d.; balance due to him, £182, 6s. 6⅓d.

1st December 1742.—" Upon a representation from the Principal and Professors of this city's University, setting forth that they were informed an attempt was made to set up a stage in this place without warrant of law: That they could not but be apprehensive that idleness and corruption of manners among the youth was likely to flow from a licentious acting of stage plays, while there were so many dissolute pieces of that sort in the English language, and the choice left to such as either from their own taste, or in compliance with the vicious relish of the multitude, were likely to choose such performances as had the most direct tendency to corrupt the morals of the audience, especially those of the younger sort: That their former observations had greatly confirmed them in this apprehension, where the performances had been frequent and the access easy: That the unhappy influence of playhouses, where there are Universities, had been apparent to the Legislature, for which reason all such in or near Oxford or Cambridge are by Act of Parliament lately discharged:—Praying, therefore, the honourable Council on these accounts to take proper measures for suppressing the same: Which having been considered by the Magistrates and Council, they authorized the Magistrates to cause prosecute the stage players before the Court of Session, who either have or shall attempt to act plays and interludes within this city or liberties thereof, contrary to Act of Parliament, and to the prejudice of the youth of this city, and do recommend to the Magistrates to cause carry on said prosecution with the utmost frugality, and to report from time to time the success therein."

VOL. LXIV.

14th December 1743. — Catalogue of the College Library, borrowed by the deceased Bailie Blackwood from the Keeper of the Library on receipt, presented in Council with the said receipt.

18th July 1744.—Letter from Dr. John Pringle, Professor of Moral Philosophy,[1] to the Lord Provost, dated Brussels, June 20th, N s., 1744, intimating that he cannot easily return to resume his office. At the time he wrote last to his Lordship, there were some hopes of an accommodation between the warring powers; "but now," says he, "since the open rupture with France, as the duration of the war is very uncertain, I can with no assurance ask any further indulgence from your Lordship and the rest of my honourable patrons." As the town had already granted him leave of absence, he could not well expect farther indulgence. He leaves the matter in the hands of the Town-Council. The Provost authorized to prepared an answer.

20th July.—The Provost's answer, expressing great respect for Dr. Pringle, but hopes he will send a letter of resignation : still they are willing to indulge him another year, if he could assure them that he would then return to his duty in the College as formerly. The patrons had now indulged his residence abroad for two years.

15th August.—Report from committee on the College affairs, that Mr. Robert Hunter, Professor of Greek, had, in consequence of an act of Council, February 10, 1742, expended upwards of £50 sterling in repairing the house he possesses in the College.

17th August.—An answer from Dr. Pringle, dated Brussels, August 15, N.S., 1744, accepting indulgence, but unwilling to promise the conditions.

The Provost to write a reply, that the Council, since they cannot have a security for his returning to the exercise of his profession in the University, desire that he would be pleased to send his resignation.

VOL. LXV.

27th March 1745.—Dr. Pringle sends a letter of resignation, dated London, March 19, 1745. The Council accept it, and recommend to Mr. William Cleghorn, Master of Arts, and son of

[1] [Dr. Pringle did not teach the Moral Philosophy class many years. He first received from the Earl of Stair an appointment to be physician to his Lordship, as Commander of the British Army. Upon the 24th of August 1742, he was constituted physician to the military hospitals in Flanders ; and in March 1744 he was made Physician-General to his Majesty's Forces in the Low Countries and parts beyond seas, as well as physician to the royal hospitals in the same countries. These situations he was unwilling to resign for the sake of retaining his Professorship.]

the deceased Hugh Cleghorn, merchant burgess of Edinburgh, who has had the charge of Dr. Pringle's class during his absence, to continue his course of lectures during the rest of the session.

Wednesday, 22d May.—Resolved that on Tuesday next, at three o'clock afternoon, the Council meet in the laigh Council-house, and that the ministers of the city be then desired to attend to give their avisamentum anent the choice of a Professor of Moral Philosophy, for supplying the vacancy in this class by the demission of Dr. Pringle, and Mr. Hutcheson's declining to accept.[1]

5th June.—Mr. William Cleghorn chosen Professor of Pneumatics and Moral Philosophy, *ad vitam aut culpam.*

5th June.—Recommended to the College committee to inquire and consider how far the several Professors observe the directions and instructions laid down to them by the several acts of Council heretofore made, and what farther directions may be necessary to be given to the Professors in time coming, and to consider this matter with all convenient speed, and report.

19th June.—Mr. William Cleghorn appears in Council and qualifies. Bailie John Yetts authorized to repair to the College and install him in the usual manner.

6th September.—Upon a memorial from Mr. Robert Hunter, Professor of Greek, setting forth that he used to make more by private teaching than all the emoluments that presently accrue to him, the salary annexed to that office being reserved to Mr. Colin Drummond, the other joint Professor during his life, the Council allow him 400 marks salary yearly during the life of Colin Drummond, joint Professor.

The Council, upon a memorial from Dr. Charles Alston, Professor of Botany, in regard there is no salary annexed to that Professorship, allowed him 500 marks annually, during the Council's pleasure, from Lammas 1746, as the Doctor has now, upwards of twenty-five years, been employed in that station, and, as such, has deservedly acquired a very great character.

---

[1] [A week after Dr. Pringle's resignation was accepted, namely, on the 3d of April, the Town-Council transmitted a presentation to the vacant chair to the celebrated Dr. Francis Hutcheson, Professor of Moral Philosophy in the College of Glasgow, who was then in the meridian of his fame. But this eminent philosopher declined to accept of the proffered preferment. It was on this occasion that Hume the historian applied for this chair; but his philosophical theories, which he had already published, effectually operated against his success.]

5th January 1747.—William Alexander, old Treasurer, elected College Treasurer for the year ensuing.

Committee named for College affairs. . . . Any five of them to be a quorum, the preses being always one.

20th January.—Mr. Joseph Ferguson preferred to Bursary of Divinity on Buchanan of that Ilk's Mortification.

Mr. John Gibson preferred to Bursary of Divinity on Mr. James Nairne's Mortification.

Mr. Thomas Hunter preferred to Bursary of Divinity on Mr. James Nairne's Mortification.

25th February.—Ralph M'Farlane preferred to Bursary of Divinity on Dr. Robert Leighton's Mortification.

George Couples preferred to Bursary of Divinity on Mr. Andrew Ramsay's Mortification.

Dugald Stewart, son to Mr. Charles Stewart, minister at Campbeltoun, preferred to Bursary of Philosophy on Dr. Johnston's Mortification.

Thomas Blacklock preferred to Bursary of Philosophy on Dr. Johnston's Mortification.

Andrew Petrie preferred to Bursary of Philosophy on Hector Ford's Mortification.

Robert Leiston, son to Mr. Robert Leiston, minister at Aberdour, preferred to Bursary of Philosophy on Hector Ford's Mortification.

John Milne preferred to Bursary of Philosophy on Hector Ford's Mortification.

Adam Watson, son to James Watson, under-janitor of the College of Edinburgh, preferred to Bursary of Philosophy on Sir Andrew Ramsay's Mortification.

John Bald, son to James Bald, merchant in Edinburgh, preferred to Bursary of Philosophy on Dr. Johnston's Mortification.

Alexander Ure preferred to Bursary of Philosophy on Dr. Johnston's Mortification.

William Gloag, son to Mr. Andrew Gloag, minister at West Calder, preferred to Bursary of Philosophy on Hector Ford's Mortification.

Thomas Blacklock preferred to Bursary of Philosophy on John M'Morran's Mortification.

25th March.—Mr. Robert Henderson, Library-keeper, demits, having held that office since November 21, 1684. Allowed to re-

tain his salary during his life, on condition that he deliver a catalogue of all the books belonging to the College Library within three
months, and make good those wanting, but in case they exceed
£10 sterling in value, then such a part of his salary shall be retained. and given to his successor during Mr. Henderson's life, as
the Lord Provost, on behalf of the city, and Mr. Robert Craigie of
Glendoick, late Lord Advocate for Scotland, on behalf of Mr. Henderson, shall jointly determine, over and above making good to the
College the value of such books as shall be found amissing. Mr.
George Stewart, Professor of Humanity, chosen Librarian, *ad vitam
aut culpam;* to have the perquisites, but Mr. Henderson to have
the salary, £33, 6s. 8d. sterling. Mr. Stewart to make out a catalogue of the Library within fifteen months from this date; and
annually to give the Council in December a list of the books purchased or gifted during the preceding year; bound to subject himself to the Council's regulations. He appears in Council, accepts
of his office, and qualifies.

The city's clerks to lend him on receipt such catalogues of the
College Library as are in their possession.

15*th April.*—Bond by Mr. George Stewart, as Library-keeper,
produced for making forthcoming the books of the Library, and
making good the other conditions mentioned in his commission.
Mr. Alexander Kincaid, bookseller in Edinburgh, his cautioner.
Letter of cautionary registered in Burgh Court books.

15*th May.*—College committee appointed to inquire into the
present state of the Library; what catalogues relative thereto are
in the College; in whose custody they are; and what books are wanting which are recorded in any of these catalogues; and what books
are in the Library, purchased or given to the College, which are
not in those catalogues; and to report.

10*th June.*—College committee to cause make an inventory of
all the instruments belonging to the city, necessary for illustrating
any branch of Natural Philosophy, that are deposited in the College,
and to take Professor Stewart's receipt, and to report.

24*th June.*—There being at present one vacant bursary in the
College on King William's Mortification, in order to supply the
same, a list of three candidates to be made out, to be presented to
the Barons of Exchequer by the College Treasurer.

3*d July.*—A like list.

22*d July.*—Mr. Robert Rutherford, Divinity bursar by a presentation on Sir James M'Lurg's Mortification, presented by John

Adam of Whitslaid, *vice patronis.* To commence at Candlemas last : for four years.

26th August.—It being represented that the Council by their act, February 9, 1726, had nominated and appointed Andrew Sinclair and John Rutherford, Doctors of Medicine, Professors of the Theory and Practice of Medicine, and Andrew Plummer and John Innes, Doctors of Medicine, Professors of Medicine and Chemistry in the College of Edinburgh, under sundry conditions and provisions mentioned in the aforesaid act : And as through some mistake or inadvertency, the said act had not been engrossed in the Principal Record of Council, and as the fact was transacted during the administration of some of the present members of Council, and recent in their memories, and fully set forth in the extract thereof, under the hands of Mr. Adam Watt, late one of the city clerks : The Lord Provost, Magistrates, and Council, with the Deacons of Crafts, ordinary and extraordinary, therefore did, and hereby do, in order to rectify the aforesaid mistake, declare the said act to be as valid in all respects, as if recorded in its proper place, and ordered the said extract to be engrossed in the present Record of Council, the tenour whereof follows : —

" EDINBURGH, *February* 9, 1726.

" The which day, the Council being convened, anent the petition given in by the above Doctors, Fellows of the Royal College of Physicians at Edinburgh, showing that the petitioners had, under the Council's protection, undertaken the professing and teaching of Medicine in this city, and under this encouragement had carried it on with some success : That if it were taught in the College by the petitioners, it would promote it more than the way in which they had hitherto undertaken it : That the sole power of instituting such professions in the College, and of electing of persons qualified to profess the same, was vested in the Council : That the promoting the foresaid profession was only what was intended by the petitioners, which would tend to the benefit and honour of this city and country : Craving, therefore, that the Council would institute this profession in the College of Edinburgh, and appoint the petitioners to teach and profess the same, as the petition bears : WHICH being maturely considered, and the Council being fully convinced that nothing can contribute more to the flourishing of this or any other College, than that all the parts of academical learning be professed and taught in them by able Professors, they were of opinion that it would be of great advantage to this College, city, and country, that

Medicine in all its branches be taught and professed here by such a number of Professors of that science as may by themselves promote students to their degrees, with as great solemnity as is done in any other College or University at home or abroad. The Council, further considering that the petitioners have given the clearest proof of their capacity and ability to reach the above valuable ends and purposes, they having already professed and taught Medicine with good success and advantage, and with the approbation of all the learned in that science here, Do therefore unanimously constitute, nominate, and appoint Andrew Sinclair and John Rutherford, Doctors of Medicine, Professors of the Theory and Practice of Medicine, and Andrew Plummer and John Innes, Doctors of Medicine, Professors of Medicine and Chemistry in the College of Edinburgh, with full power to all of them to profess and teach Medicine in all its branches in the said College as fully and freely as the said science is taught in any University or College in this or any other country: And do, by thir presents, give, grant, and bestow upon the said four Professors of Medicine, and of the particular branches thereof above mentioned, all the liberties, privileges, and immunities that at present or hereafter are or may be enjoyed by the Professors of any other science in the foresaid College, and particularly with full power to them to examine candidates, and to do everything requisite and necessary to the graduation of Doctors of Medicine as amply and fully, and with all the solemnities that the same is practised and done by the Professors of Medicine in any College or University whatsoever. And it is hereby further provided and declared, that two only of the said Professors of Medicine shall at one time have the privilege of voting with the other Professors in College affairs; and that these two enjoy the privilege of deliberating on and voting in the affairs of general concern to the College, whereanent the Professors have been in use to deliberate and vote, in manner after directed, viz.: the said Andrew Sinclair and Andrew Plummer are hereby appointed and privileged to deliberate and vote with the other Professors in their College affairs, from the day of their admission till March 1, 1727, and the said John Rutherford and John Innes, from the said 1st March 1727, to enjoy the same privilege for the succeeding year; and so by turns during their respective lives, and their continuing in office; and that this act shall take place *ad vitam aut culpam.* And it is hereby to be understood, that if their number be diminished by death or otherwise, the survivors continuing to profess and teach Medicine

2 D

shall enjoy the foresaid privileges.   And, lastly, it is hereby expressly provided and declared, that the said four Professors, or any
of them, shall not have any fee or salary for their professing or
teaching Medicine, by virtue of this present Act, or in time coming,
which shall be payable out of the revenue or patrimony which does,
or may at any time hereafter, belong to this city, whereanent thir
presents shall be a warrant.

" Extracted   (Signed)   AD. WATT."

26*th* *August*.—Considering that by the decease of Dr. John
Innes, and the valetudinary state of health of Dr. Andrew Sinclair,
Medicine cannot be so well taught in this College as hitherto; and
as Dr. Robert Whytt has for a considerable time past taught Medicine in this city's College to the universal content of all the gentlemen learned in that science, and is every other way well recommended: Therefore the Council elect him one of the Professors of
the Theory and Practice of Medicine, *ad vitam aut culpam*, in
room and place of Dr. John Innes, deceased; but with the provisions,
conditions, and limitations contained in the Council's act, February
9, 1726: Grant him all the emoluments, liberties, privileges, and
immunities appertaining to the said Professorship, particularly to
examine candidates, and to do every other thing requisite and necessary for the graduation of Doctors of Medicine: With this proviso, that
in case of the death of any of the other three Professors of Medicine, no new choice or nomination shall be made, but the Theory
and Practice of Medicine and Chemistry shall be taught by Dr.
Whytt and the other two surviving Professors: Also, that the said
Dr. Whytt, by his acceptation hereof, became expressly bound
punctually to observe and obey all the acts and bye-laws made or
to be made by the Council touching the government and administration of the College: Also, he should give regular lectures.

Ordered that Bailie J. Brown, and his committee, install the
said Dr. Robert Whytt[1] one of the Professors of the Theory and
Practice of Medicine in the said College.

2*d September*.—Mr. Matthew Stewart, minister of the gospel at
Roseneath,[2] chosen Professor of Mathematics in place of Colin

[1] [Robert Whytt, son of Robert Whytt
of Bennochy, Advocate, was an alumnus of the University of St. Andrews,
studied medicine at Edinburgh, and
took his degree of M.D. at Rheims in
1736. At this time he was in extensive
practice as a physician in Edinburgh.
In 1761 he was made first physician to
his Majesty George the Third. He died
April 15, 1766, in the fifty-second year
of his age.]

[2] [Mr. Matthew Stewart was the son

M'Laurin, deceased, *ad vitam aut culpam.* Salary, £83, 6s. 8d. sterling.

4th September.—The Lord Provost to write to Mr. Matthew Stewart, informing him of his election, and expressing that it would be agreeable to the Council to know how soon he could conveniently be loosed from his pastoral charge at Roseneath, so as to be in readiness to enter on the duties of his office against the term of Martinmas next.

VOL. LXVII.

7th October.—Committee on College affairs.

21st October.—Mr. Matthew Stewart appeared in Council, and accepted and qualified. Also took and subscribed the oath in the Council's act, September 10, 1718.

30th December.—Kenneth Bayne of Tulloch presents Charles Robertson, son to Mr. Francis Robertson, minister of the gospel at Clyne, in the shire of Sutherland, to a bursary of Divinity, upon Bayne of Tulloch's Mortification, for two years.

6th January 1748.—Andrew Petrie, son to Robert Petrie, minister of the gospel at Cannoby, Bursar of Philosophy on Lord Warriston's Mortification. Four years. Presented by Dame Grizell Baillie of Jerviswood, relict of the deceased Sir Alexander Murray of Stanhope.

9th March.—Mr. Matthew Stewart to possess the house in the College occupied by the late Colin M'Laurin, he always paying rent for the same.

Professor George Stuart, upon his petition, allowed rooms for a house in the College, having a great deal of duty in the Library, etc., and wishing to keep boarders.

The petitioner states, that, on his entry to the office of Library-keeper, he found the Library in the utmost confusion, without any catalogue but a very imperfect press one, by which no book called for could be found. The petitioner hath now finished, in three volumes, folio, an Alphabetical Catalogue, whereby any book can be found at once, to the great expense of his health. He found himself obliged to write out one for ordinary use, with a design afterwards of writing it over again, in order to make the Library

of Mr. Dugald Stewart, minister of Rothesay, in the Isle of Bute, and was born in the year 1717. He was an alumnus of the University of Glasgow, and studied theology at Edinburgh. He was ordained minister of the parish of Roseneath, on the 9th of May 1745.]

this winter subservient to the real design of it. The petitioner had gone over the whole Library three times, and written out a list of books, either lent or lost by his predecessor, to be laid before the Council when called for. And whereas Mr. Henderson, for his press catalogue alone, though of itself altogether useless, had got a gratuity of £50 sterling from the Council, the petitioner only begged a place in the College for a dwelling, to be fitted up at his own expense.

This remitted to the College committee, who report favourably; and therefore Mr. Stuart allowed various adjoining chambers on the east side of the upper College court accordingly. Remitted to the College committee to fix and ascertain the rent.

1st July.—Tack of the teinds of Dumbarney granted for nineteen years to John Craigie, younger of Dumbarney, Advocate, for himself, and in name of the other heritors of the parish of Dumbarney, containing an yearly tack-duty of 140 lbs. 18s. 4d. Scots, by and attour the minister's stipend, and eight bolls victual to the minister of Dron.

10th August.—Bursars, viz. :—

Mr. John Mackay, bursar of Divinity on Buchanan's Mortification.

Mr. James Dunsmuir, bursar of Divinity on Buchanan's Mortification.

Mr. Duncan Shaw, bursar of Divinity on Struthers's Mortification.

Mr. Alexander Cochrane, son of the deceased Mr. Hugh Cochrane, minister at Kilmaurs, bursar of Divinity on Struthers's Mortification.

Mr. Alexander Glen, bursar of Divinity on Chrystie's Mortification.

Mr. Duncan Campbell, bursar of Divinity on Ramsay's Mortification.

Alexander Elliot, son to Alexander Elliot, baxter in Edinburgh, bursar of Philosophy on Weir and Jenkin's Mortifications.

Robert Colvill, son to Walter Colvill, baxter in Edinburgh, bursar of Philosophy on Dalgleish's Mortification.

Archibald Gillies, son to —— Gillies, wright in Edinburgh, bursar of Philosophy on Hector Ford's Mortification.

William Nimmo, son to Patrick Nimmo in Whiteside, bursar of Philosophy on Hepburn and Lightbody's Mortification.

William Simson, clerk to the baxters of Edinburgh, bursar of Philosophy on Dr. Johnston's Mortification.

Alexander Thomson, bursar of Philosophy on Dr. Johnston's Mortification.

Alexander Tennent, bursar of Philosophy on Dr. Johnston's Mortification.

John Graham Pyot, son to Mr. Alexander Pyot, minister at Dunbar, bursar of Philosophy on Sir Andrew Ramsay's Mortification.

Andrew Manderston, bursar of Philosophy on Hector Ford's Mortification.

5th October.—Committee appointed on College affairs.

VOL. LXVIII.

1st November 1749.—*Inter alia*, Intimation to be made to Mr. George Stuart, Keeper of the Library, that it is the Council's pleasure he should lodge with the city clerks a Catalogue, signed by him, of the whole books in or belonging to the Library, containing also a full list of the pictures, medals, and other rarities in the Library ; and that annually hereafter, before Michaelmas, he deliver to the Council a signed Catalogue of the new books entered in Stationers' Hall, London, of which he receives a copy, to be added to the Council's copy of the Catalogue before mentioned.

15th November.—£150 sterling to be paid to Mr. Monro, Professor of Anatomy, being his bygone salary due preceding Whitsunday last, in regard the said demand cannot at present be answered out of the College funds.

31st January 1750.—It was represented to the Council that the Principal and Professors were going to choose a Printer to the University, and give him a commission accordingly. The Council find this an encroachment upon their rights, they having the sole power to choose all office-bearers in the University. The Provost therefore to write to the Principal, that there may be a meeting with the College about this, that the thing may be adjusted amicably, as the Council wish to be on an amicable footing with the College. The Provost promises to write accordingly.

7th February.—The Provost reported that he, and sundry members of the Council, had held a conference with Principal Wishart and Professors about the subject of Printer, and had shown them, from the City's records, that the Council, for upwards of a century past, had chosen the Printer to the University. Thereupon the Principal and the Professors declared that they would desist from their intention.

7th March.—Mr. William Maitland, on petition, gets £40 to enable him to proceed in publishing his History of Edinburgh.[1]

4th April.—Mr. Sands, College treasurer, produced a missive addressed to him, from Mr. George Stuart, Keeper of the College Library. With the letter, Mr. Stuart sent him an exact subscribed catalogue of the books, manuscripts, etc., in the College Library, and promised that he would annually for the future send a list of the additional books ; he said he had already written two Alphabetical Catalogues, and intended to write out a fair copy. Mr. Sands produced the aforesaid Catalogue.

A committee appointed to meet with a committee of the College, to compare the Catalogue given in by Mr. Stuart with former Catalogues of the College Library.

VOL. LXIX.

5th June 1751.—A petition from sundry students, requesting the Council would retain Mr. James Robertson, preacher of the gospel, to teach Hebrew, etc., in place of Mr. Dawson. Mr. Robertson greatly recommended by Joannes Jacobus Schultens, Professor of Oriental Languages at Leyden ; also by Dr. Hunt, Regius Professor of Hebrew at the University of Oxford. Avisamentum with the ministers ordered.

26th June.—Mr James Robertson[2] chosen in conjunction with Mr. William Dawson ; authorized to take fees. He appears in Council, accepts, and qualifies. To be installed in his office in the usual form.

VOL. LXX.

7th December.—In consequence of some dispute, the town grant a new joint commission to Mr. Robertson and Mr. Dawson ; by which Mr. Robertson, for his present encouragement, is to have the house and classroom in the College rent free, with £10 yearly

---

[1] [Maitland was a Fellow of the Royal Society. His History of Edinburgh appeared in 1753. He died in 1757, leaving a considerable fortune to his relatives in Montrose.]

[2] [At the time of his election, Robertson, from the reputation he had acquired for his knowledge of the Hebrew and Arabic languages, was offered a situation in the Dissenting Academy at Northampton, over which the well-known Dr. Doddridge presided. At first he adopted in his class Buxtorf's Hebrew Grammar ; but he afterwards published one of his own compilation, which he used in teaching. He also published a Key to the Pentateuch. He died on the 26th of November 1795.]

of Mr. Dawson's salary, and £20 more yearly from the town, during the joint lives of Mr. Dawson and himself; making in all £30 and a free house.

22d November 1752.—By act of Council, Andrew Syme, burgess of Edinburgh, appointed keeper of mortcloths, without salary, and to pay monthly 20 pounds Scots out of the perquisites of the said office to the College treasurer for the time.

VOL. LXXI.

27th June 1753.—Appointed Bailie Alexander Grant and his committee to visit that part of the College called the Common Hall, and to report and bring in an estimate of the repairs necessary thereto, under the hands of skilful tradesmen.

25th July.—Report about the Common Hall and roof of the High Library in the College. Found that the old roof is ruinous and should be renewed, and the walls raised so as to make an attic story. Estimated expense, £273, 16s. $7\frac{8}{12}$d. By this alteration, the Low Library could probably be let for upwards of £20 sterling per annum. The Council approve of the said report, with this addition, that as soon as the books can be all removed from the low old Library to the new high intended one, then the former shall be let to the highest bidder, for nineteen years, or be let for nineteen years as the Council shall think proper.

12th September.—Estimate of additional repairs for the High Library in the College, £18, 14s. 4d. Authorized to be done under the eyes of the committee.

17th October.—Estimate of additional repairs, £37, 13s. $4\frac{2}{3}$d. Agreed to.

7th November.—On a representation from Dr. John Stewart, Professor of Natural Philosophy, and Mr. Matthew Stewart, Professor of Mathematics, the town agree that, as the High Library of the College was at present repairing, the jamb adjoining to the said Library should have a flat in place of a scally roof, as presently proposed, with a parapet wall round it, so high as to be on a level with the Library roof; which would be particularly useful to the professions of the Memorialists. Estimate about £30.

21st December.—Charles Mackie, Professor of Universal History, Greek and Roman Antiquities, finding his health considerably broke, demits, it being his desire that Mr. John Gordon, a member of the Faculty of Advocates, should be conjoined with him in the said office. Intimation of his demission to be given to the Faculty of Advocates.

26th December.—A leet presented by the Faculty of Advocates to the Town-Council, consisting of Mr. John Gordon, and Mr. James Hamilton junior, Advocates. Mr. Gordon chosen, in conjunction with Mr. Mackie, Professor of Universal Civil History, and Greek and Roman Antiquities, *ad vitam aut culpam ;* with the right of survivancy to the longest liver. Thereafter Mr. Gordon, compearing in Council, accepted of the said office, and qualified.

16th January 1754.—A commission, read and signed in Council, naming and appointing Mr. Charles Mackie and Mr. John Gordon conjunct Professors of Universal Civil History, and Greek and Roman Antiquities in the University.

2d February.—Mr. John Gowdie, Professor of Divinity, resigns; and the Council order a meeting with the ministers to deliberate about a Principal and Professor of Divinity.

6th February.—Having consulted with the ministers of the city, the Council elect Mr. John Gowdie, Principal of the College, in place of Dr. William Wishart, deceased;[1] and Mr. Robert Hamilton, minister in Old Greyfriars' Church, Professor of Divinity,[2] in place of Mr. Gowdie, resigned.

VOL. LXXII.

27th March.—Commission to Mr. Gowdie, as Principal of the University, and to Mr. Robert Hamilton, as Professor of Divinity.

15th May.—On the resignation of Mr. James Davidson, and Mr. Thomas Ruddiman, the town appoint Messrs. Gavin Hamilton and John Balfour, College printers. They must take the Low Library and printing-house under it at £18 per annum, and must furnish the College Library with a free copy of what classics they shall print.

---

[1] [Dr. Wishart died on the 12th of May 1753.]

[2] [Mr. Robert Hamilton was the son of Dr. William Hamilton, who had been Professor of Divinity, and then Principal in the University. He was formerly minister of Cramond, then successively minister of Lady Yester's Church, and the Old Greyfriars'. On his election to the Theological Chair, before he could be admitted, he was required, according to a regulation which had been made by the Town-Council, to demit his charge as a minister of the city. Having performed the duties of a theological Professor nearly twenty-five years, he retired from public life, and, on the 10th of September 1779, Dr. Andrew Hunter was conjoined with him in the Theological Chair. He died on the 2d of April 1787.—See Morren's Annals, vol. ii. pp. 386-389, 399.]

19th June.—On resignation of, and representation from, Alexander Monro, Professor of Anatomy, bearing that he had taught with success thirty-five years, etc., his son, Alexander Monro,[1] is chosen joint with him. *N.B.*—He states, in this representation, that there had been more than 200 students of Physic annually for many years past at Edinburgh, and that they brought £10,000 at least annually to the town.

10th July.—Alexander Monro senior, and Alexander Monro junior, qualify in Council.

18th July.—Commission to them signed.

21st August.—Mr. William Cleghorn, on account of bad health, resigns his office as Professor of Moral Philosophy. The Council accept, and appoint that a meeting be held on Monday next at twelve o'clock, to choose a proper person in his room, and that the ministers of the city be then desired to attend to give their avisamentum.

28th August.—The Provost reports, that avisamentum of the ministers had been taken about a successor to Mr. Cleghorn, who had died since his resignation.[2]

James Balfour of Pilrig, Advocate, chosen Professor of Pneumatics and Moral Philosophy.[3]

4th September.—Mr. Balfour's commission granted.

Mr. Robertson, Professor of Hebrew, to have a house in the College, rent free, for seven years.

4th December.—Mr. John Gordon, and Mr. Mackie, demit their joint Professorship of Universal Civil History, and Greek and Roman Antiquities, and the latter proposes Mr. William Wallace junior, Advocate, for a new colleague. Their demission accepted. Gordon demitted, that he might be in a condition to accept of the Professorship of Civil Law, for which the Faculty of Advocates thought him well qualified. In his petition to the Council, he says, that he was " sensible himself that he was a better civilian than historian." Mackie in his letter to the Council says, that he was

---

[1] [Alexander Monro, *secundus*, after a long and successful career as a physician and professor, had associated with him in the Professorship his son, Dr. Alexander Monro, *tertius*, on the 14th of November 1798. He died, October 2, 1817, in his eighty-fifth year.]

[2] [Professor Cleghorn died at Edinburgh, on the 23d of August 1754, in the 36th year of his age.]

[3] [Balfour was among the first who combated the sceptical philosophy of Hume, in two treatises; the one entitled "A Delineation of Morality," and the other, "Philosophical Dissertations." He also contested the doctrines contained in Lord Kames's Essays on Morality and Natural Religion. The candour and good temper with which he wrote commanded the approbation of even his opponents.]

" advanced in years, and his health considerably broken ;" and that he was " apprehensive that he should not be in a condition much longer to give colledges [lectures] on the subject of his profession."

11*th December.*—An estimate of windows for the High Library given in and approved of. £44, 11s. 6d. sterling.

18*th December.*—Intimation of Mr. John Gordon's resignation to be given to the Advocates.

23*d December.*—Leet given by the Advocates of Mr. William Wallace and David Kennedy, Advocates. Mr Mackie demits. He and Mr. William Wallace chosen conjunct.

22*d January* 1755.—Mr. Robert Dick, Advocate, chosen Professor of Civil Law on the demission of Mr. Kenneth Mackenzie; Mr. James Veitch, Advocate, being the other person in the leet. •

29*th January* —Commission to Mr. Robert Dick read and signed in Council.

VOL. LXXIII.

30*th July.*—A new floor ordered for the new Library. The expense estimated at £45 sterling, of which the Professors generously offered to contribute £20.

19*th November.*—Dr. William Cullen, present Professor of Medicine and Chemistry in the College of Glasgow,[1] conjoined with Dr. Andrew Plummer in the office of Professor of Medicine and Chemistry. Dr. Plummer had of late been afflicted with palsy, which rendered him unable to discharge the duties of his office.

10*th December.*—Dr. Cullen accepts by letter to the Council.

21*st January* 1756.—The clerks produced in Council a Catalogue of the books in the College Library, made up by Mr. George Stuart, the present Library-keeper, and signed by him, January 1, 1750. Given to Gilbert Laurie, College treasurer, to be by him put into the hands of Mr. Stuart, upon receipt, that he may add to the Catalogue such books as have been put into the Library since the same was made up.

18*th February.*—Mr. Robert Smith's demission of the Professor-

---

[1] [It is scarcely necessary to remark, that Dr. Cullen was one of the most eminent men in the department of Medicine who have adorned the University of Edinburgh. His great work is " First Lines of the Practice of Physic ;" which was first published in 1776. It ob- tained a European reputation, and is said to have brought him about £3000 sterling. Besides other works, he published a treatise on Materia Medica, in two quarto volumes, about a year before his death, which took place on the 5th of February 1790.]

ship of Midwifery in the College of Edinburgh. Thomas Young,[1] Surgeon, chosen in his place. No salary.

Gilbert Laurie, College treasurer, demands £250, to enable him to pay Professors salaries and Bursars.

10th March.—Commission to Drs. Cullen and Plummer presented and signed in Council.

28th July.—On Dr. Plummer's death, and Dr. Cullen's resignation, the latter gets a new commission, as sole Professor of Medicine and Chemistry.

1st December.—Report of Dr. Cullen's instalment.

VOL. LXXIV.

2d February 1757.—Mr. Gilbert Laurie, College treasurer's accounts from Michaelmas 1755 to Michaelmas 1756 :—Charge, including £250 got from the late city treasurer, £1616, 19s. $8\frac{8}{12}$d.; discharge, including £414, 5s. 8d. of arrears, £1568, 15s. $9\frac{2}{12}$d. ; balance due by him, £48, 3s. $11\frac{6}{12}$d.

Ordered George Stuart, Library-keeper, to add to the Catalogue the books purchased or got from Stationers' Hall, or gifted to the Library since the Catalogue was given in by him to the Council.

15th June.—On the request of Alexander Monro senior, a new commission granted him and his son, as they were now both Doctors of Medicine, which none of them had been formerly.

23d November.—Accounts of Mr. Nisbet, late College treasurer, from Michaelmas 1756 to Michaelmas 1757 :—Charge, including £48, 3s. $11\frac{6}{12}$d. of balance, and £80 imprest into his hands, £1525, 8s. $10\frac{10}{12}$d. sterling; discharge, including arrears, £422, 2s. $10\frac{8}{12}$d., £1526, 5s. $4\frac{10}{12}$d. ; balance due to him, 16s. 6d.

VOL. LXXV.

14th March 1759.—Mr. James Guthrie, College treasurer's accounts, from Michaelmas 1757 to Michaelmas 1758 :—Charge, £1403, 13s. 8d. sterling; discharge, including 16s. 6d., balance paid to Mr. Nisbet, last College treasurer, and £419, 10s. $1\frac{4}{12}$d. of arrears, £1381, 10s. $7\frac{6}{12}$d. ; balance due by him, £22, 3s. $0\frac{6}{12}$d.

Wednesday, 27th June.—The Lord Provost having represented

---

1 [Young opened a class for students in this branch of medical practice, not confining his attention to the education of females.]

that as there is a vacancy in the Professorship of Natural Philosophy, by the decease of Dr. John Stewart, and that it is expedient
and necessary the said office should be forthwith supplied with a fit
and well-qualified person,—the Council therefore resolve that, on
Friday next, at four o'clock afternoon, the Magistrates meet in the
Laigh Council-house, and that the ministers of the city be then
desired to attend, to give their avisamentum anent the choice of a
Professor for supplying the said vacancy.

4th July.—On the Provost's report, that the ministers had approved of Mr. Adam Ferguson, he is chosen in place of Dr. John
Stewart deceased.[1]

VOL. LXXVI.

26th December.—Gilbert Laurie, College treasurer's accounts:—
His charge, including arrears and £250 impressed into his hands
by Mr. Guthrie, city treasurer, £1652, 1s. $5\frac{8}{12}$d.; his discharge,
£1584, 8s. $1\frac{8}{12}$d.; balance due by him, £67, 13s. $3\frac{6}{12}$d.

27th June 1760'—The Town-Council considering that there is
no Professor of Rhetoric in this city's University, and that the
Reverend Dr. Hugh Blair, one of the ministers of this city, has for
some time past taught that branch of literature with universal
applause; and being satisfied that the teaching of Rhetoric in the
University would be of singular use to students, and a great benefit
to the city; and knowing by experience that the said Dr. Blair is
fully qualified for that office: Therefore the Council elect the said
Dr. Blair to be Professor of Rhetoric in the University, without a
salary.

6th August.—Commission to Dr. Blair[2] read and signed in

---

[1] [Mr. Stewart died on the 12th of
May 1759. Dr. Adam Ferguson, his successor, was the son of Adam Ferguson,
minister of Logierait, in the Presbytery
of Dunkeld. He was educated at the
grammar-school of Perth and at the
University of St. Andrews. Having
studied for the Church, he acted for
some time as chaplain to the 42d Regi-
ment; and in 1757 he became tutor in
the family of the Earl of Bute. Ferguson afterwards successively filled the
Chairs of Moral Philosophy and Mathematics. He is the author of various
works. He died at St. Andrews, in
March 1816, in the 93d year of his age]

[2] [Dr. Hugh Blair, who was the
great-grandson of Mr. Robert Blair,
minister of St. Andrews, was minister
first of Collessie in Fife, and then successively of the Canongate, Lady Yester's, and the High Church, Edinburgh,
to which last he was removed in 1758.
His lectures on Rhetoric and Belles-
Lettres excited so great interest, that
his Majesty George III. was induced to
endow the chair in 1762. After having
been delivered for twenty-eight years,
they were published; Blair receiving
for the copyright £1500. He died on
the 27th of December 1800, in the
eighty-third year of his age.]

Council, and Mr. Gilbert Laurie ordered to install him as Professor of Rhetoric.

17th December.—Dr. Cullen, at the request of the students of Medicine, had, in consequence of the death of Dr. Charles Alston, agreed to teach Materia Medica for this session, should he obtain the approbation of the honourable patrons of the University. A petition from the students of Medicine to the Town-Council craving authority for this. The Council recommend to the Lord Provost to meet and converse with Dr. Cullen and the other Professors, and do as he thinks proper.

25th April 1761.—Dr. John Hope[1] elected Professor of Botany and Materia Medica, in place of Dr. Charles Alston, deceased, with salary, and to be keeper of the city's Botanic garden.

13th May.—Remit to the College committee to consider the account given in by ————, the attorney appointed by the Council, for recovering a legacy bequeathed to the city's College by Hugh Woodside, formerly of the city of Dublin, and late of Castle-town, within the diocese of Sodor and Man ; and they to report.

16th September.—Accounts of Mr. John Coutts, College treasurer, from Michaelmas 1759 to Michaelmas 1760 :—Charge, including former balance and arrears, £1499, 4s. $10\frac{10}{12}$d. sterling ; discharge, £1504, 13s. $10\frac{2}{12}$d. ; balance due to him, £5, 8s. $11\frac{4}{12}$d. Recommend now, as frequently before, to endeavour to recover arrears due to the College, particularly those due by the daughters of Sir Robert Chiesly, and James Scott, chemist.

VOL. LXXVII.

14th October 1761.—Committee on College affairs, etc. Any five a quorum, the preses always one.

9th December.—Catalogue of the College Library to be inquired after by the College treasurer, that the new books obtained since the last Catalogue was made up may be added to it.

5th March 1762.—Remit to the College committee to see what is due to Principal Gowdie's widow of the salary which was payable to her deceased husband, and to report.

10th March.—Dr. William Robertson, one of the ministers of

---

[1] [Dr. Hope, after attending the Medical classes at home, prosecuted his studies for some time abroad. On his return to Scotland he took the degree of M.D. at Glasgow, on the 29th of January 1750. He died on the 10th of November 1786.]

the city, proposed in Council as a most proper person to be
Principal, in place of Dr. John Gowdie, deceased. A committee
of the whole Council had previously met, and had unanimously
agreed to elect him. The avisamentum of the ministers had also
been taken, and they had no objection. Dr. Robertson elected.
Granted him the salary belonging to that office, and the house, with
the orchard, in the said University, as the same was lately possessed
by the said deceased Mr. John Gowdie ; but under this express
condition, that as long as he is a minister of the city, he shall not
be entitled to the sum of 500 marks allowed each of the ministers
of this city for house rent, in respect he possesses a house as Principal of the College. Dr. Robertson [1] being called upon, appeared
in Council, accepted of the said office, and took the oath *de fideli
administratione.*

7th April.—Legacy of books left by Hugh Woodside, of the Isle
of Man, to the College.

14th April.—Bailie Hog represents that he had recovered the
Catalogue of the College Library, which had been long amissing :
that he had given it to Professor George Stuart, the Librarian, to
add books got since 1757: that Mr. Stuart is now employed in
making two catalogues,—a press one, of the whole books as put in
the presses ; and an alphabetical one ; and therefore he moved the
Council for their directions thereanent : that it will be a year before
Mr. Stuart can make up said catalogues, and, when done, he proposed to give the press catalogue to the Council. Approve, and
recommend to the College treasurer to take Professor Stuart's
receipt for the said catalogue.

16th June.—£100 for repairs in the Principal's house. He is
to have no further claim during his incumbency.

30th June.—A commission from his Majesty, dated 21st of May
last, in favour of Mr. Robert Cumming, appointing him Professor
of Ecclesiastical History in the University, and third Professor of
Divinity, in place of his father, Dr. Patrick Cumming, who had resigned, was read. Mr. John Brown, treasurer, in behalf of himself,
the Magistrates, Council, and community, protests that this pre-

---

[1] [Principal Robertson, who had been
first minister of Gladsmuir, where he was
ordained in May 1744, was at this time
minister of Lady Yester's church, Edinburgh, to which he had been translated
in 1758. Not long after his election,
namely in 1764, he was removed to the
Old Greyfriars', in which he had associated with him, as his colleague, Dr.
John Erskine, in 1767. He died on the
11th of June 1793, in the seventy-second
year of his age.]

sentation shall not prejudge the town's right to the patronage of the said College. The Council agree to admit Mr. Cumming into the said office, under the foresaid protestation, saving and reserving to the city all their rights to the said College, and appoint Bailie Hog to install him accordingly.

6*th July.*—Report that Mr. Robert Cumming had been installed.

21*st July.*—A commission from his Majesty, dated 27th April last, nominating and presenting Dr. Hugh Blair, one of the ministers of Edinburgh, Regius Professor of Rhetoric and Belles Lettres in the University. Dr. Blair admitted under protest, as usual in King's presentations.

4*th August.*—Report that Dr. Blair had been installed. Council approve.

VOL. LXXVIII.

20*th October.*—Mr. Lindsay, depute-clerk, delivered at the table, to Mr. William Ramsay, College treasurer, the Catalogue of the College Library, which was put into Mr. Lindsay's hands last Council day by Mr. Hog, old Bailie.

15*th December.*—Report of repairs made in Dr. Robertson's house, to the extent of nearly £200. The Council adhere to former agreement (act 16th June last), and order only £100 to be paid.

12*th January* 1763.—Professor George Stuart demits the office of Librarian by a letter to the Lord Provost.

Mr. James Robertson, Professor of Hebrew and Oriental Languages in the College, chosen Librarian in his place, *ad vitam aut culpam.* The books to be delivered over to him with the catalogues. All the salaries and perquisites. To be obliged in the month of December every year to give in a list of all the books purchased, gifted, or which shall accrue to the College the year preceding. Professor Stuart liable to make good all the books, with every other thing belonging to the Library during his time.

15*th June.*—Representation from the Barons of Exchequer about the new Botanic garden. The Barons had made a report to the Lords of the Treasury relative to the petition of Dr. John Hope, Professor of Botany, and to the capital sum and annual expense that would be necessary to erect and maintain a Botanic garden; and particularly, had signified to their Lordships that they were informed that the present Botanic garden ₁ belonging to the town of Edinburgh might be let for £25 per annum, which would reduce the expense of maintaining the new one to the annual charge of £69, 3s. ; and that the Magistrates, in consideration of the benefit which would accrue to the public, and the town of Edinburgh in particular, from the increase of the study of Physic there, were willing that the rent of the said garden should be applied towards the expense of maintaining such new Botanic garden as might be erected in the neighbourhood of the city. The Barons, before proceeding further in the affair, expected a report on it from the Town-Council.

Remit to a committee, with power to examine into the state of the present Botanic garden, and what rent the same may be set for, and to give an answer to the Barons.

20th July.—Report by committee of a report prepared by them to be laid before the Barons of Exchequer about the Botanic garden :—That as your Lordships had made a report to the Lords of the Treasury relative to the petition of Dr. John Hope, of the capital sum for laying out the garden, and the annual expense necessary for keeping the same, etc. : In obedience to your Lordships' orders, we humbly report that Dr. Hope has two Botanical gardens at present, one at the new Port, given to the Professor of Botany by the Town-Council, during their pleasure, by their act, dated 14th February 1739; by which they also give him a house belonging to the city for his gardener to inhabit, also during their pleasure, rent free, the Professor being obliged to keep it in good order. The garden, however, is the property of the Trinity Hospital, and the city rent it for £5 per annum. The other garden is part of the garden of Holyroodhouse, granted to the family of Hamilton, which the late Dukes, and tutors of the present Duke, have permitted the Professor of Botany to enjoy. The gardener's house, given him by the city, might be let for £6 per annum. The Council, however, were willing to give annually, in all time coming, the £25 to make up the £94, 3s. necessary to maintain the new Botanic garden. The report approved of by the Council.

₁ [That is, the old Botanical garden. It was situated on the low ground east of the North Bridge, and adjacent to Trinity Hospital. It was of small extent, and the situation was not well adapted for the cultivation of plants. The new Botanical garden lay on the west side of Leith Walk. At the time this spot was well chosen, and under Dr. Hope's superintendence it was reckoned to be one of the most complete Botanical gardens in Europe. The present Botanical garden is situated near Inverleith Row, beyond Canonmills,—a situation admirably fitted in every respect for the purpose.]

7th September.—Provost George Drummond. Act authorizing the reception of the books and curiosities belonging to the Corporation of Surgeons into the College Library and Museum on certain conditions ; viz., that the members of the said corporation shall have leave to borrow books as any other *Civis*, upon their society paying £5 sterling per annum.[1] (*N.B.*—The Council here acknowledge the *Faculty* of the University.)

15th February 1764.—On the resignation of Patrick Crockat, janitor of the College, he, with John Innes, appointed joint janitors.

14th March.—Six guineas, instead of three formerly, allowed in time coming annually to the Library for coals, as there was a necessity for having two fires in the present Library, instead of one as before.

21st March.—A room in the College to be repaired for the Librarian, the expense not to exceed £6, 12s. 6d.

Wednesday, 16th May.—Mr. James Balfour of Pilrig resigns the office of Professor of Pneumatics and Moral Philosophy. The Council resolve that Mr. Adam Ferguson, present Professor of Natural Philosophy in the City's College, shall be nominated and appointed in his place.

The Council also resolve that Mr. James Russell, surgeon-apothecary in Edinburgh, shall be nominated and appointed to the Chair of Natural Philosophy, in place of Mr. Ferguson : And to take the avisamentum of the ministers of the city before the foresaid vacancies are filled up. Meeting of the Council with the ministers to be held in laigh Council House on Friday next, at twelve o'clock.

23d May.—Mr. Ferguson elected Professor of Pneumatics and Moral Philosophy, with the former salary : also authorized to take fees from the students as any other Professor in the University, notwithstanding any act of Council to the contrary; and if there be any such act, it is hereby declared to be repealed.

Mr. James Russell[2] elected Professor of Natural Philosophy.

[1] [This arrangement with the College of Surgeons has proved anything but advantageous to the interests of the University Library.]

[2] [Mr. Russell died on the 17th of October 1773. His son, of the same name, became Professor of Clinical Surgery in the University.]

2 E

They both qualify.

King's commission, dated May 5th, current, to Mr. James Balfour, Advocate, to be Professor of the Law of Nature and Nations,[1] in the room of Mr. Robert Bruce, presented and read.

Resolve to admit Mr. Balfour, under the usual protestation. Bailie John Stephen appointed to install Messrs. Balfour, Ferguson, and Russell.

4th July.—Upon petition of Dr. Alexander Monro, he gets £300 to build a new theatre. *N.B.*—In this petition the Doctor asserts that within these forty years, the Town had received from the students of Anatomy, on the lowest computation, above £300,000, and during the last twenty years, above £10,000 per annum. The Doctor advances the £300, to be repaid, £100 annually for three years.

1st August.—Act appointing £30 sterling to be paid to Mr. James Robertson, Librarian, for his great and indefatigable trouble in putting the Library in order; and the like sum of £30 sterling to be paid him next year, in full of all demand for his trouble and expense.

3d October.—William Hog, junior, elected College treasurer.

10th October.—Committee on College affairs named.

19th December.—Act agreeing to pay not only the £300, as formerly, to Dr. Monro for his theatre, but afterwards £80, 19s. 2d. in June 1768, upon his granting, before receiving the first payment (namely the first £100 of the £300), an obligation to convey to the University, at his death, his whole anatomical preparations, unless the circumstances of his family should alter, so as to make it necessary for him to dispose of them for their behoof.

9th January 1765.—Patrick Neill, upon petition, allowed to possess the ground-floor under the old Library, which was now to be fitted up for a museum. It had been used as a printing-house by him and his partners, printers, Messrs. Hamilton and Balfour, but which company had been lately dissolved.

VOL. LXXXI.

19th June.—On petition of Principal Robertson, the old Library, late a printing-house, to be fitted up for a museum for natural curiosities, at the sum of £150 sterling. The work intrusted to the College committee.

11th September.—On petition from Dr. Hope, setting forth that

---

[1] [Balfour demitted this chair in 1779, and died at an advanced age at Pilrig, on the 6th of March 1795.]

he had received considerable sums, at different times, from the Exchequer, for fitting up the new Botanic garden in Leith Walk, and craving to have the £25 per annum promised by the Council paid, due for the year preceding the 1st of May last. The Town-Council, considering that as Dr. Hope is still in possession of the Physic garden at the new Port, whereof the rent is £5 per annum, and of the gardener's house, valued at £6 yearly, he can be entitled only to £14 yearly, until he cede these to the city. After such cession, the city treasurer is authorized to begin and continue to pay him the £25 annually.

13th November.—Mr. John Erskine of Carnock, Advocate, resigns his office of Professor of Scots Law. Intimation ordered to be given to the Advocates, that they may send a leet of two to the Council. Thanks voted to Mr. Erskine for his good services.

20th November.—Mr. William Wallace resigns his joint Professorship of Universal Civil History, etc., with Mr. Charles Mackie.

A leet from the Advocates of Mr. William Wallace and Mr. Hay Campbell, Advocates. Mr. Wallace chosen in place of Mr. Erskine resigned.

4th December.—Mr. Charles Mackie resigns *in toto*. His resignation accepted, and this to be intimated to the Dean and Faculty of Advocates.

11th December.—On a leet from the Advocates of Mr. William Baillie and Mr. John Pringle, sent by the Advocates, Mr. John Pringle is chosen by the Council in place of Mr. Mackie, Professor of Universal Civil History, etc.

18th December.—Commissions to Mr. Wallace and Mr. Pringle read and signed in Council.

15th January 1766.—Petition from Principal Robertson, setting forth that the want of a sufficient number of classes or rooms for teaching had been long felt in the College, especially of late, when the number of students had considerably increased, and proposing that the walls of the old Library, now the Museum, should be raised, to furnish more apartments above, viz., one for a Natural Philosophy class, the other for an additional room to the Library. Expense, £234, 11s. 4d. The consideration thereof recommitted to the College committee, to cause execute the work.

5th February.—College treasurer's account from Michaelmas 1764 to Michaelmas 1765 :—Charge, including arrears, £1634, 11s. 9d. sterling; discharge, 1638, 19s. $10\frac{4}{12}$d.; balance due to him, £4, 8s. $1\frac{4}{12}$d.

12th February.—Upon the resignation of Dr. John Rutherford, the Council unanimously elect Dr. John Gregory[1] to be Professor and Teacher of the Practice of Medicine. Thanks voted to Dr. Rutherford for his long and faithful services, and the Lord Provost to ask the favour of Dr. Rutherford that he would continue his teaching for this course of his lectures till the same are finished.

30th April.—On Dr. Cullen's resignation of the Professorship of Medicine and Chemistry, Dr. Joseph Black, late physician in Glasgow,[2] elected in his place, with privilege to examine candidates and graduate them with all the solemnity practised or done by the Professors of Medicine in this or any other University whatsoever.

Dr. Cullen chosen Professor of the Institutions of Medicine, in place of Dr. Robert Whytt, deceased.

VOL. LXXXII.

27th August.—Proposal to have a city chamberlain chosen, to manage the city's money affairs. To act first as city treasurer. Hugh Buchan elected.

17th September.—Commissions to Dr. Cullen and Dr. Black read and signed.

26th November.—Chamberlain ordered to pay sums to tradesmen for College repairs.

10th December.—William Stewart chosen under-janitor, in place of James Watson, deceased.

VOL. LXXXIII.

2d September 1767.—David Wilkie, student of Divinity, Presbytery's Bursar.

16th December.—Town-Council's College committee to meet with a committee from the University about rebuilding the College.

---

[1] [Dr. John Gregory, who was born at Aberdeen, after practising Medicine and Surgery in his native city, settled in Edinburgh in 1765, where he soon rose to eminence, and obtained a large practice. He did not occupy the chair which he adorned many years, having died on the 10th of February 1773, in the forty-eighth year of his age. His life, written by Lord Woodhouselee, is prefixed to his works.]

[2] [Dr. Black, so celebrated for his discoveries in Chemistry, had devoted himself to the study of Medicine, and had succeeded Dr. Cullen in the University of Glasgow in the Chemical Chair. He also delivered lectures on the Institutes of Medicine in that University. He died on the 26th of November 1799, in the seventy-first year of his age. His life was written by Professor John Robison, who edited his lectures, 1803, 2 vols. 4to. See also a sketch of his Life by Dr. Adam Ferguson, in Transactions of the Royal Society of Edinburgh, vol. v. pp. 101-117.]

23*d December.*—Report from the committee. The accommodation, the various apartments, and the dimensions of each apartment, to be concerted by the Professors, that architects may be desired to prepare plans and estimates. Subscription papers to be sent to London, as many of the most wealthy and considerable persons, both of our own country and of the southern part of the Island, are assembled at London during the meeting of Parliament, and as subscriptions may be expected from both; many Englishmen of rank and opulence being now connected with the University of Edinburgh.

Sederunt the above committee :—

COLLEGE COMMITTEE.	
Bailie Miller, *Preses*.	Councillor Simpson.
Dean of Guild Learmonth.	Deacons Butter and Paterson.
Old Bailie Wright.	
Old Dean of Guild Dalrymple.	FROM THE UNIVERSITY.
Old Treasurer Hogg.	Principal Robertson.
Mr. Nicol, second Merchant Councillor.	Professor Hamilton.
	Professor Wallace.
Mr. Cleland, second Trades' Councillor.	Professor Russell.
	Dr. Gregory.

Subscription paper inserted in Town-Council Records. (*N.B.*—In the subscription paper, four Faculties are acknowledged by the Town-Council, those of Theology, Law, Medicine, and Arts.) Council approve of the intended scheme, in which the interest of the community was so much concerned. In the subscription paper it is said that " a great many students resort from all parts of his Majesty's dominions, as well as from foreign countries, to the University of Edinburgh," but that " the buildings in the said University are extremely mean and inconvenient, and several of them in a very ruinous condition." The proposal was to " provide a Library-room, a Museum, a Hall, and proper school or teaching-rooms for the several classes, as well as houses for the Principal and Professors." This, it is added, would be of national advantage, and tend to encourage literature, and to promote the flourishing state of the University.

10*th February* 1768.—Fourteen bursars chosen.

VOL. LXXXIV.

1*st June.*—Dr. John Hope resigns the office of Professor of

Materia Medica, a branch of the Professorship of Botany, which last, however, he retains, with all the salaries he had hitherto enjoyed, by a commission from the Town-Council, when chosen at first Professor of Botany, April 29, 1761.

The Provost at the same time produced in Council a commission from his Majesty, of date May 23, 1768, nominating and appointing Dr. Francis Home to be Regius Professor of Materia Medica in the University of Edinburgh.

Accept Dr. Hope's resignation, and disjoin the Professorship of Materia Medica from Botany, and admit the said commission from his Majesty in favour of Dr. Home, under the usual reservation. They then proceed to elect, nominate, and appoint Dr. Francis Home to be Professor of Medicine and Materia Medica, with all rights, etc., as any other Professor, and order a commission to be made out in his favour. Bailie Hepburn to install Dr. Home.[1]

20th July.—Petition of Professor James Robertson, Professor of Hebrew, and Librarian, in relation to his expense in making the Alphabetical Catalogue. He sets forth that he soon perceived that it would be impossible for one man to do the business of the Library, after the new regulations, and at the same time to write a catalogue of the books so soon as was absolutely necessary, to render the Library useful for the students ; he therefore hired an assistant (Mr. Duke Gordon), at £15 per annum, with board, and also three, and sometimes four, students, to be employed with himself, at five shillings per week, who for the most part dined with him during the carrying on of this work : That he having in the years 1763 and 1764 finished one copy of a catalogue of all the books contained in the presses, transcribed a fair copy thereof to lie in the Library : That in consequence of a representation by Principal Robertson, he had then received £60 sterling from the Town-Council : That in 1764 and 1765, he proceeded to cut down the first Catalogue, which was written only on one large page ; and then, with the aid of his assistant, and the students employed still at the same weekly expense, to write an Alphabetical Catalogue, which he has now finished, in four volumes folio. He hoped, therefore, that the patrons would

---

[1] [Dr. Francis Home, born on the 9th of November 1719, was the third son of James Home, Esq. of Eccles, in the county of Berwick. In 1798, he resigned his Professorship, and was succeeded by his son, Dr. James Home, who afterwards became Professor of the Practice of Medicine. He died on the 15th of February 1813, at the advanced age of ninety-three years and three months. He was the author of various works.]

consider the necessity and utility of this work, often enjoined to his predecessors, but never before accomplished, and the great expense attending it, and the time and great labour expended upon it. In consequence of his having finished the said catalogues, and the late regulations made anent the management of the Library, there had been an accession of books, amounting to £1100 sterling, since the commencement of that necessary work. During the two first years he had no salary. Praying therefore for a reward and recompense.

The facts are attested in a letter to the Town-Council, dated April 29, 1768, by Principal Robertson, by whom Professor Robertson is recommended for his great industry.

Remitted to the College committee. Bailie Hepburn reports favourably, finding a balance due to the petitioner of £85, 8s. 11d. sterling. The Council order this sum to be paid. The Provost authorized to return thanks to Professor Robertson, and further, a gratification of seventy guineas to be allowed him for his own trouble.

14*th September.*—Chamberlain's College account from Michaelmas 1766 to Martinmas 1767 :—His charge, with arrears, £1405, 8s. 5$\frac{2}{12}$d. ; his discharge, £1816, 10s. 5$\frac{4}{12}$d. ; balance, paid by the chamberlain out of the city's proper revenue, £411, 2s. 0$\frac{2}{12}$d.

12*th October.*—Committee on College affairs.

VOL. LXXXV.

12*th April* 1769.—On petition of Dr. Cullen, the town allow him and Dr. John Gregory to teach alternately the Theory and Practice of Physic during their joint lives or incumbencies; reserving to the Town-Council the full right, upon the death of either of them, or their otherwise quitting their profession, to fill up the vacancy as if the said appointment had never been made.

15*th September.*—Chamberlain's College accounts from Martinmas 1767 to Martinmas 1768 :— Charge, including arrears depending in last account, £1095, 4s. 9$\frac{4}{12}$d. sterling; discharge, £1801, 7s. 3$\frac{7}{12}$d. ; balance, paid by him out of the city's revenue, £706, 2s. 6$\frac{3}{12}$d.

VOL. LXXXVI.

20*th December.*—Alexander Wardrop, student of Divinity, son of Alexander Wardrop, in the parish of Whitburn, preferred to the Bursary of Divinity, on Convener Wardrop's Mortification.

24*th January* 1770.—Petition of Dr. Robert Ramsay, setting

forth that he had been appointed by the King Regius Professor of Natural History on the 13th of March 1767, with a salary of £70 per annum, and Keeper of the Museum in the University, and praying to be admitted Professor, under the usual reservation of the town's right in the case of Regius Professors, and to be appointed by the town Keeper of the Museum with a commission from them. Granted, on condition he conform to all the regulations of the town, and deliver to the clerk a full list or inventory of all the curiosities or rarities belonging to the University.[1]

28th February.—Council appoint the Dean of Guild and his Council to admit and receive Dr. Robert Ramsay to be burgess and guild-brother of this city, for good services done by him to the interest thereof.

VOL. LXXXVII.

29th August.—Chamberlain's College account from Martinmas 1768 to Martinmas 1769 :—Charge, including arrears, £901, 10s. ; discharge, £1837, 17s. $8\frac{7}{12}$d. ; balance, paid by the chamberlain out of town's revenue, £936, 7s. $8\frac{7}{12}$d.

19th December.—On a presentation of Captain Ninian Lewis, heir to the deceased Robert Lewis, M.D., Edinburgh, Mr. Archibald Smellie, schoolmaster in Lanark, appointed to the Bursary of Philosophy, on the united Mortifications of M'Caul and Wright, lately possessed by Alexander Wilson.

VOL. LXXXVIII.

13th February 1771.—On presentation of William Livingston of Parkhall, Andrew Bennet, son to the deceased John Bennet, surgeon in Falkirk, appointed Bursar of Philosophy, on Mitchell of Mitchills Mortification.

11th September.—Chamberlain's College account from Martinmas 1769 to Martinmas 1770 :—Charge, including arrears, £922, 10s. $8\frac{2}{12}$d. ; discharge, £2279, 3s. $10\frac{5}{12}$d. ; balance, paid by the chamberlain out of the city's revenue, £1356, 13s. $2\frac{3}{12}$d.

20th November.—The city chamberlain authorized to write a letter to the elders of Zamosc, in Poland, intimating the vacancy of a Polish student on Brown's Mortification, there having been for some years no Polish student on the said Mortification.

[1] [Dr. Ramsay died on the 15th of December 1778.]

11*th December.*—A Latin letter, signed Hugo Buchan, to the Consistory of Zamose in Poland, inviting them to send a Polish student to the College of Edinburgh, on Brown's Mortification.

29*th July* 1772.—Chamberlain's College account from Martinmas 1770 to Martinmas 1771 :—Charge, including arrears, £957, 1s. $5\frac{4}{12}$d. ; discharge, £2721, 12s. $2\frac{4}{12}$d. ; balance paid by the chamberlain out of the city's revenue, £1764, 10s. $9\frac{2}{12}$d.

16*th December.*—A letter read from Mr. Robert Hunter, Professor of Greek in this city's University, stating his having given private colleges in the Greek language in the city of Edinburgh for ten years ; and then, on the presentation of the Council, accepting of the Greek Professorship, though at that time, and for several years after, without a salary ; and his having held for thirty years that office, he hoped to the satisfaction of all concerned ; and now wishing, as he was so far advanced in years, to retire, he proposed Mr. Andrew Dalzel, present tutor to the Earl of Lauderdale's sons, for a colleague and successor.

The Council remit to the Principal and Faculty of the College, to consider if it would be advisable for the Council to grant the commission, as desired ; also to report with respect to Mr. Dalzel's qualifications for the said office.

The Lord Provost also produced in Council the minutes and report of the said Faculty, as follows :—

" COLLEGE OF EDINBURGH, *December* 10, 1772.

" Present at a University meeting, Principal Robertson, Professors George Stuart, Hunter, Robertson, Cumming, Ferguson, Young, Blair, and Russell. The meeting being constituted by prayer by Principal Robertson, preses, the Principal laid before the Faculty a letter from the Lord Provost, enclosing a letter from Mr. Robert Hunter, Professor of Greek, addressed to the Magistrates and Town-Council, wherein he represents, that having discharged the office of Greek Professor in this University, for upwards of thirty years, to the best of his abilities, and he hopes, not without success, and the approbation of the public, he now finds from his advanced age that retirement from the labour of teaching would be

a great relief to him, and therefore resigns his office into the hands
of the Magistrates and Town-Council; requesting that Mr. Andrew
Dalzel, whom he judges well qualified for the office, may be elected
conjunct Professor with him; and that the Magistrates and Town-
Council had remitted it to the Faculty of the College to consider
if it would be advisable for the Council to comply with the said request, and also to report concerning Mr. Dalzel's qualifications for
the office.

"The Principal, and several of the Professors present, informed
the meeting that they were acquainted with Mr. Dalzel, and had
such an opinion of his literature, abilities, and prudence, that they
judged him well qualified for the office. Professor Hamilton, who
was absent, sent a letter to the meeting, expressing his approbation
of Mr. Dalzel, to the same purpose. But the Faculty, in order that
they might communicate to their honourable patrons the most satisfactory evidence concerning Mr. Dalzel's abilities, appointed Principal Robertson, Professors Hamilton, George Stuart, and Ferguson,
to meet at twelve o'clock Saturday next, as a committee of their
number, to examine Mr. Dalzel, and to take trial of his knowledge
in the Latin and Greek languages, and to report to a meeting of
Faculty, appointed to be held on Monday the 14th current, at twelve
o'clock forenoon."

                    " COLLEGE, EDINBURGH, *December* 14, 1772.

" Present at a University meeting, Principal Robertson, Professors Hamilton, G. Stuart, Hunter, Robertson, Cumming, Russell,
Blair, and Black. The meeting being constituted by prayer by
Principal Robertson, preses, the Principal laid before the Faculty
a report from the committee appointed by last meeting, the tenor
whereof follows :—' *College, Edinburgh,* 12*th December* 1772.—In
obedience to the appointment of the Faculty, we took trial of Mr.
Dalzel's knowledge in the Latin and Greek languages, at considerable length. He read and explained several passages of different
Latin and Greek authors, in prose as well as verse, and gave such
satisfactory answers to the questions proposed to him, that we do
report it as our opinion, that he is well qualified for the station of
Professor of Greek in the University. (Signed) WILLIAM ROBERT-
SON, ROBERT HAMILTON, GEORGE STUART, ADAM FERGUSON.'

" In consideration of which, as well as from the personal knowledge which many of the members have of Mr. Dalzel's character,
the Faculty do unanimously offer it as their opinion, that Mr. Dalzel
is well qualified for the office of Greek; and if their honourable

patrons shall judge it proper to elect him, they are persuaded the nomination will be beneficial to the University.

" They are likewise of opinion that the long and meritorious services of their colleague, Professor Hunter, should induce their honourable patrons to grant him a recess from the labour of teaching, in the terms of his request.—Signed at Edinburgh College, December the 14th, 1772 years, by order of the Faculty, WILLIAM ROBERTSON, *Principal;* JAMES ROBERTSON, *Acad. Clericus.*"

These minutes of College being read, the Council approve, and accept of Mr. Hunter's resignation, and elect him and Mr. Dalzel joint Professors of Greek, with the right of survivancy to the longest liver of them two.

23d *December.*—Commission to Mr. Hunter and Mr. Dalzel signed in Council. They compear and qualify. The College Bailie to install them.

17th *February* 1773.—Resignation of Dr. Cullen as Professor of the Institutes of Medicine accepted. He is chosen Professor of the Practice of Medicine, in place of Dr. John Gregory, deceased. The College Bailie to install him.

The Council agree, at the desire of the elders at Zamose, in Poland, to transmit £15 sterling, as a viaticum for a Polish student to come hither on Brown's Mortification.

3d *March.*—Commission to Dr. Cullen read and signed in Council.

21st *April.*—The Council appoint the Lord Provost to write to Dr. William Robertson, desiring him to convene the Medical Faculty of the College, to give their opinion which of the following candidates is most fit for being Professor of the Institutes of Medicine, vacant by Dr. Cullen's resignation, viz., Dr. Gregory Grant, Dr. Buchan,[1] Dr. Rutherford, Dr. Duncan, and Dr. Monro Drummond. Bond by Dr. Cullen produced in Council, whereby he obliged himself, upon obtaining the office of first Physician to his Majesty in Scotland, to pay to the Professor of Chemistry, and the Professor of the Institutions of Physic in the University, one-third to each of the salary annexed to that office after deducting all expenses.

5th *May.*—Upon the report of the Medical Faculty in favour of Dr. Alexander Monro Drummond,[2] he is elected Professor of the Institutions of Medicine, in place of Dr. Cullen, resigned.

30th *June.*—Greek class to be repaired. Estimate, £19, 1s. 8d.

---

[1] [Dr. William Buchan, author of the " Domestic Medicine."]

[2] [Dr. Drummond, a native of the city of Edinburgh, in which his father was a bookseller, was at this time at Naples. See extract, 12th June 1776.]

27th October.—The Lord Provost informed the Council that the Professors had prevailed on Dr. Home to teach the Institutes of Medicine till Dr. Drummond's return from abroad; and on Dr. Ferguson to give lectures on Experimental Philosophy during the vacancy of that office by the death of Dr. Russell. Council approve of what the Professors of the University had done.

19th January 1774.—Mr. John Stevenson, Professor of Logic and Metaphysics in the University,[1] gives in a letter proposing to resign, and recommending Mr. John Bruce to be his colleague and successor.[2] Stevenson states that he had been Professor for forty-five sessions.

The Council authorize the Provost to write to the Principal, to know if, in the opinion of the Faculty of the College, this proposal would be for the advantage of the College, and their opinion of Mr. Bruce's qualifications.

26th January.—A favourable report as to Mr. Bruce. He and Mr. Stevenson chosen joint Professors of Logic and Metaphysics, with the right of survivancy to the longest liver of them two.

16th February.—Professor Ferguson requests that, as he had an offer to go abroad with a young nobleman,[3] he may be allowed to name persons to teach his classes during the remainder of the session; and recommends Dr. James Lind for the Natural Philosophy class, and the Rev. Mr. Henry Grieve, at Dalkeith, for the Moral Philosophy.

The Council refuse, and order that Professor Ferguson shall be directed to teach himself what remains of the session.

9th March.—Committee to whom it had been committed, by minute of last sederunt (March 2), to consider of a proper person

---

[1] [Professor Stevenson died in 1775, at an advanced age. During the long period of his professorship, he had trained up a greater number of young men, who afterwards distinguished themselves in the republic of letters, than any former Professor of the University. He left his library to the University. He is commemorated by Professor Dalzel in his account of Duke Gordon; by Dr. Erskine in Appendix to his Sermon on Dr. Robertson's death; by Dr. Carlyle in his Autobiography; and by the Rev. Dr. Somerville in his " Life and Times."]

[2] [Mr. Bruce, his successor, occupied this chair till 1792, when he removed to London, where he held the appointment of Keeper of the State Paper Office, and other Government situations. He died at his estate of Falkland, in Fifeshire, on the 16th of April 1826, in the eighty-second year of his age.]

[3] [This was the Earl of Chesterfield; and Ferguson, notwithstanding the refusal of the Town-Council to grant him leave of absence, accompanied this nobleman in his travels on the Continent.]

to be Professor of Natural Philosophy, report, that of all the candidates, Mr. John Robison, Professor of Mathematics and Natural Philosophy at Cronstadt, in Russia,[1] appears to them fittest. Upon which he is chosen, in place of Mr. James Russell, deceased. Bailie Brown to write to Mr. Robison.

7th September.—Mr. John Robison appears in Council, accepts his office, qualifies, and to be installed by the College Bailie.

14th September.—Chamberlain's College account, from Martinmas 1772 to Martinmas 1773 :—Charge, including arrears, £1248, 11s. $10\frac{8}{12}$d.; discharge, £3266, 1s. $8\frac{2}{12}$d.; balance due to the chamberlain, which had been paid by him out of the city's proper revenue, £2017, 9s. $9\frac{6}{12}$d.

VOL. XCII.

26th October.—Mr. John Bruce, joint Professor of Logic, appointed to teach the Moral Philosophy class in the absence of Professor Ferguson, and Dr. Andrew Duncan, Physician in Edinburgh,[2] to teach the Institutes of Medicine, in the absence of Dr. Alexander Monro Drummond, with the proviso, that this shall give neither of those gentlemen any claim of preference to any other gentleman in case of a vacancy.

5th April 1775.—The Council considering that, upon the 16th of February 1774, they had refused an application of Mr. Adam Ferguson, Professor of Pneumatics and Moral Philosophy in this city's University, wherein he had requested that he might be allowed to substitute proper persons, in what remained of his business in the College that winter, and also considering, that notwithstanding thereof he has deserted his office, and come under engagements incompatible with his discharging the duties thereof, and the act of

---

[1] [Robison was born in the year 1739, at Boghall, in the parish of Baldernock, in the county of Stirling ; the property of his father, who had been a successful merchant in Glasgow. He was intended by his father for the clerical profession ; but his own taste strongly inclined him to the cultivation of science. Previously to his appointment at Cronstadt, which took place in 1772, Robison was Professor of Chemistry in the University of Glasgow, having succeeded Dr. Black in 1766. He died on the 30th of January 1805. See Biographical Account by Professor Playfair, in Transactions of the Royal Society of Edinburgh, vol. vii. pp. 495-539.]

[2] [After teaching this class during the present and following session, Dr. Duncan continued his lectures out of the College. In 1776, he had the honour of founding the Edinburgh Dispensary ; and on the 30th of December 1789 he was appointed to the Chair of the Theory of Medicine upon the resignation of Dr. James Gregory, who was elected colleague to Dr. Cullen in the Professorship of the Practice of Physic. He died on the 5th of July 1828, in the eighty-fourth year of his age.]

the 23d of May 1764, electing Mr. Adam Ferguson into the said office being read : The Council Did, and hereby Do, rescind the said act of Council, with all that has followed thereupon, and declared the said office of Professor of Pneumatics and Moral Philosophy in the University of this city vacant.

24th May.—The Lord Provost, from his committee, in pursuance of the remittance to them last Council day, to take the letter from Mr. Adam Ferguson, late Professor of Pneumatics and Moral Philosophy, dated Blackheath, 21st April last, into consideration, and to bring in a report upon the whole, reported,—That after the bill of suspension, in name of Mr. Ferguson, had been given in, a memorial on the subject had been laid before Mr. Robert M'Queen and Mr. Robert Blair, Advocates, who had given a signed opinion, which was herewith laid before the Council ; and it was the opinion of the committee that the Council should resolve to assert their rights, and support their act of the 5th of April last, declaring the office of Professor of Pneumatics and Moral Philosophy vacant, which, the lawyers have given their opinion, proceeded on just grounds, as the report under the hand of the Lord Provost bears. Which being considered by the Magistrates and Council, they approved of the said report, and resolved accordingly.

7th June.—Upon petition of the Speculative Society,[1] the Town-Council allow them a piece of ground, twelve feet by eighteen, for enlarging the hall which the Council formerly allowed them, June 1769, to build within the College, to be solely appropriated to the use of the society ; and which was built accordingly.

Chamberlain reported that he had paid to Mr. John Bruce, who had taught the Moral Philosophy class in the College last winter, the half-year's salary, due at Whitsunday last. The Council approve, and authorize the chamberlain to pay to Mr. Bruce the current half-year's salary that shall be due at Martinmas next.

14th June.—On the resignation of Dr. Matthew Stewart, Professor of Mathematics, he and his son, Mr. Dugald Stewart,[2] are conjoined in that office, with the benefits of survivancy.

[1] [The Speculative Society was instituted in 1764 by six students of the University, for their mutual improvement in composition and in public speaking. It prospered from the first, and has continued to be eminently useful. See "History of the Speculative Society of Edinburgh." Edinb. 1845, royal 8vo.]

[2] [Mr. Dugald Stewart afterwards became Professor of Moral Philosophy in the University. He and Dr. Ferguson, who occupied the Chair of Moral Philosophy, having agreed to exchange Professorships, the new arrangement took place on the 18th of May 1785, when Mr. Stewart was elected Professor of Moral Philosophy, and Dr.

21st June.—A letter of resignation presented from Mr. George Stuart, Professor of Humanity. Accepted, and the office declared vacant. Bailie William Trotter, and Convener Thomas Simson, appointed delegates, to meet with the delegates from the College of Justice, the Lords of Session, Faculty of Advocates, and Writers to the Signet, to elect a successor to Mr. Stuart.

28th June.—Read in Council an extract of the election of Dr. George Stuart, and Mr. John Hill, Professor of Humanity in the University of St. Andrews,[1] to be joint Professors of Humanity. Minute of election, dated Advocates Library, June 28, 1775. The delegates from the Lords of Session were Lord Justice-Clerk (Thomas Miller), and Lord Stonefield; from the Town-Council as before; from the Faculty of Advocates, Henry Dundas, Lord Advocate; and from the Writers to the Signet, Mr. John M'Kenzie, depute-keeper of the Signet.

Town-Council elect accordingly.

Messrs. Andrew Dalzel, John Bruce, Dugald Stewart, and John Hill, all Professors of the University, made burgesses and guild brethren of this city.

19th July.—Provost to write to Dr. Alexander Monro Drummond, giving him notice to attend his duty in the College against the next winter session.

VOL. XCIII.

30th August.—The Lord Provost acquainted the Council, that not being able to obtain any certain intelligence where Dr. Alexander Monro Drummond, whom the Council, in May 1773, had elected Professor of the Institutions of Medicine, when he was abroad in his travels, was to be found, in order to give him intimation to attend his class, as directed by an act of Council, 19th July last, he had caused make out a memorial and queries to be laid before the city's lawyers for their advice, which he produced, with the answers or opinion of the Lord Advocate, the Solicitor-General, Mr. David Rae, and Mr. Robert Blair, Advocates; which being

Ferguson was conjoined with the Rev. John Playfair in the Mathematical Chair. Having obtained in 1810 Dr. Thomas Brown as his colleague, Mr. Stewart retired from his academical duties. He died in 1828, in the seventy-fifth year of his age. His collected works have been edited by the late Sir William Hamilton, Professor of Logic in the University.]

[1] [Professor Hill was a native of St. Andrews, where his father was minister. He died on the 7th of December 1805. He wrote a Life of Dr. Hugh Blair, which was published as a posthumous work in 1807.]

read in Council, they approved of what the Lord Provost had done, and remitted to the present and old Magistrates and Council to consider the matter and report.

6th September.—Upon report of the Lord Provost from the committee, the Council resolve not to allow the Chair of the Institutions of Medicine to be kept vacant longer than another session. And if Dr. Drummond does not appear to accept the said office before the term of Whitsunday next, it shall be declared vacant, and then supplied without loss of time. And order copies of this resolution to be delivered to Dr. Drummond's relations, and also transmitted to himself by letters addressed under cover to Sir Robert Harris, at the office of the London Exchange Banking Company.

Dr. Robertson's house to be painted, papered, etc., at £32, 2s. 2¾d.

Dr. Duncan appointed to teach the Institutes of Medicine another session.

20th September.—Chamberlain's College account from Martinmas 1773 to Martinmas 1774 :—Charge, exclusive of arrears depending in last account, £320, 16s. 6d. ; discharge, £3140, 15s. $3\frac{1}{12}$d. ; balance due to the chamberlain, which has been paid by him out of the proper revenue, £2819, 18s. $3\frac{1}{12}$d.

13th March 1776.—The Council allow Professor John Hill to possess his present house in the College, rent free, for three years, after Whitsunday next, on condition of his repairing it at his own expense.

10th April.—The Lord Provost reported that he had written to Dr. Drummond, enclosing the act of Council, and directed his letter in the manner thereby appointed, etc.

8th May.—Professor Dugald Stewart allowed to possess his present house in the College, rent free, for three years, after Whitsunday next, on his satisfying the Council at the end of that period that he has expended to the amount of the whole rent upon repairing the house.

12th June.—In consequence of a letter from Sir William Hamilton, his Majesty's resident at the Court of Naples, dated 14th May last, to Dr. Ramsay, which was read in Council, the Council conclude that Dr. A. Monro Drummond is not to accept of the Professorship of the Institutes of Medicine, therefore they declare the office vacant.

19th June.—Dr. James Gregory, physician in Edinburgh, elected

Professor of the Institutes of Medicine,[1] in place of Dr. William Cullen, late Professor thereof.

VOL. XCIV.

28th August.—Chamberlain's account of the College revenue for the year, to wit, from Martinmas 1774 to Martinmas 1775:—His charge, inclusive of arrears, £592, 5s. $8\frac{8}{12}$d.; his discharge, £3886, 8s. $10\frac{11}{12}$d.; balance due to the chamberlain, paid by him out of the city's proper revenue, £3294, 3s. $2\frac{5}{12}$d.

VOL. XCV.

5th March 1777.—The committee on College affairs reported that they had considered a missive from Professor Hamilton, with the regulations proposed by him to be observed in disposing of Divinity bursaries, and were of opinion that the following regulations should be established and observed in time coming: *1st,* That no petition for a Divinity bursary be received, unless accompanied with a certificate from the Professor of Divinity, or, in his absence, from the Principal, or from two at least of the other Professors, that the petitioner is a student of Divinity at the College of Edinburgh, and qualified to enjoy the bursary applied for; and, *2d,* That no payment be made unless a certificate be produced by the student from the Professor of Divinity, or, in his absence, from the Principal, or any two of the other Professors, bearing that the bursar attends the Divinity sessions. The Council approved of the said report, and appointed these regulations to be strictly observed for the future in disposing of Divinity bursaries.

2d April.—The Council desire Professor Robison to condescend on the most necessary instruments needed for experiments, that they may judge how far they can go in purchasing any of them.

16th April.—Professor Robison gives in a list of instruments, of which he asserts many are absolutely necessary, and offers to purchase them all immediately, if the town would allow him £300,

---

[1] [Dr. James Gregory, the eldest son of Dr. John Gregory, noticed before (p. 436, note), attained to great eminence as a physician and a Professor. He published a text-book for his students, entitled, "Conspectus Medicinæ Theoreticæ," which he wrote in Latin, although, like his colleagues in the Medical Chairs, he lectured in English. He succeeded Dr. Cullen in the Professorship of the Practice of Medicine in 1790. He died on the 2d of April 1821, in the sixty-eighth year of his age.]

to be paid £100 annually during three years; or, if the Council will furnish as many, he will accept of £220 to be paid as above.

Remit to the present and old magistrates and convener to do therein as they shall see cause.

30th April.—On report of the committee, the Council allow Professor Robison £300, to be paid him by instalments, on condition that he show, from time to time, evidence of instruments being bought equal to the sums paid, and become bound, he and his heirs, that they shall all be produced at his leaving his office.

11th June.—Mr. Hill allowed a part of the Museum for a Humanity class.

Upon the application of Professors Dalzel and Stewart, £20 allowed for fitting up the Greek class, so as to allow the Mathematics to be also taught in it. Expense not to exceed £20 sterling.

18th June.—Mr. Adam Ferguson, Professor of Moral Philosophy, allowed a seat in the Tron Church.

16th July.—The petition and representation of Dr. Monro, setting forth that, nearly sixty years ago, the Magistrates appointed Professors to teach the several branches of Medicine on the plan of the then most celebrated University of Leyden; that, in the year 1720, his father was elected Professor of Anatomy, who, in imitation of the practice of Leyden, then taught, and from that time continued to teach yearly Anatomy and Surgery in one connected course of demonstrations and lectures, and was universally considered as Professor of both branches; that, in 1754, he was appointed his father's colleague and successor, and, from 1759, had conducted the whole course of lectures, and assisted and continued to adopt the general plan pursued by his father, comprehending Surgery with Anatomy; that the teaching of Surgery has been understood to belong to his office, yet the commission granted to him and his father as joint Professors of Anatomy, makes no mention of Surgery, probably resulting from the supposition that it was comprehended under that of Anatomy: Craves a new commission, expressly bearing him to be Professor of Medicine, and particularly of Anatomy and Surgery. Granted.

VOL. XCVI.

8th April 1778.—Two James Frasers, one son of James Fraser, assistant-secretary of the Bank of Scotland, and the other son of Mr. George Fraser, minister of the gospel at Monedie, in Perthshire, appointed bursars, for three years, on the Mortification of Thomas Fraser, writer in Edinburgh, and of the city clerk's office there, on the presentation of John Spottiswood, Esq., Robert Grant and John Fraser, both Writers to the Signet, three and a quorum of the trustees appointed by the said deceased Thomas Fraser.

24th June.—Upon petition, the above term of three years prolonged to five, as the Mortification bears that Fraser's bursars are to hold it for a whole course of the College (which, as was well known, took up the space of five years), and for three years thereafter, upon their making choice of the profession of Divinity, Law, or Physic.

9th September.—Chamberlain's College account :—Charge, including arrears :—£295, 9s. 8d. ; discharge, £5461, 7s. 4$\frac{10}{12}$d. ; balance, paid by the chamberlain out of the city's revenue, £5175, 17s. 8$\frac{10}{12}$d.

4th November.—Presented and read in Council a letter from Professor Joseph Black, addressed to the Lord Provost. As trustee for Professor Ferguson in his absence, Mr. Black thought it his duty to acquaint his Lordship and the honourable Town-Council, that although when Mr. Ferguson embarked for America, where he is now in his Majesty's service,[1] he was fully persuaded that he should return home before the beginning of the approaching session of the College ; it now appears that some part of the winter may elapse before he can return to this country, and perform the duties of his office as Professor in the University. This delay of his return having been occasioned by causes which Mr. Ferguson neither could foresee nor prevent, his friends hope that it will be readily excused ; and they suggest that some other person should be appointed to teach his class during his absence. Mr. Dugald Stewart appointed to do so.

VOL. XCVIII.

5th May 1779.—Dr. Robertson allowed repairs to his house to the extent of £18s. 10s. sterling.

---

[1] [During the American war, Ferguson wrote an answer to Dr. Price's work on Civil and Religious Liberty. This recommended him to the Government. The war being unpopular at home, and the British troops unsuccesful in America, five commissioners were appointed by the British Government, in the beginning of the year 1778, to negotiate a peace with the Colonies ; and Ferguson was appointed secretary to this commission. They landed in America, but were refused a passport to the seat of the American Government.]

VI.

MR. CLEMENT LITTILL'S[1] DEED OF CONVEYANCE OF HIS LIBRARY
TO THE TOWN-COUNCIL OF EDINBURGH FOR THE COL-
LEGE.—(Page 345.)

At Edinburgh the fourtene day of October, the zeir of God
Ane thowsand fyve hundreth and fourescoir zeiris.

THE QUHILK DAY, in presence of Alexander Clerk of Balbirny,
provest of the burgh of Edinburgh, Alexander Vduart, James
Nicol, and Johnne Sym bailzeis, Johnne Harret dene of gylde
thairof, Johnne Adamesone, Henry Neisbet, Johnne Jhonnestoun,
Lucas Wilsone, Andro Stevinsone, Frances Kinloch, Robert Bog,
Alexander Oustiane, and Eduard Galbraith of the counsale, Alexander Oustiane tailzeoure, Gilbert Primrois chirurgiane, Eduarde
Hart goldsmyth, Patrik Broun skynnare, Johnne Richertsone said-
lare, Johnne Harret baxter, Johnne Blythman flescheoure, Williame
Stevinsoun wrycht, and Thomas Diksone furroure, Comperit Williame Littill, burges of the said burgh, brother and onlie executoure
constitute be vmquhile a richt honourable MAISTER CLEMENT LITILL
aduocate, and ane of the Commissaris of Edinburgh; and declarit
quhow that his said vmquhile brother, vpoun the day of his deceis,
being of perfyte mynd, and considderring with himself that he wes
to be callit frome this lyfe to the mercies of God, and be the luiffing
affectioun and greit zele borne be him to the Kirk of God, and to
the aduancement of his worde, wes justlie movit and maist cairfull
that the buikis and workis of holie scripturis in greit multitude
conqueist be him in his tyme suld nocht perische or be seperated,
Left with ane luiffing hart and mynd his haill buikis and workis of
Theologie to the richt honourable and his natiue toun of Edinburgh,
and to the Kirk of God thairin, to the effect and purpois, that sik
personis knawin of honest conuersatioun and guid lyfe (and na
vtheris), quhilkis ar and sall be willing to travell and be exerceised
in the estait and vocatioun of ministerie, or vtherwayis of dewitie
desyrous, and speciallie sik personis as ar or sall be of bluid to the
said vmquhile Maister Clement, for the aduancement of the glorie
of God and his trew and sinceir worde preichit and presentlie pro-

[1] [Mr. Clement Littill, one of the Commissaries of Edinburgh, died on the 1st
of April 1580. Commissariot of Edinburgh, February 20, 1582.]

fessit within this realme of Scotland, Sall at the plesoure and will
oulie of Maister James Lowsoun, now present minister of the said
burgh, or quhat sumeuir vther minister that salhappin to haue the
charge of [the] ministrie and of the saidis buikis efter him and in
his place for the tyme, haif frie access and ingress at all sik convenient times heireftir as the said minister present or to cum sall
think guid and expedient, and [na] utherwayis, for reding and col-
lecting the fruitfull knowlege of the saidis buikis, as it sall pleis
God to distribute his graces to the reidaris; and ernestlie desyrit
his said brother for the performance heirof and deliuerance of the
saidis buikis: Conforme to the quhilk lattir Will, The said Williame
Litill promitted the deliuerance thairof, and hes presentlie deliuerit
to the saidis provest baillies and counsale of the said burgh, the
saidis buikis haill togidder, intituled according to the particulare
Cathalog following; and in euerie ane of thame is prentit the armes
of the said vmquhile Maister Clement, with thir wordis,—

I AM GEVIN TO EDINBVRGH & KIRK OF

GOD BE MAISTER CLEMENT LITIL.

THAIR TO REMAN. 1580.

[The Catalogue of books, amounting to "threttene scoir and
aucht buikis," which follows in this part of the Deed, along with
extracts from the Town-Council Records regarding Clement Littill's
bequest, are printed as a separate article in the "Miscellany of the
Maitland Club," vol. i. pp. 285-301.]

The quhilkis buikis the saidis Provest, baillies and counsale hes
presentlie ressauit fra the said Williame; and promittis faithfullie,
and obleisses thame and thair successouris, provest, baillies, and
counsale of the said burghe of Edinburgh for the tyme, to the airis
of the said vmquhile Maister Clement, for the cairfull and faithfull
preserving and keiping of euerie ane of thame; and that at na tyme
heireftir ony of the saidis buikis to be distributed, gevin, put away
or removed, athir be credeit or vthirwayis, furth of the duelling
house of the said Maister James Lowsone, as place appointit for
thaim to remaine. Nor that nane of the saidis buikis salbe lent

nawyise furth of the said duelling hous quhair thaj ar presentlie put in keiping, bot vpoun the conditioun contenit in the act of the deliuerance of thame to the said Maister James Lowsoun, be the saidis Provest, baillies and counsale. And that compt quarterlie salbe tane of the saidis buikis as effeiris, sua that thaj may and sall remane togidder in the said place appointtit thairto, to the effect foirsaid, and in perpetuall memorie of the gude affectionate mynd of the said vmquhile Maister Clement, to the singulare comforte of the kirk of God and to all his faithful seruandis, vpoun the quhilkis premissis the said Williame askit instrumentis.

And thaireftir the said day, in presence of the foirsaidis Provest, baillies and counsale, comperit Maister James Lowsoun minister, and grantit him to haue ressauit reallie and with effect the particular buikis aboue writtin, as is contenit in the Catalloge fra Williame Littill, in name of the saidis Provest, baillies, and counsale, and to have presentlie put, ordourit and layit the same in the house and Librare maid and appointit to that effect : And thairfoir actit, band and obleist himself for releif of the toun and discharging of his dewitie in the credeit committit vnto him, to preserue and keip the saidis buikis diligentlie and faithfullie, vnlent, vndisponit, or put away to ony maner of persoune, according as the saidis provest, baillies and counsale hes bund and obleist thameselfes to the airis of the said vmquhile Maister Clement, and to be ansourable for the saidis buikis, and mak the same furthcumand to the saidis Provest, baillies and counsale, and thair successouris, sua oft as he salbe requyrit be thame thairto.

> Extractit furth of the Counsale Book of the said burgh of Edinburgh be me, Maister ALEXANDER GUTHRIE, commoun clerk of the samyn. Witnessing thairvnto my signne and subscriptioun manuale.

[It may be noticed, that in completing the arrangements for having the entire Library transferred to the New College buildings in the year 1827, it was thought proper to bring together the various books which bore the above distinctive marks of having originally belonged to Clement Littill; and these having been rebound or repaired, and stamped with his arms on the sides, they are now most appropriately placed in a separate apartment, along with the collection of Manuscripts, the Hawthornden books, and other rarities.

The following extract from the Council Register relates to the original transference of these books to the College, after the death of Lawson :—

18th September 1584.

Librarie.—The same day Ordanis the Townis Librarie skelffis and buirdis thairof to be transportet furth of the lugeing sumtyme occupeit be Mr. James Lowsoun minister and sett up in the townis College, in a hous convenient, at the sicht of Williame Littill bailzie, and to be delyverit to Mr. Robert Rollok, Maister of the said Col· lege, and he to be oblist to the custody thairof, siclyk as the said Mr. James wes oblist of before. And ordanis the Thesaurer to mak the chairges of the transporting and upsetting thairof, quhilk sall be allouit in his compts.]

VII.

EDINBURGH COLLEGE, June 8, 1798.

MEMORANDUMS for a History of the University of Edinburgh from the year 1646, where the MS. History of Mr. Thomas Crawford breaks off.

N.B.—Of Mr. Thomas Crawford's History there is a copy in the Advocates Library, in the handwriting of Mr. Matthew Crawford, Regius Professor of Divinity and Church History, as appears from a docquet at the conclusion. The original, from which this was taken, belonged to Mr. Laurence Dundas, Professor of Humanity, who had lent it to Mr. Matthew Crawford. It is probable that this original is in the possession of Sir Thomas, now Lord Dundas, whose father, the late Sir Laurence Dundas of Kerse, Bart., was a nephew or near relation of the above Professor Laurence Dundas, and inherited what fortune the Professor had left.

Another copy of this History belongs to the College Library, and is in the handwriting of Mr. William Henderson, Librarian, and bears in the title to have been given in to Mungo Wood, city treasurer, the 15th of January 1673. Probably a duplicate was so given in, and is now in the possession of the patrons of the College.

I can find no regular record or minutes of the transactions of the College of Edinburgh, posterior to this History of Mr. Thomas Crawford, till 14th of February 1733, with which date a folio volume, of pretty regular minutes of the meetings of the Senatus Academicus, commences in the handwriting of Mr. John Stevenson, Professor of Logic, who acts as secretary till the 28th of May 1734; and is succeeded in that duty by Mr. John Ker, Professor of Humanity, in whose hand the minutes are continued from the 4th of October 1734 to the 29th of July 1739; and in an unknown hand from the 23d of November 1739 to the 6th of April 1741. They are then continued in the hand of Mr. Robert Hunter, Professor of Greek, from the 26th of April 1741 to the 12th of November 1744; from which date they are carried on by Dr. George Stuart, Professor of Humanity, and Secretary and Librarian, but in too abridged a manner, being partly in Professor Stuart's own hand, and partly in that of his brother, Mr. Alexander Stuart, afterwards one of the ministers of Westkirk; and of some other person by the Professor's direction, till the 10th of March 1763, when Dr. James Robertson, Professor of Oriental Languages, enters upon the office of Secretary and Librarian, and carries on the record till the 25th of October 1785; after which Mr. Andrew Dalzel, Professor of Greek, being conjoined with Professor Robertson in the office of Secretary and Librarian, concludes the volume from the last-mentioned date, and enters upon a new volume, July 31, 1790.

A. D.

INDEX.

INDEX.

CORRECTIONS.

PAGE 59, line 8, "Robert Ker, eldest son of Lord Roxburgh," so in MS.; but it should have been " William Ker, eldest son of Robert Lord Roxburgh."

Page 62, line 16, *for* George, *read* James.

Page 75, line 16, " 23d of January," so in MS.; but it should have been " 3d of January."

Page 176, line 28, "October, 1653," so in MS.; but it should have been, " March 1, 1654."

Page 203, line 19, *for* Ward, *read* Wood.

Page 265, line 28, "the Pneumatics, Logic," so in MS.: it should probably have been " Pneumatologia."

Page 328, line 4, *for* Revas, *read* Reras.

Page 332, line 15, *for* November 20, 1737, *read* November 10, 1736.

Page 335, line 10, *for* 1727, *read* 1627.

EDINBURGH : T. CONSTABLE,
PRINTER TO THE QUEEN, AND TO THE UNIVERSITY.

Printed by BoD™in Norderstedt, Germany